Closing Death's Door

Closing Death's Door

Legal Innovations to End the Epidemic of Healthcare Harm

MICHAEL J. SAKS

AND

STEPHAN LANDSMAN

OXFORD
UNIVERSITY PRESS

Oxford University Press is a department of the University of Oxford. It furthers
the University's objective of excellence in research, scholarship, and education
by publishing worldwide. Oxford is a registered trade mark of Oxford University
Press in the UK and certain other countries.

Published in the United States of America by Oxford University Press
198 Madison Avenue, New York, NY 10016, United States of America.

© Oxford University Press 2021

All rights reserved. No part of this publication may be reproduced, stored in
a retrieval system, or transmitted, in any form or by any means, without the
prior permission in writing of Oxford University Press, or as expressly permitted
by law, by license, or under terms agreed with the appropriate reproduction
rights organization. Inquiries concerning reproduction outside the scope of the
above should be sent to the Rights Department, Oxford University Press, at the
address above.

You must not circulate this work in any other form
and you must impose this same condition on any acquirer.

Library of Congress Cataloging-in-Publication Data
Names: Saks, Michael J., author. | Landsman, Stephan, author.
Title: Closing death's door : legal innovations to end the epidemic of
healthcare harm / Michael J. Saks and Stephan Landsman.
Description: New York : Oxford University Press, 2021. |
Includes bibliographical references and index.
Identifiers: LCCN 2019051756 (print) | LCCN 2019051757 (ebook) |
ISBN 9780190667986 (hardback) | ISBN 9780190668006 (epub) |
ISBN 9780197519974
Subjects: LCSH: Medical care—Law and legislation—United States. |
Medical personnel—Malpractice—United States.
Classification: LCC KF3821 .S25 2020 (print) | LCC KF3821 (ebook) |
DDC 344.7304/11—dc23
LC record available at https://lccn.loc.gov/2019051756
LC ebook record available at https://lccn.loc.gov/2019051757

9 8 7 6 5 4 3 2 1

Printed by Sheridan Books, Inc., United States of America

CONTENTS

1. The Problem of Iatrogenic Injury 1
2. Nightmare in Dallas—The Ebola Case: A Medical Error Paradigm 5
3. IOM and Public Disclosure of the Error Problem—*To Err Is Human* 11
4. Injury Incidence: The Scope of the Problem 23
5. The Medical Malpractice Litigation System 51
6. Meditations on Medical Torts 75
7. Defensive Medicine: A Response to the Legal Response? 99
8. Error Reporting: A Flawed Panacea 125
9. Legal Innovations to Promote Patient Safety—An Introduction 137
10. Incentives—Good, Bad, and Perverse 153
11. Systems, Errors, and Responsibility—It's the System's Fault! 177
12. Regulation and Engaged Surveillance 195
13. Information Technology 233

Epilogue: The Path Forward 259
Notes 261
Index 327

1

The Problem of Iatrogenic Injury

First, do less harm.[1]

After heart disease and cancer, the third leading cause of death in the United States—and the number one cause of accidental death—is an ironic one: iatrogenic injury (avoidable, unintended harm caused by the healer). Surprisingly little investment, or even public attention, is given to this enormous problem. The stratospheric cost in lives, health, and dollars borne by victims, families, insurers, and taxpayers constitutes one of the greatest problems our society currently faces. Yet the flawed machinery rolls on, barely noticed by the public and inadequately addressed by officials whose job is to concern themselves with the public's safety.

Hundreds of thousands of preventable deaths each year and more than a million serious injuries stir little notice and less action. We are offered news stories on 42,000 yearly opioid-overdose deaths, the 21,800 annual deaths tied to radon, and the nearly 20,000 people who die prematurely each year from air pollution caused by fossil fuels. Even the 20 people killed each year by cows, the five high school football players who died last year from overexertion in hot weather, and several deaths associated with Monster Energy Drink reported to the U.S. Food and Drug Administration get their share of attention. But the looming problem of iatrogenic deaths and injuries goes largely overlooked.

Initiatives within the healthcare industry have failed repeatedly to make serious progress in reducing preventable iatrogenic injuries and deaths. The patient safety problem has thus far proven impossible for them to solve, or even to talk about candidly. The enormity of the problem is matched by the reluctance of those in the healthcare industry to come seriously to grips with it—a difficulty that is organizational and economic as well as psychological. Existing incentives are perverse and legal policies are paradoxical. The less spent on improving patient safety, the more money a healthcare organization makes. More money is earned when a patient is injured (and needs additional care) than when all goes well. The reward for costly investments in safety would be reduced revenue.

The principal economic counterforce is medical malpractice litigation, but for a constellation of reasons it has never been a sufficiently effective means of incentivizing investments in making healthcare safer. At the same time that healthcare providers detest the very existence of a system of malpractice litigation (never mind how they feel about actual lawsuits), the traditional litigation system is so favorable to the interests of the industry that its attractions dwarf aversion. Only a fraction of potential valid claims are brought, and, in the aggregate, the law requires the industry to reimburse victims only a few pennies for every dollar of externalities created by harmful error. Consequently, fundamental changes in malpractice law have never been pushed hard by the healthcare industry and probably never will be.

What the industry has done is to lobby—successfully—for tweaks that have made a system that is kind to it even kinder. This campaign has convinced lawmakers that the industry is the victim of injured patients and their lawyers, and so it is the industry that needs protection. What had always been an anemic system of compensation and deterrence has in recent decades been weakened further by several waves of law reforms. Claiming rates have been dropping steadily for several decades so that today the number of malpractice claims brought per physician has been cut by nearly two-thirds. Like responding to the problem of car crashes by pulling the highway patrol off the roads, the reforms have further reduced incentives for investment in safe healthcare.

But debates over tort law and tort reform are a distraction from the real problem that needs solving: how to reduce harm to patients. Tort law fails future patients by its inadequacy in producing needed incentives for safety. Tort reform fails future patients by sheltering the healthcare industry from scrutiny and accountability, further reducing incentives for safe care, and assuring that the problem of iatrogenic injury and death will remain with us for a long time to come.

The aim of this book is to explore strategies the law could undertake that look beyond conventional malpractice litigation. A new generation of innovative laws might harness the insight that more can be achieved by attending to higher levels of organization, by correcting perverse incentives, by encouraging the use of appropriate new technology, and pursuing other innovations. We make no claim to offering a complete or best solution. We hope, instead, to arouse a new and more constructive conversation that will lead to more effective solutions and greater patient safety.

After introducing the issue of patient safety in Chapters 1 and 2, we describe the problem of iatrogenic injury—its discovery, disregard, eventual public unveiling, and its extent—in Chapters 3 and 4. Chapters 5 through 8 examine the conventional legal responses to the problem of avoidable patient injuries and deaths and counter-responses. The final five chapters of the book explore some innovative possibilities for promoting patient safety: replacing perverse incentives with more beneficial ones, systems thinking, examples of successful (and unsuccessful) regulation, and the harnessing of information technology.

AUTHORS

Michael Saks, whose doctorate is in experimental social psychology, began his career as a psychology professor with a focus on research design and statistical analysis, conducting studies on legal policy questions. Within a few years he was drawn so far into those issues that, after studying at Yale Law School, he relocated to the legal academy, where he has spent three-quarters of his professional life, still trying to improve legal policy and practice with the methodology and knowledge of empirical behavioral science research. Among other works, he co-authored the multivolume treatise, *Modern Scientific Evidence: The Law and Science of Expert Testimony* and *The Psychological Foundations of Evidence Law*. His book-length article, *Do We Really Know Anything About the Behavior of the Tort Litigation System—And Why Not?* has been the most-cited law review paper on the tort system for a generation. His extensive work on forensic science and the law helped advance the National Research Council's groundbreaking project, *Strengthening Forensic Science in the United States: A Path Forward*. Currently, he is Regents Professor at the Arizona State University where he is on the faculties of the Sandra Day O'Connor College of Law and the Department of Psychology and a fellow of the Center for Law, Science and Innovation. His courses in law, behavioral science, and research methodology have been taught to judges, lawyers, and law professors, as well as to law students, graduate students, and occasionally medical students.

Stephan Landsman is a graduate of Harvard Law School. He is the author of five books and over 60 law review articles, most concerned with questions of civil justice or the functioning of the American jury system. He began his legal career as a trial lawyer representing those seeking assistance through the federal Legal Services program. He became a law professor in 1976 and, since then, has taught at the law school level in the United States, England, and India, most recently as the Robert A. Clifford Professor of Tort Law and Social Policy at DePaul University College of Law. Throughout his career he has participated in the representation of clients in a wide variety of civil cases. He successfully advocated before the United States Supreme Court in *City of Akron v. Akron Center for Reproductive Health*, 462 U.S. 416 (1983). More recently he has participated in a range of medical malpractice cases, airline crash suits, pharmaceutical products liability litigation, claims arising out of the 9/11 terrorist attacks, and the improper use of dark money campaign contributions to influence candidates for judicial office. He is a long-time member of the American Bar Association and drafted its *Principles for Juries and Jury Trials*. Apart from his work on civil justice, he has authored *Crimes of the Holocaust, The Law Confronts Hard Cases*, an examination of a series of criminal prosecutions of Nazis and their henchmen after World War II.

2

Nightmare in Dallas — The Ebola Case

A Medical Error Paradigm

The best interest of the patient is the only interest to be considered.[1]

At about 10:30 PM on the evening of September 25, 2014, a man came into the emergency room at Texas Health Presbyterian Hospital in Dallas complaining of a headache, fever, and stomach pains.[2] He was briefly questioned by a triage, or screening, nurse at about 11:30 PM and was found to have a temperature of 100.1°F. About an hour later, at 12:30 AM, he was more formally interviewed by a member of the emergency room nursing staff.[3] The man's name was Thomas Eric Duncan. He was 42 years old and, in heavily accented English, told the nurse he had recently arrived from Africa. The nurse entered Duncan's information into the hospital's electronic records system. Shortly before 1 AM emergency room physician Dr. Joseph Meier began his evaluation of the patient. He noted that Mr. Duncan had both abdominal pain and a "sharp" headache, but despite the materials noted in the medical records, found him "negative for fever." Dr. Meier described the patient as "a local resident" (another observation at odds with the electronic record).

At 3 AM, Mr. Duncan's temperature spiked to 103°F, but within a quarter hour the doctor wrote in the hospital record: "Patient is feeling better and is comfortable with going home."[4] At 3:30 AM the patient's temperature was down to 101.2°F, and he was discharged with an antibiotic prescription to address what the doctor diagnosed, despite a negative computed tomography scan, as sinusitis—a swelling or inflammation of the sinuses.

Mr. Duncan went home but was rushed by ambulance back to Dallas Presbyterian 55 hours later, on the morning of September 28, with a temperature of 103°F, along with violent vomiting and diarrhea. He was again examined in the emergency room and, this time, it was noted that he had recently been in Liberia, where the Ebola virus was raging. The emergency room nurse and doctor who saw him, employing an existing hospital "algorithm," tentatively diagnosed Ebola.[5] Mr. Duncan was immediately isolated and tests were undertaken to establish the nature of his illness. On September 30, the Ebola diagnosis was confirmed. The caregivers at Dallas Presbyterian struggled to save Mr. Duncan's life, but he died on October 8.

The hospital staff caring for Mr. Duncan had virtually no training in the treatment of Ebola or similar illnesses.[6] Although Dallas Presbyterian, along with other hospitals throughout the United States, had been advised by the Centers for Disease Control and Prevention on July 28, 2014, of the risk of the appearance of Ebola in America and, on August 1, had received a directive to prepare an Epidemiology Emergency Policy to deal with Ebola-infected patients, the hospital had taken few steps to address such an eventuality. Nurses involved in Mr. Duncan's case had not been instructed how to deal with highly infectious diseases and, according to one treating nurse, had to do research on the Internet to determine what protective gear to wear and what measures to take to protect themselves.

The news of Mr. Duncan's illness made local and national headlines. It also set off something of a panic in the Dallas area.[7] Unlike virtually any other sort of medical error, the media paid the case the closest attention—in all likelihood because of the threat of mass contagion. The hospital found itself under enormous pressure to explain why it sent an Ebola-infected man home untreated. On October 1, the day after Mr. Duncan's illness was definitively diagnosed, the hospital released a written statement indicating that when Duncan was seen in the emergency room, he had no more than a "low grade fever" in conjunction with "stomach pains" and that his symptoms "did not warrant admission."[8] This statement was not only inaccurate; it also failed to address the hospital team's critically important mistake in not taking into account Mr. Duncan's recent arrival from Africa.

Later that day, as media pressure mounted and health worries escalated in Dallas, the hospital held a televised press conference featuring Governor Rick Perry along with Dr. Mark Lester, the hospital's Zone Clinical Leader and an executive vice president of Texas Health Resources, the corporate entity that owned and operated Dallas Presbyterian.[9] At this event, Governor Perry sought to reassure the citizens of Dallas that governmental units were carefully monitoring the situation, most particularly in relation to school children who may have come in contact with others who had spent time with Mr. Duncan. The governor praised Dallas Presbyterian and, by his presence, sought to assuage fears that the hospital was a dangerous center of contagion.

When the hospital's representative, Dr. Lester, spoke, the picture became considerably less rosy. He admitted that the emergency room nurse doing intake knew that Mr. Duncan had recently arrived from Africa—a significant piece of information that should have triggered inquiry about the possibility of Ebola.

He conceded that all had not gone well in Dallas Presbyterian's emergency room communications regarding Mr. Duncan's travels: "Regretfully that information was not fully communicated throughout the full team."[10] The implication was that someone, perhaps the intake nurse (the lowest level member of the Dallas Presbyterian healthcare treatment team), had made an error and Duncan's recent arrival from Liberia "wasn't factored into clinical decision-making." Such a communication problem was a convenient explanation. It exonerated higher-ups— the treating physician and hospital—from responsibility for any mistake, at least with respect to the initial diagnosis.

On October 2, under unrelenting media pressure, the hospital changed its story.[11] In a newly drafted statement, the hospital blamed the communications failure on a "flaw" in the electronic data recording system that deprived the initial physician, Dr. Meier, of the critical travel data. In this way, the hospital seemed to make an effort to shift the focus of responsibility from anyone on the staff to the system that served the hospital's information processing needs.

The no-one-made-a-mistake hypothesis would not hold. Pummeled by negative news reports, on October 3, the hospital's leaders finally admitted that the information about Africa had been available to the entire treating team: "The patient's travel history was documented and available to the full care team in the electronic health record (EHR) including within the physician's workflow."[12] This meant that the team, and most particularly the attending physician, had erroneously disregarded critical information in making the original diagnosis. The hospital's inability to effectively identify and articulate the staff's mistake was probably not an institutional effort to cover up its fault but a reflection of an ingrained and reflexive resistance to recognition of and public candor about medical error.[13] This lack of effective assessment and candor could not withstand the intense media pressure generated by the widely held belief that the hospital's mistakes had exposed hundreds of Dallas residents to a deadly virus. (Ironically, that belief was not particularly well founded, since only those coming into contact with Mr. Duncan after he became critically ill were in danger of contracting the virus by contact with his bodily fluids.) It was at about this point that Texas Health Resources, the hospital's parent, sought outside assistance by hiring one of the premier crisis-management public relations firms in the country, Burson-Marsteller, to manage the difficulties the organization was facing.[14]

Dallas Presbyterian's problems were far from over in early October. The perception of its incompetence was amplified when it was discovered that two of the hospital's nurses had contracted Ebola. What the public saw was a highly fallible institution that had erred in diagnosing a deadly virus, seemed incapable of telling a straight story about its mistakes, and was unable to protect its own staff. It was at this juncture that the hospital changed its approach and admitted to having made a serious mistake. The hospital went one step further and apologized for its errors.[15] On October 16, the Chief Clinical Officer of Dallas Presbyterian's parent corporation, Texas Health Resources, Dr. Daniel Varga, replacing the apparently ill-informed Dr. Lester, testified by video hook-up to a congressional committee.

He flatly declared: "We did not correctly diagnose [Mr. Duncan's] symptoms." He added: "We are deeply sorry."[16]

What Dr. Varga did not comment on was the lack of preparation at Dallas Presbyterian and the cause of the errors made by the staff. More alarmingly still, Dr. Varga noted that Nina Pham, one of the treating nurses, had contracted Ebola but that the hospital did not "know precisely how or when she was infected."

In the wake of all this, Duncan's family filed suit against the hospital, claiming that Dallas Presbyterian had committed medical malpractice in diagnosing and treating him. The general consensus in the legal community was that this would be a very difficult suit to win despite the hospital's admission of error and Duncan's death in circumstances where earlier treatment would have offered a reasonable chance of saving his life. The reason was a "tort reform" enactment adopted in Texas in 2003 that gave the emergency room staff and hospital immunity from liability for their negligence unless their behavior was "willful and wanton."[17] In other words, patients injured by emergency room malpractice could never win lawsuits unless they could show the treating staff's determination to harm them or the healthcare worker's callous disregard of clearly known peril. Although the legal deck was stacked against them, Duncan's family had the attention of the country's press. Dallas Presbyterian entered into a settlement for an undisclosed amount with the family rather than face public scrutiny of its mistakes or be heard to argue that, despite its admitted errors, it owed the Duncan family nothing.[18]

Dallas Presbyterian won its bet that apology and public relations spin would restore its reputation. The turning point, according to knowledgeable onlookers, was a *60 Minutes* segment focused on the courage and decency of the hospital's staff during the Ebola crisis.[19] This seemed to persuade Dallas and the nation that all had been fixed in Texas.

Throughout this episode, there was virtually no discussion of the larger problems brought to light by the nightmare in Dallas. In this book, we shall look at some of those problems and suggest that they exemplify flaws in the American healthcare system that contribute to the deaths of up to 400,000 hospital patients every year.

An important thing to note about the Duncan case is that it played out before a national audience informed at every turn by an active and inquiring press. This is virtually never the case with respect to the overwhelming majority of deaths caused by medical error. For every highly publicized case of a Thomas Eric Duncan, or of the famous science writer, Betsy Lehmann, killed by a massive overdose of chemotherapy drugs, or of the immigrant girl Jesica Santillion, dead because of the transplanting of organs of the wrong blood type, there are literally tens, perhaps hundreds, of thousands of cases to which the media pays no mind.[20]

When such instances do come to public attention, the evidence suggests that some institutions will engage in the sort of blame game on display in the early days of the Dallas Ebola crisis. If possible, blame will be placed on the patient.[21] (Hints of this may be seen in the Duncan case with respect to questions raised about the accuracy of some of his answers to emigration questions.)[22] Failing that, the focus will often fall on low level healthcare workers, most particularly nurses. If these strategies fail, a modern trend, and one we will explore in some detail, focuses on the "system." In Dallas, this meant targeting the electronic records system. If it could be blamed, then no one was really responsible. In this way, criticism could be deflected to the anonymous programmers, designers, and installers of a faceless technology.

Failing these blame-shifting strategies, it has become increasingly common for treaters faced with claims about error to admit fault and apologize. This seems like an important step forward, but we will argue it is seldom premised either on concern to improve care or genuine remorse. There is a belief, widely disseminated and discussed in the medical community, that apology reduces the likelihood of malpractice suits and the amount of the compensation ordered to be paid to injured patients.[23] While the Duncan family suit does not precisely fit this pattern, apology played a role in it, too. In Dallas, the maneuvering was not of the victims. It was aimed, on the apparent advice of a globally famous advertising and public relations firm, at restoring the credibility and reputations of an 898 bed hospital in Dallas and the far larger corporation that owned it.

Although society's traditional line of defense against medical errors involving negligence has long been the malpractice lawsuit, we will show that the medical malpractice case is a dying breed. The insights that might be derived from it for the improvement of care have generally been ignored. In many states tort reform legislation has effectively gutted the malpractice remedy for most victims.[24] In light of the challenge of medical error and the ineffectiveness of malpractice lawsuits, we will seek in the second half of the book to identify ways in which the error problem might be addressed through economic incentives, government surveillance, and technological change.

3

IOM and Public Disclosure of the Error Problem—*To Err Is Human*

> Health care is not as safe as it should be. A substantial body of evidence points to medical errors as a leading cause of death and injury.[1]

The spreading challenge of injurious medical error and the healthcare industry's failure effectively to deal with it were products of developments that began at the conclusion of World War II. It was then that medical and pharmaceutical advances, in conjunction with already established improvements in sanitation and living conditions, opened up the prospect of overcoming diseases that had ravaged society for centuries. Science seemed to have revolutionized healthcare.

Medical advances led to increased clinical success and soaring medical prestige.[2] This combination did little to encourage awareness of, let alone a desire to address medical error. Added to this were the profession's long-standing traditions of resistance to outside oversight and reluctance to criticize the work of fellow doctors.[3]

From early on in the postwar era there was a desire, in an increasingly prosperous America, to spread the blessings of the new medical miracles to an ever-wider segment of the population. To this end, in 1965 Congress established the Medicare and Medicaid programs. These programs would, eventually, underwrite the cost of care for as much as 32% of the population by guaranteeing medical access for a large majority of elderly Americans and most of those receiving federally supported public assistance. Despite the government's dramatically increased role in the financing of medical care, it was effectively barred from regulating the quality of care by the terms of the new legislation, which prohibited "any supervision or control over the practice of medicine or the manner in which medical services are provided."[4] This prohibition was insisted upon by leaders of the American Medical Association as its price for cooperation with the program. The demand was driven by its ongoing efforts to insure medical practitioners' independence and their exclusive control over the delivery of care.

DISCOVERING AND IGNORING A PROBLEM

It should come as no surprise that, in these circumstances, problems regarding patient safety would not be thoroughly explored. Although the mid-1960s produced preliminary warnings about iatrogenic harm—injury or illness caused by medical care—there appeared to be little desire or motivation within the healthcare industry to pursue the issue. The first real signal of difficulty that registered in the medical world came with the rise of medical malpractice claim filings in California in the early 1970s. Although these claims signaled the possibility of a serious problem in the treatment system, that was not how they were interpreted. Alarmed by the rising cost of medical malpractice claiming, the California Hospital and Medical Associations, at the urging of the doctor-lawyer Don Harper Mills, began an examination of medical error by reviewing 21,000 closed medical files from 23 California hospitals.[5] The purpose of this review was to substantiate the belief that there were very few genuine medical errors, that lawyers were pursuing spurious claims and that it might be of financial benefit to doctors if the medical malpractice system were abandoned in favor of the then-popular notion of relying on a no-fault mechanism. Such an approach could compensate the genuinely injured without irksome litigation or the intrusive demands of the victims' lawyers.

What the California research disclosed came as a surprise to the investigators. The records revealed a great deal of injurious medical error, so much as to suggest that there were more than 10,000 error-caused deaths per year in California hospitals as well as many times that number of injuries. These findings produced a troubling reaction in the California medical establishment. The effort to enact a no-fault program was quietly dropped, and in 1975, in its place, the California Hospital and Medical Associations championed a money-saving scheme entitled the Medical Injury Compensation Reform Act (MICRA) that would cap medical malpractice victims' noneconomic compensation (in other words, payments based on psychological harm, or pain and suffering, rather than lost wages or medical expenses) at $250,000.[6] The effect of this scheme was to cut significantly medical malpractice awards in California (by up to 30%), most particularly awards to the elderly, infants, minor children, and stay-at-home mothers (none of whom could prove lost wages or similar financial losses). Thus, the California healthcare industry opted for a program that could save money at the expense of the most vulnerable of legitimate victims. At the same time, the legislation took no steps to address the underlying malpractice problem. The MICRA capping scheme endures to this day—its original $250,000 cap (set in 1975, remember) becoming more onerous with each passing year.

Apart from adjusting their lobbying and legislative strategy, the healthcare associations did nothing to respond to the problems identified in their own data. In fact, the data themselves were, more or less, buried. They were not made available at all until two years after MICRA had been enacted and what was published for general consumption was a technical summary without the critical findings.[7] The findings languished in obscurity until Professor Patricia Danzon of the Wharton School at the University of Pennsylvania, discovered and analyzed them and incorporated them in her 1985 book, *Medical Malpractice: Theory, Evidence and Public Policy*.[8] There she pointed out not only the alarming rate of treatment-connected injury but the small number of medical malpractice claims filed in reaction to it in California.

The problems of high rates of medical error and suits filed to recover damages because of it did not go away. In the early 1980s, however, providers remained convinced that the problem was mostly about grasping lawyers and disingenuous patients.[9] Faced with a surge of malpractice-related issues, the State of New York sought the assistance of a team of Harvard University researchers to examine conditions in that state.[10] The Harvard team began its work in 1984 and reviewed a random sample of 31,000 closed files drawn from 50 hospitals. In light of professional skepticism, the study was designed in a manner calculated to take an extremely conservative approach in assessing error. The study's findings mirrored those in California. Researchers found a deeply troubling error rate of 3.7%. About one in four of those errors could be classified as negligence and about 14% led to the death of the patient. A follow-up study found that only 2% of the injured sued to recover damages.[11] In other words, this vast and painstaking examination revealed that while there was an enormous amount of medical error, only a tiny fraction of it led to malpractice litigation.

The bad news about the problem of medical error continued to mount as the 1980s wore on. In 1985 Danzon drew attention to California. By 1988, four public agencies released similar findings about the quality of American healthcare in general (the agencies included the Prospective Payment Assessment Commission, the Physician Payment Review Commission, the U.S. General Accounting Office, and the Office of Technology Assessment).[12] The message was underscored in 1991 when the most prestigious journal in American medicine, the *New England Journal of Medicine*, published the New York findings of the Harvard study group.[13] The publication of this article was watershed moment in the history of the patient safety movement, the point when it could no longer be doubted that members of the healthcare industry knew that they faced a serious problem because of the error-based harm being done to patients. Yet, despite the overwhelming evidence, there was little response. As one of the authors of the Harvard study and a leading champion of patient safety, Dr. Lucian Leape, concluded, the study's findings "were essentially ignored."[14] This was, in some ways, more disturbing than what had taken place in California a decade earlier. There, data were at first withheld and then quietly filed outside the reach of most of the profession. In 1991, by contrast, the leading journal in medicine published an article with the most significant and reliable data, generated by the most prestigious researchers, that documented a huge safety problem. The industry's communal response was to turn its back on the data. The medical world seemed to be saying that safety was not particularly important.

MANAGING THE BUSINESS OF HEALTHCARE

While all this was going on the business of medicine was undergoing convulsive change. The traditional method of billing in the healthcare industry was fee-for-service; in other words, doctors and hospitals did what they felt was necessary and charged what they thought was appropriate. It was a system that produced ever-escalating expenditures driven by patient demand arising from an idealized notion of what medicine could accomplish, as well as the powerful financial incentives providers had to boost income by prescribing both more services and more sophisticated services. Skyrocketing costs triggered a set of legislative initiatives to foster managed care, the central idea of which was placing control of expenditures in the hands of third parties like insurance companies and other care managers like health maintenance organizations (HMOs), rather than the doctors and hospitals that provided care. Savings could be secured because managers were empowered to restrict the sorts of treatments offered and the size of the expenditures permitted for each covered individual. The managers made their profit by fixing premiums to be paid by the insured (or their employers) that covered not only the estimated cost of care but a tidy sum for those overseeing the program. Managers could boost their profits by cutting the cost of care below that estimated as the basis for the premiums. Unfortunately, this created powerful incentives for managers to shortchange the insured by placing excessively restrictive limits on access to medical care. Despite the problems posed by these incentives, the percentage of Americans participating in managed care grew from 5% in 1983 to 50% a decade later.[15]

Many of the insurance company and HMO plan managers vested with control over medical spending were protected by congressional legislation under the Employee Retirement Security Act (ERISA), which was passed in part to protect the provision of healthcare benefits to covered workers. Under the terms of the act, managers were insulated from virtually all state laws related to benefit distribution.[16] This preemption or negation of state law–based oversight meant there was very limited legal machinery to police what plan managers did. Denials of benefits and allegations of bad faith in the handling of claims could only be challenged in federal court before federal judges whose review was, by design, perfunctory. Claims of manager misconduct leveled both by patients and doctors soared, and there was a growing societal perception that plan managers were abusing their authority for monetary gain.[17] This perception was reinforced by stories about intentional bureaucratic delays that proved fatal to patients who could not get treatment approved and refusals to recognize the medical legitimacy of proven therapies.[18]

Organized professional medical associations and consumer groups joined in concerted political action seeking to curb the power of the managers and, by the early 2000s, had succeeded. The contest for control of treatment was a bitter one and was only won when the U.S. Supreme Court relaxed the restrictions on suits against misbehaving healthcare managers.[19] Ironically, in light of organized medicine's long-standing opposition to malpractice actions, it was the expanded reach of such proceedings that signaled the triumph of the profession over the managed care operators.

The managed care fight had several unfortunate consequences with respect to the problem of medical error. It fueled public skepticism about the quality of healthcare but gave providers a scapegoat in the form of greedy insurance companies. This deflected attention from the problems the industry itself was causing. The problem was compounded in 1993–1994 when the Clinton administration's single-provider healthcare proposal was soundly defeated thereby setting back any prospect for government regulation of quality and safety.

CONFRONTING AND DEFLECTING THE COSTS OF HARM

That said, the medical error issue did come to public attention in another guise. The cost of malpractice insurance shot up in many medical specialties, most particularly obstetrics. Some physicians faced the prospect of the loss of coverage altogether. The American Medical Association, state medical societies, and their political allies responded to this crisis by seeking to reduce the availability and scope of medical malpractice actions. This did nothing to address the volume of injuries being suffered by patients. Its objective was the cutting of insurance costs. A number of so-called tort reform restrictions were adopted in many states. The leading legislative step was the capping of noneconomic damages as had first been implemented in California in 1975. Other steps included placing limits on plaintiffs' attorney's fees and the creation of various screening devices to restrict the sorts of claims that could get to court. These initiatives did nothing to improve the quality or safety of medical care. Indeed, they may have had the opposite effect by reducing incentives for doctors and hospitals to protect patients from harm. Not only were incentives to be careful undermined, the economics of malpractice litigation was changed. Because of the new rules, lawyers representing injured patients in many states faced greater difficulty in winning cases and recovering substantial awards. In light of the cost and difficulty of bringing medical malpractice cases, many lawyers turned away from pursuing such claims. The result was the filing of fewer suits and the undercutting of the didactic and deterrent benefits they might provide. In states like California, it became exceedingly difficult for elderly or child patients to find a lawyer willing to represent them even when there was little doubt that they had been injured by negligent mistreatment.

Certain healthcare experts concerned with medical error sought alternative ways to pressure the medical industry into taking steps to improve safety. One approach these experts thought promising was the publication of safety-related statistics by government regulators. The idea was that these data would provide consumers with information that allowed them to make treatment choices based on which hospitals and doctors seemed most careful and, in turn, that the workings of the market would exert pressure to improve on those who were less safe. This "medical facts" strategy was perhaps most vigorously pursued by

Dr. Mark Chassin when he served as the New York State Health Commissioner, from 1992 to 1995. Under his leadership, the New York State Department of Health rated institutional performance concerning a variety of treatments and issued reports to the public. The effort seemed to have some effect on cardiac treatment facilities. Those hospitals with the lowest ratings slowly began to improve. Research, however, indicated that even in this focused and narrow context it was not consumer reaction through patronage that drove safety improvement but medical center pride and a desire not to be seen by other specialty units as offering substantially inferior care.[20] The gains outside the cardiac treatment context were extremely modest and held little promise of major systemic improvement. By the mid-1990s, it was clear to researchers and reformers alike that consumers would not, in most cases, base their selection of care providers on safety data and that consumer action would not produce substantial improvement in care.

The ad hoc group of safety reformers seemed to be facing an intractable problem. Their studies had clearly demonstrated the widespread and devastating impact of medical error, but neither the healthcare industry nor the public appeared to take the findings seriously. What developments there were seemed to be moving away from enhanced safety, whether it was restrictions on malpractice claims or the resurgence of medical independence from any serious form of oversight. In this deeply troubling setting, Dr. Lucian Leape prepared an article entitled, "Errors in Medicine."[21] It was Leape's cry of frustration, as the co-author of the Harvard/New York studies, at the failure of the profession to attend to the challenge of medical error. He likened medicine's situation to what, in the airline industry, would be the almost daily crashing of jumbo jets (based on the number of lives lost). He compared the medical profession to the operators whose actions resulted in the partial meltdown at the Three Mile Island nuclear power plant. Leape's article appeared in one of the leading medical periodicals, *Journal of the American Medical Association (JAMA)*. However, reflective of hostility to any news about medical error, *JAMA*'s editor was so fearful about professional reaction to the piece that he had it released during the Christmas holidays when fewer readers would take notice and the outside media were likely to be preoccupied with other matters. The editor, Dr. George Lundberg said he believed the question to be critical "but feared that I would lose my job if the public media hit hard on it."[22] This sounding of the alarm, like those before it, was ignored.

Perhaps the story of medical error was not quite so invisible as Dr. Leape suggested. In 1995, the popular media began a series of reports on medical mistakes. Press pieces during that year focused on surgeries where the wrong arm or leg was amputated, the wrong breast removed and, perhaps most disturbing of all, where medical missteps led to the untimely death of a patient. No such incident was more widely discussed than the death of the health and science writer, Betsy Lehman, due to an overdose of a toxic chemotherapy agent administered at the world famous Dana-Farber Cancer Institute in Boston. Lehman's death gave a human face to the discussion of the casualties of medical mistake, making the problem far more salient and personal.[23]

Ferment also roiled the ranks of safety advocates. They had failed to convince the medical establishment that it had to act on safety. Their publications in the most prominent journals had not triggered change. Their efforts to enlist consumers in the campaign to demand greater safety had not gotten any real traction. In addition, efforts to establish guidelines to improve the quality of practice (with concomitant gains in patient safety) were under sharp attack as demonstrated by an incident that arose after the Agency for Health Care Policy and Research (AHCPR), a governmental body set up by Congress in 1989 to fix practice guidelines, prepared a protocol regarding spinal fusion surgery. That protocol was attacked by a group of orthopedic surgeons as an inappropriate intrusion on medical independence. While the guidelines had the better of the science, the surgeons had the better of the politics. They took their complaints to Congress and persuaded the legislators not only that the federal agency was wrong, but that the AHCPR ought to be disbanded. Its budget was cut drastically, and it was eventually replaced by the Agency for Healthcare Research and Quality (AHRQ). The message seemed clear—traditional research, consumer action, and government regulatory efforts would not be able, on their own, to secure improved quality or safety. The prevailing impression of the infallibility of medical judgment remained, more or less, intact. [24]

With these challenges as a backdrop, safety and quality advocates gathered at the Annenberg Center in California in 1996 to discuss strategy.[25] It should be noted that while the advocates of enhanced safety and the champions of improved quality were close allies at this time, their goals were not entirely in harmony. The quality advocates saw their push for guidelines and reform of medical routine as the key to improvement in medicine. They viewed safety as important but thought its enhancement would be a positive side effect arising out of proper quality control. They considered the science of medical safety to be underdeveloped and its pursuit a distraction from broader practice improvement. The safety advocates, on the other hand, saw themselves as facing an immediate crisis that threatened tens of thousands of patient lives, a crisis in need of immediate attention. These differences were not critical as the two groups sat down together but would cause serious difficulty when safety issues became a cause célebrè at the end of 1999.[26]

The Annenberg meeting helped spark energetic efforts on a number of fronts. The American Medical Association (AMA), no particular friend of the safety advocates, felt the pressure of concern about error and in July of 1997 created the National Patient Safety Foundation (NPSF), with a mandate to explore the issue.[27] (The AMA would cut the NPSF loose in 2005.) The NPSF was joined by other organizations in focusing on quality and safety issues including the National Quality Forum (NQF), created in 1998, to pursue the sort of guidelines research no longer easily undertaken by government agencies[28] and the Institute of Medicine (IOM), a private body associated with the National Academy of Sciences. In this period, the IOM received substantial private foundation funding to explore and report on the safety question.[29] The Annenberg group held a follow-up meeting at Harvard's Kennedy School of Government in 1997. [30] All of this attention to safety coalesced into a plan to undertake a concerted campaign regarding the issue, in part, inspired by the inquiry conducted into the catastrophic destruction of the space shuttle Challenger.[31] Public examination of the shuttle disaster had disclosed a chain of systems failures leading to the explosion of the spacecraft and the loss of its crew. The inquiry and attendant report garnered wide praise and resulted in substantial safety improvement at NASA. It was hoped that a similar strategy might yield genuine improvement in healthcare.

Heightened sensitivity to safety was manifested on a number of other fronts. In 1996, Congress enacted the Health Insurance Portability and Accountability Act (HIPAA) to accomplish several goals, including protection of medical privacy and continuation of health insurance coverage.[32] The legislation also contained a safety initiative of some note, the National Practitioner Data Bank. This mechanism was intended to gather negative information about medical practitioners including malpractice awards and loss of license or exclusion from participation in government-funded healthcare programs like Medicare. The idea was to be able to identify "rotten apple" doctors so that the harm they caused could be curbed. This approach reflected the belief that most medical malpractice was committed by a small number of bad doctors who could be identified and disciplined or removed from practice. At around the same time, the primary hospital accrediting body, the Joint Commission on Accreditation of Healthcare Organizations (JCAHO—now simply called the Joint Commission), embraced the so-called sentinel event program, which employed a threat of accreditation sanctions to require careful examination of patient deaths or serious injuries not related to the natural course of the patient's illness.[33] JCAHO began by focusing on 11 events that should never happen. The idea was to improve safety by getting rid of outlier treatment problems through the exertion of pressure on caregiver institutions to look at and, it was to be hoped, improve their practices.

In 1998, the effort to secure patient safety reform gained additional momentum when a number of prominent business leaders joined with medical experts and others in an effort to spur safety and quality improvement through an organization called the Leapfrog Group.[34] This broadening of the safety coalition to include those who paid for medical care expanded the movement's social significance and potential clout. The enlarged group came together at the Annenberg Center for a second meeting to explore strategies to spur improvement. They were joined by several private foundations including the Howard Hughes Medical Institution, the Kellogg Foundation, and the Commonwealth Fund, all of which were committed to help finance the effort. The upshot of all this was the commissioning of the IOM to prepare public reports concerning the extent of the problem of medical error and designed to persuade America of the need for reform.

THE IOM REPORT

The first product of the IOM's efforts was a document entitled *To Err Is Human*.[35] The authors of this report faced a serious challenge. Past scholarly efforts had gained little traction, including the California research from the 1970s, the

Danzon analysis of those data in the 1980s, the Harvard/New York study in the late 1980s, and a follow-up study in Colorado and Utah begun in the early 1990s. The findings about medical error had been validated and reinforced by studies using very different methodologies including on-site observation and examination of the quality of care in other countries.[36] The message, although consistent and alarming, seemed to have virtually no effect on the healthcare industry. In light of this, the drafters of the IOM report made the fateful decision to reach beyond the industry and take their case directly to the public.

This meant crafting a report that could appeal to a nonprofessional audience, a task best served by using a number of public relations strategies like attention-grabbing imagery, personal anecdotes, and claims that would stick in people's minds. To further these goals, the report emphasized one particularly alarming statistic—that medical error resulted in between 44,000 and 98,000 deaths a year in hospitals.[37] Scholars on all sides of the safety debate have noted the limited utility of this bit of data. On the one hand, as we have already noted, these numbers were produced by a methodology so conservative as to understate medical error by a factor of five or more. On the other, the figures do not account for the inherently poor survival prospects of many patients (often those harmed are very sick), nor do they focus on settings other than hospitals or harms other than a patient's dying. Yet, as has often been noted, no story has the same intensity of impact on public perception as news of an untimely death. The death of the celebrity journalist Betsy Lehman and the indefensible error that killed eight-year-old Ben Kolb during minor surgery were the first things noted in the IOM's report.[38] The report has been described not only as sensational but as something of a "Hail Mary" pass on the part of its authors. IOM drafters sought the boldest and most dramatic gesture they could imagine—one that bypassed providers and sought to galvanize public concern.

The release of *To Err* developed into a huge media event.[39] Several days before the December 1, 1999 official release date, the chief health correspondent for NBC television news, Robert Bazell, became aware of its dramatic contents and, on November 29, announced its findings on national television. This "scoop" set off a mad scramble among other media outlets to pursue the story. For most of the next week, newspaper, television, and radio reporters explored the threat of medical error. While these reports could hardly be described as scientific, they did make the public aware of the issue in the most emphatic way. A poll conducted at the time found that more than half of all Americans (an astonishing figure for any news story, let alone one about scientific data) were aware of the IOM's conclusions.[40] Whatever else *To Err* accomplished, it made people confront the safety problem.

The report championed four core proposals: (i) that the medical error problem was a national issue rather than simply a matter of local concern; (ii) that to understand the problem, and begin to address it, there was a need to encourage error reporting on a nationwide basis; (iii) that professional practice guidelines to direct various courses of treatment needed to be developed; and (iv) that errors should not be understood as the failings of a few incompetent healthcare providers but as breakdowns in the complex system that provides medical care.[41] It is easy to recognize in these proposals challenges to some of organized medicine's most dearly held traditions, most particularly those around physician control and reticence concerning outside reporting and oversight. Despite the strength of the data, doctors were inclined to reject its conclusions and resist efforts to find solutions. A poll of physicians taken not very long after the release of the report found them estimating less than 5,000 error-caused hospital deaths per year although the IOM's hard-to-refute number was 10 to 20 times larger.[42] (Later research using the global trigger assessment technique would point toward 400,000 iatrogenic hospital deaths per year).

Critics of the IOM's work found unusual allies. Chief among them was Troyen Brennan, the leader of the Harvard group that gathered the New York data. Dr. Brennan sharply attacked the wrongful death statistic claiming (probably correctly) that it was intended to "harness a public fascination with accidental death."[43] The illness and fragility of those dying were, according to Brennan, underweighted in compiling the data. He also noted the absence of a "control group" in the core analysis and the inconsistencies between evaluators reviewing the patients' files. While much of this criticism is sound, it exaggerates the unreliability of the data-gathering method, the very method Brennan and his Harvard team had themselves used in studying New York and, later, Colorado and Utah. It also failed to take into account the data relying on different methodologies that came to similar conclusions.

Despite the criticisms, *To Err* created a groundswell of concern. Within a week of the release of the report, the Clinton administration directed federal agencies to begin working to implement its proposals.[44] (The speed of this reaction suggests prior communications with the authors and a shared agenda.) This was, in short order, followed by sympathetic responses from the Presidential Quality Interagency Task Force (QUIC) and the General Accounting Office (GAO) as well as administration efforts to get a national reporting system up and running. On other fronts, too, safety initiatives were undertaken. The hospital accreditor, the JCAHO, expanded its sentinel event program and began an initiative to conduct unannounced hospital inspections. There was also widespread agitation for a reduction of resident hours in light of studies suggesting that long shifts for young doctors resulted in many serious errors (as well as auto accidents on their trips home).

Despite these steps, medical commitment to safety reform, never robust in the first place, soon vanished. This was, first, a reflection of the industry's accurate perception that the public and press focus on the issue would wane and leave healthcare providers free to reassert their own agenda. High on that agenda was a second cycle of tort reform to curtail medical malpractice litigation in light of an insurance scarcity problem that came to a head in 2001. Pushed by President Bush and the new administration, the focus shifted from safety to the vilification of medical malpractice plaintiffs and their lawyers. Congress continued its resistance to guidelines and science-based medicine. In 2004, as it had in 1999, the national legislature used its fiscal power to curb guidelines development. It instructed the AHRQ to devote all its resources to information technology rather than clinical practice.[45] Although safety advocates put a brave face on matters, by the middle of the first decade of the new century, *To Err* and its insights about medical mistakes were all but forgotten, although the problems of iatrogenic death and injury had not, by any measure, been fixed.

4

Injury Incidence

The Scope of the Problem

In almost no other field would consumers tolerate the frequency of error that is common in medicine.[1]

Don Harper Mills, MD, JD, was a mosaic of law and medicine. Born in Beijing and raised in Cincinnati, he spent his professional career in Los Angeles. He was a physician and an attorney and, in the 1970s, a member of the editorial board of the *Journal of the American Medical Association*. He was a pathologist who taught at the University of Southern California School of Medicine. Mills was also actively involved in forensic science, and in 1986–1987 he ascended to the presidency of the American Academy of Forensic Sciences. He also was the medical director of the County of Los Angeles Medical Malpractice Program, where he was in charge of claims management for the public hospitals and clinics of LA County. In addition, Mills headed a consulting firm concerned with medical risk management, a role in which he worked with medical malpractice insurance companies and their clients to try to reduce their exposure to malpractice lawsuits.

Errors and consequent harm happen.[2] A lab mix-up leads to the wrong patient being assigned the diagnosis of breast cancer and getting a mastectomy that she does not need. A patient becomes infected with a life-threatening bacterium. A wrong dose is given, and a once-normal child suffers life-long brain damage. A brain tumor needs to be removed, but the surgeon confuses left with right. Sometimes such errors lead to lawsuits.

In the early 1970s a "medical malpractice crisis" erupted, meaning that insurance companies dramatically raised the price of insurance for doctors, hospitals, and others in the healthcare industry or refused to provide insurance at all. The most immediate action by the healthcare industry and its insurers was to send their publicists and lobbyists out to influence public opinion and to seek changes in law that would make lawsuits more difficult to bring or to win or that would at least keep compensation to victims low.

THE CMA/CHA STUDY

At the same time, ideas for more fundamental, longer-term solutions were being explored. Jointly, the leadership of the California Medical Association and California Hospital Association (CMA/CHA) was thinking about the possibility of radically changing the system of compensating victims of medical injury. Could the centuries-old tort system—through which victims of accidental injury filed their claims for compensation with a court of law—be replaced with something else? Under the current system, only harms resulting from *negligently* caused injuries were compensable. That is, caused by acts or omissions that depart from the standard of care that the typical healthcare provider would have delivered under the circumstances. Determining which actions and omissions were negligent and which were not often required a lengthy and complicated process involving costly work by lawyers and expert witnesses on both sides of a case. CMA/CHA leaders wondered if a no-fault system—an idea that was gaining popularity in healthcare policy thinking around the country—might provide a more stable and less expensive means to compensate injured patients. They hoped for a compensation system that could be handled administratively and almost automatically: no lawsuits, no lawyers, no courts, and no juries.

Before they were ready to propose such a reform, however, they wanted to be able to anticipate how such an alternative system was likely to play out. They and the insurance companies knew how many lawsuits were being filed in court as well as how many claims were negotiated and settled without any formal filing. What they did not know was how many patients were actually being injured or killed, how the harms occurred, where in the system most of the trouble was happening, and so on. They needed research, and they asked Don Harper Mills to lead the study.

Mills's top lieutenants for the study were individuals who, like him, were trained in both law and medicine: John Boyden, MD, LL.B., of Salt Lake City, David Rubsamen MD, LL.B., of Berkeley, and Harold Engel MD, LL.B. of Los Angeles. They had to negotiate cooperation and ground rules with a representative sample of California hospitals, design a records sampling process, develop a review and coding system, and with the "assistance of outside experts providing medical auditing, data retrieval, and actuarial and biostatistical services, [select] a random sample of 20,864 patient charts from 23 representative California hospitals," then screen the patient records, evaluate them, and analyze the gathered data.[3]

The title of the report they presented to the CMA/CHA in 1977 hinted at its purpose: *Report on the Medical Insurance Feasibility Study*.[4] Although the findings could have been nothing other than crushing to the researchers and their sponsors, their worries were only hinted at. Even before presenting any findings, the report mounts a defense, reminding readers that workplace accidents and auto accidents injure and kill people, too, not only medical care; warning that those who regard "the medical profession and the hospital industry [as] the 'bad guys' in the current malpractice litigation crisis" will find that the data from the study "reinforce that conclusion," but urging that people appreciate that, in risking to find what the study found, "California's health care team took that risk in an attempt to secure more knowledge about its services for the benefit of society. That this Study was done at all reflects favorably upon the foresight and dedication of these professionals."[5] They tell us in every way but coming right out and saying it that the findings delivered dreadful news to the people who paid for the study and who did the study—not to mention to patients, families, health insurers, and the rest of society.

Mills and his colleagues discovered that 4.65% of inpatients in California hospitals at the time suffered what they termed a "potentially compensable event," that is, harm "caused by health care management." With 3,011,000 admissions to California hospitals per year, that meant 140,000 people suffered from harms caused by the care they were receiving. The researchers calculated that all but 28,000 of those injuries were temporary, but 5,400 involved serious permanent disability and 13,600 were deaths.

Nevertheless, the Mills team—led by medically trained lawyers (or legally trained doctors) who had extensive experience evaluating malpractice claims from the defense perspective—concluded that only 17% of the 140,000 California hospital patients who suffered harm had cases strong enough and serious enough that they would be taken on by plaintiffs' lawyers and in which legal liability could properly have been found. That translated to only 0.08% of all hospital patients. Still, it came to 23,800 patients, more or less.

Mills and company did not need to tell their readers what this meant, and the report does not address the policy implications. Those whose daily lives were immersed in managing malpractice claims instantly realized that for every 10 malpractice suits that could properly have been brought on behalf of an injured patient, only one actually materialized into a legal complaint. And that they currently faced only 1 case for every 60 that would have been eligible for compensation under a no-fault system.

The realization that the number of patients injured during their hospitalizations, or even the number of *negligently* injured patients, was very large while the number of lawsuits was very small, meant that the tort system was keeping costs to the healthcare system low and costs to injured patients high. A no-fault system would multiply the number of compensated patients many times over.[6] If the existing malpractice litigation system was regarded as unpleasantly expensive by the healthcare industry, a no-fault system would impose a far greater cost burden by transferring much more of injured patients' losses back onto the industry than the existing system had been doing.

One might think that such unexpected, game-changing findings would lead to a major article in a leading journal, or a book, or a press release. Instead, the Report hid in plain sight for nearly a decade. The year following the report's release, Mills published a summary of its findings in what was arguably the most appropriate as well as the most obscure of journals, the *Western Journal of Medicine*—essentially, the journal of the California medical community.[7] The full report was offered for sale to the public through a small San Francisco publisher.[8] The first time the Mills team's findings were cited in the medical or any literature was 1984,[9] but awareness of the research started to grow in earnest with the publication of a 1985 book on medical malpractice by Wharton School economist Patricia Danzon.[10]

Don Harper Mills, for his part, seems to have been torn between loyalty to his medical colleagues and concern for preventing harm to future patients. He wrote of the courage of the medical and hospital associations for sponsoring the research and of the risks that inevitably accompany medical care. But at the same time he was the first to see the real problem clearly: previously unimagined numbers of patients were being injured and killed. He quietly urged that the methods of sampling and classifying and measuring harm that his team had developed be adopted within every hospital to evaluate its own iatrogenic incidence rates and to use that as feedback to guide them to identify causes, introduce preventions, and bring those frightful numbers down.[11] He urged increased use of hospital-based peer review, shielded from discovery, to identify problem procedures and problem physicians and to take corrective steps rather than waiting to be confronted by harmed patients after the damage was done.

It would be a long time before the study's findings would lead to any initiatives to reduce the numbers by developing programs to promote patient safety, in California or elsewhere. Indeed, it would be a long time before there would be anything resembling candid discussion of the problem.

ADDITIONAL STUDIES OF MEDICAL ERRORS AND INJURIES BASED ON PATIENT RECORDS

The CMA/CHA study was not the first by the Mills team. Several years earlier, Mills and his colleagues had worked with the U.S. Department of Health, Education and Welfare (HEW) to begin to develop the methods he employed in the California study. The HEW project, which Mills regarded as a pilot study, reached the finding that hospital medical care caused injuries to about 6% of patients and that about one-third of those (2% of all patients) were harmed negligently and therefore could have brought valid legal claims. Of course, only a small fraction of them did.[12] The lessons of those research projects—if they had been learned at all—were soon forgotten.

The subsequent brood of studies was prompted by the next "medical malpractice crisis," in the mid-1980s. Public debate over the problem and what to do about it prompted the deans of the Harvard School of Public Health and the Harvard Law School to invite several of their colleagues to form the Harvard Medical Practice Study (HMPS) Group to conduct an interdisciplinary analysis of medical malpractice problems with a goal of recommending solutions to the nation.[13] The Study Group's members debated with each other for more than a year. Then, it dawned on us that we were mired in these controversies because we suffered from the same information gap that was afflicting legislators and courts asked to choose from this policy menu. The case for these proposals rested almost entirely on anecdotal evidence, too easily tailored to the predispositions of the protagonist.

Eventually we concluded that as scholars in a university, our responsibility and our comparative advantage lay in doing the kind of research that could fill this yawning gap in the malpractice debate. Accordingly, we mapped out an ambitious study that for the first time would come to grips with all the major facets of this problem. Only after immersing ourselves in this process of empirical discovery and analysis would we be in a position to offer our views about how to improve the law's treatment of medical care.[14]

The group's proposed study—built upon and designed to improve upon the work of Mills and his colleagues—was pitched to officials in government and organized medicine in Massachusetts, the obvious site for the research. The researchers tried to convince those officials of an obvious point: "Governments should know something about the real world of medical injury and malpractice litigation before they enact reforms that profoundly affect the fates of patients, doctors, and lawyers for decades to come."[15] But their offer to carry out the research in Massachusetts was refused because a malpractice reform bill supported by both the governor and the Medical Society was pending in the legislature. Any delay—even for real-world information to illuminate the problem and guide solutions—risked confusing lawmakers and lobbyists with the facts and certainly would delay the adoption of a law poised for approval. The researchers turned to the State of New York, where the Commissioner of Health, Dr. David Axelrod, recognized the need for more solid answers. The proposed study was welcomed and the State committed $4 million to pay for it.[16]

The heart of the study was much like that carried out by the Mills team. The medical records of approximately 31,000 patients treated in 51 New York hospitals in 1984 were reviewed. The hospitals were a representative sample of the state's acute-care nonpsychiatric hospitals. Through careful sampling and subsequent weighting, the researchers could extrapolate the findings to the state's 2,600,000 hospital patients that year. The records were screened by medical records analysts trained to identify possible *adverse events*, defined as "unintended or unexpected harmful consequences of medical intervention."[17] Those adverse events found were then reviewed by at least two physicians who again assessed whether the injury should be properly regarded as adverse; judged whether the injury was attributable to negligence and, if so, the gravity of the negligence; and evaluated the disability level caused by the injury. Disagreements were resolved by one of six senior physicians on the project.[18] Additional data were gathered, notably interviews with hundreds of patients and doctors as well as reviews of claim files opened by malpractice insurers on any patients whose records were part of the study.

The essential findings were that 3.7% of New York hospital patients (nearly 99,000 people) suffered adverse events, and nearly 28% of those were due to negligence. In other words, slightly over 1% of the patients, more than 27,000 individuals, appear to have been victims of medical malpractice.

Table 4.1 breaks these data out by severity of the disability suffered by the patient. Notably, the more severe the harm, generally speaking, the more likely it was to have been negligently caused. Also important to note is that although 14% of the adverse events caused death and 3% produced major permanent disability, 71% of those who suffered from adverse events had injuries from which they recovered in six months or less. Those numbers became the key to the Harvard team's policy recommendations. They found a way that a no-fault compensation system might work. Under their proposal, those whose disabling injuries healed in less than six months would receive no compensation. For everyone else, no-fault malpractice

Table 4.1. DISABILITY CAUSED BY ADVERSE EVENTS, NEW YORK STATE, 1984

Disability	Adverse events N	%	Negligent adverse events N	%	Adverse events due to negligence %
Minimal (recovery 1 month)	56,042	57	12,428	46	22
Moderate (recovery 6 months)	13,521	14	3,302	12	24
Moderate (recovery >6 months)	2,762	3	817	3	30
Permanent (1%–50% disability)	3,807	4	869	3	23
Permanent (>50% disability)	2,550	3	877	3	34
Death	13,451	14	6,895	25	51
Not determinable	6,477	7	1,989	7	31
Total	98,610	100	27,177	100	28

NOTES: Totals differ from sums of columns because of rounding. Table adapted slightly from Weiler et al.

SOURCE: A Measure of Malpractice: Medical Injury, Malpractice Litigation, and Patient Compensation by Paul C. Weiler, Howard H. Hiatt, Joseph P. Newhouse, William G. Johnson, Troyen A. Brennan, and Lucian L. Leape, Cambridge, Mass: Harvard University Press, Copyright © 1993 by the President and Fellows of Harvard College

insurance would pay 100% of medical costs and 80% of lost earnings (up to 200% of the average earnings level in the state), but nothing for general damages (pain, suffering, disability, disfigurement, loss of enjoyment of life).

The Harvard researchers followed up their count of negligent iatrogenic injuries by linking those patient records to malpractice insurance company records. Their findings, shown in Table 4.2, reveal some important facts about what those victims of injury or their families do in the insurance-claiming system. Taking the data on their face,[19] we see that, among the 30,121 patient records, the Harvard reviewers judged 280 to have involved negligently caused injuries. Of those, only eight became files opened by insurance companies (not necessarily lawsuits—insurers would open a claim file if a doctor or hospital notified the company of a harmful error that *might* become a claim).

What is clear is that the overwhelming majority (more than 97%) of negligently injured patients seek no compensation for the losses they have suffered from negligent care. This is not a number that doctors, hospitals, or insurers would know without a study to find out how many patients could properly have sued but never did. At first, it might seem a comforting number to potential defendants and their insurers. But after a moment's reflection one realizes that it shows how easily the world could blow up in the faces of malpractice insurers. If, instead of 3% of negligently injured patients bringing claims, 6% did (still a tiny proportion), that would be experienced as a doubling of claims. If only a quarter of negligently injured patients filed claims, that would constitute more than an eightfold increase over what the healthcare industry and its insurers were accustomed to.

Finally, if we look at the situation from the more limited perspective normally available to insurers (only half of Table 4.2), here is how the world appears: 47 claims (or potential claims) have emerged. Of those, only eight appear to actually involve negligence. That looks like a ratio of five unwarranted claims for every one valid claim. What insurers would not be aware of (without studies of this kind) is that for every case they believe should not have entered the system but has, there are seven cases (272 divided by 39) that could properly have entered the system but never did. In short, without studies like these, even people intimately involved in the system have seriously limited—distorted, it is fair to say—understandings of its true nature.

The Harvard researchers carried out further studies in two other states: Utah and Colorado.[20] In those states, combined, they found 2.9% of hospital patients suffered adverse events, and, of those, 27.5% were due to negligent care.

Table 4.2. NEGLIGENT ADVERSE EVENTS AND CLAIMS, NEW YORK STATE

	Claim filed?		
	No	Yes	
Negligent adverse event	272	8	280
No negligent adverse event	29,802	39	29,841
	30,074	47	

To sum up, based on the medical records review approach to counting adverse events, it appears that somewhere between 3% and 5% of hospital patients suffer from harm caused by their medical care. Of these adverse events, about 28% are due to negligence. This means that about 1 hospital patient out of 100 suffers from harm that would qualify as medical malpractice (negligently caused harm). Applied to the 35.1 million annual hospital patients[21] in the United States currently, that would work out to between 1,053,000 and 1,755,000 victims of adverse events, of whom between 147,420 and 245,700 die and another 28,000 to 46,000 suffer permanent total disability. Continuing the extrapolation from the Harvard findings, meritorious malpractice suits could be brought by approximately 351,000 of those patients, although only about 10,000 actually materialize. These figures are necessarily approximations, since extrapolation to the nation must be made from a handful of studied places to a varied landscape. The actual numbers could be lower or higher. Even within New York State, the adverse event rate varied considerably from one studied hospital to another.

Other research, at other times and in other places, arrived at findings that were similar or even more worrisome. Using the same records review approach, in 2010 the Office of the Inspector General of the U.S. Department of Health and Human Services (DHHS) reported a study limited to Medicare beneficiaries in hospitals. The research found that 13.5% of those patients suffered serious adverse events, with 1.5% resulting in death—meaning about 180,000 Medicare patient deaths a year from adverse events. The cost of treatment for adverse events added 3.5% to inpatient costs—or $4.4 billion over the year. The physician reviewers judged 44% of the harmful events to have been clearly or likely preventable.[22] To extrapolate these results to the total hospitalized population, one would need to more than double the number of patients under consideration.

Many of the previously discussed numbers might seem high to readers who have heard the oft-quoted figure from the Institute of Medicine's (IOM) report, *To Err is Human: Building a Safer Health System* (2000), namely, that annual patient deaths from hospital care numbered "as high as 98,000." That report borrowed heavily from the Harvard project, extrapolating from the New York, Utah, and Colorado data to the nation as a whole, and arrived at a figure of between 44,000 and 98,000 deaths annually from healthcare gone awry.

As we soon will see, those numbers actually are conservative and for all kinds of reasons. First, it's important to realize that those data were from the mid-1980s, reported in the 1990s,[23] and reiterated by the IOM in 2000. Today, decades later, although the number of nonfederal acute care hospital inpatients has not increased,[24] for various reasons, the number of tests, scans, and procedures performed per patient *has* increased.[25] At the same time, no revolutionary improvements in patient safety have come along to bend the iatrogenic injury curve downward.[26] So the numbers have had nowhere to go but up.

Moreover, careful readers would have noticed that two sentences after giving those oft-quoted figures, the IOM report went on to read:

> These extrapolations likely underestimate the occurrence of preventable adverse events because these studies: (1) considered only those patients whose injuries resulted in a specified level of harm; (2) imposed a high threshold to determine whether an adverse event was preventable or negligent (concurrence of two reviewers); and (3) included only errors that are documented in patient records.

The third point, about patient records, means that errors and injuries kept out of the records by providers would never be counted. This is an issue addressed by other studies, which sought to overcome that limitation, and we describe some of those in the following discussion.

Debates over whether the counts over- or understate the number of preventable deaths seem on balance to favor the likelihood of undercounting. For example, the high-water mark could have been 140,400 preventable deaths, not 98,000 (78% of deaths, rather than the 51% ultimately reported), but caution led the researchers to exclude many of the deaths from the preventable category.[27]

Commentators have pointed out that the HMPS approach to records review was "implicit" (doctors reviewing the records used their own largely unguided judgment in evaluating what they saw in the records), the reviewers were not specialists (who might have seen more shortcomings of care), standards of care do not always have a consensus (so whether care was negligent or not is an argument that needs to be had), and reviewers could not have known about adverse outcomes that did not emerge for months or years after the events recorded in the records.[28]

Finally, the IOM report points out that only hospital activity was studied, meaning that many of the errors and harm suffered by patients in the United States were not captured at all:

> These figures offer only a very modest estimate of the magnitude of the problem since hospital patients represent only a small proportion of the total population at risk, and direct hospital costs are only a fraction of total costs. More care and increasingly complex care is provided in ambulatory settings. Outpatient surgical centers, physician offices and clinics serve thousands of patients daily. Home care requires patients and their families to use complicated equipment and perform follow-up care. Retail pharmacies play a major role in filling prescriptions for patients and educating them about their use. Other institutional settings, such as nursing homes, provide a broad array of services to vulnerable populations. Although many of the available studies have focused on the hospital setting, medical errors present a problem in any setting, not just hospitals.[29]

DISAGGREGATING ADVERSE EVENTS

Later in this chapter we will look at some of the efforts to count adverse events that might have eluded studies relying on the patient chart reviews. But before moving on from the patient record–based numbers, let us pause to zoom in on the incidence of major subcategories of adverse events. (See Table 4.3.)

Treatment, Especially Surgery

Among the more obviously negligent surgical adverse events that take place are wrong-site and wrong-patient surgery, anesthesia-related errors, retained foreign objects, and surgical burns and fires.[30]

Somewhere in the United States a surgeon "leaves a foreign object such as a sponge or a towel inside a patient's body after an operation 39 times a week, performs the wrong procedure on a patient 20 times a week and operates on the wrong body site 20 times a week." In other words, an estimated "80,000 of these so-called 'never events' occurred in American hospitals between 1990 and 2010."[31]

The term *never event* was first introduced in 2001 by Ken Kizer, former CEO of the National Quality Forum (NQF), in reference to particularly shocking medical errors that should never occur. Over time, the list has been expanded to signify adverse events that are unambiguous (clearly identifiable and measurable),

Table 4.3. TYPES OF ERROR

Diagnostic
Error or delay in diagnosis
Failure to employ indicated tests
Use of outmoded tests or therapy
Failure to act on results of monitoring or testing
Treatment
Error in the performance of an operation, procedure, or test
Error in administering the treatment
Error in the dose or method of using a drug
Avoidable delay in treatment or in responding to an abnormal test
Inappropriate (not indicated) care
Preventive
Failure to provide prophylactic treatment
Inadequate monitoring or follow-up of treatment
Other
Failure of communication
Equipment failure
Other system failure

SOURCE: IOM (2000); Leape et al., *Preventing Medical Injury*, 19 Qual. Rev. Bull. 144 (1993).

serious (resulting in death or significant disability), and usually preventable.[32] Death occurred in 6.6% of these cases. Those figures came from the National Practitioner Databank (NPDB)—a database of malpractice payments and settlements, along with other concerning information about healthcare providers, such as loss of license, loss of admitting privileges, and negative actions by private credentialing bodies. Consequently, the counts were "likely on the low side." Other research, casting a wider net by reviewing 138 empirical studies, suggests the actual number of surgical never events that occur is two to three times greater than what was found in the NPDB.[33] Because retained objects can cause pain, abscesses, intestinal fistulas, obstructions, visceral perforations and sometimes death, those foreign objects need to be removed. The Centers for Medicare and Medicaid Services calculated the average price of removing one of these items at $63,631.[34]

In the HMPS of New York State, 48% of adverse events occurred in association with a surgical procedure.[35] The leading causes among those were: wound infections (14%), acute technical complications (13%; e.g., operative injury, bleeding, wound problems), and later-emerging technical complications (11%; e.g., vascular graft thrombosis, retained common duct stone). The Utah–Colorado replication had similar findings, with 45% of all adverse events involving surgical inpatients. About half of such errors were regarded as preventable.

If we count wound infections under infections (see the following discussion), rather than under surgery, then only about 34% of adverse events are attributable to surgery (48% minus 14%). Even then, surgery remains the major locus of harmful errors in the healthcare setting.

One research project studied four different surgical services (general surgery, vascular surgery, combined general surgery and trauma, and cardiothoracic surgery) at a university teaching hospital and found the following.[36] Complications occurred in approximately a third of surgeries, of which 13% to 21% (depending on the surgical service) were major, with deaths occurring in 2% to 3% of cases and between a fifth to a half of those deaths being judged by peers to have been preventable. Overall, these surgical adverse event rates were two to four times greater than what had been found in the Harvard research. As in the Harvard projects, however, almost half of them were judged to be the result of provider error.

Infection

When sick people are gathered together in hospitals, something of a perfect storm inevitably forms: patients with weakened immune systems are surrounded by germs that are bountiful and easily spread by caregivers. According to the Centers for Disease Control and Prevention (CDC), "On any given day, 1 in 25 hospital patients has at least one healthcare-associated infection."[37] Healthcare-associated infections (HAIs) are monitored by the CDC and reported in its HAI Prevalence Survey. In a recent year, it reported that about 722,000 HAIs were contracted in acute care hospitals in the United States, causing the deaths of 75,000 patients during their hospitalizations.[38]

One form of bloodstream infection, severe sepsis with a major complication, was the second most frequently billed diagnosis submitted by hospitals to Medicare in 2013, amounting to more than 398,000 cases and growing by the year. Treating those infections cost Medicare $5.6 billion in 2013.[39]

Considering all hospitalized adults, not only Medicare patients, a review of 26 studies calculated the costs of the five most common and preventable infections among hospitalized patients.[40] The study concluded that about 441,000 infections occur among hospitalized adults in the United States every year for a total cost to treat of $9.8 billion. Surgical-site infections and ventilator-associated pneumonia each accounted for about a third of the total costs, followed by central line bloodstream infections (19%), *Clostridium difficile* infections (caused by a bacterium that results in severe diarrhea; 15%) and catheter-associated urinary-tract infections (less than 1%). Bloodstream infections from central lines (long tubes inserted in a large vein to deliver medication, fluids, nutrients, or blood) were the most expensive infections to treat, costing $45,814 per case. Ventilator-associated pneumonia was second, at $40,144 per case. Surgical-site infections cost $20,785 per patient to treat. *Clostridium difficile* infections cost $11,285 per case. Least costly to treat was catheter-associated urinary tract infections, at $896 per case.

Not all infections are the result of preventable errors, of course, although many are. Healthcare workers can easily transport infections from one person to another. But one of the easiest and most effective preventives—washing hands—is skipped by caregivers one-third to one-half the time.[41] Three kinds of infections are considered so preventable that they made Medicare's "never" list: central-line associated bloodstream infections, urinary tract infections, and infection with *Clostridium difficile.*

Medication: Wrong Drug, Wrong Dose, Wrong Patient

Since its establishment in 1938 through to the end of 2013, the U.S. Food and Drug Administration (FDA) approved 1,453 drugs. Up until the 1950s, the FDA approved an average of four new drugs per year. From the 1950s to the 1980s it averaged 10 per year. Since the 1980s, that average climbed to 20 new approved drugs per year.[42]

Over the decades, medications have increased in their power to provide health benefits, along with the potential to cause harm.[43] The number and complexity of modern pharmaceuticals makes it easy for two (or more) drugs that work fine by themselves to do harm when taken together. Prescribers need to be aware of all the drugs a patient is already taking if they are to avoid giving the patient an additional drug that will not get along well with the others. Pharmacists and nurses are the next in line to foresee potentially dangerous interactions before the medication is supplied or administered. This is one area where computers can provide enormous help. But there are far easier errors to be made. Some drugs have confusingly similar names, so the wrong one can accidentally be prescribed, supplied, or administered. A wrong drug or wrong dose can be administered to the right patient. Or the right drug in the right dose can be given to the wrong patient.

The ease with which disaster can occur is exemplified by the case of a two-and-a-half-year-old boy who entered a medical facility for a routine bronchoscopy to remove a sunflower seed that went "down the wrong pipe." During the course of treatment, he was given an injection of 10 milligrams of morphine as a sedative. But the dose was much too large for a child of his age and weight. Within a few hours, he lapsed into a coma and remained unresponsive for several days. The overdose depressed his breathing, insufficient oxygen reached his brain, and permanent damage resulted. When the child entered the hospital, he was normal and healthy, able to walk, speak in sentences, ride a tricycle, and was toilet-trained. On leaving the facility, he suffered spasticity, rigidness, impaired hand-eye coordination, impaired balance, impaired motor-skills, impaired speech and vision, mental disability and convulsions, and he was no longer toilet-trained. His impaired mental, sensory, and motor abilities were permanent. An uncomplicated medication error changed his life and that of his family forever.[44]

Such errors are not rare. A study of medication errors in hospitalized children concluded that such errors are a major cause of death and injury of young patients. "Due to small volumes of solution involved, even a large error may occur with an unsuspiciously small dose."[45]

Adults can be harmed by medications almost as easily. A woman in a Boston hospital underwent a brief surgical procedure intended to relieve pain from a back injury. The neurosurgeon wanted to confirm that tubing that had been threaded into her spine was correctly placed. To improve imaging, he requested a special dye that was safe to inject into the spine. The hospital pharmacy did not have that dye, so it sent up a different one. The nurse handed it to the surgeon, saying, "This is what they have." The surgeon read the label—too quickly—missing the warning: "Not for intrathecal use" (not to be injected into the sheath that encloses the spine). He proceeded to inject the dye and completed the operation. When the patient awoke, she was suffering from severe pain and seizures. A day later she was dead.[46]

A major study of medication errors occurring in association with surgery was reported in 2015. In the study sample, 3,675 medication administrations occurred in 277 surgeries, with 193 errors resulting in adverse events. At least one error occurred in 45% of the surgeries, of which nearly 80% were preventable.[47]

In the HMPS, 19% of adverse events were medication-related. Nearly a fifth of those were the result of what the physicians reviewing the patient records viewed as substandard care (or what the law calls negligence).

Other research involving two Boston teaching hospitals found that 1% of adverse drug events were fatal, 12% were life-threatening, 30% were serious, and 57% were significant. Forty-two percent of those classified as life-threatening or serious were regarded as preventable. The errors involved many types of drugs: analgesics, antibiotics, sedatives, chemotherapeutic agents, cardiovascular drugs, and anticoagulants.[48]

A report from the IOM examined medication errors in all kinds in healthcare settings.[49] In hospitals, on average at least one medication error occurred per hospital patient per day. The extra medical costs of treating those drug-related injuries was conservatively estimated at $3.5 billion a year (just in medical costs—not other losses to the patients, such as lost earnings). The IOM review found errors to be common at every stage, from prescription to preparation to administration of the drug to monitoring the patient's response.

Diagnosis

Diagnosis can present caregivers with the mystery stories of medical practice. One such case was of a five-year-old boy, who appeared healthy, except for three ugly sores—on his face, calf, and elbow—that prompted his dad to take him to a dermatologist.[50] The sores were red, raised, and scaly. His pediatrician had tried unsuccessfully to treat the sores with several antibiotics. The father told the dermatologist that the boy had been hospitalized for pneumonia a few months earlier. The pneumonia had been treated with antibiotics, first by mouth and, when that didn't help, later by intravenous antibiotics. His breathing was made difficult by fluid that filled the sac around his right lung. More than a cup of thick fluid was slowly drained by inserting a tube into his right side and between his ribs into the sac. The bug that caused the illness was not identified, but the patient felt much better, and was sent home on antibiotics. He had been doing well for weeks until the skin sores started to appear.

Other than the three sores, the dermatologist's exam found the boy to be normal. She suspected the cause to be some kind of infection. But antibiotics had already been given for the most likely bacteria and even some to treat antibiotic-resistant staph aureus (MRSA), if that was the culprit. Perhaps the boy had a different bacterium, a cousin of the one that causes tuberculosis. Or perhaps he had been colonized by some type of fungus. Some of those infect the lungs before turning to other parts of the body. The dermatologist biopsied the sores. The pathologist found a fungus present among the skin cells, but not which particular fungus. A fungus that could cause pneumonia and sores was dangerous enough to infect bones, brain, and eventually to kill. (Moreover, all the antibiotics the child had been given previously were useless against fungi.)

The dermatologist sent the boy to an infectious disease specialist. Two common types of fungus, which live in soils in different parts of the United States, cause both lung and skin infections. The infectious disease specialist and his resident inquired about the child's whereabouts and activities—travels, visits to orchards, farms, petting zoos. The resident zeroed in on a visit to the grandparents' vacation home in a new development (clue: disturbed soil). Most significant, two dogs in that community had died recently—from infection by one of those soil fungi. Once the identification was confirmed by the pathology lab, the patient began a six-month course of treatment targeting the specific fungus. Within days, the skin sores started to disappear, providing further confirmation of the diagnosis.

The TV show *House* and magazine column *Diagnosis* are so interesting as they are, in part, because they intentionally defy the medical maxim, "When you hear hoofbeats, think of horses, not zebras."[51] It's not much of a mystery if the solution is obvious. But we'd all prefer not to be so mysterious to our doctors. And, fortunately, properly trained diagnosticians provided with the necessary information should arrive at correct diagnoses most of the time.[52] Errors tend to occur when incorrect assumptions are made, steps are skipped, information is overlooked or not obtained, tunnel vision takes over, conclusions are reached prematurely, or, of course, the diagnostician has been confronted with a zebra. Think about the Ebola case in Dallas, discussed in Chapter 2 of this volume. When doctors act as detectives, they risk making the same mistakes as do police detectives: generating a hypothesis they become too pleased with too soon, *looking* for evidence that confirms that hypothesis, and disregarding or discounting evidence inconsistent with the favored hypothesis, rather than testing the hypothesis as scientists are trained to do—by actively looking for potentially disconfirming indications.

A 2015 review of the problem of diagnostic errors throughout the healthcare system, not only in hospitals, was conducted by the IOM, and its findings and recommendations were published in a report titled, *Improving Diagnosis in Healthcare*.[53] The IOM committee did not find adequate research to put a number on the industry-wide incidence of harm-causing diagnostic errors, calling that lack of sufficient sound research one of the study's most surprising and troubling findings. The committee did, however, suggest that "countless" patients are harmed and that "most people will experience at least one diagnostic error in their lifetime, sometimes with devastating consequences."

The IOM report put a figure of between 6% to 17% on the incidence of hospital adverse events attributable to diagnostic error. That conclusion was based on studies, such as the HMPS, that reviewed patient records. In the HMPS, 8.1% of adverse events were attributed to incorrect diagnoses, but 17% of *preventable* errors were diagnostic mistakes.

The report canvassed familiar suspected causes of diagnostic errors: poor judgment (such as taking unjustified shortcuts, including making superficial assumptions), poor coordination of care, rushed visits, unclear communication with patients, misread or misplaced X-rays or lab tests, health records that can't be easily shared, even recent experiences that skew doctors' thinking, causing them to get stuck on an incorrect diagnosis. Remedies for most of these are not beyond reach.

Perhaps surprisingly, intensive care units (ICUs) appear to host a disproportionate number of missed diagnoses. A 2012 study out of the Johns Hopkins University School of Medicine reviewed the findings of 31 studies describing a total of 5,863 autopsies to compare potentially fatal misdiagnoses in ICUs to those in the general inpatient population. The autopsies revealed that 28% of the patients had a missed diagnosis at the time of death and that in about 8% of those the misdiagnosis was serious enough to have caused or contributed to the patients' deaths. The ICU errors were about half again as frequent as those in the general hospital patient population. Extrapolating to the national ICU patient population, the researchers concluded that up to 40,500 critically ill patients die annually as a result of clinicians in ICUs failing to diagnose hidden life-threatening conditions such as heart attack or stroke.[54]

BEYOND HOSPITAL RECORDS

The harmful errors we have discussed to this point were usually found by chart review—research teams scrutinizing patients' records in hospital files. Relying on patients' medical records is to some degree limiting, perhaps very limiting. Medical records do not plainly announce errors and the damage they have caused, and sometimes practitioners make active efforts to conceal their errors from the record to avoid responsibility.

In whatever spheres of life we might inhabit, including at home, how many of us eagerly disclose our mistakes, especially those that make us look careless or stupid, particularly when the slip-up led to a harmful or costly outcome? Similarly, healthcare providers often keep their missteps under wraps—so much so that an important focus of patient safety experts has been to try to find ways to promote disclosure so that ways to prevent future errors can be found.[55]

As children, most of us had already become experts on avoiding responsibility for our mistakes. Social psychologists Carol Tavris and Elliot Aronson captured and analyzed a broad range of such behavior—from the trivial to the tragic—in their unexpectedly entertaining book, *Mistakes Were Made (But Not by Me)*. Most important, perhaps, is these authors' focus on our ability to persuade *ourselves* that we did nothing wrong or are not responsible for what went wrong, regardless of whatever the objective evidence to the contrary might be.

In reviewing medical records through his work in risk management, Don Harper Mills discovered that some doctors changed hospital charts in an effort to conceal their part in mistakes that led to harmful outcomes. Mills teamed up with a colleague from the forensic sciences to write an article recommending the use of forensic document examiners to help detect fraudulent changes in medical records. Mill advised, "There are instances of injudicious and fraudulent alterations of medical records which can be detected by the document examiner and can be supported by physical evidence."[56] Today's computerized medical records might make the detection of fraudulent changes harder or easier, depending on the system's design.

Because of the limitations of medical records as sources of information on adverse events, at least two different approaches have been developed to try to capture more fully and more accurately the numbers and kinds of harmful medical errors that occur in hospitals. These studies find much higher levels of iatrogenic injury than those relying exclusively on what gets written into medical records.

One approach is to come as close as possible to directly observing patient care. This research strategy puts observers on the wards to conduct more direct, real-time monitoring of patients and providers, gathering intelligence on what's happened to patients that may not be recorded in their charts. The disadvantage of such studies compared to records reviews alone is that they are more labor intensive and costly and require more time.

One such study was reported in 1981, having been carried out in a general medical service of a university teaching hospital in Boston. In addition to a careful review of each patient's record, "identification of iatrogenic issues was supplemented with staff questioning of clinical personnel who cared for the patient and with information obtained from utilization review coordinators who were evaluating the patients' needs for continued hospitalization." That study found that 36% of patients suffered an injurious adverse event; 9% were victims of "major" iatrogenic harm, and 2% of such cases resulted in death.[57] A similar hospital observation study conducted in Chicago found that errors were made in the care of nearly half of all patients, and of those, about a fifth caused serious injuries.[58] These findings suggest the number of adverse events overall is *10 times* what had been found by any of the records-review studies and that 15 to 20 times as many patients suffer major permanent disability or death.

A second alternative approach to finding adverse events uses patient medical records, but researchers proceed somewhat more like archeologists or detectives seeking out facts that might be hidden from view:

> The [Institute for Healthcare Improvement's] Global Trigger Tool [for measuring adverse events] uses specific methods for reviewing medical charts. Closed patient charts are reviewed by two or three employees—usually nurses and pharmacists, who are trained to review the charts in a systematic manner by looking at discharge codes, discharge summaries, medications, lab results, operation records, nursing notes, physician progress notes, and other notes or comments to determine whether there is a "trigger" in the chart. A trigger could be a notation indicating, for example, a medication stop order, an abnormal lab result, or use of an antidote medication. Any notation of a trigger leads to further investigation into whether an adverse event occurred and how severe the event was. A physician ultimately has to examine and sign off on this chart review.[59]

Automated versions of such tools are in development.[60] Meanwhile, in one study, the Global Trigger Tool was applied to the records of adult patients admitted during a single month in 2004 at three large U.S. tertiary (specialized) care centers that had "well-established patient safety programs" "focused on improved detection of safety incidents and adverse events through patient safety reporting programs, and special tools built around advanced electronic health record systems used within all three organizations."[61] In fact, the three hospitals had won awards or other recognition for their patient safety initiatives. The names of the hospitals were kept confidential, but we learn that one was an academic hospital and two were community-based teaching hospitals; one was in a midsize city in the West, one in a large city in the Midwest, and the third in a large city in the

Northeast. The study found an overall adverse event rate of 33.2%.[62] The most serious harms and deaths accounted for a little over 8% of all adverse events.

Another application of the Global Trigger Tool was aimed at determining whether progress was being made in patient safety.[63] The researchers sampled and analyzed records from 10 hospitals in North Carolina over the period from January 2002 to December 2007. The overall adverse event rate was found to be 25.1%, with only a hint that patient care was becoming safer over time.[64] Of all the harms identified, 13.8% were permanent or life-threatening or caused death.

These alternative approaches to counting adverse events found, overall, about 10 times as many as had been found by the more conventional medical records reviews (the CMA/CHA and HMPS research), and between 8 and 10 times the number of major permanent disabilities or deaths. Importantly, they suggest that the results of studies that relied exclusively on the type of records review employed by Mills and the Harvard teams markedly undercount the actual incidence of adverse events. The problem of iatrogenic injury in hospitals is larger than is generally concluded.[65] But even these larger, more tightly woven nets still capture only what occurs in hospitals. Healthcare is also provided in other settings.

BEYOND HOSPITALS

Because not all healthcare is delivered inside of hospitals, not all healthcare-associated errors and injuries occur inside of hospitals. All outpatient care, including that provided in doctors' offices, skilled nursing facilities, rehabilitation hospitals, nursing homes, and the increasing number of outpatient surgical centers are overlooked by the studies we have discussed thus far. Since about 30 times as many outpatient visits occur annually as there are hospitalizations, ample opportunity exists for errors to be made outside of hospitals. Counting outpatient errors and injuries is harder to do, which goes a long way toward explaining why there is so little of it. But some glimpses have been obtained. Compared to the 35 million hospital patient admissions each year in the United States, there are 900 million visits to physicians' offices. The error-injury profiles are, of course, different in different settings.[66]

Whereas surgical errors rank at the top of the sources of adverse events for hospital inpatients, followed by infections, evidence suggests that medication is the major source of trouble in the outpatient setting. One study found that adverse drug events occurred in 25% of primary care patients and that 11% of them were preventable.[67] The IOM's report on medication errors concluded that medication errors harm at least 1.5 million patients each year. That is more than triple the number of harmful medication errors found to occur in U.S. hospitals annually.[68]

Diagnostic errors are another large concern. The IOM has estimated that annually 5% of adults experience a diagnostic error in outpatient care—which puts the total in the millions. Autopsies spanning decades have found that diagnostic errors contribute to approximately 10% of patient deaths.[69]

Outpatient surgery and other procedures are increasing rapidly, and there is no reason to think the rates of error, injury, and death are any less than what has been found in hospitals. For example, ambulatory surgery centers have been found to have infection control policies that are more lax than those of hospitals.[70] Almost as many procedures are performed in ambulatory surgery centers as in hospitals (in the most recent published estimates, 22.5 million versus 25.7 million, respectively).[71]

To learn what kinds of malpractice actions occur in the outpatient context, researchers from Cornell Medical College analyzed data in the NPDB. Focusing on malpractice payments, they found nearly as many payments being made for injuries incurred in outpatient settings as in hospitals (43.1% were for injuries in outpatient settings, 47.6% in inpatient settings, and 9.4% for occurrences that carried over from one setting to the other). Two-thirds of the payments were for major injury (36.1% of payments) or death (30.6%). In contrast to the hospital setting, the leading type of error in the outpatient setting was diagnostic (45.9%), and the second most common involved nonsurgical treatments, especially medication errors. Medication errors accounted for 1 out of every 131 deaths in the outpatient setting, but only 1 out of 854 inpatient deaths.[72]

The Office of the Inspector General in the DHHS studied the incidence of medical injuries and deaths of patients in skilled nursing facilities (SNF).[73] A SNF is a postacute care facility that patients can be discharged to if they need continuing nursing and rehabilitation care following hospitalization for an injury or illness but no longer need the level of care provided by a hospital. Such facilities are certified to receive compensation through Medicare, and therefore Medicare has an interest in the quality and cost of the care its beneficiaries receive.[74] At the time of the data collection in 2011, about 20% of all hospitalized Medicare beneficiaries went to one of the 15,207 SNFs in the United States for posthospital care. For the services SNFs provided to 1.8 million beneficiaries, Medicare paid $28.4 billion.

The research was carried out by conducting a review of patient medical records, with an eye for adverse events. About 33% of Medicare beneficiaries suffered an adverse event during their SNF stays—11% of them temporary (requiring medical intervention, but causing no lasting harm); the rest were more serious, requiring extended treatment, endangering survival, or contributing to the patient's death (1.5% of patients). The adverse events were related to medication (37%) or ongoing resident care (37%) or were infections (26%). Physician reviewers determined that 59% of the adverse events were clearly or probably preventable. Much of that preventable harm resulted from substandard treatment, inadequate monitoring, or failure or delay in providing needed care. Over half of the residents who experienced harm returned to a hospital for treatment, which was estimated to cost Medicare an additional $2.8 billion that year.

In 2016, the DHHS Inspector General reported a similar study of adverse events in rehabilitation hospitals,[75] with similar findings: 29% of patients suffered some kind of adverse event resulting from their care, almost half of those were preventable, and almost a quarter of those patients had to be transferred to an acute care hospital for treatment of the adverse event.

Although far from a mirror image of what occurs inside of hospitals, the varied kinds of treatment leading to uncounted injuries and deaths that occur outside of hospitals clearly need to be added to the more salient findings of preventable injuries that have been found to occur in hospitals if we are to gain a complete picture of the scope of the problem of patient safety.

BEYOND INADVERTENCE

The discussion thus far has been concerned with inadvertent errors and accidental injuries. Is there another category we need to consider—a more intentional kind of harm to patients?

More than occasionally, a caller to the radio program *Car Talk* would ask about some costly work that had been done on the caller's vehicle, but which had not solved the problem or otherwise made the caller wonder why the mechanic did this or that to the car. The show's hosts, Bob and Ray Magliozzi of Cambridge, Massachusetts, would laugh boisterously and explain to the car's owner that those repairs probably were necessitated not by the needs of the car so much as by the mechanic's need to make a boat payment.

Suppose the same sort of thing happened in a different industry: healthcare. Suppose some doctors some of the time performed surgery—fusions of vertebrae, meniscus repairs of knees, hysterectomies, coronary bypasses, and others—on patients who could not be expected to derive any benefit from the treatments. The procedures were performed, rather, because the doctors performing them were driven by profit, not by the best interests of their patients. Suppose further that those surgical procedures went smoothly. They didn't fix anything that needed fixing, but the patient recovered from surgery without complications and went on with life unburdened by any lasting harm—other than financial. The only thing wrong with the treatment is that it was not needed in the first place and therefore conferred on the patient no benefit.

How should we classify such occurrences? They would not show up in studies of adverse events. The patient has been harmed, but not in the way that we normally think of iatrogenic harm. Indeed, the doctor's malpractice insurer probably would resist paying for the defense of a lawsuit resulting from knowingly unneeded (but otherwise uneventful) surgery because the insurance contract does not insure the doctor for intentional harms, only for accidental harm. If not malpractice, what kind of legal claim would a patient (or the patient's health insurer, or a government insurer) bring in the case of an operation performed for no purpose other than to enrich the doctor and hospital? A suit for civil fraud would be in order. Or perhaps for the intentional tort of battery: cutting tissue without obtaining proper informed consent.[76] Or a prosecutor might indict for the criminal analogs of fraud and battery.[77]

It's not hard to find cases in which a maverick doctor, a practice group, or even a larger healthcare organization have transgressed so badly in the quest for more money that (if caught) they wind up paying back substantial sums in overcharges to insurers, paying fines, being barred from participation in Medicare, or even being prosecuted criminally. Here are some examples. They are at once extreme and yet not rare.

- An Indiana cardiologist and his two partners were the three most highly reimbursed cardiologists in Indiana, billing Medicare for $5 million in a single year. It turned out that needless surgical procedures were performed on 300 or more patients, often multiple procedures per patient. As the chief of cardiovascular medicine at the Cleveland Clinic and former president of the American College of Cardiology, Dr. Steven Nissen, explained, "Cardiology, whether we like it or not, is generally a big moneymaker for hospitals. We are still a fee-for-service system, and that creates, in my view, misaligned incentives among some physicians to do more procedures and among some institutions, particularly in areas where there is not tight medical supervision, to turn a blind eye and enjoy the high revenue stream."[78]
- The Ashland Hospital Corporation in eastern Kentucky repaid $41 million to settle allegations that unnecessary cardiac procedures had been performed and billed to Medicare and Medicaid.[79] Same story at Tenet Healthcare, which repaid $54 million for unnecessary cardiac procedures on patients at just one of its hospitals.[80]
- The Hospital Corporation of America (HCA) was found to be performing unnecessary (and potentially dangerous) cardiology work. Some cardiologists at several of its hospitals were unable to justify many of the procedures they were performing. In some cases, the doctors entered false information into patients' medical records to make it seem the procedures were necessary (asserting blockages of 80% to 90% when later investigation revealed the blockages actually were 33% to 53%). At one hospital, half the treatments were performed on patients without significant heart disease. In one of a series of settlements reached with the U.S. Department of Justice, HCA paid $1.7 billion in fines and repayments. The lesson was not learned: similar problems arose in subsequent years.[81]
- At Health Management Associates (HMA), a for-profit hospital chain based in Naples, Florida, emergency room doctors were pressured to admit at least half of the Medicare and Medicaid patients they saw. Scorecards were posted where all of the ER physicians could see who was meeting their admissions targets, who was close, and who was "failing." The hospital chain's goal was to make money by admitting patients whether or not they needed hospitalization. This was just one of a variety of stratagems HMA invented to try to maximize the money it could collect.[82]
- Despite the dangers of radiation from powerful computed tomography scans, hundreds of hospitals across the country unnecessarily scanned the chests of their Medicare patients twice on the same day. Radiologists

say that performing two scans in succession is rarely necessary. At leading teaching hospitals, the rate of such repeated scans is about 1%. At the hospitals under investigation, the rate was 80%.[83]

In all of these cases of unnecessary testing or treatment, patients either are harmed outright (such as by surgery) or exposed to known risks (such as radiation) or exposed to potential risks (such as the kind of injury that might be recognized as an adverse event).

These extreme examples distract us from a far larger and less obvious problem, one that has been studied experimentally by Dan Ariely, a professor of psychology and behavioral economics at Duke University's school of business. In a series of experiments examining dishonesty, Ariely and his colleagues developed a research paradigm through which they could test various factors that produce less or more lying and cheating. In the basic paradigm, participants were given easy math tasks that they would be able to solve given enough time, but the tasks were boring (so motivation was low) and the time allowed was not sufficient. Participants would be presented with a set of 12 numbers between zero and 10, each given to two decimal places (e.g., 4.62, 7.51) and they have to pick out the two that sum to 10. They were given 20 sets of such numbers and had four minutes to complete them (no one finishes them all). At the end, they were paid based on how many they solved correctly.

One important difference between experimental groups was who had the responsibility for counting the number of correct answers. Half the subjects gave their answer sheet to an experimenter who scored it. The other half scored the answers themselves and were told to take their original answer sheet with them to recycle. Subjects in the "recycle" condition reported significantly more answers correct than those in the "experimenter-counts" condition. That is, they cheated when they were allowed to report their own scores. Within this basic paradigm, various experimental interventions were tested. For example, before doing the math task, half the subjects were asked to spend two minutes writing the Ten Commandments (from memory), while the other half were asked to write down the names of 10 books that they had read in high school. For subjects in the "experimenter-counts" condition, which list they wrote had no effect on their reported math scores. But for those in the "recycle" condition, it was the subjects who wrote the 10 book names who cheated more; the scores of the subjects who wrote out the Ten Commandments were no different from those in the "experimenter-counts" condition. In another variation, college student subjects who signed the university honor pledge on the math task sheet also didn't cheat.[84]

Ariely explained one of his most important findings this way:

Across all of our experiments, we've tested maybe 30,000 people, and we had a dozen or so bad apples and they stole about $150 [in total] from us. And we had about 18,000 little rotten apples, each of them just stole a couple of dollars, but together it was $36,000. [That's] actually a good reflection of what happens in society.[85]

One real-world example of the little-rotten-apples phenomenon occurred at the gift shop in the Kennedy Center for the Performing Arts, in Washington, D.C., where $150,000 had been embezzled. An investigation did not find one major thief, but small amounts of pilferage by dozens of mostly elderly volunteers among the 300 who worked at the gift shop.[86] Small losses add up.

How might the little-rotten-apples problem work in healthcare? One thing to realize is that, depending on the circumstances, some or a lot of room exists for discretionary judgment in evaluating a patient's condition and the need and options for treatment. Ambiguity can exist in the measures of a patient's condition, in what the condition is, in when a condition crosses the line into likely-could-benefit-from treatment, and in where that dividing line is and how fuzzy the line is. Reasonable variations in judgment can shade into unreasonable ones. Where an obviously healthy uterus is removed from a woman presenting minor complaints, that would readily be viewed as deliberate unnecessary surgery.[87] But consider a more ambiguous situation, described by a New England ophthalmologist: "My old partner . . . was asked by a friend of his . . . at what level of vision do you do a cataract operation? And he said, well, if there's one ophthalmologist in town, its 20/200. If there are two ophthalmologists in town, its 20/80. If there are three ophthalmologists in town, its 20/40."[88] In other words, the needs of the providers (for business) rather than the needs of patients can drive utilization of services.

Looked at more broadly, a tension can exist between the interest of providers in providing certain services or performing certain procedures (for which they will be paid) and the best interests of patients, who might require less intensive interventions (in contrast to what is most remunerative for the provider) or none at all. As long as the need for treatment and the supply of treaters are in balance, the market serves the needs of both parties to the transaction. Trouble arises when the need for services and the supply of providers get out of balance. If there are too many patients with a given problem and not enough providers, patients will have to wait to get the care they need. On the other hand, if there are more providers than patients who need them, then the pressure builds to give patients tests and treatments that they don't need.[89]

Researchers from the Dartmouth Institute have made some astonishing discoveries about the provision of healthcare. The story begins as a medical detective mystery.[90] Led by Dr. Jack Wennberg, founding editor of the *Dartmouth Atlas of Health Care*, the research team collected data on every medical transaction in an area, a state, or a region. As they looked at the pattern of health services being provided, they saw that medicine was practiced differently from one locale to another, and the differences were considerable. People in one town might have their hemorrhoids removed five times more often (per capita) than people in a nearby town. The same was true for numerous other procedures, such as tonsillectomies, hysterectomies, mastectomies, cataracts, or prostate surgery. Wennberg found such differences in his own community:

We live right on the boundary between Stowe and Waterbury Center, Vermont. And if my kids had been going to the school system in Stowe, they would have had a 75% chance of getting their tonsils out. If they'd gone to the Waterbury School where they actually did it was about 20%.[91]

Why did doctors make the treatment decisions they made? The first place to look for an explanation of those wide differences in practice patterns was, of course, the patients. Did patients have different health problems in different communities and regions? Or more serious cases of the same problems? The research found that health conditions across the patient populations did not differ enough to begin to explain the differences in medical practice.

If the reason was not differences in the patients, could it be differences among the doctors? Physicians and surgeons in Maine, intrigued by Wennberg's findings, decided to try to find the explanation. They met several times each year, by specialty, to try to solve the puzzle. Initially, they strongly suspected it was their training—what they learned in different medical schools or residencies and brought with them into their practices. But it turned out that despite their differences in training, they largely agreed on the proper way to approach the health conditions with which their specialty dealt, what criteria should be met before doing one or another procedure. Other hypotheses were suggested. Could it be differences in local medical culture, fear of lawsuits, temperament (eagerness to take action), other things?

In the end, the answer was the last thing the doctors wanted it to be, and no one wanted to talk about: money.[92] Financial incentives explained why some doctors did more surgery for the same conditions than their peers did, chose more expensive (more remunerative) procedures over less expensive ones, and persisted in doing procedures that had been studied in randomized trials and found to be worthless to patients.[93] It was the doctors' interests that explained those anomalies in healthcare delivery, not the needs of the patients. Related to our central concern, those choices expose patients to unnecessary risks and harms. Moreover, even when no adverse events occurred, patient outcomes generally were no better when more was done rather than when less was done.[94]

Over the years, the Dartmouth Institute for Health Policy and Clinical Practice has documented dramatic differences in the provision of medical care around the United States—explainable not by the needs of patients but by the supply of services available—and collected their results in *The Dartmouth Atlas*.[95] The Dartmouth researchers refer to this, somewhat euphemistically, as supply-sensitive care:

> Supply-sensitive care refers to services where the supply of a specific resource has a major influence on utilization rates. The frequency of use of supply-sensitive care is not determined by well-articulated medical theory, much less by scientific evidence; rather, it is largely due to differences in local capacity, and a payment system that ensures that existing capacity remains fully deployed. Simply put, in regions where there are more hospital beds per capita, patients will be more likely to be admitted to the hospital. In regions where there are more intensive care unit beds, more patients will be cared for

in the ICU. More specialists will result in more visits to specialists. And the more CT scanners are available, the more CT scans patients will receive. The Dartmouth Atlas has consistently demonstrated these relationships.[96]

While the Dartmouth researchers have been concerned primarily with ineffectiveness (excessive treatment does not lead to better health outcomes) and waste ("Supply-sensitive care also accounts for more than half of all Medicare spending."), they also recognize that the delivery of medical care that serves the economic interests of providers rather than the health needs of patients increases the risk of harm: "Hospitals can be dangerous places, where patients face the risk of medical error, adverse events, and hospital-acquired antibiotic-resistant infections."[97] "Patients who receive care for conditions that would have never caused a problem can only experience the risk of the intervention."[98] Treatment that a patient would not have consented to had the patient known it offered no benefit is itself a harm, even if the patient does not suffer an adverse event. But it is a harm that will go uncounted by research focused on injurious medical mistakes.

AT THE END OF THE DAY, HOW BIG IS THE PROBLEM?

Extrapolating from various studies to a national incidence of avoidable injuries and deaths caused by medical management leads to a range of different conclusions, any of which should be cause for abundant concern. The focus usually is on deaths, although the large number of serious and permanent injuries should be deeply concerning as well.

If the 13,600 deaths caused by medical (mis)management in California hospitals found by the CMA/CHA study in the mid-1970s were extrapolated to the United States as a whole at that time, the number of deaths nationally would have been around 163,200.[99] The other major chart review studies, by the Harvard team—summarized by the IOM, as finding "as many as 98,000" avoidable deaths nationally in the mid-1980s—were reanalyzed by four of the Harvard researchers, including Lucian Leape and Troyen Brennan, who suggested that the number of preventable deaths was as high as 140,000.[100]

Martin Makary and Michael Daniel, of the Johns Hopkins University School of Medicine, combining major studies of several types conducted after the IOM report (from 1999 to 2013), calculated "a mean rate of death from medical error of 251,454 a year."[101]

We noted that the patient chart reviews employed in those studies are something like a net with holes so large that many adverse events slip through. Studies using more intensive approaches found the number of serious injuries and deaths to be 15 to 20 times as high as what is found using patient record reviews alone. Another technique, the Global Trigger, found about 10 times as many adverse events as the earlier records reviews. John James, a retired NASA toxicologist turned medical error researcher, reviewing the four major Global Trigger studies available, concluded in 2013 that deaths from "preventable adverse events" numbered somewhere between 210,000 and 440,000.[102]

All of those studies and reviews of studies limited themselves to what happens to inpatients in nonfederal acute-care hospitals. Beyond those patients, we noted, were patients receiving diagnoses, treatments, and surgeries in various nonhospital settings: doctors' offices, outpatient clinics, free-standing surgical centers, skilled nursing facilities, rehabilitation hospitals, and nursing homes. Regarding what happens in those settings, the research is far more limited. But a few facts that we discussed provide an inkling.

First, the annual number of outpatient surgical visits in the United States currently is more than four times the number of hospital patients admitted for surgeries. Although surgeries in hospitals would, in the aggregate, be for more serious and risky conditions, the sheer number of surgeries outside of hospitals offers ample opportunity for preventable errors to occur. Second, approximately 1.8% of patients in skilled nursing facilities died as a result of the care they received (or needed but did not receive). This alone adds another 90,000 deaths, more or less, to the total. Third, the IOM study of medication-related injuries concluded that three times as many harmful medication errors occur in healthcare delivered outside of hospitals as inside them. Fourth, nearly as many payments to compensate patients for iatrogenic harm were made for injuries incurred in outpatient settings as in hospitals. Two-thirds of those payments were for major injury or death. The leading type of error in the outpatient setting was diagnostic, and medication errors in the outpatient setting accounted for 1 out of 131 deaths (compared to only 1 out of 854 inpatient deaths).

In light of those facts, however incomplete, a conservative estimate would be that as many preventable deaths and serious injuries occur in healthcare settings outside of hospitals as occur inside of hospitals.

Those expanded and additional sources of harm suggest the need to multiply the number of injuries and deaths. If we doubled IOM report's conservative, and oft-quoted numbers, we would be looking at between $34 to $58 billion in annual economic loss to patients, families, insurers, and taxpayers. A more recent study (employing estimates totaling 187,000 deaths and 6.1 million injuries annually in and out of hospitals) found the likely cost of harmful adverse events to be somewhere between $393 billion and $958 billion. That is an amount equal to between 18% and 45% of total U.S. healthcare spending in 2006.[103]

Finally, consider the problem of unnecessary care—patients subjected to surgery that was not needed as well as being given tests, scans, medications, and treatments that offered patients no benefit while exposing them to risks of harm. We suggested that the vast majority of these unnecessary treatments would not be captured by any of the studies designed to find adverse events. Even unnecessary surgery, in and of itself inherently injurious, would be overlooked unless it resulted in an adverse event. We also suggested that the line dividing beneficial from unnecessary testing and treatment is a difficult one to draw. But the work of the Dartmouth Institute and of other researchers has shown that about 30% of healthcare spending in the United States is worthless because it offers patients no benefit.[104] That implies an enormous quantity of harmful or risky tests and procedures that has gone uncounted by the usual studies. This is an area in need of much more research. And the solution to it will call for approaches quite different from those usually contemplated by patient safety experts.

In sum, there can be no doubt that a serious problem exists and remedies are needed. This is true whether the number of adverse events suffered by patients is taken to be at the low end of the range (44,000 to 98,000 preventable deaths suffered by hospital inpatients) as found through chart review research, or the higher end (250,000 or 440,000 deaths). And even more troubling, if the direct observation and Global Trigger approaches provide the more accurate measures, they lead to estimates of injurious errors that are higher than those in the IOM report by a factor of about 10. (The increase associated with deaths is less dramatic: about twice as many if the Global Trigger results are correct, and about five times as many if the direct observation studies are correct.) And, of course, double those if we add adverse events occurring outside of the acute-care hospital setting. And far more if we add unnecessary treatments.

In an effort to infuse those mere numbers with greater impact, patient safety experts have sometimes expressed the incidence of preventable deaths resulting from medical errors in terms of jumbo jet crashes.[105] Since the news media, the public, and officials of various kinds are stirred with concern whenever a commercial airliner crashes—but are not roused by people dying quietly one by one, spread across the nation's healthcare system—the analogy is meant to function as an attention grabber.[106] Patient deaths due to medical error equal as many as six or more jumbo jets crashing every single day of the year. The very lowest estimates would translate to one jumbo jet crashing about every third day.

Dr. Mark Chassin, currently president and CEO of the Joint Commission (formerly the Joint Commission on Accreditation of Healthcare Organizations), compared the error rates in healthcare to those of other industries:

> If the performance of certain high-reliability industries, whose standards of excellence we take for granted, suddenly deteriorated to the level of most health care services, some astounding results would occur. At a defect rate of 20 percent, which occurs in the use of antibiotics for colds, the credit card industry would make daily mistakes on nine million transactions; banks would deposit 36 million checks in the wrong accounts every day; and deaths from airplane crashes would increase one thousand-fold.[107]

As Dr. David Hyman and co-author Professor Charles Silver comment, "An error rate of 20% would be intolerable in the business settings identified, but error rates as high as 79% have been observed in health care."[108]

The CDC does not include deaths due to iatrogenic injuries in its monitoring of the "leading causes of death in the United States." But, if it did, even the very lowest of the estimates would place medical error third on the CDC's list, while the highest counts would rival the top spot.[109] So, whatever number we take to be *the* incidence of avoidable deaths and serious injuries suffered by patients in our nation's healthcare system, we are led to the conclusion that the problem is either extremely serious or considerably worse than that.

5

The Medical Malpractice Litigation System

[T]he litigation system seems to protect many patients from being injured in the first place. And since prevention before the fact is generally preferable to compensation after the fact, the apparent injury prevention effect must be an important factor in the debate about the future of the malpractice litigation system.[1]

When a patient suffers a serious, preventable, accidental injury in the course of receiving medical care, what options does the law offer? And what usually happens? Typically the process presents many hurdles for injured patients, and the outcomes are far less favorable than most people would guess. Many, perhaps most, injured patients are not at all sure that what happened to them was an iatrogenic injury, and the same is typically true for the families of patients who unexpectedly died. Some errors are glaring, of course (wrong surgery, wrong patient, wrong site), but many more are ambiguous to patients and their families, if not invisible. Something is seriously wrong with the patient, but is this because the wrong drug or the wrong dose was administered? Or because a scalpel slipped and severed something that should not have been severed? Or because a surgical instrument was "retained" inadvertently? Returning from the hospital, the patient never again is able to urinate: Was that a normal risk of the procedure or the result of an error?

Doctors and hospitals generally do not disclose to patients when errors are made. Procedures that turn out badly typically are spoken of as undifferentiated "complications." The vast majority of the time, error or not, negligence or not, such patients do nothing. Without protest, they live with their conditions and whatever has been done to their lives and their finances. This response is known as "lumping it." Some injured patients start asking around; maybe a friend of a friend is a nurse who works in a hospital, and offers some insight or opinion.

A small subset of these patients searches for and finds an attorney whose practice includes medical injuries. The attorney screens these cases, turning away most of them before or after conferring with a medical expert. If the injured patient's case is accepted by an attorney, the vast majority of those will end through some kind of pretrial resolution, such as a negotiated settlement. In cases that do go to trial, typically in front of a jury, the jury usually decides in favor of the defendant (the doctor or hospital). Plaintiff patients who do win at trial will often see the jury's award reduced by the trial judge or reduced through further negotiations before an appeal is filed, after which an appellate court might reduce the award of damages further if not set it aside entirely. The tiny fraction of successful lawsuits resulting in "blockbuster" awards, the ones that make the newspapers, do not reflect what happens in most cases.

The previous brief sketch of the progression from medical injury to legal resolution is fleshed out thoroughly later in this chapter, which examines medical malpractice law and litigation. But first we will look briefly at the origins and purposes of tort law—most simply understood as "accident law." Then we expand that understanding of the nature and function of tort law by looking at the system through the lens of economic analysis. Next, we look at the more specialized rules that apply when the accidents at issue occur in the context of healthcare (also known as medical malpractice liability or medical professional negligence). The chapter will then trace the flow of cases into and through the system using the findings of empirical research.

ORIGINS, NATURE, AND PURPOSE

Medieval common law did not draw a clear distinction between criminal and civil wrongs—both involved unjustified harm to an innocent victim. Over time—due partly to the intellectual development of the common law (coming to appreciate that intentional harms and accidental ones should be treated differently, for reasons of both morality and social engineering) and partly due to technological advances (which created more and more dangerous risks that increasingly resulted in accidental injuries)—tort law and criminal law diverged.

Glimmers of a separate law of torts can be seen in the eighteenth century, but became more clearly and fully developed in the nineteenth and twentieth centuries. Tort law was necessitated by and evolved in tandem with technological advances and the growth of modern industries. Tort law evolved to meet the needs of our individualistic and market-based society (as opposed to more communitarian and regulated societies), and therefore has become most highly developed in the United States. Tort law allows businesses, professionals, and all of us in our quotidian lives a broad zone of freedom to act, stepping in only after harm occurs, to consider whether a harm-doer should or should not be required to compensate the victims of that harm. Correspondingly, where tort law shrinks, governmental, or quasi-governmental regulation tends to expand.

Conduct that produces or merely risks harm, has a moral aspect, lacks socially redeeming value, and is accompanied by intent to produce the injurious outcome or by awareness of a high likelihood of harm or indifference to a recognized risk of harm (thereby justifying such notions as blameworthiness, guilt, and punishment) became crystallized into the criminal law.[2] By contrast, injury-producing conduct that arises inadvertently out of otherwise socially productive activity (transportation, product manufacturing, construction, and healthcare, to name a few) are addressed by the law of torts. Like other Anglo-American civil law (such as property law and contract law), notions such as immorality, stigma, blameworthiness, guilt, and punishment have a small role to play, if any at all.[3]

This centrally important distinction between tort law and criminal law seems to be blurred in the perceptions of some who become defendants in tort suits. For example, in his autobiography, legendary auto manufacturing executive Lee Iacocca wails about the damages his company had to pay for dangerous cars that caused terrible harm to some of their customers, arguing that the law had unjustly overreached because neither he nor his employees ever "intended" to do anyone any harm.[4] Mr. Iacocca is implicitly suggesting that "*intent* to cause harm" should be an essential basis for liability; that the law should intercede on behalf of injury victims only when the harm-producing conduct is criminal in nature; and that victims should otherwise bear their own losses (rather than being compensated by the company that caused them harm).

Similarly, some propose to distinguish between "good" doctors (those who try their best to do safe and competent work, but occasionally slip up or overlook something, cause a harmful accident, and then get "nabbed" by the tort system) and "bad" doctors ("unqualified, unmotivated or reckless"[5]), who are the ones the tort system should concern itself with. A doctor who *recklessly* causes the death of a patient commits the crime of manslaughter. Prosecutors generally prefer to leave even those cases to the civil side of the legal system, to tort litigation. But the law does sometimes employ the criminal remedy for the "bad" doctors.[6]

The tort system maps quite differently than those who would make corrupt intent or bad character its touchstones. Both good and bad drivers can have accidents. From one incident to the next, the tort system treats the good and the bad drivers equally, although presumably the bad drivers will more frequently bring themselves to the attention of the tort system. So, a sort of "natural" tendency exists for the less competent to be dinged more often than the more competent. Industries are expected to respond to the tort system's responses by taking feasible steps to reduce accident risks. Delivery companies could hire drivers with better safety records. Insurers could experience-rate drivers or fleets and set their insurance rates accordingly.[7]

Additional attributes of tort law are revealing. Most of the conduct with which criminal law is concerned is so objectionable to society that a crime can be committed even when no harm befalls any victim. Aiming a gun at a person and pulling the trigger but missing—even if the intended victim remains completely unharmed and even unaware that a shot was fired—constitutes the crime of attempted murder and carries a harsh sentence.

By contrast, because the conduct with which tort law is concerned is regarded altogether differently (it has social value), it is treated altogether differently. Only the occurrence of actual harm can give rise to a tort. A potential tortfeasor whose conduct is careless and dangerous, but who in the end has caused no harm, has done nothing that is recognized as wrongdoing by tort law. Furthermore, criminal law is classified as public law, the harm done is to society and not just to the injured individual, and so criminal actions are brought by public prosecutors. Tort actions, on the other hand, are private law and can only be brought by the individuals who suffered the loss.

The previously described distinctions characterize the heartland of each of those two legal domains. Blame, guilt, stigma, moral failing, and punishment are aspects of criminal law, not tort law. Tort law's heartland is unintentional accidents that occur in the course of socially desirable activity. At their borders, however, criminal law and tort law seep into each other a bit. Some torts are intentional, and those can give rise to *punitive* damages (this resembles criminal law). An intentional assault can be responded to by both a criminal prosecution and a tort action that adds punitive damages to compensation for the victim's losses. And a few crimes require only lack of awareness (i.e., negligence) when awareness is required (this resembles tort law). But these exceptions, few and far between, underscore our characterization of the respective heartlands of these two legal realms.[8]

The essential purposes of tort law are usually said to be compensation and deterrence.[9] The compensation function should be obvious from the preceding discussion. We have said little of deterrence. Deterrence in tort law should not be confused with deterrence in criminal law. Since torts do not generally involve awareness of the risk of the coming harm, deterrence cannot mean to consciously refrain from causing the harm. Deterrence in tort refers to the incentive effects that the requirement to pay for damages will have on future efforts toward and investment in safety. These are the subject of economic analysis.

ECONOMIC ANALYSIS

Legal scholars as well as economists have been interested in the micro-economic dimensions of tort law.[10] When an accident occurs, the loss falls initially on the victim. If nothing else is done, victims of accidental injury will bear their own losses: medical expenses, disability, lost earnings, property damage, and so on. The challenge for tort law is to define the conditions under which the losses ought to be shifted to the injurer. The questions posed by economic analysis have centered around what the economic effects are of any given set of legal rules for cost-shifting, what economic effects ought to be the goals of tort law, and what rules best effectuate those goals.

Consider the pizza delivery business as an example. In an effort to meet the needs of customers and to earn their patronage, pizza delivery services aim to deliver pizzas as quickly as possible. Accordingly, they adopt practices and incentive systems designed to accomplish that goal. Those practices can lead (and have led) to delivery personnel driving too fast and less safely than they otherwise would.

What happens if the law does nothing when pizza delivery crashes occur, leaving the cost on innocent accident victims? Pizza delivery services that drive the fastest will earn the most profits—up to some point where the cost of their own vehicle repairs cancels out the additional profits. Also, costs will be created for people outside the transactions of the pizza industry—costs of medical care for the personal injuries, property damage, death, lost future earnings, etc.—which will be borne by the crash victims, their first-party insurers, employers, families, and taxpayers (depending on the private and social insurance programs available to victims). Those costs, termed externalities, are part of the total cost of doing business that the law (by doing nothing) allows the pizza industry to transfer to others, creating a subsidy for the pizza industry.

Instead, tort law could require pizza delivery businesses to compensate *all* victims of the accidents they cause in the course of their deliveries (a situation termed "strict liability" or "no-fault," because establishing liability requires only proof of causation). Legal historians believe that for centuries before the mid-1800s, all direct and immediate harms were decided under this kind of rule. Under this tort policy, economic analysis suggests that pizza delivery services would drive *too* carefully—so afraid of taking chances or speeding that many hungry customers would wait too long to receive too many cold pizzas. That, too, is a social cost. Victims would no longer be subsidizing the delivery of pizzas, but pizza delivery services would not be as efficient and effective as they could be.

Rather than compensating no one or everyone who is injured by a pizza delivery vehicle, what tort law has typically done in this kind of situation is to set "negligence" as the threshold for evaluating when losses should be shifted from victims to injurers.[11] Negligence, or fault-based, liability became firmly established in the United States in the middle of the nineteenth century.[12] Negligence can be defined as a failure to exercise the degree of care that would be used by the ordinary reasonable person under the particular circumstances. A more quantitative but no less familiar definition of negligence is known as the Learned Hand formula: $B < PL$, meaning that conduct is negligent if the burden (B), or cost, of avoiding the accident is less than the losses (L) suffered by the plaintiff (P) discounted by the probability of the incident's occurrence.[13] This is what tort law means by "fault" or "unreasonable conduct." Yet another articulation of the same concept has been embraced by safety experts: the Johnston substitution test, which focuses attention on the other side of the very same coin.[14]

Negligence is not a moral judgment. It is an economic efficiency judgment. Students of the economics of tort law have argued that negligence is the ideal threshold for distinguishing cases in which losses should be left on the plaintiff from those where losses should be shifted to the defendant. "[T]he dominant function of the fault system is to generate rules of liability that if followed will bring about, at least approximately, the efficient—the cost-justified—level of accidents and safety."[15] That is, total economic welfare for society is maximized by identifying the dividing line that produces the minimum combined total cost of accidents and accident avoidance. Negligence is that dividing line. From the Learned Hand formula, it is easy to see why. When losses to a plaintiff can be prevented by the expenditure of a relatively small additional investment by the defendant, society benefits by preventing wasteful costs in the form of the victim's damages. When avoiding losses to an injury victim could be prevented only by the defendant's investment of an excessive sum in prevention, then it does not make economic sense (for society) to have that investment made, and the loss should remain on the plaintiff.

Economic efficiency and societal wealth maximization are not necessarily the Holy Grail. All legal rules are choices, based on various considerations and having various impacts. Negligence has its critics. Some of them point out that from a compensation perspective, it leaves a large number of innocent victims of preventable accidents with nothing. Victims of accidents that were slightly nonnegligent (by the Learned Hand formula: B was slightly greater than PL) are entitled to no compensation, and must bear all of the losses created by someone else's error or carelessness. All cases that fall below the negligence threshold are to be decided for the defendant, and that is a lot of accidental injuries. This strikes thoughtful critics of negligence as unfair and unwise, and they argue that many more innocent victims of the inadvertence of others should be compensated than occurs under the conventional fault-based rule. This was part of the reasoning that led New Zealand to replace its negligence-based tort law with a national no-fault system in 1972.[16] From a deterrence perspective, some critics of negligence believe that by allowing so many harms to go uncompensated, insufficient incentives are created for at least some industries to invest sufficiently in accident prevention. Society should be willing to pay a little more than the economically efficient minimum to achieve greater safety and prevent more lives from being damaged or destroyed. That can be accomplished by setting the threshold for finding liability lower than the line drawn by negligence. Evidence that our society values life and limb and freedom from pain and disability more than is implied by the negligence standard is the amount of our GDP we devote to healthcare. Before we get too far ahead of ourselves, however, let's return to the implications of negligence-based tort liability.

When costs are sometimes shifted to defendants, interesting and useful things happen. Shifting a sufficient portion of the costs of accidents to defendants places those costs on those who are in the best position to take steps to prevent accidents and, also important, those in the best position to figure out how to do so most efficiently. The law does not say what to do; it merely places the incentives where they will do the most good. Defendants (especially repeat players within various industries) find themselves confronted with something closer to the total costs of their activities. That is, the costs they had externalized onto others in society are "internalized" back to them. Defendants and prospective defendants are in the best position to evaluate how best to manage those costs—something they have no incentive to do unless the costs are internalized. They might decide to continue to work as before, continuing to generate negligent injuries at the same rate as before. Or they might decide to make certain investments (behavioral or technological) to reduce the incidence of the most frequent or most expensive kinds of harm. Tort law leaves the choice to them. From a business's viewpoint, as judge and professor Richard Posner has put it, "When the cost of accidents is less than the cost of prevention, a rational profit-maximizing enterprise will pay tort judgments to accident victims rather than incur the larger cost of avoiding liability."[17] And that is not a bad explanation, from an economic perspective, of why the healthcare industry has not invested more in patient safety.[18]

At bottom, the law is indifferent to the decision any given defendant or industry makes. But the law assumes enough economic rationality that they will make the choice that is best for them (the most cost-efficient choice) and, therefore, the choice that is best for society. As we already noted, the choice that minimizes tortfeasors' combined damages costs and accident costs is the choice that moves toward "the efficient—the cost-justified—level of accidents and safety." Thus, in the eyes of economic efficiency analysis, the goal of tort law is not to eliminate all accidents and their associated costs. Rather, tort law seeks to minimize the total cost of accidents plus investment in accident avoidance—in other words, to help society find the optimal level of safety, not the maximum level of safety.

Tort costs—whether paid in the form of insurance premiums or paid directly by a defendant tortfeasor ("self-insurance")—are in essence a pass-through from customers to persons who are negligently injured by the relevant activity.[19] The funds are collected by and held briefly by the potential tortfeasor, but originate with the customers and are earmarked to pay for accident compensation.[20] That is yet another aspect of tort law's compatibility with the marketplace. Imagine that the industry-wide cost of paying damages to the victims of zealous pizza delivery drivers averages $50,000 per shop per year. Each pizzeria will obtain that amount by increasing the price of pizza pies commensurately.[21]

The potential tortfeasor has choices about how to handle those potential costs most efficiently and profitably. At its most efficient, each pizzeria finds the optimal balance of investments in safety and exposure to liability to minimize the total costs it needs to set aside for accidental negligent injuries (usually with an insurer). Some pizzerias might choose to require safe delivery practices. Pizzerias that are more successful in approaching that minimum can use their savings either to increase profits or to lower their prices (making them more competitive).

On the other hand, unfortunately, this arrangement creates the illusion that all of the funds collected for tort purposes are intended for the pizzeria owners and that if they can stop those funds from being spent on crash victims, they can keep all of those savings as profit. Were the pizzerias' trade association able to persuade the legislature to bar suits by victims of pizza delivery crashes or to limit payments to victims to a fraction of their actual losses, market forces would tend to push prices lower. So not all, or not much, of the savings would remain in the pockets of the pizzeria owners, as they had hoped.

Nothing works perfectly, in law or in healthcare, but in a sufficiently free market, tort law is expected to nudge an industry's practices toward an efficient balance of injury costs and safety costs, toward minimization of the total costs of accidents and accident prevention.

THE MEDICAL ACCIDENT SUBSPECIES OF TORT LAW

To prevail in a typical tort case requires a plaintiff to prove that the defendant was under a *duty* of care that the defendant *breached* by conduct that was *negligent* and that *caused* some nontrivial *damage* to the plaintiff. In a typical tort case, the duty owed is to anyone and everyone who might foreseeably be affected by the tortfeasor's actions. If a reasonable person in the defendant's situation would have acted in a safer manner, which likely would have prevented the injury from occurring, the defendant would be considered negligent. If any one of those elements is not proven to exist, the case is decided for the defendant and the loss remains on the victim of the injury.

In the medical injury context, important additional restrictions have traditionally been placed on the legal formula just described. First, whereas the typical tort defendant owes a duty to the world, the malpractice defendant owes a duty only to his or her patient, which means a person who is in a contractual relationship with the provider.[22]

Second, the existence or absence of negligence in nonmedical torts is assessed by laypersons (the jury), often using nothing more than their collective life experience to determine how the ordinary reasonable person in the relevant circumstances would behave. In other words, jurors supply the standard of care without instruction by experts. In contrast, the standard of care for a healthcare provider must be supplied by experts from the same professional community as the defendant. Whether or not the defendant failed to perform up to that standard is also a subject of testimony by experts. Unlike most tort cases, without a suitable expert to propound a professionally informed view of the situation, a malpractice plaintiff's case typically would end before it begins.

The courts sometimes invented special doctrines to protect certain fledgling industries from liability while they were struggling to establish themselves on sound commercial foundations. Railroads of the nineteenth century were the archetypal example of this practice. Special rules such as the fellow servant doctrine[23] and assumption of the risk[24] barred many potential claims by injured railroad and manufacturing workers. In the arena of medical injury, the courts developed rules such as the charitable immunity doctrine (which insulated many hospitals from liability), the strict locality rule (requiring the plaintiff to obtain an expert from the same geographic community as the defendant physician), and advantageous wrongful act accrual dates for statutes of limitations (ending the time period following the injury when a claim may be brought).

Such special protections need not be permanent. With the passage of time, the economic success of protected industries combined with the further development of their technologies, practices, and other circumstances can lead to the eventual withering of the rules that had helped the industry reach a more economically sound stage of development. For example, the strict locality rule allowed any given community of physicians to make malpractice cases nearly impossible to bring against one of their members by refusing to provide expert testimony in cases arising in the locality. At the same time that such "conspiracies of silence" created pressures to modify or abolish the locality rule (so injured patients could find outside experts to explain why their care was below acceptable standards), so did continuing medical education and communication and other innovations. It became increasingly medically unnecessary, as well as legally inappropriate, to protect pockets of doctors from having to be competent by more contemporary and more widely accepted professional standards.

The definition of negligence is one of utter relativism. Actions or inactions are negligent if they are less safe than what the community of others would do in a given situation. The standard changes with changes in technology, beliefs, and practices of the reference community, the particulars of the situation and context, and so on.

In the medical context, therefore, the definition of negligence depends entirely on what the profession, or a relevant subpopulation within the profession, considers to be appropriate under the given circumstances. Not that identifying the applicable standard, or standards, is straightforward. But the law defers to medicine to say what its standard is. This leads to a seeming paradox: over time, the better able medicine becomes to treat illness and injury, the easier it is for a physician to practice negligently. When there is little that a doctor can do (because little is known and technological tools are few), doing little or nothing is not negligent. But the more that medical science learns and the more tools that exist, the more that doing nothing, or not enough, or not the right thing, constitutes negligent care.[25] So we have the seeming paradox that the better medicine gets, the more negligence there is. But it isn't paradoxical. The moment knowledge and technology advance so that something beneficial can be done for a patient, practitioners must do that something and do it properly, else they have performed negligently.

Many industries that have grown large enough to afford lobbying have sought to reduce the law's capacity to hold them accountable to the public, with the ultimate hope of escaping from the risk of liability altogether. The incentive for doing so could not be clearer: the less money that is required to be transferred to persons harmed by an industry's errors, the more money members of that industry might be able to keep in their own pockets. For professionals, perhaps especially in the world of American healthcare, there is a further incentive. A highly trained professional, whose socialization has been into a culture where independence of judgment and action are highly prized and where traditionally accountability within the field largely ceases once training ends,[26] is more than a little annoyed by the idea that some ordinary citizens (juries) are going to sit in judgment over whether or not the doctor performed properly.[27]

ELEMENTS OF THE LITIGOTIATION PROCESS

As cases move through the litigation process, their movement from one decision node to the next is propelled less by decisions made by formal decision makers, like judges and juries, than by negotiated agreements made between the disputing parties. Negotiation is the dominant activity in litigation. This led a leading scholar of the subject, Marc Galanter, to coin the term "litigotiation."[28]

What everyone who is concerned about the malpractice liability system should want to know, and needs to know if they are to think meaningfully about the system, is how many cases could or should properly enter the system, how many do enter, what happens to them along the way, how they end, the cost of producing those outcomes, what effects the process and its outcomes have on things that matter, and whether what society gets is worth the cost. Perhaps the litigotiation process is efficient and effective. Perhaps not. To find out, we need to pay attention to the systematic empirical research that provides these evidence-based descriptions.[29]

What goes on at any given stage of the litigotiation system can be understood only in relation to what occurred at the decision nodes that preceded it and that later stages provide feedback to inform decisions at earlier stages.[30]

Initiation of Claims by Victims

As we saw in Chapter 4 of this volume, by any measure, the annual incidence of medical adverse events in the United States, negligent or otherwise, is huge—totaling more than all other causes of accidental injury and death combined. But the proportion of those that become filed lawsuits is tiny. The vast majority of potential valid claims that drop out do so at this first decision node; most victims of medical injury take no action to obtain compensation.[31]

Focusing only on adverse events occurring in hospitals (the best-studied healthcare arena), by the most litigious estimates (i.e., the numbers that suggest the highest rate of filing malpractice lawsuits by injured patients),[32] for every 100 adverse events, 4 malpractice insurer claim files are opened; for every 100 *negligent* adverse events, 17 claim files are opened.[33] These are the high water marks of claiming. As the denominator is replaced with more complete incidences of adverse events,[34] the claiming rate fades almost to the point of vanishing.

Compare this behavior to that of an automobile owner who takes his car in to the shop for some repairs, and when he returns for it learns that in the course of working on the car, the mechanic has accidentally damaged it to an extent that it will never run properly again, cannot be repaired, and the damage is permanent. Would the great majority of car owners simply take their battered vehicle home, without complaint and without asking for compensation for the damage? Yet that's what people do when their bodies suffer comparable damage in hospitals.[35]

To students of the malpractice litigation system over the past 30 or more years, one of the most interesting questions has been, "Why do so few victims of medical injury bring claims?" Why do the vast majority of victims and their families take no action? They quietly accept the injuries, suffering, disability, and losses, or they turn to insurers or government for financial help. What they do not do is demand accountability from those who caused their injuries.

If they are not suing those who injure them, what are they doing? One study that examined how nearly 200 patients dealt with medical care they considered to be seriously unsatisfactory found that 26% did nothing, 46% changed doctors, 25% complained to their doctor directly, and 9% contacted lawyers although none of them ultimately filed suits.[36]

More general research on people's responses to tortious harms found that such injuries are transformed into disputes only after the victims traverse several stages of processing the problem: naming, blaming, and claiming.[37] First, the victim must recognize that a harm has occurred and define it as a damaging change from normal or expected (*naming*). Next, the victim must attribute the cause of the harm to some person or other entity (*blaming*). And finally, the person must make a decision to confront the harm-doer and demand recompense (*claiming*). Fewer and fewer victims of tortious injury reach each succeeding stage.

Medical injury is one of the most difficult areas of torts in which to name, blame, and claim. While an injury in itself will alert the driver of a car or the user of a tool that something is amiss, a medical patient is less likely to know whether a condition following treatment is normal or unexpected; if unexpected, whether it was caused by the medical intervention; and, if so, whether to take any action. Interviews with patients who felt they had received poor medical care found that in the aftermath of the care the injured patients consulted family, friends, and professionals, including nurses or doctors they might know in an effort to understand the nature of their condition and what caused it.[38]

Many go no further—do not complain to the doctor or hospital, do not visit an attorney. One reason is that our legal process is not self-starting but requires victims to initiate and pursue their cases. That is a hurdle many people find daunting. Many are especially reluctant to complain to or about high-status professionals. Many like their doctors too much to complain. Even people with sufficient education, status, and assertiveness to complain and press a claim often choose not to have to relive the events, preferring to put the experience behind them sooner rather than later and to adapt to their new, postinjury lives.

Attorney Filtering of Cases

Those relatively few victims who wish to press their claims cannot realistically do so unless a lawyer agrees to handle their case, and lawyers try not to accept a case unless they see an acceptable probability of gain for themselves in doing so.

The basic economics of malpractice cases are not hard to understand. As a litigation category, malpractice cases have long required an unusually large dollar investment (compared to other kinds of personal injury or wrongful death cases), and the investment is made by plaintiffs' attorneys. Malpractice cases require consulting medical experts to evaluate those cases that pass preliminary screening by the attorney; other experts must be hired to prepare for and possibly testify at trial; a greater investment of an attorney's time compared to other types of tort cases. Expenses are paid out of the attorney's funds, and they are reimbursed, if at all, out of the proceeds of a settlement or verdict. The result is that a malpractice case must have a higher expected return (compared to other personal injury or wrongful death cases) to be worth an attorney accepting it.[39] Many of the reforms of recent decades (see Chapter 6 of this volume) have aimed to add additional burdens to the effort and cost of litigating as well as to reduce the prospects of a successful outcome for plaintiffs. The result has been to push the threshold for accepting a case higher and higher.[40]

Those economic incentives and disincentives compel plaintiffs' lawyers to perform a valuable service for doctors and hospitals. Lawyers will seek cases with strong evidence of negligence and causation, and clients whose injuries are severe. Weaker cases will be declined. Without economically self-interested lawyer gatekeepers, more claims and weaker claims would become lawsuits. This selective acceptance further reduces the number of actionable injuries that actually become litigated cases.[41]

Systematic empirical studies of lawyer case screening behavior are fewer and farther between than of most other aspects of the malpractice litigation system because this activity is more private: an injured patient or family member phones or visits lawyer's office, records and other information are obtained, and attorneys make decisions. None of that is public. But what studies exist confirm the expectations of a substantial degree of economic rationality. In a study of attorney screening practices involving tens of thousands of contacts with clients seeking representation, attorneys rejected 80% of prospective malpractice claims (compared to 70% for other kinds of tort cases).[42]

Another study that examined plaintiffs' attorneys' responses to requests from prospective medical malpractice clients reached similar findings. Of 730 total calls received by these lawyers' offices over 10 randomly selected days, medical records were obtained for 90, most of which were then reviewed by a consulting expert. The physicians' reviews led to 53 more rejections because they "were felt to have had insufficient damages (42%) or lacked negligence on the part of the healthcare provider (26%)." For various reasons, additional cases were rejected. In all, only 3% of the original 730 inquiries led to an eventual claim being filed; 97% were declined.[43]

Despite those screening efforts, the decision to file is imperfect because information in possession of the plaintiffs' attorneys and their consulting physicians is incomplete. Some "good" cases inevitably are rejected, and some "bad" cases are accepted, at least for a while. Note the asymmetry. A good case that is rejected by plaintiffs' attorneys will rarely if ever be resurrected. But a bad case that is accepted can be discarded at some subsequent stage. Put a bit differently, erroneous rejections of cases are unlikely to be corrected, while erroneous acceptances are likely to be corrected because they are under continual evaluation.

Pretrial Disposition

Once an attorney accepts a case, the defendant's insurer and its lawyers join the conversation. The filing of a claim permits the defendant's representatives to respond to the plaintiff's reading of the case and permits the plaintiff's attorney to engage in civil discovery to learn more about a case than was known prior to filing. These exchanges allow both sides to assess and reassess the relative strengths of their cases.

Lawyers (and parties) are reluctant to give over control of a case to third party decision makers (judges and juries). If the two sides can agree within reasonable bounds on the strength of the evidence and the value of a case, they will settle it themselves. Of the cases that have entered the legal process through the gatekeeping of the plaintiffs' lawyers, this is the stage at which around 90% of them are resolved and disposed of.

What is the resolution of those cases? Using data from 60 U.S. medical malpractice insurers, one study found that of all cases that led to the opening of an insurance company file, 64% were eventually dropped, withdrawn, or dismissed; 27% resulted in a settlement with a payment to the plaintiff; and only about 8% proceeded to trial.[44]

Although those numbers show considerable winnowing of cases in this pretrial stage (92% of claim files exit the system), some caution is required before we can infer more than that. For one thing, the usual sources for counting cases inevitably involve some undercounting and some overcounting. The insurer's "claim files" contain more cases than will actually become complaints (lawsuits) filed by plaintiffs, because insurers open a file merely if informed by an insured that an incident occurred or might have occurred. So some of the cases that "drop out" were never actually in to begin with. On the other side of the ledger, court files contain fewer than all of the cases that actually have been processed and resolved by litigotiation. That is because some number of cases have been resolved and paid without a lawsuit ever being filed with a court. The best estimate of these that we have found is that for every trial verdict, roughly eight cases are settled prior to the filing of a complaint.[45]

But many of those 64% of cases that were dropped, withdrawn, or dismissed surely are not statistical illusions, but cases that plaintiffs' lawyers started out thinking were "good" cases. They have no incentive to invest resources in cases that will only cost them time and money. So what happened? At the time of filing, full information is not available to plaintiffs' lawyers, and by the end of the pretrial phase much more has been learned. Even then, information is incomplete because neither side does the more thorough investigation and preparation it will do on those cases that actually go to trial. This is an imperfection in information gathering and analysis. But to do otherwise would be inefficient. Both sides invest what they regard as sufficient time and effort for current purposes, not all possible time and effort. There is no point in overinvesting in research, depositions, and so on in every case when only a fraction of them will go to trial. So mistakes get made. Doubtless, plaintiffs' attorneys come to believe that cases they initially thought were worth accepting lack solid evidence of negligent medical management. But mistakes go in the other direction as well. For example, a study of 6,000 closed insurance claims found about half of the cases that were dropped by plaintiffs without payment "would have produced an award for the plaintiff if taken to verdict."[46]

Perhaps the most useful question that can be asked *and answered* about what is going on in this pretrial phase is whether cases are being disposed of in the correct directions: Are meritorious cases receiving compensation and nonmeritorious cases being dropped, withdrawn, or dismissed without payment? All else equal, are stronger plaintiff cases settled for larger amounts than weaker ones? Put simply, what is the correlation between case strength and disposition pretrial?

A number of studies (mostly carried out by medical and healthcare policy researchers) have been conducted in which independent evaluators reviewed insurance company closed claim files in an effort to evaluate whether the dispositions go in the directions to which the medical record evidence points regarding the insured's responsibility for the plaintiff's injury. Insurance law scholar Tom Baker has reviewed insurance closed claim studies, and we summarize his summaries.[47]

Overall, in cases where negligence was found by case reviewers to be present, about 90% of claimants received some payment. Where the evidence was ambiguous, about 65% received some payment. And in cases judged defensible, nonmeritorious, or some similar classification, roughly 20% to 25% received payments (although the variation across studies was wide: from none receiving payment to 42%). The amounts paid were strongly correlated with the strength of evidence of negligence and the severity of injuries. On average, paid settlements compensated malpractice plaintiffs with less than half of their economic losses.[48] The negotiators appear to be reaching agreements that reflect the evidence—discounting damages by the likelihood of an eventual verdict favoring the plaintiff.

One such study, by David Studdert, Michelle Mello, and Atul Gawande, provides graphic indication of these patterns.[49] The researchers drew a random sample of 1,452 cases from five liability insurers' files and had physician reviewers evaluate the extent to which evidence in the cases supported the conclusion that medical error caused the plaintiff's injuries. They concluded that the malpractice system reached the "right" result about three-quarters of the time. The confidence of their medical reviewers that a harmful medical error had occurred was highly correlated with the likelihood that payment was eventually made to the plaintiff. This is evident in Figure 5.1, which relates the reviewers' ratings to the likelihood of compensation in these cases. The greater the evidence of negligent medical management, the greater the likelihood that a plaintiff received some compensation for the injury: across six levels of reviewer judgment of increasingly clear evidence of negligence, likelihood of payment increased monotonically: 19%, 32%, 52%, 61%, 72%, and 84%. The authors also found that improper payment denials were a far more serious problem than were improper payments.

The process and the results described are far from perfect, but they strongly suggest the system, generally, produces rational judgments about what is to be done with the cases. An expensive and time-consuming way to produce outcomes, to be sure, but in terms of relative merit based on the facts, the outcomes appear quite reasonable.[50]

Worth bearing in mind is that even medically trained reviewers in the more placid context of the research we have been summarizing sometimes disagree with each other about whether a negligent error had occurred or not.[51] With room

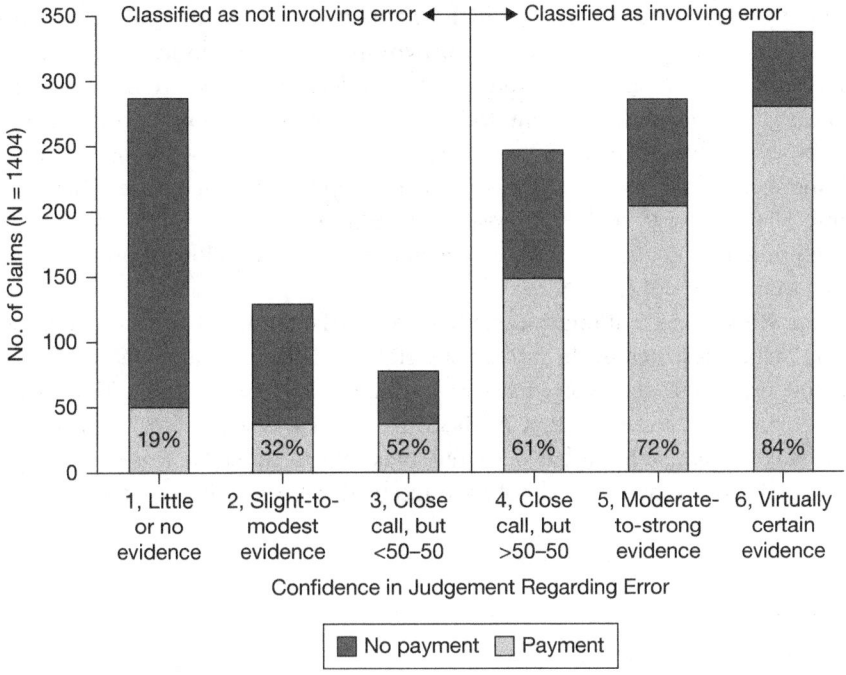

Figure 5.1. Relationship between physician ratings of evidence and probability of payment to plaintiff.
SOURCE: David M. Studdert, Michelle M. Mello, Atul A. Gawande et al., CLAIMS, ERRORS, AND COMPENSATION PAYMENTS IN MEDICAL MALPRACTICE LITIGATION, 354 NEJM 2029 (2006). (Copyright © 2006, Massachusetts Medical Society. Reprinted with permission from Massachusetts Medical Society.)

for such debates, the coherence of results, overall, is that much more noteworthy. Because their resolutions do not have the benefit of perfect understanding of the facts of the cases and the inferences that flow from those facts, both sides hedge their bets and cut their losses. Payments are sometimes made even when the defense side thinks there probably is no negligence and sometimes cases are dropped even when the plaintiff side thinks there probably is negligence. Both sides do the best they can with the information they thought was worth acquiring. The pretrial process reduces uncertainty, but some uncertainty remains. And that is a good thing, too, because a moderate amount of uncertainty facilitates settlements.[52]

Trials

As we saw half a dozen paragraphs ago, only about 8% of insurance company claim files eventually became trials. Other research has found roughly similar amounts. A study by the National Center for State Courts of all types of tort cases found that, overall, 4.8% were resolved by trial, while 11.1% of medical malpractice cases required a resolution at trial, making them more resistant to settlement than any other type of tort.[53] Most likely, that is because medical malpractice insurance policies typically contain provisions that give physician defendants more control over settlements than other tort defendants. Whereas lawyers and insurers tend to make settlement decisions based on their rational, economically-driven evaluation of the cases, physician defendants are, understandably, driven by more emotional needs, such as pride and reputation. The result is that they more often refuse to settle than insurers would. Accordingly, malpractice insurance premiums are higher than they would be if that additional power to force cases to trial did not exist.

The types of medical injury cases that reach trial tend to involve the most serious harms. Research by the Bureau of Justice Statistics[54] found that 90% of medical malpractice trials involved severe, permanent injuries or death. That makes sense when one considers that medical malpractice cases are costly to litigate. Unless considerable harm has occurred, meaning considerable losses by the patient, plaintiffs' lawyers would not have accepted the case to begin with.

Verdicts

What are the outcomes of medical malpractice trials? Let's pause to think about what we would expect the data to look like if the litigotiation system were working in ideal fashion. We delve into this analysis in part because even small amounts of unpredictability in trial verdicts is sometimes mistakenly viewed as showing irrationality on the part of the judge and jury. Note that we say *judge* (as well as jury) because, in a civil trial, judges have the authority to set aside any civil verdicts they regard as being in error. Any civil verdict that the judge lets stand is presumably considered by the judge to be a reasonable one.[55]

If full knowledge and complete rationality informed the settlement stage, then cases with evidence that supported plaintiffs would be settled in their favor, and the stronger and clearer that evidence the more favorable the resolution in the plaintiff's favor would be, and vice versa. The consequence would be that only the most ambiguous, too-close-to-call cases would proceed to trial. What trial outcomes should be expected when a set of cases fitting that description comes to trial? The answer has to be: random. Under the described state of the system, trial verdicts showing random, unpredictable outcomes would do nothing more than to confirm that the pretrial phase of the litigotiation system is working properly.[56]

On the other hand, any positive correlation between observed and predicted outcomes—predicted by judges' suggested verdicts or by neutral experts rating the strength of evidence of negligence—would be evidence not only of factfinder rationality but also that cases were leaking from the pre-trial settlement phase into the trial phase that, in a more perfect world, would have been resolved prior to trial.[57] And that is what is found—not the random *trial* outcomes that a perfect *settlement* process would produce.

Research on judge–jury concordance generally has found agreement to approach 80%—with more of those cases involving verdicts for plaintiffs than for defendants, by a ratio of about 5:3. When judges and juries disagreed with each other, there was no systematic skew favoring plaintiffs or defendants for either type of decision maker.[58] The first and most famous study of this type was by legendary University of Chicago social science and law scholars Harry Kalven and Hans Zeisel.[59] Later replication reached similar conclusions.[60] More recent data on verdicts in the 75 largest counties in the United States found that the parties to civil cases generally each win about half of their cases. More specifically, plaintiffs won in 51.6% of tort cases overall.[61]

The verdicts in medical malpractice jury trials are dramatically different. Plaintiffs win only about 25% of trial verdicts in medical malpractice cases.[62] Why do juries find for plaintiffs so much less often in malpractice cases compared to other kinds of personal injury cases?[63] David Hyman and Charles Silver[64] offer an incentives-and-systems explanation:

> What is needed is an explanation for why trials often occur in cases with low likelihoods of success, even though plaintiffs and defendants agree on the litigation odds. Professional malpractice insurance, which sometimes requires consent of the insured to settle a case, is one possible explanation. Suppose a plaintiff has a 25 to 35 percent chance of winning a case with large damages. Normally, an insurer would attempt to settle a long-shot case like this one by offering a payment discounted in light of the litigation odds. A consent-to-settle clause prevents an insurer from doing so without a doctor's permission, and a doctor might object to avoid the reputational, reporting, and insurance consequences that accompany a malpractice settlement. If no settlement offer is forthcoming, a plaintiff and his or her attorney will face a stark choice: drop a case with a non-trivial likelihood of success, or try the case knowing that the odds favor the defendant. Predictably, the decision to try will be made when the expected damage award exceeds the marginal cost of going to trial. Also predictably, plaintiffs will lose most long-shot cases, but will do well when they win. Thus, both high plaintiff loss rates and high verdicts in a few long-shot medical malpractice cases can be explained.

Support also exists for the idea that jurors come to malpractice trials favoring defendants, if only in the sense that they require more proof of negligence from malpractice plaintiffs than they do from other tort plaintiffs. Studies of malpractice insurers' evaluations of their own cases indicate that half of the cases that insurers judged to favor plaintiffs were nevertheless decided by juries in favor of the defendants.[65] If so, we need an explanation of why this reality does not seem to be reflected in pretrial settlements so that the trials of cases that do not settle fall closer to the expected 50:50 ratio at trial. The answer might be the one suggested by Hyman and Silver (medical malpractice defendants hold insurers back from settling cases they would rationally choose to settle). Or it might also be that signals of which cases (out of a set of otherwise winnable plaintiff cases) will be rejected by jurors are too complex, lost in the noise, and hard to decipher. Because settlements dominate the system, any given attorney takes very few cases to trial each year, and in malpractice there are even fewer. One needs more exposure to the signals to decipher them than lawyers get.

Compensation Awards

Jurors are instructed that, if they find in favor of the plaintiff, they are to award damages sufficient to make the injury victim "whole"—that is, to put the plaintiff in as nearly the situation he or she was in before the accident, to the extent that money can substitute for a lost leg, organ failure, brain damage, blindness, or whatever the accidental harm might have been, or to compensate a family for a loved one's lost life. Clearly, this can be a difficult calculation to make.

Some of these damages are easier to gauge than others: the value of lost earnings; medical expenses required to diagnose, treat and rehabilitate the victim's injuries; and other out-of-pocket costs necessitated by the injuries (so-called economic or special damages). Other damages, referred to as "noneconomic" or "general" damages are harder to estimate with precision: physical pain, mental suffering, disability, disfigurement, and loss of enjoyment of life.

To say that the latter are "noneconomic" is only to say only that they are not traded in the marketplace. There is nothing about them that inherently precludes specification of their prices. Economics tells us that a price can evolve out of market exchanges for *anything* that is traded on markets. After all, thanks to markets, people are able to determine predictable prices for different smearings of paint on canvas. If we bought and sold organs and appendages or the right to blind another person, we would know the market value of those losses, at least on average.[66]

That the law wishes to make persons whole, treating us as unique individuals entitled to personalized assessments of our losses, can only be viewed as one of its admirable features. On the other hand, the law does not give jurors the tools they need to accomplish that goal with any kind of precision. Jurors must make those estimates with very little guidance. Not only is the market value of the "noneconomic" losses unknown to jurors (and to everyone), they are not even given the benefit of learning what other juries have awarded for similar injuries in the same or similar circumstances. Arguably, that could be done and it would produce more stable, predictable, vertically equitable, jury-generated awards,[67] but the law currently prohibits the provision of such information to jurors.[68]

The problem is not so much with the jurors, but with the (lack of) information they are provided. This is well illustrated by one experiment in which randomly selected jury-eligible laypersons—as well as judges and lawyers who litigate personal injury cases—are presented with dozens of different injuries ranging widely on different dimensions. They were asked to rate those injuries on the pain, suffering, disability, and disfigurement they thought were associated with each injury. Those intuitive ratings by the laypersons of the multidimensional horrors of injuries were as stable and predictable as those made by judges, defense lawyers, and plaintiffs' lawyers responding to the same injuries.[69] These findings suggest that people have shared and stable reactions to the multidimensional dreadfulness of different kinds of injuries, whether they have been dealing with them professionally for decades or are asked to ponder them for the first time.

The problem arises when people are asked to convert those injury estimates into compensation dollars. Now the awards made by the laypersons are decidedly less predictable ($R^2 = 0.23$) than those of judges ($R^2 = 0.42$), plaintiffs' lawyers ($R^2 = 0.48$), or defense lawyers ($R^2 = 0.58$). These findings suggest that the translation from injury ratings to dollar awards requires some kind of cognitive framework, whether developed through experience or perhaps by being provided with some kind of decision aid.[70]

Nevertheless, both jury simulations and studies of databases of actual tort awards find a high degree of what is referred to as vertical equity: the more severe the injuries, the higher the awards, and vice versa. Horizontal equity is harder to achieve; that is, plaintiffs with similar injuries receive varied awards.[71] Keep in mind, as we discuss these issues further, that the medical injuries that come before juries are almost always severe—90% of them deaths or injuries that are serious and permanent.[72]

How close do jury awards come to matching the actual economic losses of medical malpractice plaintiffs? The answer is that, on average, plaintiffs recover about half of their economic losses.[73] Moreover, they fall short in an interesting pattern. Like tort awards of all kinds, they overcompensate those with the smallest losses; as losses grow larger and larger, they undercompensate more and more. That is, the jury award is a continuously shrinking fraction of increasingly large losses.[74] This pattern is shown in Figure 5.2.

And what of noneconomic, "pain-and-suffering" awards? At the end of the day, noneconomic damages constitute less than a quarter of medical malpractice awards. The most careful study of the question found that, on average, jury awards in medical malpractice cases exceeded the economic losses of the injury victims by only 22%.[75] That is an interesting number because it represents a smaller portion of the award than normally will be contractually owed by plaintiffs to their attorneys in legal fees.[76] This parallels other research making even more clear that the role played by general damages is to cover legal fees.[77]

Numerous studies, approaching these questions from different angles, reinforce these findings and sometimes hint at cognitive phenomena that explain the patterns observed. First, many awards require extrapolation to future years. Although considerations of inflation and interest require compounding to reach the correct future amounts,[78] without help from explicit calculation aids, people tend strongly toward linear guesstimation of future values. This leads to the pattern of increasing shortfall evident in Figure 2.[79]

Second, experimental evidence has found that jurors tend to discount awards as a hedge on their uncertainty that they have made the correct liability judgment.[80] Since cases that go to trial (rather than settling pretrial) tend to be cases

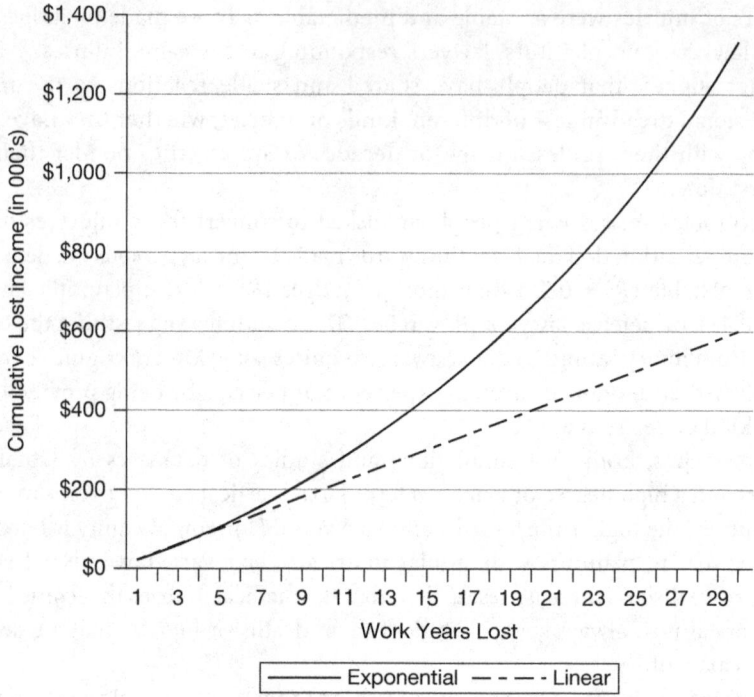

Figure 5.2. Estimating the value of future lost earnings.
SOURCE: Michael J. Saks, DO WE REALLY KNOW ANYTHING ABOUT THE BEHAVIOR OF THE TORT LITIGATION SYSTEM—AND WHY NOT? 140 U. Penn. L. Rev. 1147 1219 (1992).

with ambiguous evidence of liability, they are perfect candidates for this kind of discounting. And because they tend toward the severe end of the loss spectrum, the discount will take quite a bite out of the award.

Third, an unusual opportunity to assess lay jury awards was created when, as part of its reforms capping medical malpractice awards, Indiana instituted a professionally administered patient compensation fund to decide all losses above $100,000, rather than allowing juries to decide those larger awards. Contrary to expectations, malpractice awards in Indiana came to average one third higher than those of its neighbors, Michigan and Ohio, which retained traditional malpractice systems.[81] The most likely explanation is that the professional administrators were better able than jurors to calculate damages accurately, with a correct understanding of the effects of inflation and *without* improperly discounting the award for uncertainty about liability.

We have been discussing averages, which reflect how the system overall is operating. But variability certainly occurs, and high-end outliers can be far more extreme than low-end outliers, simply because the low end has a natural floor and the high end has no ceiling. As the next subsection makes clear, trial award outliers at the high end are good for little more than headlines and lobbying. The next stage of the legal process is ready to cut them down.

Adjustments Following Verdicts

After the jury announces its award, more litigotiation stands between plaintiffs and their recoveries. Under traditional procedures, defendants may and often do request that trial judges reduce jury awards (remittitur), and plaintiffs may request increases (additur, available in some state courts).[82] Judges grant remittiturs much more often than additurs. In addition, defendants can appeal to a higher court to have the award reduced or overturned altogether. Each such move creates uncertainty, and uncertainty breeds negotiation. So, even after the jury award is in, plaintiff and defense attorneys often continue to negotiate (reductions in) compensation amounts. In what the reader should recognize as a now-familiar pattern, the higher the jury award, the greater its eventual reduction likely will be.[83]

Even without the intervention of judges, widely honored practice places a de facto cap on damages. The final agreed-upon damages amount rarely exceeds the physician defendant's liability insurance policy limits. That is, no matter how high the damages ultimately awarded by the jury, judge, or legal system, the plaintiff will get no more than what the doctor is insured for.[84] Unsuccessful malpractice defendants rarely are required to pay anything out of their own pockets.[85]

On top of the traditional rules and practices are the medical malpractice reforms of the past several decades. Many are aimed at reducing the size of compensation awards or increasing the plaintiffs' costs (which also reduces a plaintiff's compensation). These are discussed in the next chapter.

SUMMARY AND CONCLUSION

Each stage of the litigotiation process reduces the number of cases that transition to the next stage and refines the remaining pool of cases. At the outset of the process, an enormous number of true positive claims never materialize by not being offered to plaintiffs' attorneys, or by being rejected by plaintiffs' attorneys as having an insufficient expected return on the attorneys' investments in those cases. Of cases that do cross the threshold into the system, at each successive stage, cases are categorized and re-categorized, progressively removing the clearest cases—both those with strong evidence of negligently caused serious injuries and those lacking such evidence—from the system, compensating the former and denying the latter.[86]

Here is an illustrative, numerical summary of that winnowing process that takes true positive medical injury cases to and through trial. The following data represent estimates for hospital patients for the year 2010 in one state, with a population of 6.4 million and 710,000 hospital admissions.[87] (The reader can extend the estimates to the United States as a whole, with a population of nearly 50 times as many people, patients, and victims of medical injury.)

26,000—patients suffering injuries from adverse events
8,600—patients suffering injuries from negligent adverse events
4,300—patients with moderate or greater injuries (half of which are deaths)
500—claims filed
40—trials commenced
10—verdicts favoring plaintiffs
0 (approximately)—receiving compensation at least equal to plaintiffs' losses

Thus, for every claim filed, there were more than 50 adverse events in hospitals, about 17 negligent adverse events, and nearly 9 moderate-to-more-serious negligent injuries (half of which were deaths).[88]

For every case that proceeded to trial, there were about 650 adverse events that occurred in hospitals, 215 negligent adverse events, and nearly 110 moderate-to-more-serious negligent injuries (half of which were deaths).

From the perspective of how often injurers are called to account for the accidental harm they have caused, the tort system is unusually kind to healthcare defendants. It always has been, and has been made more so, by the reforms of recent decades. Fewer than 2% of the victims of adverse events bring claims for compensation; fewer than 6% of the victims of negligent adverse events bring claims; and fewer than 12% of the victims of relatively serious negligent adverse events bring claims.

The tort system generally returns very little of the costs that have been imposed on victims of accidental injury. A national-scope Rand Corporation study calculated the direct and work-loss costs resulting from nonfatal accidents of all kinds in the United States.[89] About half of the victims' losses were expenditures on direct costs, mostly medical care for the injuries; about half were from lost earnings due to inability to work. About 62% of direct losses were paid by one form of insurance or another (first party health insurance, worker's compensation, government assistance). About 33% of lost earnings were compensated by some form of disability insurance. The tort system obtained reimbursement of only 7.7% of the accident victims' losses.

For injuries sustained receiving healthcare, the picture is even more extreme. In the aggregate, between less than 1.0% and 3.8% of the costs suffered by medical injury victims are returned by the tort system.[90]

Researchers who have studied the workings of the tort litigation system, including those who have focused on malpractice litigation, have come to the conclusions that:

> If one focuses on outputs, the liability system does much better than conventional wisdom suggests; it sorts the wheat from the chaff reasonably well. Focusing on those who initiate claims, patients treated negligently recover damages far more often than patients who were treated nonnegligently. There is also a well-established severity gradient: Payments increase with injury severity. . . . Unfortunately, most patients are undercompensated, and those with the most severe injuries suffer the biggest gap between provable injuries and the amounts they recover.[91]

In addition, most victims of iatrogenic injury receive nothing, most often because they take no steps to enter the system, and the great majority of those who do try to bring suits are excluded by plaintiffs' lawyers who don't want their cases.[92]

If the system is viewed as "erratic," that has to be because out of the large number of negligent injuries suffered by patients, only infrequently are those responsible made accountable, and it is not obvious to them why they can err with impunity most of the time but not all of the time.

The major concern about the malpractice litigation system should be whether it accomplishes what could be its most important goal: keeping patients safe by creating an environment that promotes investment (and not only in dollars) in preventing iatrogenic harms. How well does it do on that dimension?

6
Meditations on Medical Torts

Prevention (or deterrence, as some prefer) is a most worthy but dismayingly elusive goal in all systems.[1]

When we cause harm, especially inadvertently, we humans seem to have two instinctual reactions that propel us in opposite directions. One is to make amends, to assist those we have accidentally injured, in the process restoring our own psychological and moral balance. The anonymous author of the following letter, who simply had the misfortune of being in the wrong place at the wrong time, could have been replaced by happenstance with any one of us. And yet he (or she) is the poor soul who has remained haunted for decades, still seeking expiation.

> Thirty years ago, I was in a car-and-moped accident. I was driving the car. The police determined that the moped driver, a preteen with no driving experience, was at fault. A passenger on the moped, also a preteen, died the next day from her injuries. At the funeral, the parents made clear that they would not accept my apology and condolences, and that they never wanted to hear from me again.
>
> Over the years, I've thought about the accident and have wondered how the parents are doing. A few years ago, I found the child's obituary in a newspaper archive and discovered the parents' names. I thought about reaching out to them; I don't want them to think I've forgotten or that I don't care. But the memory of their shoving me away at the funeral has held me back. Also, I care about their feelings and don't want to reopen old wounds.
>
> More recently I discovered the names of the child's siblings. I imagine that hearing from me might not be as difficult for the siblings as for the parents. Should I contact them, or should I respect the parents' refusal from decades ago?[2]

Most of us don't need the law to tell us to do what we can to help, and most of us most of the time can work out a solution without the law's intercession. Ironically, in the world of healthcare injuries, this instinct seems strangely hushed. Special programs have started to be developed to introduce healthcare institutions and providers to the notion that victims of accidental medical injuries ought to be approached promptly and honestly and offered help.[3]

Our second instinct is to evade responsibility. We might fear consequences and try to hide from our victims and the authorities (think hit-and-run drivers). But, more deeply, to realize that we have hurt someone inadvertently makes most of us feel terrible. If we can convince our friends, our colleagues, and ourselves that we were not the cause of the harm, or were the cause but are not responsible for it, we have found another way to feel better about the accident. This second reaction seems to be the dominant one in the culture of American healthcare.

When we want to, we can be ingenious at arguing for our nonresponsibility—denying causation, or fault, or shifting responsibility to someone or something else.[4] Perhaps we are so good at that because we began our training in blame-avoidance almost as soon as we were old enough to act and to talk. Auto insurance companies sometimes receive explanations from their insureds against whom claims have been made for causing crashes. One company received a letter from a policyholder who crashed into a tree. The letter writer explained that *the tree was coming right at him*, and there was nothing he could do to avoid it. The human capacity to justify and excuse ourselves is almost limitless.[5]

American tort law comes actively into play only when the injurer and the injured cannot reach their own mutually satisfactory resolution. It also exerts some indirect influence by waiting, just over the horizon, with its rules and its procedures, offering some gyroscopic guidance to the informal discussions that might be taking place. In this book, we are concerned first and foremost with patient safety and with tort law only insofar as it makes a contribution to patient safety.

THE BEHAVIOR OF THE TORT LITIGATION SYSTEM

Previous chapters summarized the evidence-based picture of medical malpractice and the law's response in some detail. Here is a postage-stamp summary.

Preventable injuries in the healthcare setting are abundant, so many of them that errors and slip-ups kill enough of us each year to rank as America's number three cause of death. The annual costs of those injuries and deaths (paid by victims, their families, their insurers, and taxpayers) total in the scores of billions of dollars. At most, only a tiny percentage of those cases enter the tort system.[6] An even smaller percentage of patients (of course) receive any reimbursement for the losses caused by their calamitous encounter with the healthcare industry. In the end, the civil justice system returns only a few percent (at most, under 4%) of the billions that are externalized[7] annually onto victims and the wider public (through insurance and government programs). Injured individuals who do receive compensation generally receive less than their economic losses, and the greater their losses the greater the proportionate undercompensation. The tort system is slow (resolutions typically take several years) and inefficient (in the sense that every dollar transferred from the injurers to the injured carries a transaction charge of roughly another dollar), although perhaps is surprisingly efficient from a population–of–patients–level deterrence perspective (discussed further later in this chapter).

What all of that processing effort and its accompanying costs buy is a reasonable job of sorting cases into those for which the evidence supports a decision to compensate and those for which the evidence does not—*after* cases get past the first step or two of sorting. The great mass of negligently injured patients never even consult lawyers about their cases, and most of those who do are turned away.[8] So, the great majority of cases that would otherwise have been entitled to compensation disappear from the tort reimbursement system without ever really entering it.

As filed cases move through the process, most are resolved without a trial—dismissed, dropped, or settled. The size of a settlement reflects the strength of the case and, of course, the magnitude of the plaintiff's losses. Cases with the strongest and weakest evidence of liability settle most readily; more ambiguous cases, unsurprisingly, are more resistant to settlement. If the pretrial sorting process worked perfectly, the cases that arrived in court would be toss-ups. And, therefore, jury verdicts on liability would seem to be random. The fact that they are not—evidenced by a considerable agreement between jury verdicts and what judges say they would decide in the same case—is an indication of the settlement process's imperfection. In malpractice cases, for a variety of reasons, juries' liability verdicts tend to favor defendants.[9] Jury awards—which might seem unpredictable when we focus on a single case—turn out to be quite predictable in the aggregate: half the variation in damage awards can be predicted by knowing a single fact: the dollar cost of treating the victims' injuries.[10] Further reviews (by trial judges), negotiations (among counsel), and appeals (before appellate judges) most often reduce damage awards further. When all is said and done, plaintiffs who receive any compensation rarely see anything more than the limits of a defendant's insurance policy, regardless of the actual losses they have suffered, and usually a good bit less. When the sun sets on a case, only the insurance company will be writing a check.

In addition to that description of how cases flow (or don't) through the litigotiation system, tort law has also been doctrinally kind to defendants of all stripes, and especially so to healthcare industry defendants—even before recent decades of successful lobbying for protective rules applicable only to them. For example, courts invented doctrines (e.g., charitable immunity) to insulate hospitals and doctors from liability. Unlike other types of tort cases, medical malpractice cases cannot even begin unless a valid contractual relationship exists between the plaintiff and defendant.[11] Rather than shifting the cost of injuries to defendants for *all* accidents they cause, they are liable only for those in which their carefulness fell below a reasonable minimum standard ("negligence"). Unlike other tort cases, the specification of that standard of reasonable care has to be proven through the expert testimony of another provider.

We need to reflect on what all of this means for the bigger picture of society's interest in being protected from medical accidents and the law's role in that.

DOES THE TORT LITIGATION SYSTEM SECURE REIMBURSEMENT FOR LOSSES SUFFERED BY VICTIMS OF INJURY? ("COMPENSATION")

Despite the hypnotically repeated mantra that the tort system has two chief purposes—compensation and deterrence—is it really a compensation system? A moment's reflection on the empirical evidence should convince anyone that compensation is not a principal function of tort law, nor could it (without radical transformation) ever work effectively as a compensation system. "[T]he tort system does a miserable job of compensating victims of medical malpractice."[12] If society really wants to compensate a large portion of those injured by accidents, an altogether different system would need to be created.[13]

Readers might find this odd. After all, the system appears to be about whether or not dollar losses should be borne by injured plaintiffs or shifted to the defendants who allegedly injured them. Plaintiffs enter the system in search of compensation for their losses. Potential as well as actual defendants, certainly of the professional and corporate kind, make substantial investments (in lobbying as well as litigation) to try to avoid reimbursing injured plaintiffs for their losses.[14] That certainly seems to be about compensation versus the effort to avoid paying compensation.

Moreover, among the conclusions insurance law scholar Tom Baker reached after extensive interviews with plaintiff and defense side personal injury attorneys, were these:

> For practicing lawyers, tort law in such cases appears to be *almost entirely about compensation*, except in the egregious case. In the egregious case, the lawyers are more likely to describe "going for blood" [i.e., seeking damages not only from defendants' insurers, but from the defendants themselves] in retributive terms than they are to discuss deterrence. The one exception is the case in which the "wrong" is the failure to purchase (enough) insurance, and there the deterrence is directed not at unsafe behavior, but at insurance purchasing. Thus, at least according to the practitioners of the art, it seems that tort law in action is less concerned with deterrence than tort doctrine and theory would suggest.[15]

What we have here is the difference in understanding a system that comes from looking at the trees versus looking at the forest. To understand the part being played in the tort system by the quest for and the defense against paying compensation, we need to gain some altitude. The lawyers Baker spoke with were on the forest floor thinking intensely about individual trees (cases). That is not necessarily what the system writ large uses those cases to accomplish. To offer a cruder but clearer analogy: What the cogs in the machine are thinking about does not tell us what the machine is doing and, by inference, what the machine's purpose is. Not only in cases of iatrogenic injury, in all types of personal injury (with the exception of auto crashes),[16] the tort system has never returned more than a fraction of the losses sustained by tortiously injured persons.[17]

If the tort *system's* compensation function is small, what is it doing that is large? The only possible answer, if there is an answer, is *deterrence*. In our view, the best evidence-based account that can be offered to explain what the tort system is doing is this. It is sampling various categories of injuries that occur in society and the activities that produce those injuries. The promise of compensation for tortious personal injury and property loss lures the needed samples of victims into the tort system. What the law does with those cases announces to the world what price is to be set on *future* tortious injuries. And not only the dollar cost of compensation (which, by the way, had already been paid when potential defendants paid their liability insurance premiums), but the inconvenience, annoyance, embarrassment, diminished reputation, psychic pain, and whatever else might be visited upon defendants by the process. To accomplish its deterrence purpose, every case of tortious injury does not have to be compensated fully or at all. A more or less constant trickle of salient reminders might suffice to stimulate some marginally greater level of precautions against preventable harm.[18]

One might view what we have described as a failure of the tort system: it does not and cannot accommodate more than a fraction of those who have been accidentally injured by others' failure to take the steps necessary to prevent the harm. It leaves the vast bulk of losses on the innocent victims.

At the same time, what we've described could be viewed as the genius of the tort system. For a surprisingly small price—if measured as the average cost *per injury prevented*—it generates potentially massive and widespread deterrence. Considering how few cases the tort system actually touches (relative to the incidence of negligent iatrogenic injury), and how little money (relative to total costs externalized) it actually returns to injured patients, the dread of the tort system that apparently is felt by doctors and other healthcare workers is quite remarkable. So remarkable, that the tort system has been described as "a mouse with an otherworldly roar."[19]

One indication of the impact of that roar is that doctors have been found to greatly overestimate the risk of being sued.[20] They believed that 45% of adverse events led to malpractice claims (actual rate, 4% or less) and that 65% of negligent adverse events led to litigation (actual rate, 13% or less). Those large misperceptions partially make up for the very low rate at which tort claims actually are brought. Achieving the same impact entirely economically—perhaps by compensating many more of the negligently injured or perhaps by adding a multiplier to each tort settlement or award and thereby clawing back a larger fraction of the externalities that any industry or activity imposes on society and its members, especially so with the healthcare industry—would cost huge sums and require a much larger administrative workforce than is actually required by the existing tort system.

Put simply: compensation plays a small but essential role in achieving the tort system's real and central purpose: deterrence.

DOES THE TORT LITIGATION SYSTEM MAKE HEALTHCARE SAFER? ("DETERRENCE")

If deterrence is the chief purpose of the tort system, then a logical question to ask is whether it accomplishes that purpose. The short answer is that no one knows, and it's hard to imagine how anyone could obtain a reasonably solid answer. But before we explore the path to those conclusions, we should first clarify what deterrence means.

The simplest and best synonym for deterrence is *motivation for prevention*. The word "deterrence" sometimes confuses, in part because it implies different things in different legal contexts. In criminal law, deterrence typically means dissuading people from *intentionally* or *knowingly* committing crimes by threatening to punish those contemplating rape, robbery, murder, or other crimes. In the realm of accident prevention, it has to mean something more subtle, because accidents have more to do with lack of awareness of critical circumstances than with intent. (Those who say "But I didn't intend to cause harm; it was just an accident and therefore I should not be held responsible" are confusing tort law with criminal law.)

If our image of the archetypal tortfeasor is a careless driver or a homeowner or shopkeeper who waited too long to repair a loose railing, then it might make sense to think that those individuals could be motivated by the prospect of a tort lawsuit to exercise greater care—thus reducing the probability of such accidents.

Most of the time, however, except for auto crash cases, defendants are corporations, governments, and other organizations, coordinating the interdependent activities of numerous actors. The same is even true of medical malpractice litigation.[21] For organizational defendants, it makes sense to think of deterrence as the impact that the prospect of tort liability might have on their decisions whether to invest more or less or nothing at all in preventing accidents—by purchasing safer equipment, providing safety gear, reorganizing people and work tasks, improving the content and methods of training—or perhaps not? For such collectivities, investments in safety, rather than individual attentiveness, are the most important effects sought by accountability in tort law.

Organizations and Individuals

When the Indiana University Caving Club emerged from a cavern they had been exploring, they padlocked the entrance shut and headed home. No one noticed that one club member was missing. Freshman Lukas Cavar had become separated from his group, got lost in the cave and decided to stay in place until the others came to find him. When the passage of time brought nothing but solitude, he found his way to the cave entrance only to confront a locked gate. For nearly three days he survived on a few snack bars and the sticky insides of their wrappers, shivered, dodged bats, and spent hours licking moisture from the walls of the cave to try to prevent dehydration. He typed out good-bye messages to loved ones on his signalless cellphone. By the third day, feeling extremely weak, he considered eating cave crickets. That night, the club's leaders returned and rescued him.[22]

If the club did not have protocols requiring expedition leaders to count heads entering and exiting, pairing spelunkers with buddies to keep track of each other, and other safety precautions, or failed to effectively train their members in such protocols, then the organization could be viewed as responsible for the near-tragedy. But, as the caving club's president stated afterwards, "We have a series of rigorous protocols in place that are supposed to prevent situations like this, but they are only effective if followed. We had a failure in our leadership to closely follow all these safety procedures. The risk that our member was exposed to as a result of these failures is a vivid reminder of why we have protocols."[23] Thus, when an organization does everything that could reasonably be expected of it, and an individual who was supposed to follow safe procedures disregards them or executes them poorly, then responsibility would seem to fall on the individual who failed to perform.

One might, however, argue that the organization could have done a better job of selecting its expedition leaders or making sure they knew what to do and did it. Additionally, in law, under most circumstances, the torts of employees and other agents are imputed to the organizations for which they work. Thus, even when an individual has clearly caused the harm, the organization is considered responsible to the victim. The healthcare industry is unusual in the extent to which it has engineered itself to keep the torts of physicians and some other workers from becoming the legal responsibility of larger organizational units.[24]

Empirical Studies of Tort Deterrence

Research studies designed to test for the hypothesized deterrent effects of the tort system are few,[25] spread across various categories of accident types, and their designs are unavoidably weak—meaning that they cannot support strong inferences about the impact of tort liability on safety, be it positive (an effect detected) or negative (no effect).[26] Think about what a first-rate study of the question might look like. If researchers could, they would take all of the states of the United States and randomly assign half of them to have a tort law regime and half of them not to. Over a period of time, the behavior of people and organizations could be monitored, counting the incidence of accidents, injuries, and deaths. By comparing the states with tort law and the states without it, we could see whether having tort law makes a difference.

With that ideal (and impossible) experiment as the touchstone, it's easier to see how close actual studies have come, or failed to come. Some studies have examined the effect of different legal rules on accident-related fatalities, for example, comparing workers' compensation systems to the common law tort regimes they replaced within a state. The usual finding has been that imposing workers' compensation premiums on companies led to a decrease in fatalities.[27]

Another approach has been to compare the incidence of accidents or fatalities associated with different tort rules that exist in different states. States with contributory negligence rules were compared to states with comparative negligence, finding safer driving in states with the contributory negligence rule.[28] Others have compared states with no-fault auto compensation systems to others with conventional negligence–litigation–based tort law. The results have been mixed, but tend to find that fatalities are higher in states with no-fault.[29]

New Zealand's Abolition of Tort Liability

Perhaps one can make a starker comparison by looking at a common-law nation that abolished nearly all of its traditional tort system in favor of a no-fault, universal insurance system, as New Zealand did starting in 1974.[30] In New Zealand, tort suits are prohibited for virtually all accidental injuries, including "medical treatment injuries," and instead are generously compensated by a government agency, the Accident Compensation Corporation.[31] Each accident type is funded within its own domain: levies are imposed on drivers to fund the account that pays for auto crashes; business owners, for workplace accidents; healthcare organizations and professionals, to pay for medical injuries; and so on. Not unexpectedly, under such a system, claims and costs have gone up, but New Zealanders believe their more expensive system is well worth its price.[32]

Healthcare-caused injuries have presented the greatest challenges for the Kiwi system's architects, and have required considerable tweaking over the years, including adding back the element of negligence to keep costs from spiraling. The New Zealand system also requires a high degree of accountability of providers and organizations to a government agency that has the power to investigate, discipline, or order corrective measures to prevent repetitions of the problems that led to an injury. Error reporting is required, but apparently that had long been a part of Kiwi medical practice. "Error reporting in New Zealand is a regular part of the medical culture; acknowledgment of injuries in patient records is extremely high. Truthful, consistent error reporting provides opportunities to evaluate quality of care problems, a sharp contrast with the United States, where such reporting is rare."[33]

The difference, however, might not be as sharp as suggested between our two compensation systems, which tells us something about accident law and disclosure. A study of patients in the United States found that only a quarter of those harmed by medical errors had had those errors disclosed to them by their caregivers. The comparable rate of disclosure in New Zealand appears to be about

40%.[34] That is an important not-so-much-of-a-difference. It suggests that tort law might not be the barrier to improved disclosure that many assume it to be. There might be "many reasons why physicians do not report errors, including a general reluctance to communicate with patients and a fear of disciplinary action or a loss of position or privileges."[35]

How does New Zealand compare for safety?[36] New Zealand's rate of adverse events has been found to be about triple that found by the Harvard research team in New York, Colorado, and Utah. On the other hand, adverse events in the United States were more lethal, with deaths occurring about three times as often.

Global Comparisons

A much more expansive approach to international comparison of legal responses to accidental injuries was a study by researcher Michael Smith.[37] Using motor vehicle and nonmotor vehicle fatality rates over a period of 50 years from 113 countries, Smith compared mortality rates in nations with different legal systems. Where legal responses were based on English common law, motor vehicle accident fatality rates were lower than those in countries using French civil code systems or former members of the Soviet Union and Eastern bloc countries; vehicle accident fatality rates in countries whose legal systems are based on Scandinavian civil codes do not differ from those in common law countries. For nonmotor vehicle accidents, fatality rates were lower under common law systems than under every type of civil code system: lowest in common law nations, higher in French, then German and then Scandinavian civil code countries, and highest in former Soviet and Eastern bloc countries.

Evaluating the Studies of Tort Law's Effects on Safety

All of the studies described so far suffer from the problem that they are correlational (observational), not experimental. Whether the comparison is between jurisdictions with different laws, between many jurisdictions with many different laws, or within a jurisdiction that changed its law between time 1 and time 2, inferences cannot be drawn without considerable ambiguity. Competent researchers are well aware of this challenge.

The reduction in workplace fatality rates after worker's compensation systems replaced fault-based tort litigation might have been the result of imposing more certain costs on employers. But it might, instead, reflect other changes over time, including other laws and other safety-related practices and equipment (stemming from other forces). Moreover, the finding is not consistent across studies.

The fact that no-fault auto insurance has been found sometimes (but not in all studies) to be associated with an *increase* in highway deaths could mean that no-fault gives drivers reduced incentives to drive safely. But it could, instead, be telling us that states with a more serious driving problem are more tempted to try something new. Comparisons between states must struggle with the problem that states that choose one rule differ from states that choose the other rule in numerous ways, from weather to culture to geography to economic characteristics and beyond, and those differences are changing over time.

Does Smith's comparisons among the legal systems of 113 different nations mean that common law tort litigation is a superior deterrent to accidents? Perhaps. But, as Jonathan Cardi and his colleagues comment, "Smith's study almost certainly fails to control for a host of potentially confounding variables (e.g., vastly differing cultural norms, different types of cars, population density, etc.), and using gross fatalities as a measure of deterrence poses significant limitations for the study's validity."[38]

One can compare another common law legal regime–New Zealand, which took a far-reaching turn away from torts–in an attempt to test whether, overall, the American tort system is better (or worse) at facilitating safety. But whatever is found must confront the problem that New Zealand differs from the United States in countless other ways. Still other problems might be found in the research methods: perhaps the American research set a higher threshold for counting something as a medical adverse event, or to be negligent, or perhaps the fact that the Kiwi healthcare providers were by custom more forthcoming in disclosing errors (voluntarily writing them into patients' records) might have made their errors easier for reviewers to identify and so appear to be more numerous.

All of this is a familiar research problem: comparison is essential, but finding apples-to-apples comparisons in nonexperimental settings is a challenge. The problem is no less familiar in medical research. For example, in trying to determine whether hormone replacement therapy for postmenopausal women was helpful or harmful or had no effect, observational research led to the conclusion that estrogen supplementation was a good idea. Higher quality experimental designs eventually revealed that such treatment actually was dangerous, but not before decades of estrogen replacement had caused tens of thousands of unnecessary breast cancers, heart attacks, and strokes in women.[39]

A radically different approach is the randomized experiment but, on the topic of whether tort law deters, such a study can be done only through simulation.[40]

Studies of the Effects of Tort Law on Patient Safety

Studies aimed specifically at the question of whether the existence of potential malpractice liability promotes greater safety in healthcare, or whether reforms that weaken tort law reduce patient safety, are usually no better off than correlational studies of tort deterrence more generally. When comparing one rule here and a different rule there, or a higher frequency of litigation here and a lower frequency there, and trying to associate those differences to differences in the level of patient injuries, one has to be assuming at least this much: that the differences in litigation have been stable and that healthcare organizations and providers are aware of those differences in levels of litigation and have been reacting to them. But you don't have a comparison between places with tort law versus places with no tort law. Instead, you have places with a little more tort law versus a little less tort law. Are practitioners likely to adjust their estimates a bit upward or a bit downward to reflect the legal differences being compared (how would they know?) and then adjust their level of precaution accordingly? Hovering above those small differences you have the existence of the general, overarching tort system, and providers' general awareness of that overarching system, which might be the main (and vague) thing practitioners are aware of. Doctors have been found to greatly overestimate the litigation risk that they face,[41] and they are not sensitive to (or not aware of) the differences in liability risk between one rule in one locale or jurisdiction and another.[42] So it seems heroic of researchers to expect to find effects of changes in the law. Were we to find changes in either direction, they might be the product of any one or more of dozens of other programs, initiatives, incentives, and rules pressing toward safer practices or toward practices that are less safe, few if any of which are being accounted for.

What would help most to tease apart the confounds would be data sets that gather consistent data over time, so that as changed laws change litigation risk, we could observe how healthcare safety practices change (or don't) in the law's wake. What we need are moving pictures; what we have are snapshots. So far, the research has been stuck with too many confounding variables that might be masking real effects or creating the appearance of effects that do not exist.

Enough complaining about the challenge of obtaining coherent, meaningful findings from such research. What does the research that has been done appear to find? The overwhelming conclusion of a review of research on the effects of various tort reforms on patient safety was, for nearly all of them, "too limited to draw conclusions."[43] So, we are left empty-handed, not knowing one way or the other.

But wait, a glimmer of empirical light has appeared. One recent research project studied what happens when, over time, tort law is weakened: Does its hypothesized deterrent effect decline?[44] Zenon Zabinski and Bernard Black looked at the effect on patient safety of adopting caps (limiting general damage awards) in five states (Florida, Georgia, Illinois, South Carolina, and Texas), which were also compared to control states (which did not adopt the caps reform—thereby allowing trends due to other factors to be taken into consideration). As a measure of safety practices, the researchers used the Patient Safety Indicators (PSI) instrument, developed by the Agency for Healthcare Research and Quality. The research found that in states with caps on damages, the level of safety as measured by the PSI declined.

> We find a gradual rise in rates [of errors and harm] for most PSIs after reform, consistent with a gradual relaxation of care, or failure to reinforce care standards over time. The decline is widespread, and applies both to aspects of care that are relatively likely to lead to a malpractice suit (e.g., PSI-5; foreign body left in during surgery), and aspects that are unlikely to do so (e.g., PSI-7; central-line associated bloodstream infection). The broad relaxation

of care suggests that medical malpractice liability provides "general deterrence"—an incentive to be careful in general.[45]

Somewhat contrary in its implication, but also finding impact of *the right kind of* tort actions, is recent research by Michael Frakes and Anupam Jena. They found that when courts abolished the "locality rule," thus requiring providers to adhere to a national standard, providers rose to meet the higher clinical standards to which they would be held; furthermore, that improved quality has some sticking power.[46]

If a conclusion can be drawn about medical malpractice liability based entirely on the research that exists, leaving aside popular assumptions and lobbyists' rhetoric, it would be that the litigation system (a) enhances patient safety, although far too weakly to be a complete solution, and, ironically, (b) makes its contribution to safety at low cost (defined as cost per iatrogenic injury prevented).

ANECDOTAL EVIDENCE

Unfortunately, the state of knowledge is such that the most revealing evidence on tort law's deterrent value is perhaps the anecdotal.

Not too many years ago, anesthesiologists inadvertently killed 1 patient in every 5,000 owing to the way anesthesia was administered and how the patient's oxygenation was monitored. Distressed by their high malpractice premiums, a national group of anesthesiologists undertook a project designed to help figure out what they were doing that was killing so many patients and causing brain damage in many others. One important source of insight for the committee were the tort claim files in past cases. The committee made important discoveries about what was going wrong and how to fix it. Before long, the incidence of death from anesthesia fell to one in 250,000—a fifty-fold reduction in patient deaths! As safety went up, malpractice premiums plummeted; anesthesiology went from being one of the costliest specialties to insure to having among the lowest premiums. The head of the project said: "The relationship of patient safety to malpractice insurance premiums was easy to predict. If patients were not injured, they would not sue, and if the payout for anesthesia-related patient injury could be reduced, then insurance rates should follow."[47] Without the pressure of tort liability, one wonders when and how this dramatic improvement in patient safety would have occurred.[48]

A paradoxical sort of evidence comes from the oft-heard argument that tort law has led to defensive medicine, which arguably is wasteful of resources and risky for patients. But if healthcare providers are, indeed, engaging in defensive medicine, then they *are* responding to tort law's deterrent impact. The "defensive medicine" concern is actually that tort law *overdeters*, that it leads to excessive precautions. But that would confirm its ability to motivate providers to invest effort at being safer. The contradiction between arguing that medical malpractice litigation has no power to motivate change toward safer practices and also that it generates widespread defensive practices, is obvious. Which of these, if either, is true is the more challenging and important question.[49]

One can draw a straight line from tort liability to the advent of the patient safety movement. Without the pressure of tort litigation, the major studies of the incidence of preventable iatrogenic injury (e.g., the California Medical Association/California Hospital Association research and the Harvard Medical Practice Study [HMPS]) would not have been undertaken. Without the findings of those studies, the report of the Institute of Medicine, *To Err Is Human*, would not have been written and published. And without the Institute of Medicine (IOM) report, it is hard to see how the patient safety movement would have been launched. As a leading member of that new field has said, "prior to the IOM Report, we were doing next to nothing to make patients safer."[50]

DOES THE SYSTEM TARGET THE RIGHT EVENTS?

Deterrence would be less effective if the litigation system targeted too many incidents of nonnegligent injury and missed too many incidents of negligent injury. That would send, as they say, "the wrong signal" to prospective tortfeasors and undercut the goal of stimulating prevention of harmful errors. The point was made by a captivatingly simple analogy provided in an important book by Paul Weiler and his HMPS colleagues about the realities of iatrogenic injury and the law's responses. The comment was that the malpractice litigation system is like a traffic cop who "regularly [gives] out more tickets to drivers who go through green lights than to those who go through red lights."[51] This image suggests something worse than random and, according to David Studdert and Michelle Mello, "This pronouncement of the tort system's inaccuracy in matching compensation awards to the merits of claims has become a staple in policy debates over medical liability reform. Assertions that the system is a lottery in which compensation awards are little better than random are commonly heard from the medical community and others who advocate far-reaching reforms."[52]

Unfortunately, the traffic cop imagery has served to mislead more than to illuminate. Importantly, Weiler and colleagues said more about those traffic lights, and on the very same page where they introduced the analogy.[53] What they explained was that, because the vast majority of cars went through the green, and only a few percent through the red, even a highly accurate process (even one that is 99% accurate) would produce a larger *number* of cars ticketed for going through green than ticketed for going through red. "With that difference controlled for," they explained, "the odds that a careless driver will get a ticket, or that a careless doctor will be sued, *are far greater* than the odds faced by their careful counterparts."[54] "[B]oth the reality and the perception of that [deterrence] signal have a pronounced tilt in the proper direction." But the metaphor stole the show so thoroughly that most people who talk or write about it get the point backwards.

According to the HMPS data, which intentionally set a high threshold for considering an adverse event to be negligent,[55] doctors who caused a negligent injury were 22 times more likely to have claims filed against them for such events than doctors who had not caused negligent injuries. If this were a medical test for diagnosing the presence of a disease, such a level of accuracy (what is termed a likelihood ratio; here, it is 22) would be considered "large and often conclusive" for diagnosis.[56]

Continuing the medical testing analogy, if the tort system were attempting to diagnose a negligent iatrogenic injury (which it is), it would be said to have a *specificity* of 99.9%. That is, it rules out 99.9% of the cases that should be ruled out. That's up there with the best lab tests for disease detection (better, for example, than tests for influenza and prostate cancer). The problem is that the "test" is terrible at detecting negligent-adverse-injury cases: its *sensitivity* is only 2.9%. That is, only 2.9% of negligent adverse events become claims for compensation.[57] We might usefully wonder why negligently injured patients aren't screaming at the medical malpractice litigation system more loudly than the healthcare industry does.

The data of Mello and Studdert,[58] which examine only malpractice claims that reached insurance companies, yielded a sensitivity of 73.5% and specificity of 71.8%.[59] That means getting it right nearly three-fourths of the time. Not perfect, to be sure, but not as bad as some medical tests.[60]

Biochemical tests might be an inappropriate standard for comparison to tort litigation. Litigation is humans "diagnosing" torts. How do *humans* do at diagnosing disease? Performance varies a lot with the disease and the patient. (The ease of tort diagnosis also varies with the case.) In one study, doctors got the easier diagnoses right 55.3% of the time, and the difficult ones right 5.8% of the time.[61] In another, nine cases were presented for diagnosis to 72 fourth-year medical students, 72 second- and third-year internal medicine residents, and 72 general internists with medical school faculty appointments. The experienced physicians reached correct diagnoses 49% of the time; residents, 44%; and medical students, 26%.[62] Error rates higher than those in Mello and Studdert's study of medical malpractice "diagnosis" have been found in studies of diagnoses of skin diseases,[63] psychiatric illnesses,[64] gynecologists' interpretations of the diagnostic significance of positive mammograms,[65] and others.

The level of "diagnostic" errors in the tort system are often condemned. When equally imperfect, and worse, findings emerge in studies of medical diagnosis, researchers and commentators talk of how challenging the task is or about tweaking a measure's cut-points to improve the trade-off between sensitivity and specificity or the need for more research or training or innovation to help improve performance. When the health industry discusses the imperfections of the tort system, the solutions are rarely so constructive. When it is the tort litigation system under discussion, the glass is not viewed as an encouraging three-quarters full, but as a calamitous one-quarter empty.

As we noted in the preceding chapter, the chief problem in sorting tort cases is really that, because private law is nonself-starting, most valid cases never get out of the starting blocks, and many that do take the initial step are screened out by lawyers as offering insufficient expected returns on their professional investment. By the lights of the HMPS data, 97% of *valid* claims never materialize.[66]

As a result, those researchers found that the probability that a doctor who *did not* cause a negligent injury would be sued was 0.0013 (13 chances in 10,000). And the probability that one who *did* cause a negligent injury would become a defendant was 0.029 (290 chances in 10,000). Of the few cases that endure long enough to be resolved by a trial verdict, about three-quarters are decided against patients—because, as Studdert and Mello note, of a "pervasive tendency to deny compensation to all claims, regardless of merit."[67]

THE BEHAVIOR OF THE TORT LITIGATION SYSTEM ACCORDING TO THE HEALTHCARE INDUSTRY

An anecdote circulated years ago about the renowned economist John Kenneth Galbraith, close friend and adviser to John F. Kennedy, who sat next to the president as the two explained their ideas for improving the U.S. economy to the roomful of prominent economists they had assembled to discuss the matter. Kennedy hoped to win their backing for his proposed policies, but the room's consensus was far from approving. At one point, Galbraith leaned close to Kennedy and whispered, "This is not going well." Kennedy replied into Galbraith's ear: "Don't worry. We get to write the report."

Only that anecdote enabled one of your authors to make sense of what he experienced at a meeting of advisers to the secretary of the Department of Health and Human Services (DHHS) during the Reagan years. A high-ranking official in the department invited me to Washington to be one of a broad gathering of outside advisers who met with DHHS officials to discuss possible policy responses to what was widely thought to be a malpractice liability crisis. I did not look forward to the meeting. We advisers were asked to focus on the facts of the situation, the data. Judging from the picture being painted in the news, relying on pronouncements from government and industry officials, I expected to be a lonely voice. What those officials were saying and what the data said seemed to emanate from different universes. To my amazement and relief, virtually all of the other advisers, and some DHHS staffers, were equally aware of the actual data and regarded it seriously. Instead of rowing against the tide, I found myself sailing along with most of the others. I left the meeting with the sense that—at least on this issue—facts, evidence, and data would prevail over narratives invented to advance an industry's agenda. I was even more amazed, however, when the official DHHS report on the subject was published. Although our names were listed as consultants, none of the facts, data, or studies that we advisers had shared with officials at the meeting were even mentioned in the report, much less relied on to guide policy. They had evaporated. Almost as soon as I started wondering how such a thing could have happened, I imagined one health department official remarking to another, "This is not going well." And the other replying, "Don't worry. We get to write the report."

Readers of the first few chapters of this book might have started to suspect that many of the pronouncements of healthcare industry officials, their advocates, and their friends in government describe the problem of iatrogenic injury and the law's responses in ways that are at a considerable remove from the facts as found by empirical research. The healthcare industry has started to rely increasingly on evidence-based medicine. But not yet on evidence-based policymaking. Next we list some of the industry's pronouncements.

The tort litigation system

- encourages patients to file frivolous lawsuits.[68]
- sues doctors at a rate far above the incidence of real malpractice events.[69]
- creates malpractice insurance crises because of spikes in malpractice litigation (that is, abrupt increases in claim frequency and size of payments).[70]
- is an unpredictable lottery.[71]
- is misdirected at individual responsibility when systems are responsible for most errors in the healthcare system.[72]
- permits sympathetic juries to unjustifiably give the insurance company's money to injured people.[73]
- encourages juries to award far more in damages than justified by plaintiffs' losses.[74]
- places doctors at risk of bankruptcy.[75]
- drives physicians from states without malpractice tort reforms, leaving patients without sufficient numbers of providers.[76]
- frightens doctors and other healthcare providers into hiding errors, thereby preventing the transparency needed to solve the very serious problem of iatrogenic injury.[77]
- is chiefly responsible for skyrocketing healthcare costs, mainly by causing the practice of defensive medicine.[78]
- has no deterrent effect.[79]
- fails to compensate more than a fraction of (negligently) injured patients.[80]

The final item on that list is the most demonstrably true of the assertions, and the most ironic. The evidence supporting it was discussed in the preceding chapter. The irony is that most of the tort reforms that the healthcare industry has promoted and state governments have instituted have been designed to make it *even more difficult* for injured patients to obtain compensation. (See Tables 6.1 and 6.2.) That is the central point of malpractice law reform. To convince legislatures to put more roadblocks in the way of negligently injured patients by arguing that the darned tort system has put too many roadblocks in the way of injured patients is more than a little paradoxical. As we will shortly see, that is the very feature of the tort system that is kindest to the healthcare industry and has led to its continued embrace of the tort system, despite

Table 6.1. FIRST-GENERATION MALPRACTICE REFORMS (WIDELY PROMOTED BY HEALTHCARE ORGANIZATIONS)

Aimed at the size of recoveries ("severity")
 Periodic payments of damages
 Collateral source offset
 Joint and several liability changes
 Caps on general or total damages
 Punitive damages limits
 Ad damnum clauses restricted

Aimed at the number of suits
 Pretrial screening panels
 Shortening statutes of limitations
 Attorney fee controls
 Certificate of merit
 Defense costs awardable

Aimed at increasing plaintiffs' difficulty (or costs) of winning
 Expert witness requirements
 Informed consent limits
 Professional standard of care asserted
 Res ipsa loquitur restrictions
 Statute of frauds for medical guarantees

Aimed at functioning/cost of judicial process
 Mediation
 Arbitration
 Notice of intent to sue
 Precalendar conference required
 Preferred scheduling

Insurance Reforms
 Patient compensation funds
 Joint underwriting associations
 Limits on insurance cancellation
 Mandates for liability coverage
 Reporting requirements

SOURCES: Randall Bovbjerg et al., *Valuing Life and Limb in Tort: Scheduling "Pain and Suffering,"* 83 Northwestern Univ. L. Rev. 908 (1989); Eleanor D. Kinney, *Malpractice Reforms in the 1990s: Past Disappointments, Future Success?* 20 J. Health Polit. Pol. 99 (1995); Frank A. Sloan and Lindsey M. Chepke, Medical Malpractice (2008).

its unending criticism of the tort system. Moreover, if the healthcare system wanted patients who suffered negligent adverse events to be compensated, it could simply do so, without exchanging so much as a postcard with the tort litigation system.

More generally, however, we should all be able to agree that if anything is bad and needs to be modified or thrown away—be it a legal policy, a medical

Table 6.2. SECOND-GENERATION MALPRACTICE REFORMS (GENERALLY OPPOSED BY HEALTHCARE ORGANIZATIONS)

Use of medical practice guidelines to set the standard of care
Scheduling of damages
Mandated use of alternative dispute resolution methods in lieu of tort
No-fault approaches
   Limited no-fault early compensation
   Neo-no-fault early compensation
   Pure no-fault approaches
Enterprise liability
Private contract to implement malpractice reform

SOURCE: Eleanor D. Kinney, Malpractice Reforms in the 1990s: Past Disappointments, Future Success?, 20 J. Health Polit. Pol. 99 (1995).

procedure, or a pair of uncomfortable shoes—it should be possible to describe the actual problems that need solution, rather than resorting to the invention of problems that do not exist. Many or most of those asserted problems were at one time attempts to find plausible explanations for unpleasant conditions (e.g., periodic spiking of malpractice insurance premiums). Let's be generous and call those hypotheses. But hypotheses need to be tested. And, once they've been tested by a reasonable amount of research of reasonable quality, and no support has been found, or the findings establish the contrary, we might expect false narratives to be set aside and the inquiry to move on, in search of more constructive hypotheses. But that is not how things have worked.

One lobbying strategy has been to keep repeating beguiling narratives, whether or not they are supported by evidence. Another strategy is to concede that the new evidence radically changes the picture but insist that the old solution will solve the newly recognized problem. Thus, the American Medical Association (AMA) for a time, most vigorously in the 1980s, condemned tort law and demanded its reform or abolition on the grounds that harmful errors in healthcare bordered on nonexistent, and therefore virtually all tort claims were invalid if not altogether frivolous. In the wake of empirical research on the incidence of preventable injuries and deaths in hospitals, that narrative could no longer stand. So one day the AMA announced that it was changing its position.[81] In the new narrative, tort law had to be altered or abolished *because* the problem of iatrogenic injury was so large and so serious. Fear of lawsuits was said to be preventing what was needed most to improve patient safety: candid disclosure of problems that led to injuries so that solutions could be devised.[82] The picture changed entirely—from safe-as-can-be to carnage—but the proposed policy change remained the same.

More paradoxically, the tort system serves the economic interests of the healthcare industry to such an extent that seeking to change it fundamentally is not something that its leaders are likely to ever want to do.

THE HEALTHCARE INDUSTRY'S LOVE-HATE RELATIONSHIP WITH TORT LAW

The one thing we thought we could be sure of is that everyone in the healthcare industry, especially doctors, hates tort law, malpractice litigation, and related stressors. As part of their larger project, Paul Weiler and his Harvard colleagues interviewed 739 physicians, who "expressed great distress, even anguish, over having their professional performance and competence attacked."[83] Some insist that no amount of reform of the tort litigation system will ever be enough; it has to be eliminated entirely, because "no matter what kind of traditional curbs we put on our legal system, physicians . . . are still subject to potential malpractice suits."[84] In an article that deeply ponders what might justifiably be done to make the law more accommodating to doctors, Ellen Wertheimer's first sentence puts the matter bluntly: "It is at this point axiomatic that doctors hate lawyers."[85]

Physicians' emotions about this one subject often have overtaken their otherwise informed judgment. In a review of Robert Wachter and Kaveh Shojania's book devoted to the problem of patient safety, *Internal Bleeding: The Truth Behind America's Terrifying Epidemic of Medical Mistakes*, an otherwise highly favorable reviewer comments that "Even the good-natured tone of *Bleeding* becomes apoplectic in its chapter on legal liability." And, significantly, "they misunderstand it, too."[86] Ravings about things that are not so is not the most direct path to improvements. But it certainly makes one's feelings known, and for some lawmakers, that is more than enough.

Comprehend their fear and loathing or not, let's take as a given that healthcare providers despise the tort system. The question, then, becomes why the healthcare industry's leaders have not devoted more effort to trying to abolish it. The industry has worked at weakening the tort system (as it applies to themselves) but not killing it. Why? The answer seems to be that it would be hard to invent a system of supposed injury compensation (with or without deterrence) that could be more generous to the industry.

We've already seen the most glaring benefits: A tiny fraction of suspected (and actual) negligent adverse events suffered by patients is taken up by the tort system. In what other compensation system can one imagine that it would be normal for a mere 11% of patients who have suffered adverse events causing "Grave Permanent Total Disability" to seek recompense?[87] For injuries that do become claims, at every step through the process, the advantage, on average, remains with healthcare defendants. Recent reforms have added to those advantages. That translates into scores of billions of dollars of costs that the healthcare industry externalizes onto victims and the rest of society that it is never asked to reimburse.

Whenever the industry begins to flirt with some other system, it soon seems to remind itself of what a splendid deal it already has, and ends the affair. That is what happened as far back as the 1970s when the California Medical Association and California Hospital Association started to dream about an administrative compensation system of some kind to replace malpractice litigation. It abandoned those reveries as soon as its research revealed that a horrifically large number of patients in California hospitals were being killed or suffered permanent or grave disability, whereas only a small fraction of those victims brought claims, and an even smaller fraction had to actually be compensated. From the viewpoint of writing checks to injured patients and the families of decedents, the tort system is as close as one can realistically come to no system.

The same realization has struck repeatedly and again quite recently. Legislation to replace medical malpractice litigation with a no-fault administrative system known as the "Patient Compensation System" (PCS) was introduced in a number of legislatures around the country, among them Georgia and Florida, promising to lower healthcare costs by reducing the need to practice defensive medicine while also compensating more injured patients. Judging from their blog posts, frontline doctors loved the idea. But at its November 2016 meeting, the AMA voted to support state medical societies in *opposing* PCS legislation. One reason for that opposition is the now familiar one: "the number of claims could increase," for example, "by as much as 840% under the legislation proposed in Florida."[88]

The skyrocketing of claims that would arise from an administrative compensation system does not necessarily imply skyrocketing costs. Limits of various kinds could be placed on injury payouts, for example, schedules of compensation, discounts on total awards, caps on general damages or on total awards. That would solve the math problem, but it could create new pressures on legislatures as growing numbers of injured patients and their families would begin to see more clearly how shabbily they are being treated—something that is far less visible in the tort process. Administrative no-fault systems like PCS, with cost controls that protect the industry, in effect, say: Filing is easy, and in due time you'll receive a check for a fraction of the costs you were burdened with. Tort says: You may file (if you can find a lawyer who thinks your case is worth taking), and you could be entitled to full compensation for your losses (but in the end you will probably not receive anything close to that). Everyone who needs to know these facts knows them; if not workaday healthcare providers, the people running their industry obviously do.

Beyond the numerical (fewer cases) and financial benefits that tort law bestows on the healthcare industry, when the curtain comes down on private enforcement, it tends to go up on government enforcement to replace the regulatory effect that is thought to have been lost. So, the death of tort law, history suggests, will lead to increased regulation of healthcare in an effort to raise the level of patient safety, and possibly even an increase in criminal prosecutions for the most egregious iatrogenic harms. Every industry has within it tendencies to seek a profit advantage against competitors and the public: insider trading, cheating on product quality or purity, cartels, stealing trade secrets from competitors, or evading accountability for harm.[89] Without some counterforce, all would be at the mercy of the most clever or cutthroat of the businesses. The principal counterforce, after market competition, is the law. And if one of the law's tools (e.g., tort) is disabled, others tend to arise to fill the gap.

Some or many doctors also want to be in a position to fight any allegation that they provided less than first-rate care, and tort law gives them the right and the power to do that. One of the architects of the proposed healthcare financing reforms of the Bill Clinton era recounts one physician's opposition to a plan that would have relieved individual doctors of having to face lawsuits: "I have a constitutional right to be sued and you can't take it away from me."[90]

For these and other reasons, the leaders of the industry, including physicians' groups, always return to the conclusion that tort liability is the best deal in town, and they hold to it, even though they hate it, and even though other systems could be more efficient, more humane to injured patients, and in some ways more agreeable to providers. But just because, on balance, you love the tort system better than its alternatives doesn't mean you don't want to alter it.

CHANGES IN TORT LAW AS APPLIED TO THE HEALTHCARE INDUSTRY ("MALPRACTICE REFORM")

In pursuit of its escape from accountability, the healthcare industry has been unusually successful in recent decades in persuading state legislatures to make changes in tort law and legal process as it pertains to them. The major changes are listed in Tables 6.1 (first-generation reforms) and 6.2 (second-generation reforms). Overall, the reforms have succeeded in cutting the number of malpractice claims by nearly two-thirds over the past several decades.[91]

Most of these reforms, especially the "first generation," are aimed at reducing the number of patients who can bring claims, making the traditionally tiny proportion of injury victims who do so even tinier, and to reduce the amount of compensation that can be received by those whose claims succeed. Reviewing the empirical research on the effects of these reforms, Allen Kachalia and Michelle Mello found that few of them, at least on their own, contributed to the reformers' chief goals of reducing the number of injured patients who brought claims, reducing payments to them, and keeping malpractice insurance premiums down.[92] The reform with greatest impact has been caps on damages, which has been found to produce "substantial savings" on payments to victims and to have imposed a "modest restraint on growth of malpractice premiums." Makes sense, doesn't it? Limit the amount you have to pay out to any given victim, and you reduce the total amount you have to pay out.

So, capping damages, not surprisingly, has become the favorite reform. More than half the states have adopted limitations of one form or another on awards of noneconomic damages, and some have done so for total damages (economic as well as so-called noneconomic). These caps have reduced mean payment per claim by as much as 40%.[93] These reductions have, in turn, led to lower malpractice insurance premiums—although not as low as hoped because insurers have been cautious about reducing rates.

Granting the industry its goal of keeping more money in its own pockets, caps are the cruelest way to accomplish that goal. Caps do not reduce the compensation of all successful claimants by some fixed percentage, or by some sliding percentage, or withhold compensation from those who need it the least (because their losses are the least). It is patients with the most severe injuries who are made to carry the greatest burden of subsidizing the industry. Patients with the least severe injuries and losses receive their full compensation. A patient whose wrong foot was cut off, for example, might receive the entire general damages award determined by a judge and jury. But the patient whose spinal cord was inadvertently severed would almost certainly receive only a fraction of her award. Caps focus on the most tragically injured malpractice victims and require them, and only them, to forego compensation that a court would otherwise have concluded was proper for their losses.[94] Furthermore, over time, a cap cuts deeper and deeper, which a proportional slicing would not. The $250,000 cap that California placed on general damages in 1975 translates to only $53,000 in today's dollars.

At the same time that they are protecting industry profits, very few of the reforms are aimed at preventing patients from being injured or killed. Of the few that might contribute to that goal, Kachalia and Mello's review of the literature mostly found too little research on possible quality-of-care effects to draw any conclusions. Subsequent research described earlier in this chapter, by Zabinski and Black, found that caps led to a relaxation of patient safety practices, and "[t]he decline is widespread."[95]

There is nothing unlawful or unethical in the healthcare industry's promotion of these reforms, except perhaps if you consider all of the statements the industry has made to legislators and the public claiming to be acting in the interest of patients when it really is acting almost entirely in its own interest. But that, too, is what industries do when they are trying to manipulate the law to boost their own profits without producing any additional value. Such behavior is familiar to economists and public-choice theorists, and they have given it a name: "rent-seeking."[96]

When asked to evaluate the goals that the law might be able to promote in regard to iatrogenic injury, the most highly rated choice of most groups–doctors, defense lawyers, plaintiffs' lawyers, torts professors, and the public—is to facilitate communication within the healthcare industry, the better to find ways to prevent future harm.[97] Hyman and Silver have taken a careful look at the effects of the tort law regime on such communication. They found, contrary to familiar assertions, that tort law has not reduced the amount of disclosure and communication (compared to times and places where tort law was less active or absent). Nor have tort reforms increased it.[98] Worth noting is that every other industry has worked at, and made great strides in, improving the safety of both workers and the public without needing to be sheltered from tort liability.

Some excellent arguments have been made for the virtues of one or another type of nonlitigation no-fault systems,[99] and some research suggests that such systems are likely to better achieve the things most people would like to see the law accomplish.[100] But, as previously noted, those have never been sufficient to break up the enduring romance between tort litigation and the healthcare industry.

BOTTOM LINES

From the viewpoint of patient safety, which is our touchstone, the inadequacy of the tort system could not be more obvious. Medical malpractice litigation has made an insufficient contribution to the prevention of iatrogenic injury and death. That was true even before the orgy of tort reforms seen in recent decades. Hundreds of thousands of deaths and a million preventable injuries each year cannot be considered acceptable—not for the healthcare system and not for the legal system. The law can and should do more, and the latter chapters of this book explore some of the possibilities for finding legal tools, beyond tort law, that might help make a bigger dent in the problem.

To say that the entire solution to "America's terrifying epidemic of medical mistakes"[101] is not being found in tort law does not mean that none of it is being found in tort law. Notwithstanding considerable rhetoric generated in support of these propositions, evidence is scarce that the tort system makes no contribution to patient safety or that it does more harm than good.[102] Tort law might, in fact, be making a substantial contribution at a surprisingly low cost. Even if its contribution is modest, to think that eliminating tort law, or continuing to weaken it, will produce improvements in patient safety is, in light of available evidence, a counsel of foolishness. We do not abolish the highway patrol because many drivers continue to drive unsafely.

What is needed is addition, not subtraction. No one approach produces all the safety that is desired in any sphere of activity. As Yale law professor Peter Schuck has noted, "All systems . . . have had to adopt auxiliary measures—information, education, administrative regulation, instinct for self-preservation, technology, market effects (including reputation), professional discipline, and other behavioral influences—to augment the call for accident prevention."[103] Not least is what the healthcare industry can achieve through its own patient safety initiatives ("the patient safety movement"). The more that is accomplished by those efforts, the less work any of the other methods need to accomplish, including the tort system.

7

Defensive Medicine

A Response to the Legal Response?

Physicians in states with strong tort reforms and in states lacking those reforms articulated identical views regarding malpractice risk.[1]

Defensive medicine is a puzzle. It is almost universally regarded as a dreadful problem, a bane of the healthcare system, an evil committed by healthcare providers, suffered by patients, paid for by all of society, and blamed on the tort system.

Defensive medicine is said to be difficult to define but, for the moment, can be thought of as the practice of ordering medically unnecessary tests and performing needless procedures for purposes unrelated to the well-being of patients. Defensive medicine is "employed explicitly for the purposes either of averting a possible law suit or [if a law suit were filed] of providing appropriate documentation that a wide range of tests and treatments has been used in the patient's care."[2] One needn't be a medical expert to recognize this as a "deviation from sound medical practice."[3]

Defensive medicine is a mystery to serious researchers and a necessity for healthcare industry lobbyists. During a panel discussion about "public discontent" with tort law, one participant raised the issue: "[W]hat about the problem of defensive medicine? The general counsel of a New York hospital told me that from 15% to 25% of their services are done solely to provide a possible defense in a lawsuit." Others agreed. But another panelist replied by asking the naked emperor question: "I would like to know where can we go for documentation of defensive medicine? Where are the independent studies that show us what defensive medicine really is—beyond a catch phrase, what it means in reality, and how we can evaluate it? Where can we go beyond the assertions of interested parties?"[4]

Indeed. How do we actually know anything about it? Who discovered it, and how? What is the evidence for it? For its costs? That it even exists? How do we

Note: Portions of this chapter originally appeared as an article in Health Matrix: Journal of Law-Medicine, published by Case Western Reserve University School of Law. The article is entitled The Paradoxes of Defensive Medicine and is included in Volume 30. This material is reproduced with the permission of Health Matrix.

know that defensive medicine is an economic and behavioral discovery and not merely a rhetorical one?

A TOOL FOR ADVOCACY

That defensive medicine is a useful tool for healthcare industry lobbyists is easy to understand. Nothing else about it is. The lobbyist's goal is to bring about changes in law that advantage the client industry by increasing its revenues or reducing its costs. The direct economic costs of the medical malpractice system are small. The total amount of malpractice insurance premiums collected (from doctors, hospitals, and other providers) reflects most of the costs required for the defense of the nation's malpractice claims: compensation payments, legal fees, profits for insurance companies, administrative costs, and anything else.[5] That total represents one-quarter of one percent of all expenditures on healthcare (i.e., $9.2 billion out of $3.5 trillion[6]). That $9.2 billion constitutes a mere 2.4% of all liability insurance premiums paid for *all* activities in the United States (by businesses and individuals combined). Yet it comes from the industry that collects 17.9% of our GDP. Ironically, the industry that pays proportionately so little to insure itself against the cost of accidents is the same industry that generates more accidental death and injury (as a byproduct of its work) than the combined total of all other human activity in the nation.[7] As seen earlier, the great bulk of the costs of those accidents are externalized from the healthcare industry onto the shoulders of victims and their families, first-party health insurers (i.e., health insurers), and taxpayers through government insurance programs.

How can a lobbyist persuade a legislature to help make that highly favorable gain-loss profile even more favorable to the industry? The key is to turn that small number into a far larger number. And the concept of defensive medicine is what supplies that far larger number. Healthcare providers, mostly physicians and hospitals, the lobbyist's argument goes, are so afraid of becoming defendants in malpractice suits that they lard needless tests and procedures onto the nation's annual healthcare bill. No one knows how much all of those wasteful tests and procedures really cost us, but speculative amounts are offered by proponents who, given the nature of their assignment, reach for the largest numbers they can assert short of triggering disbelief or amusement. The most extreme of those imaginary numbers transforms the approximately one-quarter of one percent of healthcare costs into something a legislator might be induced to worry about.

Various estimates have been advanced. Philip Howard—founder of Common Good, an organization which promotes the idea of removing medical malpractice disputes from conventional courts—floated the figure of $100 billion in 2003 (in 2018 dollars: $137 billion).[8] His estimate was flayed as "grossly exaggerated"[9] by physician and legal scholars David Hyman and Charles Silver, and they explain why in considerable detail.[10] Undeterred, others outbid Howard. A 2003 U.S. Department of Health and Human Services (DHHS) report gave figures of $70 to $126 billion (in 2018 dollars: $96–$173 billion).[11] The American Tort

Reform Association asserted annual defensive medicine expenditures of $200 billion (in 2018 dollars: $210 billion).[12] Topping that, the healthcare economics firm BioScience Valuation has put the amount above $480 billion annually. And Jackson Health System, a healthcare organization based in Miami, did even better, with a figure of $650 to $850 billion (in 2018 dollars: $713–$933 billion).[13] For those looking for a solution to the problem of America's exorbitant healthcare costs, those are the kinds of numbers that can attract some attention.[14]

If defensive medicine actually does exist in something like the form and extent often supposed, then it not only wastes vast resources; it also adds to the dangers confronting patients, as they are subjected to needless tests, radiation, medication, sometimes surgery, and other low-value and no-value care. By calming doctors' fears, medical malpractice reform would, runs the argument, save hundreds of billions of dollars of worthless healthcare expenditures and protect patients from the risks associated with healthcare they do not need.

WHY COMMIT AND WHY ADMIT?

Not very long ago, doctors denied engaging in defensive medicine. Today they are eager to assert that they do. We will examine the empirical evidence later. For now, the question is why would a healthcare provider choose to pursue defensive practices? And, having committed defensive medicine, why admit to it?

Why Might Doctors Engage in Defensive Medicine?

The reasons for defensive practices seem obvious at first. As discussed elsewhere in this book, the healthcare industry is organized in a way that loads as much of the cost burden of iatrogenic injuries as possible onto physicians and their insurers, even when much of the cause and the capability to prevent is within the control of larger organizational units.[15] If you are a provider on whom that burden falls, you probably want to do something to lighten it.

If you could reduce the chances that your house would burn down or that your car would be in a crash, and you could accomplish that (a) by spending someone else's money (the patient and the patient's health insurer) and (b) pay yourself a bonus for taking the trouble to spend other people's money, would you? The greater a physician perceives the risk of a malpractice lawsuit to be, the more tests and other procedures the physician orders, the more money that physician and the industry get to charge, and the more the risk of being sued is reduced.[16] The desirability of the practice, at least for the practitioner, seems beyond debate. Wouldn't you be crazy not to?

But perhaps the self-serving benefits of defensive medicine are not so clear as they seem. How are doctors to know which actions actually will be protective? They can guess. But there is little or no empirical evidence on what extra actions reduce the risk of—what? What are they trying to reduce the risk of? Of a claim being filed (a case being initiated)?[17] But only a fraction of 1% of hospital admissions become claims, and a smaller fraction for patients seen out-of-hospital. Of losing a case? The vast majority of filed malpractice cases are disposed of without a trial anyway.

How is it that defensive practices can help when one of the most-mentioned reasons for defensive practices is said to be that patients and the litigation process are so unpredictable? Paradoxically, then, engaging in defensive practice bespeaks a belief in the existence of patient and legal system predictability—the alleged absence of which is the reason for engaging in defensive practices in the first place. And, if the defensive practice is effective at reducing the risk of lawsuits by reducing the risk of harmful error, then it sounds less like a defensive stratagem and more like good medical practice.

Perhaps defensive practices are the product of superstition—in the psychological and anthropological sense. Superstitious behavior is found in all societies and cultures.[18] The great anthropologist Bronislaw Malinowski, while studying the people of the Trobriand Islands, made a discovery about the causes of superstitious behavior. Malinowski observed that the islanders had no superstitions connected with performing activities in which the relation of actions to outcomes was predictable and frequent. Activities that were unpredictable and carried the risk of harm or loss, however, were accompanied by superstitious practices. Fishing in the lagoons yielded a predicable amount of fish and was safe, and to this activity no magic, no superstitions, were attached. Fishing in the ocean, on the other hand, offered the chance of making an especially large haul of fish, but also the risk of coming home empty-handed, or not coming home at all. Ocean fishing was accompanied by superstitions and magic. We can see the same pattern in our own society. For example, baseball players have no superstitions in connection with fielding (which they accomplish successfully 98.4% of the time[19]); their superstitions cluster around the less predictable activity of batting (which they accomplish successfully only 24.8% of the time).

And perhaps something similar is true of defensive medicine. Lawsuits against doctors are so rare relative to the number of patient contacts, and rare even when the doctor is in fact responsible for a serious negligent adverse event,[20] that almost any behavior one engages in could seem to have a correlation (albeit an illusory correlation) with the fact of not being sued. An extra computed tomography scan might seem to keep lawsuits at bay. But so might wearing a protective necklace of garlic bulbs. The connection between actions and harms leading to lawsuits is unpredictable: the same errors and harm that usually do not produce a malpractice suit once in a great while do produce one. And a lawsuit, whatever its disposition, is a dreaded experience. There is nothing (evidence-based) that is dependably known to reduce that very small risk to an even smaller one. So perhaps defensive practices arise to provide a *feeling* of control over an uncontrollable situation. That is what humans tend to do when faced with high stakes and uncontrollable risks; it's not just for Trobriand Island fishermen and baseball players.

Evidence that defensive practices actually reduce lawsuits is quite scarce.[21] *Belief* that defensive practices fend off lawsuits, however, is said to be common.

Eventually, perhaps, defensive practices of various kinds become part of the culture of the healthcare industry, not just something a few individuals decide to do of their own invention. Physicians and other providers are advised by teachers or colleagues, or have read, that self-protection is a good idea.

Or perhaps their lawyers advise them on how to practice medicine. Some years ago one of your authors attended a meeting of a medical school with its teaching hospital on the topic of medical malpractice. At this large, well-attended gathering, one of the speakers was the hospital's lawyer, who previously had been that state's attorney general. One piece of advice he offered the assembled medical students and faculty and staff was that, if in doubt, they should deliver babies by cesarean section. Why? Simple, he explained: Because he'd much rather defend a lawsuit for a needless cesarean in which the baby came out healthy than a case for the failure to do one that resulted in a damaged baby.[22]

Perhaps the logic of diagnosis and treatment teaches a doctor that some actions will almost certainly reduce the risk of harm and therefore of a suit. But such obvious benefits—to the doctor because they are benefits to the patient—make those actions strange candidates for inclusion in the category of "defensive medicine." Keeping patients safe and healthy should be the central goal of the healthcare industry. Recall that the best definition of defensive medicine is that it helps the doctor while doing little or no good for the patient. Where is the line that divides well-intended low-value care from self-dealing defensive practice? Surgeon and author Atul Gawande tells of the time his own child, who had fallen down some stairs, was taken to an emergency room (ER) for examination, given a computed tomography (CT) scan, examined, observed, and cleared to go home. Gawande explains that he "bullied the doctor into admitting" his son to the hospital for 24 hours and obtaining a repeat scan. "The next day, the scan and the patient were fine."[23] Suppose the ER doctor had ordered that extra care without being pressured to do so. (Some in fact do so.) Was the supposedly excessive causation "defensive"? Or was it the kind of care that a doctor prefers for his or her own family, but which (presumably based on the research evidence) is cost-ineffective and therefore normally foregone? That extra care might be wasteful, but can it be said to be "defensive"?

Gawande's story also reminds us that sometimes nervous patients or families want more than is thought to be needed, and doctors sometimes comply with the patients' wishes. Is *that* defensive medicine? Gawande has given another example, of a patient who was scheduled to have her thyroid removed because it contained microcarcinoma—tiny, slow-growing cells that could, but were very unlikely to, become cancerous. She wound up in his office because the surgeon who was planning to remove the gland was absent owing to his own health issues. Gawande explained to the patient why the risk of cancer was minimal, the risks of harm from the surgery, and the unpleasantness of life without a thyroid. They could monitor the thyroid, and if the cells started to grow, it could always be removed later. The reader thinks how lucky she was to have crossed Gawande's path and been spared needless surgery. But the patient couldn't bear the thought of even a miniscule risk of cancer and soon after had her thyroidectomy anyway.

Or consider this. In one of our law school classes, the topic of the moment was what a doctor should do when a patient asks for a medication that the doctor knows will be useless for the patient's condition, but the patient is not convinced and insists on trying the drug. A medical student in the class (who was also a law student) said that she would write the prescription that the patient wanted. The student explained: the patient will go elsewhere and find another doctor to write it. Better to keep the patient's business and try to work with the patient over time to guide the patient to prefer more beneficial treatments. Thus, unnecessary treatment, with its waste and risks of harm, is not always and everywhere a result of the desires of the doctor. Patients sometimes manage to put themselves at risk and waste healthcare dollars, and their doctors merely go along.

While some defensive practices may nevertheless benefit (or at least not endanger) patients, other defensive actions impose potential or actual harm on the patient—radiation, infection, falls, harmful drug reactions. In these circumstances, doctors sometimes increase the risk of harm and therefore of a lawsuit—the very thing they were hoping to avoid. So, from the provider's viewpoint, a trade-off is being made: the same actions that might decrease the risk of a lawsuit in some ways simultaneously increase the risk in other ways.[24] Presumably the tradeoff is seen by the provider as favoring the interests of the provider, else the defensive action would not be taken. That, at least, would have to be the rational defensive practitioner's decision calculus.

Why Would Anyone Admit to Engaging in Defensive Medicine?

It is one thing to engage in defensive practices, but quite another to admit to the deed. So why do so? Why not just do it and keep quiet about it? After all, ordering tests or treatments when the doctor believes that the procedures offer no, or minimal, prospect of benefit to the patient, but mainly serve the doctor's interests, are illegal as well as unethical. Billing for needless services is a form of healthcare fraud. The Medicare claim form, for example, requires providers to certify that the services shown on the form were medically indicated and necessary for the health of the patient. If the doctor does not believe the services are medically necessary, the claim is false.

The principal gain for the provider usually said to be the goal of defensive medicine (protection from a lawsuit) is a fraudulently obtained benefit. A prosecutor who had evidence of such behavior would see criminality in it. If the prosecutor wanted to act, one charge could be criminal fraud.[25] Since the act exposes the patient to risk of injury, the physician could also be charged with the crime of reckless endangerment.[26] If the defensive practice subjects the patient to wounds or radiation, the prosecutor might see the crime of assault and battery—because the patient was subjected to injury without having granted valid informed consent.

Leaving aside the civil or criminal liability, defensive medicine violates principles of medical ethics.[27] One ethical precept of medicine is that, "A physician shall . . . be honest in all professional interactions." Moreover, physicians are duty bound to report "to appropriate entities" colleagues they find "engaging in fraud or deception." Most important, the AMA's Code of Medical Ethics instructs that "a physician shall, while caring for a patient, regard responsibility to the patient as paramount." Defensive medicine turns all of that on its head: the interests of the physician are set above those of the patient by an act of fraud.

Let's return to the question: Why admit to engaging in defensive medicine? If you were a physician and you realized that you routinely, intentionally did things that were unethical and illegal, universally condemned as wasteful of precious healthcare resources, a "deviation from sound medical practice" and potentially harmful to the patients who place their trust in you, would *you* take every opportunity to proclaim your misdeeds from the rooftops and the op-ed pages?[28]

In fact, there was a time not very long ago when doctors did not take kindly to the suggestion that they were practicing defensive medicine. The accusation was regarded as an insult, an accusation of misconduct, and the response was denial, not enthusiastic affirmation. Medical commentary in the early 1970s spoke of "the spectre of defensive medicine, with the connotation that actions were motivated primarily by the desire to avoid malpractice liability,"[29] arguing that it was not happening.

Don Harper Mills was part of an AMA Board of Trustees' conference on medical costs in 1964, and it was his task to try to determine how much the malpractice litigation system was contributing to the costs of healthcare. "It was easy," he said, "to establish the cost of [liability] insurance as a direct effect of malpractice litigation on health care, but it was much more difficult to consider the indirect costs that physicians might induce through the mechanism of defensive medicine."[30] He surveyed physicians and from them he learned that about 25% of X-rays were, in the view of the doctors, unnecessary. But the doctors said they were being performed not because of malpractice concerns, but in response to pressure from patients who had been injured in accidents and whose lawyers were preparing cases against motorists or others alleged to be responsible for the patient's injuries. As to laboratory tests, he found that no more than 5% were thought by doctors to be unnecessary, and of those only a fraction were being ordered out of "medicolegal concerns."

A 1980 study found "medicolegal factors" to be involved in only 1% of laboratory tests and, even for those relative few, defensive practice was not the only factor said to motivate the test being ordered. Supporting the conclusion that malpractice fears did not cause doctors to order needless tests, the authors of that research added the observation that, "this study was conducted shortly after a large increase in professional liability insurance costs . . . which was accompanied by extensive public and professional debate on the problem of malpractice litigation."[31]

A 1971 paper reviewed the literature on defensive practices, finding "the most significant allegation" to be "the threat of malpractice litigation raises the cost of medical care by inducing physicians to overutilize diagnostic and treatment procedures."[32] Citing half a dozen studies, the review concluded that "the allegation that a physician responds to the increased threat of a malpractice suit by practicing defensive medicine has not been verified." Original research by the authors of the 1971 paper asked physicians in North Carolina and California to respond to hypothetical scenarios. That research detected some defensive medicine, "but the practice is not extensive and does not have as significant an impact as previously alleged." Most of those engaged in what appeared to be defensive practices argued that whatever protection a test or treatment might offer the doctor was outweighed by the medical benefits they provided to patients. One interesting defensive practice that developed in response to the perceived threat of malpractice litigation was to keep more "detailed records of examinations and treatments." Most of the doctors in the study felt that the innovation of keeping careful patient records had medical as well as legal-defense benefits. "Defensive medicine is good medicine," a 1974 article in the Journal of the American Medical Association argued.[33] In short, they said they didn't do it—until they started saying they do.

What changed? The ethos of advocacy changed. From the latter 1970s onward, as industry leaders and lobbyists sought to promote tort reforms by blaming high costs on defensive medicine, which was in turn blamed on fears of tort litigation, physicians apparently realigned their own story.

Today, the existence, the magnitude, the cost, and the evils of defensive medicine are touted widely and loudly by the healthcare industry. Now, most doctors insist they and their colleagues are practicing defensive medicine. "Nine out of 10 physicians reported practicing defensive medicine" "in an effort to avoid lawsuits" reported one large healthcare organization of a survey it had conducted.[34] A follow-up study, by the Gallup Organization, found that 73% acknowledged "they had practiced some form of defensive medicine in the past 12 months," and these "[p]hysicians attribute 26% of overall healthcare costs to the practice of defensive medicine."[35] In another study of 824 specialists in surgery, obstetrics, neurosurgery, emergency medicine and others, 93% reported practicing defensive medicine, such as ordering unnecessary CTs, biopsies, and MRIs (magnetic resonance imaging) and prescribing excessive antibiotics.[36] A more recent study found that 91% of physicians believe that defensive medicine exists, resulting in the administration of "more tests and procedures than necessary."[37] In a broader study of drivers of healthcare costs, the author "consulted surgeons, internists, anesthesiologists, family physicians, emergency physicians, and medical subspecialists. Many identified defensive medicine as their primary reason for ordering additional tests, estimating that it was responsible for 20% to 50% of their orders."[38] Whether or not physicians actually do practice defensively on such a scale, nowadays many seem to think that they do, or at least are eager to say that they do.

The spokespersons and lobbyists for the healthcare industry, who promote the existence and the impact of defensive medicine and do not hesitate to emphasize how terrible it is, do not wonder whether it exists or not. Industry advocates insist that it does and, what's more, they have a solution for it. Their remedy is (more) malpractice liability reforms to ease doctors' fear of lawsuits, which will enable them to wean themselves from their defensive ways.

But here is a puzzle. On the one hand, when fraud investigators detect healthcare providers prescribing unnecessary tests, treatments, and other procedures, they are charged with healthcare fraud, compelled to pay restitution, barred from filing future insurance claims, and/or prosecuted criminally.[39] But if they engage in the same conduct, motivated instead by fear of having to participate in a legal process where their insurer might be required to compensate a negligently injured patient, then the response of news media, the public, lawmakers, and perhaps even patients is sympathetic concern for the anxious physician. In both scenarios, such providers elevate their own interests above those of their patients and they profit from doing so.[40] Their conduct is equally illegal and unethical in either scenario. But, while the protagonist in one scenario is viewed as a malefactor; in the other he or she is seen as a worried victim deserving forgiveness, compassion, and (as advocates hope) legislated relief.

Indeed, if the healthcare industry's spokespersons are correct, defensive medicine far overshadows the most recognized types of healthcare fraud. All kinds of conventional healthcare fraud (i.e., fraud other than that associated with defensive medicine) constitute the single most expensive category of insurance fraud in the United States, currently estimated at about $40 billion per year.[41] If the exponents of the costs of defensive medicine are correct, then defensive practices extract at least an equivalent amount in healthcare fraud, and possibly well over 20 times as much.[42]

DOES DEFENSIVE MEDICINE ACTUALLY OCCUR?

For serious researchers, the defensive medicine hypothesis has been a challenging mystery. Although physicians once insisted that it didn't exist, perhaps it did. And though today they insist it does exist, perhaps it doesn't. Researchers want to know if defensive medicine is really being practiced. What has emerged from their research could be described as a mosaic of inconsistent and contradictory findings, with most of the tiles in the mosaic simply missing. The main questions to be asked are, Do healthcare providers really engage in defensive medical practices? If so, *how much* is it done and *how much* waste and harm does it generate? And, if that amount is substantial, what effective and efficient steps can be taken to reduce the problem?

The best current answer to the first two of those questions is that no one has the answers, at least not any based on sound data. Thoughtful researchers regard the answers as being remarkably elusive—for good reason, as we are about to see.[43] The consensus in the field is that, if defensive medicine exists, whatever its extent, the dollar cost of wasteful procedures attributable to defensive medicine is a thin shadow of what the industry's campaigners argue. Consequently, even under the most optimistic estimates, reforms of tort law would not be able to make much of a contribution to bringing down America's unusually high healthcare costs.

Let's unpack those findings and conclusions. The essential challenge to researchers is that because multiple motives overlap and overlay each other, the research must somehow disentangle a set of confounded motives. When a doctor orders a test or recommends a procedure, what has driven that choice? It could be self-protection. But it could instead, or in addition, be to serve the needs of the patient. Or it could be the desire to make money. Under the fee-for-service model that has dominated American healthcare, the more services provided, the more the industry can bill. As countless researchers, policy analysts, reformers, and commentators have pointed out, all of the motivating factors in the healthcare system—not just money, but medical training, professional norms, patient desires, and almost everything else—support doing more: test more, scan more, treat more.[44] Defensive medicine is only one of a number of causes of excessive and unnecessary care. How is one to separate the motivation of lawsuit fear from those other forces that all push in the same direction? In the absence of mind readers, how is one to sort those out? If multiple motives operate simultaneously, can they ever be sorted out? That is the challenge researchers face.

Another problem is definitional: What counts as defensive medicine? If healthcare providers feel pressure to do medically desirable things to avoid malpractice—for example, wash hands, follow good medical practices, keep accurate patient records—is that "defensive"? Some think so, and will say they are practicing defensively. But if that is what is happening, at least for them the malpractice system is working as intended and producing desirable effects: it has created incentives to practice effectively and safely. This can work the other way around: practices that have little value for patients but are thought to protect the doctor might come to be routine, with many practitioners not realizing that these were originally defensive tactics. Doctors using such procedures might think they are not acting defensively, just following standard practice, when what they are doing could be understood as defensive practice. Or, what if a doctor realizes a given diagnostic or treatment procedure has potential value for the patient as well as providing a potentially defensive benefit for the doctor? Is that "defensive" or not?

The Congressional Office of Technology Assessment (OTA) in 1994 proposed this definition of defensive medicine, which has often been employed ever since: "Defensive medicine occurs when doctors order tests, procedures, or visits, or avoid high-risk patients or procedures, primarily (but not necessarily solely) to reduce their exposure to malpractice liability."[45] Other definitions have adopted variations such as

- "positive" defensive medicine (aka: "assurance behavior": taking extra steps) and "negative" defensive medicine ("avoidance behavior": refraining from treating certain patients or using certain procedures);
- whether the defensive practice is conscious or unconscious; or
- whether the action is taken solely or primarily for the doctor's benefit rather than the patient's.[46]

The definition that requires the least mind reading is Frank Sloan and John Shadle's more economic one: "only care for which expected cost exceeds expected benefits" counts as defensive medicine. Whether conduct is "defensive" or not will sometimes, or often, depend on the definitional lens through which the behavior is being viewed.

The studies that have been undertaken on defensive medicine fall into three basic groups. One type, *direct physician surveys*, simply asks providers what they do and why they do it.[47] A second type, *clinical scenario surveys*, presents doctors with descriptions of patients and their health problems and asks them to choose from a set of options what clinical actions they would take and to indicate what factors led to their choices. The third type consists of *multivariate statistical analyses of existing data sets*, which could reveal the impact of malpractice risk on actual utilization of medical services.

Each of these types of research, owing to their own particular strengths and shortcomings, have fallen short of providing sufficiently sound and complete answers to the most important questions about defensive medicine. One general problem that can haunt any type of study is the "file drawer problem,"[48] a consequence of one important type of publication bias wherein studies that find no effects (X does not cause Y) are less likely to be accepted for publication than those finding an effect (X causes Y). For example, imagine you are a researcher who hypothesizes that singing in the shower prevents cancer. You have carried out 17 studies that show no protective relationship between singing and cancer, so those wind up in your file drawer (if not your wastebasket). Your eighteenth effort yields the kind of findings you had been hoping for, and those results find a home in a journal. When the world searches the literature to see whether singing protects against cancer, the one positive study will be found. The 17 null findings will not. This kind of selection bias also means that the one finding that did get published likely was a false conclusion resulting from random noise leading to erroneous rejection of the starting assumption of no difference ("null hypothesis")—what statisticians refer to as type I error.[49] Other researchers will be unable to replicate your finding that singing prevents cancer, and that is a serious problem for building knowledge.

For present purposes, the file drawer problem means that, of equally well-done studies, those finding an effect are more likely to become part of the literature than those not finding an effect. Limited and contradictory as the body of research on defensive medicine is, it is all that anyone has with which to try to answer the question: Does it exist?

Direct Physician Surveys

As we have seen, several decades ago physicians responded to surveys asking about their defensive practices by overwhelmingly denying that they engaged in them at all. Rather, they said, they ordered tests and procedures for reasons of sound medical practice. Sometime in the 1970s their answers began to turn around. Today, the same professional populations overwhelmingly insist that they *do* engage in defensive practices, generating rates of reported defensive medical practice, as we noted earlier, that sometimes exceed 90%.[50]

What such percentages mean is more than a bit mysterious. Perhaps the leap from low numbers to high numbers describes the reality of different times and different behavior. Or, perhaps what has changed is the politically correct answer to the question. For strategic reasons, what was once a badge of shame has become a badge of honor, or at least of solidarity. What people actually did, what they say they did, and why (they say) they did it are not always in synch, to put it mildly. On consequential topics, survey respondents are quite capable of answering strategically, or in line with their tribe's current norms—rather than offering their most candid response.[51] In the research business, this is known as "social desirability bias." People want to look good to others, especially those whose opinions matter to them, but even to pollsters.

These are only the most obvious of the methodological weaknesses of self-report surveys.[52] Others include low response rates, especially by busy professionals; recall biases; heuristic biases; and questions that could not possibly elicit meaningful answers.

Typically, physician surveys have low response rates,[53] which allows respondents with stronger feelings about the subject matter to be over-represented in the sample. The resulting sampling bias could drive up the "average" amount of defensive practice reported.

Aside from statistical distortions resulting from sampling difficulties, a variety of psychological distortions play havoc with self-reports.[54] Even were respondents trying their best to provide the most candid answers they could, instant recall of the choices they made in each case over a defined period of time, or mentally averaging them, or some such, is impossible. Efforts to provide answers also suffer from unintentional cognitive biases. For example, when asked to estimate the frequency of occurrence of something, our minds equate the ease (or difficulty) of recall with higher (or lower) frequency (the *availability* heuristic, as it is known to cognitive scientists). If survey respondents have heard others offer guestimates (as doctors almost certainly have), they will tend to conform their own guestimates to those they have heard before (the heuristic of *anchoring*).[55]

Direct physician surveys pose questions that are vague or general, inviting responses that are similarly so: Does fear of malpractice liability influence your choice of procedures? Have you engaged in defensive medicine in the past year? How often do you employ defensive practices (not at all, sometimes, often, very often)? Such questions and their response options cannot reveal how many procedures, of what kinds, under what circumstances, and with what costs or benefits, are defensive. Respondents usually are left to self-define defensive medicine—it means whatever each respondent thinks it means. When 93% of doctors say that *sometime* in the preceding year they did *something* to *someone* that they felt was defensive in nature, we still know very little about how common or how costly the problem is.

People have difficulty ascertaining their own motives much more than we think we do. Whatever the real cause of our behavior, we are capable of quickly inventing a plausible explanation which might or might not have influenced what we did.[56]

Serious researchers are skeptical about the usefulness of the just-ask approach to learning about the incidence of defensive practices. The OTA review considered the direct physician survey results to be "highly suspect," especially due to something researchers today would call "priming"—the questions "invariably prompt responding physicians to consider malpractice liability as a factor in their practice choices." That is, if the question cannot be asked without raising concerns for litigation and defensive medicine, then the answers that are elicited will be infected by concerns about, and efforts to connect answers to, litigation and defensive medicine.

If it's difficult to accurately access the roles of competing factors in one's own decisions, how are respondents supposed to accurately discern what their colleagues did and why they decided to do those things? Nevertheless, pollsters will ask questions whether they are answerable or unanswerable. And, because people responding to surveys can generate answers to any question they are asked, answers will come forth, and surveys of belief and opinion are sure to generate data. This happens even when those being polled do not know, and could not know, the actual answers to the questions asked. Queried whether space aliens exist, 60% of respondents answered, "yes." When those respondents were then asked to compare the intelligence of space aliens and earthlings, 47% asserted that the extra-terrestrials were more intelligent, 13% thought they were less intelligent, and 40% thought we were "about the same."[57] Can such findings be taken as a serious guide to the IQs of space aliens?

Similarly, doctors can be, and have been, surveyed and asked to estimate the costs of defensive medicine. Although respondents are in no position to know what decisions countless other doctors have made, for what medical conditions, with what motivations, and at what cost, they nevertheless give answers—although they are merely guesses.

But look at what can be done with those guesses! Jackson Healthcare conducted its own survey of doctors and asked them to estimate the overall percentage of healthcare costs that were attributable to defensive medicine.[58] Answer: 34%. Jackson then hired the Gallup Organization to repeat the survey (with, presumably, better design and sampling). The new answer to the percentage-of-healthcare-costs question: 26%. The next step is to multiply those guesses by the total cost of healthcare, and one can assert conclusions of the kind Jackson Healthcare did: "A report from The Centers for Medicare and Medicaid Services recently estimated overall U.S. healthcare spending in 2009 to be $2.5 trillion. If physician estimates are accurate, according to Gallup and Jackson surveys, between $650 billion and $850 billion are being spent each year due to defensive, or lawsuit-driven, medicine."[59]

How seriously can this approach be taken? OTA concluded after its extensive review of such surveys that they had little value: "Survey-based estimates of the national cost of defensive medicine advanced by researchers at several organizations are unreliable and potentially biased."[60] Although simple surveys of complicated issues are notorious for providing little in the way of meaningful information, they are nevertheless frequently employed because they are relatively cheap and easy to do. This is not to say that direct-ask survey studies cannot be of value when they inquire about something on which the respondents are well-informed, and ways are found to obtain candid answers. But, on the topic of defensive medicine, such surveys have been useful mainly to lobbyists.

Clinical Scenario Surveys

An alternative approach is to present descriptions of specific cases to samples of physicians and asking how they would handle them: what tests, what treatments, and why. Responses to broad, general survey questions and more concrete and specific clinical scenarios can produce dramatic differences in results.[61] Different research approaches can lead to opposite conclusions.

In the defensive medicine context, case scenarios have been designed to allow researchers to infer whether the respondents' clinical choices deviate from what is medically appropriate in ways that protect the doctor more than they benefit the patient.

Compared to the surveys described earlier, scenario studies are few and far between for the same reasons that direct-ask surveys are so numerous: cost and difficulty. Actual medical knowledge is needed to prepare the scenarios and to evaluate the responses. (By contrast, asking, "Have you practiced defensively in the past year?" is a snap.)

Scenario surveys can be conducted without prompting or priming, that is, without conveying that "this study is about defensive medicine and how you feel about malpractice litigation," thereby evoking respondents' thoughts and feelings about those issues. On the other hand, these surveys too reveal only what respondents say rather than what they do. But a major virtue of the scenarios is that they are so specific. Instead of a vague count of how many doctors feel they acted defensively, or believe that their colleagues have been doing so, the doctor reacts to a specific description of a patient with specific health problems. Specificity is also a weakness of the scenario approach: they are so specific that the responses cannot easily be generalized to other patients and other conditions. To obtain a more complete picture of how much defensive medicine is (impliedly) practiced, a wide range of scenarios would have to be presented to many different doctors. The OTA's conclusion from the scenario studies it reviewed and the new studies it conducted was this: "Although it is possible to identify particular clinical situations in which defensive medicine plays a relatively major role, it is impossible in the final analysis to draw any conclusions about the overall extent or cost of defensive medicine."[62]

Most of the clinical scenario studies by OTA and others were chosen and "specifically designed to increase the likelihood of defensive response by physicians." Thus they were not representative of most diagnostic situations doctors would encounter. Even so, doctors responding to these scenarios did not employ defensive practices much or at all.[63] Certain scenarios, however, did arouse more cautious responses than others. "The scenario with the greatest evidence of defensive medicine was a case of a 15-year-old boy with a minor head injury resulting from a skateboard accident. In that case, almost one-half of all respondents reported that they would order a CT scan, and 45% of those who said they would order it would do so primarily out of concern for malpractice."

The contrast between the scenarios that did and those that did not elicit defensive practices can potentially help refine our understanding of when doctors do and when they don't act "defensively" and why. The previous case example represents a situation in which the risk of missing a serious diagnosis is small, but if one is missed the outcome could be catastrophic. Under such circumstances, doctors were inclined to worry about error, harm to the patient, and malpractice liability—and do more testing than they thought strictly necessary.

On the one hand, that appears to be defensive behavior prompted by fear of litigation, because most CT scans carried out under such circumstances will find the brain was undamaged. On the other hand, perhaps this is where an excess of caution (and additional expense) benefits the patient by ensuring that serious brain damage is not in the process of developing. Recall Dr. Gawande's insistence, earlier in this chapter, that his son get the extra testing and observation in a very similar situation.

In another study using clinical scenarios, researchers hunted for correlates of excessive resource use.[64] They wondered if a relationship might exist between apparent defensive practices and the physicians' own malpractice claims history. Might those who had been sued previously be more vigilant about avoiding future suits? The research found no evidence of such a relationship. The only variables found to be consistently correlated, across multiple scenarios, were doctors' attitudes toward cost consciousness (those who were more concerned about costs kept costs lower) and their subjective estimates of the probability that they were dealing with a potentially severe health problem (those who saw higher risks of severe harm to a patient tended to want to do more—as in the head injury cases—as one would expect).

Overall, "[i]n clinical scenario surveys designed specifically to elicit a defensive response, malpractice concerns were occasionally cited as an important factor in clinical decisions; however, physicians' belief that a course of action is medically indicated was the most important determinant of physicians' clinical choices."[65]

The contrast between the conclusions reached based on direct-ask surveys versus those from clinical scenarios illustrates how powerful an impact research design can have on what a study finds. Yet another, and wholly different, methodological approach is to stop asking doctors what they say they have done or what they say they would do, and to try to look at what they actually do.

Multivariate Statistical Analyses

The third research approach consists of statistical analysis of existing databases pertaining to the volume of tests and procedures that doctors order (typically measured in dollars of Medicare expenditures) in states with different levels of malpractice risk. Malpractice risk in these studies has been measured by malpractice premiums, incidence of lawsuits, or tort reforms. The basic idea is that where malpractice risk is lower doctors should be less fearful, will therefore practice less defensively, diagnose and treat less intensely, and consequently cause fewer healthcare dollars to be spent—all else equal.

"All else equal" is the Achilles heel of this approach. Two pre-existing groups—in contrast to an experiment where two or more groups are created equal by random assignment to treatment conditions, and then treated differently so the treatment's effects can be compared—are never equal. People in a state with, say, higher malpractice premiums might also have a population of Medicare recipients who are older or poorer or differ genetically (more people of Scandinavian ancestry here, Asian there), or for some other reason differ in the health problems they have, or where other changes in the state have occurred (such as other legal reforms), thereby confounding the tort reform of interest.

Relying on healthcare spending to reflect the quantum of defensive medicine presents a more unusual problem. As discussed earlier, treatment intensity varies as a function of the supply of healthcare services, not only patients' health needs. Moreover, the blurry line between healthcare fraud and defensive medicine has methodological implications. Studies that have compared Medicare billings to patient records have found that the billings can overstate healthcare actually provided, sometimes by a considerable amount—a discrepancy of 60% to 90% depending on patients' diagnoses.[66] According to healthcare fraud expert Malcolm Sparrow, researchers who equate Medicare billings with medical services actually provided are missing the distorting effect of fraud on their data.[67] Thus, in places where Medicare fraud is higher, spending will be higher, and researchers can mistake that for defensive medicine being greater.

If the level of fraudulent billing could be controlled for, then a finding that providers in a state with a certain tort reform billed for fewer Medicare dollars than providers in a state without that reform would be consistent with the hypothesis that malpractice risk explains the difference. But it would also be consistent with having sicker patients who therefore need more care, which requires more spending. Or different cultures of practice intensity, or differences in supply of and demand for services, or any of numerous other confounding variables that could make it appear that the cause of spending differences is defensive medicine when something else might be driving the cost differences instead of or on top of the legal changes of interest.

So, researchers must disentangle the possible cause of interest from the unknown confounding variables by making statistical adjustments using measures of those potentially confounding variables. (That is the "multivariate" part of the approach.) Those adjustments are neither simple nor straightforward. The study might not have collected data on a critically important confounding variable. Or the statistical model might under-adjust for its impact.

Erroneous conclusions that can result from inadequately controlled observational studies can be dramatic, as medical researchers know well. For example, studies using such research designs led to the conclusion that estrogen replacement was beneficial to post-menopausal women.[68] As the reader might recall from Chapter 6 of this book, the methodological risk was that women who sought and obtained hormone replacement differed in various ways from those who did not—perhaps being essentially healthier, wealthier, and taking better care of themselves in numerous ways. Better health outcomes for those women might seem to be attributable to the estrogen when in reality they were attributable to those confounding factors. Eventually, better designed research (randomized controlled trials) discovered not only that hormone replacement was *not* the cause of better health outcomes, but that it was dangerous for many women. Incorrect conclusions about estrogen based on findings from multivariate, observational (correlational) research designs had already led to tens of thousands of avoidable breast cancers, heart attacks, and strokes.[69]

Despite its imperfections, the multivariate approach has the virtue of dealing with the behavior of actual doctors making real choices about treatment of real patients—not merely what doctors in surveys say they have done or would do. Keeping reasonable cautions about confounds and file drawers and so on in mind, let's review the multivariate studies.

Studies and Their Findings: Cesarean Sections

One popular line of such studies looked at cesarean sections, because an obstetrician's preference for delivering a baby vaginally or surgically is thought to be especially sensitive to the malpractice risk climate. The thinking was that where the risk of malpractice litigation was higher obstetricians would perform an increased number of cesareans. Taken together, the results of those studies are inconclusive. Some did find higher cesarean delivery rates where malpractice risk was greater.[70] Other studies found little evidence that cesarean rates increased in response to higher malpractice risks or costs, or they found *decreases* in the rate of cesareans (in contrast to the expected increases).[71]

At the pinnacle of insightful inconclusiveness, at least one research team found a relationship but wondered whether it reflected improved practice in response to higher malpractice risk. A climate of greater malpractice risk was associated with increased use of electronic fetal monitoring, more diagnoses of fetal distress, and more consequent use of cesarean deliveries. But whether increasing cesareans reflected good or bad medical practice under such circumstances, the researchers were not prepared to say: perhaps increased concern about litigation led to safer practices, which led to an increase in cesareans where they were actually needed and consequent better outcomes for patients.[72]

Studies and Their Findings: Cardiac and Other Medical Procedures

Looking at other medical procedures, mixed results emerge. Some studies have found evidence that wasteful spending ordered by doctors is at least somewhat correlated with the level of malpractice risk faced by those doctors. The earliest of these studies, and one which sets the high-water mark for findings of a defensive medicine effect, was conducted by Daniel Kessler and Mark McClellan.[73] Kessler is an attorney and economist; McClellan a physician and economist who held several major posts in the George W. Bush administration, including administrator of the Centers for Medicare and Medicaid Services. Their study looked at the effects of state malpractice law reforms on Medicare spending for hospital patients being treated for acute myocardial infarction (AMI) or new ischemic heart disease (IHD) in the years 1984, 1987, and 1990. They found that what they termed "direct" tort reforms (damages caps, abolition of punitive damages, elimination of mandatory pre-judgment interest, changes in the collateral source rule[74]) were associated with a 5% to 9% annual reduction in medical expenditures for patients with those two conditions. And those reductions occurred "without substantial effects on mortality" or greater need for readmission for AMI or IHD—suggesting that the additional care being delivered was of little benefit to patients. "Indirect" reforms combined (including such changes as limitations on plaintiff attorney contingency fees, mandatory periodic payments, joint and several liability and patient compensation funds) reduced Medicare payments by 1.8%. The elimination of joint and several liability—replacing it with a proportionate share liability rule—resulted in a small increase in Medicare spending.

If their results could be generalized to all healthcare costs, not just treatment of two heart conditions for Medicare inpatients, then defensive medicine could account for a substantial amount of wasteful healthcare spending.

Later studies built on, expanded, and improved upon Kessler and McClellan's initial work in various respects, such as by including more illness conditions than just two types of heart disease, outpatient as well as inpatient spending, physician spending as well as hospital spending, private as well as Medicare spending, covering longer time periods, using larger samples, and trying to control for additional confounding variables.

One of those studies was a follow-up by Kessler and McClellan themselves. In this study they looked at the population of Medicare beneficiaries with heart disease from 1984 to 1994, finding that liability-reducing "tort reforms" reduced defensive practices, but also that managed care could substitute for liability reform. More specifically, they found that noneconomic damage caps were associated with a 4.2% decrease in spending for AMI patients and a 4.4% decrease in spending for IHD patients (contrasting with 5.8% and 8.9%, respectively, from the initial study). They also found that "malpractice pressure" had a greater effect on diagnostic procedures than on treatments). Moreover, the follow-up found that managed care stanched the excess spending about as well as tort reform did.[75]

A study by researchers at the Congressional Budget Office studied Medicare patients treated for a broad range of conditions, but "failed to find any impact of state tort laws on medical spending."[76] Another Congressional Budget Office (CBO) study, looking at a broader set of spending measures, from 1980 through 2003, and employing more statistical controls, found that caps on noneconomic damages resulted in no reduction in overall healthcare spending, but did reduce Medicare inpatient spending. The study also found that the replacement of joint and several liability with proportionate share allocation of liability resulted in a 4% *increase* in overall Medicare spending.[77] The CBO's conclusion was that the evidence was weak or inconclusive that tort reform could reduce defensive medicine).[78]

Health economists Katherine Baicker and Amitabh Chandra found little evidence of changes in treatment patterns for several different treatment protocols for Medicare enrollees, or for overall expenses in Medicare programs associated with increases in liability insurance premiums.[79] Another study by Baicker and colleagues found that "higher malpractice awards and premiums are associated with higher Medicare spending, especially for imaging services," but those increases represented less than 0.6% of aggregate spending).[80]

Frank Sloan and John Shadle, both economists who focus on analyzing healthcare issues, extended Kessler and McClellan's approach by looking at Medicare payments over a longer time period (1985–2000), expanding the range of health conditions beyond heart disease, treatment settings that included outpatients as well as inpatients, and adding additional controls (notably the health status of the patient). They found no statistically significant reduction in healthcare payments, concluding that Kessler and McClellan's findings "do not generalize to other reasons for hospital admission" and that "it seems inappropriate to conclude that tort reforms implemented to date succeed in reducing non-beneficial care."[81]

J. William Thomas, a scholar of health management and policy led a research team that studied 35 clinical specialties to assess whether and how much malpractice liability reforms would reduce healthcare spending. They concluded that "defensive medicine practices exist and are widespread, but their impact on medical care costs is small," finding that, across all 35 specialties, "if medical malpractice premiums were to be reduced as much as 30%, defensive medicine costs would decline no more than 0.4%".[82]

A health policy research team of economists and an attorney, led by Leonard J. Nelson III, conducted a study focusing almost exclusively on the impact of damage caps and concluded that "it is not clear that caps will significantly reduce healthcare costs or that any savings will be passed on to consumers."[83]

Legal scholar Ronen Avraham and colleagues found a 3% to 5% reduction in intensive cardiac interventions following adoption of familiar tort reforms (including damages caps), and estimated a total reduction of about 1% to 2% across the entire healthcare system. Like Kessler and McClellan (2002), they also found that managed care could eliminate the excess spending caused by defensive practices.[84]

Health economists Darius Lakdawalla and Seth Seabury used jury awards in malpractice cases as the measure of litigation pressure and found that where trial awards were higher medical expenditures were higher (presumably from defensive practices).[85]

Leading a research team that included an economist, a physician, and two data-oriented legal scholars, Myungho Paik studied how Medicare spending changed after Texas adopted comprehensive tort reform in 2003, including a strict damages cap, by comparing spending in Texas counties with high claim rates to spending in counties with low claim rates. The study found no decline in spending in the high litigation risk counties relative to the low-risk counties. Relative to national spending trends, if anything, spending increased postreform. "In sum," the study concluded, "we find no evidence that Texas's tort reforms bent the cost curve downward."[86]

In an expanded study, Paik and colleagues reanalyzed the effects of tort reforms, particularly damages caps, of the mid-1980s and found no change in Medicare spending as a consequence. They also analyzed the effects of the imposition of caps in nine states during the "third wave" of tort reforms (2002–2005). They found no significant impact on Medicare Part A (hospital) spending but did find an approximately 4% *increase* in Medicare Part B (physician services) spending (rather than the predicted reduction in spending when liability fears are reduced).[87]

Another study, by another interdisciplinary team of economist, physician, and legal scholar, led by Ali Moghtaderi, found little to no association between the existence of caps and Part A and B spending nor between caps and a range of cardiac testing rates and interventions.[88]

Most worrisome, of course, is the possibility that reducing or removing the risk of tort liability reduces safety for patients. Of the studies that tested for that outcome most found no effect, but a few reached findings that raise concerns. Reviewing research that examined mortality as a function of tort law reforms in 2009, the CBO[89] found evidence that malpractice law reforms led to a small increase in the nation's overall death and injury rate—translating, at the time, to approximately 5,000 additional deaths and 400,000 more injuries. Similarly, another study by Lakdawalla and Seabury,[90] although finding that where jury awards in malpractice cases were higher medical expenditures were higher (presumably from defensive practices), also found that patient mortality was *lower*, leading these researchers to conclude that defensive practices were beneficial to patients[91]—and therefore tort reforms aimed at reducing physician liability expenses were not cost-effective. Economists Janet Currie and Bentley McLeod found that the introduction of noneconomic damages caps *increased* the rate of cesareans (rather than the intuitively expected decrease), as well as increasing preventable complications of labor.[92] More recently, Zabinski and Black, as you might recall from the preceding chapter, found that imposing caps on general damage awards triggered gradually rising rates of harmful errors (measured using the Agency for Healthcare Research and Quality's Patient Safety Indicators instrument).[93]

Legal scholar and economist Michael Frakes and economist Jonathan Gruber, who was one of the principal architects of the Patient Protection and Affordable Care Act, sum up the same body of multivariate studies that we have just reviewed, saying, "Collectively, the above findings paint a varied picture of both the size and existence of defensive medicine."[94]

ONE ALMOST QUASI-EXPERIMENT

Frakes and Gruber recently reported their own ingenious study, which improves upon the multivariate approach by finding circumstances which can almost be said to be quasi-experimental.[95] They designed their study around an idiosyncrasy of the U.S. military health services: active-duty personnel who believe they have been injured through negligent care have no right to sue for compensation, whereas other patients (e.g., families of active-duty personnel, retirees, and their family members) face no such bar to their malpractice claims.

In essence, from one patient to the next, the very same military treatment facilities (MTF) and their staff face two different worlds, one with and one without the possibility of malpractice liability. It's almost a true experiment. But because patients in the two groups differ in ways that might confound observed differences, or other mechanisms that might be responsible for observed differences, the researchers also used multivariate analyses to try to remove possible confounding statistically. But their approach comes closer than any other to an apples-to-apples inquiry. If caregivers at MTFs order more tests for their patients who possess the right to sue than they do for patients who have no right to sue—as much else equal as the research could manage—then those differences likely result from defensive practices rather than something else. In addition, another basis for comparison arose when some base hospitals closed and military patients had to turn to nonmilitary hospitals for care.

To summarize Frakes and Gruber's main findings, on several different measures of treatment intensity, patients at on-base MTFs who could not sue received 4% to 5% less care than those who could sue. In circumstances where doctors had less discretion whether to treat or not, the effect of liability immunity was reduced by 1% to 2%. In regard to patients for whom doctors were not immune from suit, diagnostic procedures were far more likely to be ordered than nondiagnostic procedures. All but two nondiagnostic procedures showed no differences in frequency in the care of patients who were, versus who were not, able to sue. Those two—gastrointestinal and orthopedic admissions (which were only marginally significant)—suggested that providers were *less* likely to order those procedures for patients who had the power to sue. Interestingly, all else equal, MTFs treated patients at a lower intensity than private hospitals did.[96] Frakes and Gruber's study also permits an estimate of the maximum savings that might be realized if the healthcare industry were completely immunized from tort liability, which we discuss in the concluding section.

DISCUSSION

The notion of defensive medicine presents a series of paradoxes. The most aggressive advocates on behalf of the healthcare industry insist that healthcare workers routinely behave unethically,[97] recklessly,[98] wastefully, and fraudulently by engaging in defensive practices.[99] But, they urge, potential remedies should not be focused on those engaged in such behavior because they do what they do out of fear—a fear of being compelled by the law to reimburse patients for losses resulting from preventable iatrogenic harms. Instead, they argue, the solution is to remove the source of the fear—in other words, to further insulate the healthcare industry from legal and financial accountability. Doing so, they promise, will make the evils of defensive medicine and any wasteful spending that results from it disappear. By contrast, those who would persist in applying conventional accident law to the healthcare industry do not seem to believe that healthcare providers behave so badly as the industry claims.

Also paradoxically, the industry's argument implies a legal system that has a powerful influence on behavior. By the lights of the defensive medicine concept, physicians and other providers are being overdeterred by the tort system. With helpful data and thoughtful adjustments, a legal tool so able to move behavior should be able to be used to steer providers to deliver better and safer healthcare, rendering litigation less necessary, reducing provider fears, making defensive practices unnecessary, and sending wasteful healthcare expenditures downward.

Another paradox, of a different order: if providers are caught ordering unnecessary tests, treatments, and other procedures, thereby fraudulently increasing their incomes, they are charged with healthcare fraud, required to return their ill-gotten gains, and are confronted with civil penalties if not criminal charges.[100] But if they engage in essentially the same behavior under the flag of "defensive medicine," then the response tends to be sympathetic concern for the fearful physician. In both scenarios, healthcare providers elevated their own interests above those of their patients and profited from doing so. But what at one moment evokes scorn for fraud and self-dealing, a blink of an eye later is seen as a cry for help.

One of the most remarkable facts about defensive medicine is how successful the promotors of the notion have been in persuading legislators and the public of its existence, its seriousness, that it is key to solving the problem of exorbitant healthcare costs,[101] and that the only cure for it worth discussing is to reduce the healthcare industry's legal-financial accountability. That, despite empirical evidence for the hypothesis which, until Frakes and Gruber's study (and perhaps still), could only be viewed as contradictory and uncertain. Paik and colleagues explain the situation this way: "The defensive medicine 'story' is both plausible and politically convenient. . . . This story lets physicians lobby for, and politicians support, an easy reform (limit lawsuits) rather than take the hard steps needed to limit healthcare cost growth." Despite limited evidence of the story's validity, "the belief that tort reform will reduce healthcare spending still drives much policy analysis in this area."[102]

Exponents of the defensive medicine hypothesis have put forward fantastic numbers, the most extreme of them approaching a trillion dollars, on air-thin bases. But even serious and sober studies have found their way to numbers at the high end of where the empirical evidence can take us. In their effort to calculate the *total* national cost of the medical liability system in the United States—from administrative costs to damages payments and everything in between—health policy scholar Michelle Mello and colleagues,[103] arrived at a figure of $45.6 billion (in 2008 dollars) for defensive medical practices ($38.8 billion by hospitals and $6.8 billion by physicians) and $10 billion for all other malpractice litigation system costs added together.

Obviously, that is vastly less than the survey-based guestimates of $650 to $850 billion (as much as $933 billion in today's dollars). But Mello and colleagues built their estimate of the defensive medicine components around Kessler and McClellan's (1996) high-water-mark analysis.[104] Had the Mello team averaged in the other studies, many of which found more modest fear-of-litigation effects and others none at all, their estimate of costs attributable to defensive medicine would have been lower still.[105] They do note that the quality of the sources for their estimate of defensive medicine costs was unavoidably one of the weakest of all cost components in their study. They classify the quality of that evidence as "low." The generally shaky quality of the underlying evidence might be the most important lesson to take from our entire exploration of the hypothesis of defensive medicine.

So much for costs. What about benefits? Mello and colleagues recognized that from the cost of defensive practices one has to subtract the benefits secured by malpractice litigation. The most notable of these would be *savings from injuries and deaths prevented*. If that benefit exceeds the cost of defensive medicine, then the system provides a net gain to society. On this vital matter, they write: "It is important to note, however, that our calculations ignored benefits arising from this spending."[106] That figure is a known unknown. From a dollars-and-cents perspective, it does policymakers little good to know the costs of any system or policy unless the benefits that those costs purchase for society are also known. And so, another curiosity of this debate has been an obsession with costs accompanied by a disregard of benefits.[107]

Perhaps the chief concern of policymakers is how to bring down America's astonishingly high healthcare costs.[108] To the extent that defensive medicine exists, how much can reducing or eliminating it contribute to bending the cost curve downward? Looking across the landscape of policy options for bringing healthcare costs under control, while ensuring broad access to care and promoting innovation, James Mongan and colleagues, in a study published by the New England Journal of Medicine, rated malpractice reforms as having the "lowest potential for cost savings" because, combined, the "direct costs of malpractice premiums" and the "estimated costs of 'defensive medicine' are not major factors in overall health care spending."[109] More recently, Frakes summed up the research community's consensus as being "that medical malpractice reform is unlikely to be a meaningful source of healthcare cost containment."[110]

Frakes and Gruber have provided the approximate upper bound of savings that might accrue from reduced defensive practices if malpractice liability were abolished entirely, which is under 5%.[111] The *costs* that would be associated with abolition, including a rising incidence of iatrogenic injury, are unspecified, as discussed earlier. Thus, whether abolition would lead to net savings or net increased costs is unknown.

Why isn't the conversation about other, larger sources of wasteful expenditures in healthcare? Using the Mello team's estimate of the cost of defensive medicine, the portion of total healthcare spending attributable to defensive practices is 1.5%.[112] But that represents only a fraction of the approximately 20% to 30% of total healthcare expenditures that are squandered on low-value and no-value services.[113] If the major concern is to reduce healthcare costs by reducing wasteful spending, attention might more fruitfully be given to the problems that account for more than 90% of the waste, and less on the one that accounts for 5% to 7% of the waste. The laser-beam focus on defensive medical practices suggests that the industry's main interest is not in reducing wasteful spending on healthcare through reducing in defensive medicine.

If defensive medicine is itself a particular concern, whatever the reasons, attention could be given to more effective ways to reduce it. Hyman and Silver have noted, "If tort reformers were genuinely worried about defensive medicine and desired to prevent it, they would offer vastly different proposals from the ones they now endorse. Concern about unnecessary tests and procedures, for example, might lead them to call for evidence-based treatment guidelines specifying when and if certain tests need to be performed."[114] As research described above has suggested, managed care can be as effective as tort reform in reducing defensive practices. Insurers could identify worthless practices known to be associated with defensive medicine and refuse to pay for those. Healthcare fraud investigators could include among their targets the most common defensive practices. Accountable care organizations, on the rise, or other forms of valued-based payment arrangements might, by their very nature, drive down defensive practices along with other low-value care.[115]

One of the most illuminating findings of researchers is that tort reforms have had little impact on the perceptions of healthcare providers about the legal environment that they inhabit. If providers are insensitive to the specific tort rules under which they practice, if they do not know which versions of which reforms exist where they practice, they cannot accurately adjust their estimation of malpractice risk. Instead, they simply have and hold onto a generalized fear of becoming a defendant in litigation. To the extent this describes providers' state of knowledge, it means that the economic and psychological signals sent by a given tort reform, or package of them, tend to be overwhelmed by noise.

That is what a team of health system researchers, led by Emily Carrier, found: levels of malpractice concern were generally high and unrelated to the actual level of lawsuit risk in the state where physicians practiced.[116] "These results suggest that many policies aimed at controlling malpractice costs may have a limited effect on physicians' malpractice concerns"—and therefore on practice behavior and costs.[117]

Relatedly, Hyman and Sage have discussed the "habits and beliefs" of physicians, which "seem unaffected by evidence regarding the actual likelihood of a lawsuit or the level of potential damages."[118] This is consistent also with findings of physicians' overestimation of lawsuit risk[119] and general "anxiety about medical malpractice litigation and liability," which has been described as "pervasive . . . erroneous . . . and irrational."[120] The insensitivity of healthcare providers to actual levels of litigation risk has led Hal Scherz, surgeon and president of the advocacy organization Docs4PatientCare, and Wayne Oliver, executive director of the advocacy organization, Patients for Fair Compensation, to suggest that "[t]he only way to eliminate defensive medicine is to make it impossible for doctors to be sued for medical errors."[121]

Another, quite different, scenario aligns coherently with existing empirical evidence, and it is consistent with an image of healthcare providers as thoughtful professionals seriously concerned about their patients' well-being, without pitting their patients' interests against their own.[122] This scenario is that sick patients fall along a continuum ranging, at one extreme, from clearly suffering from a condition that requires a particular treatment strategy to clearly not suffering from the condition at the other extreme. For those clear cases, no defensive practices need be employed. Cases near the middle, characterized by the greatest uncertainty, where the risk of error is high, will be more likely to prompt defensive behavior, especially for a condition where an erroneous diagnosis would lead to a disastrous outcome. Under such circumstances, non–cost-beneficially optimal, "wasteful" diagnostic testing is most likely to be undertaken.[123] Whether that is done to protect the physician or the patient might be impossible to disentangle. Doctors might say they thought they were acting defensively. But they were simultaneously making sure that the patient was protected from the harm of error. Under such circumstances, the line that divides defensive medicine from good medical practice fades.

An example of that kind of situation would be a head injury. If the patient suffered a potentially dangerous head injury that could have been detected with more testing and observation, but it is not caught, the result for the patient could be disastrous. That's what the doctors responding to OTA's head injury case scenario were almost certainly thinking about when they proposed to order "excessive" testing. That is certainly what Atul Gawande was worrying about when his son was taken to the ER after a fall. Furthermore, it is consistent with research finding that "the strongest effect of greater malpractice pressure is in increased use of imaging services, with somewhat smaller effects on the use of other discretionary, generally low-risk services such as physician visits and consultations, use of diagnostic tests, and minor procedures."[124]

If that is what most defensive medicine looks like, it is not irrational, not especially wasteful, and not something many of us patients would wish to put a stop to. Perhaps much if not most defensive medicine stands at the confluence of two streams—defensive practice and good medical practice—flowing together and becoming one, indistinguishable.

8

Error Reporting

A Flawed Panacea

We commonly believe that physicians maintain a conspiracy of silence.[1]

A central component of the safety improvement strategy outlined by the Institute of Medicine (IOM) in *To Err Is Human* is the immediate establishment of a mandatory nationwide state-based publicly accessible reporting system for grave medical errors (death or serious injury), alongside voluntary confidential reporting mechanisms to deal with lesser problems, particularly near-miss events (ones in which harm was narrowly avoided).[2] The reporting proposals expanded upon the disclosure strategy the IOM drafters had themselves adopted when they drew the nation's attention to what was then thought to be up to 100,000 iatrogenic deaths a year in hospitals. The authors of *To Err* presented reporting and public disclosure of serious harm as a means of holding healthcare providers "accountable."[3] It was hoped that these disclosures would prompt investigations, create incentives for better care and compel greater expenditures on safety. However, accomplishing this would require overcoming resistance to reporting within the healthcare industry. Instead of relying on confidential provider processes to deal with substantial errors, regulators and the public would be informed of major mistakes, enabling outside evaluation and response—precisely the approach used by *To Err* itself. Reporting had other attractions as well. While reporting would certainly not be cost-free, it would be far less expensive than immediately creating a set of mandates to make the delivery of care safer. It would also be easier to implement. A state-based national reporting system might be organized quickly in light of the reporting requirements already in place in many jurisdictions and the ongoing operation of the Joint Commission's sentinel event program established in 1996. Moreover, serious event reporting is neither a foreign nor exotic idea. It mirrors a traditional approach widely used in medicine—the peer-conducted review of treatment problems through mortality and morbidity (M&M) conferences held in a variety of settings, including during the training of young doctors.[4]

The IOM vision employed a mix of reporting systems scaled to address issues of varying severity. The first was the previously described mandatory system. When there was a serious iatrogenic injury, the IOM plan was to promote an organized systemic response. To that end hospitals and other healthcare-providing organizations would be made responsible for the submission of information rather than individual physicians. This, at least theoretically, would take the focus off of individual responsibility and instead focus attention on institutional action. State government agencies charged with regulatory responsibility would be the first to receive the hospital-generated reports, thus facilitating analysis of the information and government oversight of healthcare provider follow-up action. If a state chose not to participate in the IOM proposed system, the federal Department of Health and Human Services would act in its stead. (The problem was viewed as simply too serious to be left unattended.) The mandated reports would also be made available to the public, thereby enlisting public pressure to help spur improvement.

This portion of the IOM proposal was both courageous and naïve. It was brave in that it directly challenged the healthcare industry's deeply entrenched tradition of withholding information about iatrogenic injury as well as fears of lawsuits and disparaging media reports. *To Err* stated, "The public . . . has the right to be informed about unsafe conditions."[5] This was a very different notion of who should control medical information and how that information ought to be used. It was naïve in its assumption that there would be sufficient political and financial support at the state or federal level for such an approach.

The second reporting proposal was to promote the development of voluntary reporting systems for less serious events and "near misses." The focus here was not on publicity or public accountability, but on amassing enough data to help inform the safety improvement effort through the statistical identification of potentially dangerous situations. Information submitted to the voluntary reporting system would be treated as confidential, since the objective was not public or regulatory engagement but encouragement of the broadest range of professional discussion about safety by removing such impediments as fear of legal sanction or peer-directed discipline. Here the safety experts would be in charge and given every possible assistance in formulating safer practices. No single voluntary system was proposed, but rather a range of different approaches was to be encouraged, allowing the most effective to be identified and promoted.

ERROR REPORTING IN AVIATION

The chief inspiration for the two reporting mechanisms was the safety system developed in commercial aviation. The IOM team did not propose copying the airline industry systems, but did suggest that they were worthy of close attention. In connection with mandatory reporting, the authors of *To Err* noted the very thorough and public investigations mounted by the National Transportation Safety Board (NTSB) of all air crashes resulting in death or serious aircraft damage, notwithstanding the certainty of follow-on tort litigation to assess liability for negligent acts. With respect to the creation of a voluntary individualized near-miss reporting mechanism, the efforts of the Federal Aviation Administration (FAA) were repeatedly referenced and praised.[6]

The central element of the FAA program is the Aviation Safety Reporting System (ASRS). It is "a voluntary, confidential incident reporting system used to identify hazards and latent system deficiencies in order to eliminate or mitigate them."[7] Its key focus is on harnessing aviation worker input to achieve improved safety outside the serious crash context and it really seems to work. Among the reasons for its success, according to the IOM team, is that it is overseen by a neutral and honest broker, the National Aeronautics and Space Administration (NASA), rather than the FAA. This arrangement minimizes filers' concerns that they will face discipline from the FAA and accentuates the goal of future safety improvement rather than punishment for past mistakes. The system also appears to demonstrate the importance of confidentiality. No breaches of confidentiality are said to have occurred since the inception of the program in 1976, and this is credited with encouraging a very robust level of reporting. The ASRS system treats filings with the utmost seriousness, responding with alerts, warnings, and careful analysis. This gives filers a sense that their submissions are important and have a real impact on safety.

There are three important factors, not specifically mentioned in *To Err*, that are likely to have enhanced the attractiveness of ASRS. The first is that near misses are far more frequent than actual accidents (an estimated three to 300 times more frequent),[8] thereby providing a truly enhanced opportunity for analysis and improvement. Second, the system fosters immediate and factually grounded submissions because of its simple and rapid (five-day) filing requirements. Third, reporting provides a positive emotional experience for filers by encouraging both a philanthropic sense of contributing to the improvement of the system and a therapeutic release by allowing filers to air their own mistakes.[9]

Lucian Leape has suggested that the analogy between the airline industry and medicine is overstated.[10] In his view the differences between the two make the application of aviation solutions of questionable value. There is ample reason to recommend Dr. Leape's point and it raises substantial concerns about using a system like ASRS in medicine. The commercial aviation industry is both legally and logistically very different from medicine. Commercial flying is overseen on a national basis by a single federal agency, the FAA. The agency controls operations and oversees all that is done in commercial flying. By contrast, medicine has no single governmental regulatory body. Hospitals and other healthcare providers are touched by local, state, and federal regulations but remain largely independent. The sort of direction and control provided by the FAA is absent, rendering the operation of a coordinated program of reporting and change far more difficult to implement.

The difference in the legal approach to accidents between the two industries is striking. There is virtually no doubt about discovery and legal liability in the wake of the crash of a commercial aircraft. Such events never escape notice. The likelihood of the assignment of liability is virtually assured by tort doctrines like *res ipsa loquitur* (Latin for "the thing speaks for itself"). This doctrine allows a finding, without any evidence beyond the incident itself, that a commercial jet liner crash will not happen without negligence. The initial inquiry into every crash is conducted in a public proceeding overseen by the NTSB. These rigorous examinations generate a clear, and difficult to deny, declaration of responsibility. The legal situation in medicine is nothing like this. Many, perhaps most, potentially harmful events happen at times and in circumstances that may inhibit discovery. There is no high-powered investigative body waiting to examine untoward events. The likelihood of winning a medical malpractice tort claim is quite small and depends on the expenditure of a great deal of money by an injured patient or, more likely, her attorney. The incentive to report in such an opaque and unresponsive system is substantially reduced.

Internal differences regarding the operations of the industries further weaken the comparison. In aviation, pilots are highly motivated to address potentially dangerous situations. Should their aircraft crash they are likely to be the first to die. Healthcare providers do not face such risks. Their mistakes do not threaten their physical well-being. The motivation to report and, thereby, to improve practice is thus reduced. The airlines that operate commercial aircraft are relatively few in number. Thanks to this, consolidated oversight is challenging, but feasible. By contrast, there are literally thousands of hospitals and healthcare systems scattered throughout the country in every state and every conceivable setting, collectively rendering care to millions of Americans. Keeping track of, let alone directing, this far-flung and decentralized industry presents difficulties well beyond those the FAA faces. Airline passengers are served in large groups, flight by flight. They present few individual problems. Patients, on the other hand, must be handled one at a time. It has been estimated that each patient's care involves thousands of decisions. Coordinating all this is well beyond anything airlines do. While the number of flights is substantial, it cannot compare with the number of patient treatments rendered. Dr. Leape has estimated that while the ASRS system receives 30,000 reports a year, a similarly constituted medical system might receive well over a million.[11]

ACQUIRING AND USING SAFETY REPORTS IN HEALTHCARE

Assuming that submissions to a medical reporting system could be effectively gathered and analyzed, there remains the serious question of how exactly to utilize this information to improve healthcare. With airlines, pilot training focuses intensively on safety and pilots' on-the-job performance is, more or less, controlled by checklists, guidelines, and protocols into which safety improvements may be fitted. The situation in medicine is quite different. Safety training is spotty, and many providers resist standardized checklists and guidelines, instead preferring to rely on personal experience and prior practice. The integration of new safety insights into such a system is far more challenging than in aviation. Even assuming such an objective could be achieved, the cost of maintaining an ASRS-like reporting system would be enormous. Some years ago it was estimated that the ASRS system spends, on average, $70 per submission.[12] Applied to medicine, this would suggest an operating cost of hundreds of millions of dollars a year, a sum unlikely to be forthcoming without substantial changes in the current political mindset. In all, the aviation model seems only modestly helpful when considering the tools available in medicine to improve operations. All of the foregoing assumes that the touted efficacy of the airline reporting systems is genuine. While there is good reason to think the system works in most cases, there have been situations where marginal air carriers have pressed pilots and others not to file reports about risks. One of the authors of this book worked on litigation involving the stifling of reporting that contributed to a deadly crash.

The technical challenges in setting up a reporting solution to medical error, whether modeled on another industry's approach or not, are substantial. At the outset, there is a need to fashion an extensive set of definitions to guide reporters as they prepare their submissions.[13] Without such definitions, the materials submitted are likely to be little more than a useless hodgepodge of little or no practical value in identifying dangerous practices or tracking the scope of specific problems. To be useful the definitions must be specific enough to facilitate the identification of discrete problems but not so narrow as to exclude observations arising in a number of different treatment contexts. The definitions must be clear and simple enough so that reporters can learn to apply them accurately. The difficulty of interevaluator disagreement in appraising medical error has dogged safety research and was one of the primary criticisms of the seminal Harvard research on hospital-based errors in New York, Colorado, and Utah.[14] If the challenge was difficult in the narrow confines of a small group of well-trained and carefully supervised researchers, it is likely to be a great deal more problematic among practitioners asked to evaluate their own experience. This difficulty is not impossible to manage, but it does create a significant impediment to the implementation of a reporting system. It is one reason that some experts have called for adoption of simplified reporting mechanisms that do not evaluate all errors but focus on narrowly defined "never" events.[15]

Assuming an adequate definitional structure, the number of reports that such a medical system might generate presents another serious technical problem. If the system uses a narrow focus concentrating on never-events, there is a substantial likelihood of so few reports that there will be insufficient data for analysis. Never-events are rare. Their occurrence in any single hospital or other healthcare delivery system is likely to be infrequent. Useful analysis will demand intersystem aggregation. This is not impossible but presents an extra set of challenges, involving integration of reports from a number of independent sources across a wide geographical area and different practice settings. At the other end of the spectrum, reporting regimes have often been found to produce too many reports of an essentially trivial nature.[16] This flood of information may clog the reporting system, making the identification of serious problems difficult and the burden of effective analysis costly. It has been noted that too much reporting reduces the quality of the process. Getting the volume and focus of reporting right is a challenge. There is a substantial risk of not obtaining necessary data or of getting so much data that the system cannot serve its diagnostic purpose, thereby discouraging filers disappointed by the lack of useful feedback.

The most essential actors in any reporting scheme are those expected to file reports. The system has nothing to work on without their input. The cultural impediments to reporting will be discussed later in this chapter. Here it may be useful to consider the logistical barriers to the filing of reports. A number of surveys have been undertaken to identify the reasons potential filers in medical reporting systems do not act. Many of those surveyed have said that they were either unaware of the existence of the reporting system or unclear about how it operated.[17] Any mechanism that is expected to be effective must incorporate careful training of those expected to participate. Beyond such initial barriers lay a number of other logistical impediments. Many potential filers, especially physicians, state that they are simply too busy to prepare and submit reports.[18] The pressures on doctors to productively and profitably use their limited time makes this a very serious technical hurdle. The time expenditure problem is often combined with a sense among doctors that they are burdened with too much paperwork and will do what they can to avoid it. Faced with serious time constraints, and in treatment contexts where there are a number of caregivers, many physicians will delegate reporting chores or assume that others have filed the requisite reports, thereby posing a challenge of coordination and conscientiousness.[19]

The timeframe for reporting may also impact would-be filers or compromise the reliability of any information received.[20] Insistence on immediate reporting can produce hurried submissions or thwart filing altogether. On the other hand, allowing delay may degrade the quality of the reports as memories fade and distractions intrude. The form used for reporting may create further barriers. If a form is too complex, it may undermine the willingness of staff members to cooperate. But, if the form is too simple it may not generate the level of detail necessary for effective evaluation.

Studies make it clear that reporters are far more likely to embrace systems that yield work-related benefits. The benefit to be derived from reporting is feedback that makes practice safer. If such feedback is not forthcoming the cost/benefit calculus is likely to swing in the direction of not filing. A system that does not provide useful feedback is not only likely to discourage filing but to foster disrespect for the whole safety effort. (The staff's common-sense refrain: "Others don't care about the system; why should I?")

If properly managed, reporting can produce information that is exceedingly valuable in identifying problems. The IOM's drafters saw reporting as essential not only to problem identification, but also to measuring safety progress over time. The IOM's hope of using reporting to benchmark safety improvement has provoked a good deal of technical criticism. Troyen Brennan, among others, has noted that the sort of reporting envisioned by the IOM provides no denominators (the numbers of treatments rendered) so as to make possible the calculation of error rates.[21] Without such data, calculations claiming to measure improvement (or its opposite) are not reliable. Considering all this, it should come as no surprise that those who have examined the effectiveness of medical reporting regimes since the IOM's call for their establishment have been disappointed with the results.[22] The technical hurdles have not been definitively overcome and only the "easiest" problems—those posed by certain never-events—have been addressed.

CULTURAL BARRIERS TO REPORTING

The barriers to reporting are not exclusively technical and logistical. Medical culture has posed a set of challenges that have also stifled reporting. A knowledgeable observer has pointed out that, in essence, "all reporting is voluntary."[23] If those expected or required to report are intent on resisting or evading such an obligation they will, generally, succeed. Medical errors can be hidden and the evidence suggests that they are frequently left unreported. Traditionally, as a number of studies have noted, peer assessments concerning medical errors were not written down. Charles Bosk, in his celebrated sociological study of the training of young surgeons, *Forgive and Remember*, examined how the educational process made use of the M&M conference as the key mechanism for the discussion of missteps and mistakes.[24] Bosk found the discussion and criticism to be vigorous, resulting in the admission of error, but no records were kept, no reports were filed, and no follow-up investigations were undertaken. It should be noted that even the robust discussion of error observed by Bosk may be an anomaly. A number of other scholars have found that M&M conferences are often desultory affairs with little focus on error.[25] It would appear that, as a matter of custom, if error is addressed it is only done in a private and undocumented exchange kept strictly within professional ranks. This is consistent with the well-established ground rules of medical etiquette that evolved in the nineteenth century prohibiting public criticism of fellow physicians and urging solidarity within the profession.[26]

Medical resistance to reporting is grounded in more than tradition. There is also a financial issue. Doctors' livelihoods depend on the granting of practice privileges and the referral of patients. It is a widely shared belief that both of these may be jeopardized by error reporting.[27] It is a commonly held view among physicians that an error report is likely to have a negative effect on a physician's reputation. A sullied reputation is, in turn, likely to interfere with appointments and referrals. So public criticism of the performance of a doctor or a public admission of an error may be viewed as a very real threat to that doctor's livelihood. Reputation turns on information (whether accurate or not). The dissemination of negative information about performance is widely viewed as career-threatening. This is a substantial inhibition to reporting. That inhibition is likely to be compounded if there is a chance that a medical malpractice claim will be filed. Such claims, if upheld, are said by many doctors to be career destroyers.[28] In 2004, well after the disclosures of *To Err* and the fight over managed care, a poll asked doctors what they thought to be the greatest problem currently facing medicine. The majority of respondents cited medical malpractice claims.[29] The accuracy of this view, its potential for exaggeration, and the true impact of malpractice suits are matters we explore elsewhere. Here it is important to note that many doctors believe such claims are a calamity and deeply fear any disclosure.

The rhetoric used by otherwise levelheaded physician-analysts about malpractice claims is astonishingly out of character. A very knowledgeable and effective analyst of patient safety issues is Dr. Robert Wachter; his book, *Internal Bleeding*, is one of the most thoughtful available on the subject. Yet when he and his co-author, Dr. Kaveh Shojania, discuss medical malpractice, caution and measured judgment are seemingly tossed aside. Medical malpractice is described as a "Sword of Damocles" poised over physicians' heads.[30] Wachter writes of malpractice: "[E]very physician knows that his or her career can be ruined with a single slip,"[31] that it is part of "an orgy of blame"[32] in our society, that malpractice litigation has "increasingly demoralized and depressed"[33] doctors, and that any report to the National Practitioner Data Bank (NPDB) treats named physicians "like sex offenders."[34] In sum, he asserts that the law's reaction to malpractice is "lunacy."[35]

The hard data suggest that these claims are simply unfounded. The likelihood of the filing of a malpractice claim is miniscule, particularly in light of the scope and seriousness of medical error. When such claims do go to trial doctors win more than 70% of the time—far more than just about any other category of defendants.[36] Notions of an "orgy of blame" neglect to take into account the documented reluctance of virtually all injured patients to file claims and the reluctance of juries to find doctors liable. The idea that the confidential reporting system established by the NPDB is, somehow, a monstrous imposition, seems to fly in the face of Dr. Wachter's enthusiasm for reporting solutions and concern over problem physicians. Similar views have been expressed by Dr. Troyen Brenan who, despite his insightful work on the seriousness of the problem of error in hospital care as revealed in the records of New York, Colorado, and Utah hospitals, has repeatedly described medical malpractice litigation as the chief impediment to finding a solution to the problem of iatrogenic injury[37] (a claim at odds with evidence from places like New Zealand and England where an absence or scarcity of medical malpractice actions has not resulted in greater safety).[38]

Doctor analysts, despite their insights into the profession, share a professional bias that may interfere with measured judgment on this topic. The values that might produce such bias are easy to identify. Malpractice actions tend to force the judgment of outsiders onto the medical field, thus second guessing the professionals. That sort of intrusion has been anathema to doctors since the nineteenth century, if not before. It undermines doctors' control of medical care, thereby posing a threat to the core principle around which training and practice have been organized. When the real emotional and temporal costs of malpractice litigation are added to these deeply held cultural attitudes about authority and control it is not surprising that the doctor-analysts paint such a lurid, if inaccurate, picture of medical malpractice. Such rhetoric not only reflects but also reinforces the fears that inhibit the admission of error and willingness to expose one's action to scrutiny. To this list of fears should be added medical professionals' anxiety about the media. The news stories about the medical errors that killed Betsy Lehman led to substantial penalties for the caregivers involved.[39] The same was true in the much-publicized case of Jesica Santillan, whose organ transplant surgery was botched at Duke University Hospital.[40] Wachter noted that such news reports, with their outsized and often ill-informed coverage, alarm doctors (and patients too, eroding their trust in medicine) and reinforce their reluctance to report.[41]

Such reticence arises not only from the cultural views shared among doctors but also from the institutional culture of hospitals. For decades hospital administrations have viewed medical error as a threat to reputation and financial success. To address this threat, beginning in the 1970s hospitals added a new administrative branch to their staffs—risk managers. These individuals were tasked with keeping hospitals and their caregivers out of legal and media trouble.[42] The way they went about it was by keeping tight control over error-related information. They undertook internal investigations after injuries occurred to determine if there was a risk of liability. They then did all in their power to see that the information did not get out to patients, their lawyers, or the public. While it has been suggested that risk managers have begun to move away from a reactive role and toward patient safety efforts to head off problems, it is far from clear that any sort of reporting program outside the confines of the hospital would meet with their approval. Unfortunately, it will always remain in the immediate financial and institutional interest of hospitals to curtail distribution of negative information, even if down the road its distribution could facilitate safety improvement.

In some instances, reporting systems and peer evaluation have not only failed but been corrupted and used to punish filers for sharing information about errors. Disclosure can lead to a complainant's termination from employment in apparent retaliation for a report.[43]

Such incidents, and the subsequent lawsuits that have documented them, call to mind the story of Dr. Ignaz Semmelweis. In the mid-nineteenth century, Dr. Semmelweis was working as an assistant to the director of the maternity wards of the General Hospital in Vienna. At the time, 10% of the ward's new mothers were dying of puerperal, or child bed fever.[44] It was Dr. Semmelweis who finally identified the cause of its rampant spread: physicians were not washing their hands properly. But his claims were flatly rejected by the profession. It was said that his assertions were sullying the reputation of physicians. He was forced from his position. His protests about unsanitary practices eventually led to his incarceration in a mental hospital and subsequent death while institutionalized.

In the recent past some aggrieved American medical professionals formed the Semmelweis Society to offer assistance to doctors being harassed for reporting errors or patient injury.[45] No matter what one concludes about the actual incidence of such cases,[46] it is easy to see why many doctors might view reporting as professionally dangerous. Out of fear of reprisal, many may wish to avoid any form of reporting whatsoever. It might also be noted that even the much-vaunted airline reporting systems have faced problems albeit with intimidation of potential reporters.

By any measure, long established medical reporting mechanisms have not proven effective. Some of the problems encountered in the traditional M&M conference have already been mentioned. While the Bosk study of surgical resident training suggests that such conferences, at least internally, address serious errors, other reports raise questions about whether the usual M&M conference accomplishes even that. A study of such conferences found that only one hour in four was devoted to the subject of error. Even when error was discussed, it was in the most perfunctory way.[47] The frequent result of these meetings, the study reported, was to shift blame for any problems encountered to other hospital departments. The doctors participating in such meetings often act sympathetically toward their colleagues when reviewing their work. A New Jersey examination of closed case files found peer review strongly "biased" in favor of doctors.[48] Even when an error is found, the likely result is a ritual "tongue lashing," without any corrective follow-up.[49] Although Bosk entitled his book *Forgive and Remember*, it would seem that the M&M conference is not devoted to remembering but forgetting. Bosk remarks in his conclusion that "[t]his account makes clear that . . . silence is not merely a feature of professional–client relations, but that it is also a feature of . . . the Mortality and Morbidity Conference."[50]

Bosk concluded that M&M conferences "serve as a model of the lesson 'we don't tell tales.'"[51] This is what Bosk's surgical residents were trained to do. It should be noted that this "conspiracy of silence" is perpetuated despite the existence, in most states, of legal protections that make the proceedings and conclusions of M&M conferences confidential.

More recent efforts at creating reporting mechanisms have also failed. This has been the experience of the NPDB. It was first established as part of the HIPAA legislation and began operating in 1996. The legislation requires reporting of medical malpractice awards, license revocations or suspensions, medical staff discipline, and exclusion from Medicaid or Medicare reimbursement. Despite the clarity of the NPDB mandate, one study found that the vast majority of hospitals in 31 states did not file a single report during the first decade of the data bank's operation.[52] Doctors and their legal representatives have utilized a wide range of settlement and other strategies, both within and beyond the NPDB rules, to avoid the "black mark" of the filing of a report.[53] They have generally met with a sympathetic institutional response. In the end, the procedures set up to identify troubled physicians have been thwarted—this despite the fact that the process guarantees confidentiality from public disclosure. In light of all this, William Sage, a leading healthcare scholar, has suggested that society would be best served by abandoning the NPDB.[54]

The Joint Commission sentinel event program provides another example of a recent reporting initiative that has not proven effective. The original idea of the program was to identify a limited number of never-events and require hospital-conducted root-cause analyses of them. All this was to be reported to the Joint Commission. The program initially made reporting mandatory. This requirement was quickly dropped in face of protests by the American Hospital Association (the largest and most influential such organization in America) and others.[55] At the core of the objectors' articulated concerns was a fear "that such reporting could be legally discoverable thereby increasing . . . liability."[56] Legal worries and, perhaps, deeper cultural antipathy to reporting, led to a challenge that persuaded the Joint Commission to abandon its mandatory program in favor of a voluntary one that "encouraged" reporting but did not insist on it. It should come as no surprise that the sentinel event program suffered from serious underreporting. From 1995 to 2004, 3,000 events were submitted for Joint Commission review, a figure representing perhaps 1% of the serious errors that occurred.[57] During the first five years of the program there was approximately one report filed for every 53 institutions under the Joint Commission's jurisdiction (there were 19,000 such institutions).[58] The Joint Commission eventually sought to expand the number of never-events covered by reporting and analysis requirements but was forced by its constituents to declare a "moratorium" on the listing of new events because "hospitals felt overwhelmed."[59] Since there was no filing requirement it would appear that what felt overwhelming was conducting any serious analysis of these additional never-events. In light of the number of error-caused deaths and serious injuries documented in various studies, it seems clear that the Joint Commission never-event program has not been an overwhelming success. Its reach has been repeatedly circumscribed by those required to report. The Joint Commission's sensitivity to the wishes of those it accredits and laxity about chronic safety problems led the Medicaid program in 2008 to insist on the opening up of the "accreditation market" to competition.[60]

State reporting systems, even with mandatory requirements and confidentiality guarantees, have also performed poorly. One of the states that has been most committed to improving patient safety is Massachusetts. It adopted a compulsory scheme for the reporting of error-related deaths and serious injuries. While it is unclear exactly how many incidents of this sort occur annually in Massachusetts, the number of reports filed during each of the first five years of the program was between 400 and 500.[61] In light of national statistics it has been estimated that the annual number of error-related deaths in Massachusetts is between 1,000 and 2,250.[62] The gap between these figures suggests that even in Massachusetts, reporting is not approaching anything like completeness. In fact, when injuries are factored in, it has been estimated that Massachusetts receives reports on about 4% of eligible events.[63] These results are not particularly encouraging about the prospects for the creation of effective reporting regimes, even for the most serious sorts of events and even if reporting is required by law.

CONCLUSION

In each of the previously discussed reporting contexts there have been substantial guarantees of confidentiality. In none is there evidence of serious breaches of confidentiality that have led to legal liability. Yet, in all of these settings healthcare providers have avoided reporting. Claims about fears of breached confidentiality seem to provide a pretext for resistance to reporting. The available evidence suggests that whatever is done about confidentiality will have little effect on reporting and that providers will continue to resist reporting regimes. In New Zealand, when medical malpractice litigation was replaced by a no-fault system, doctors still did not disclose errors with the frequency that they should have and were predicted to.[64] The same is true in England where both confidentiality and tight limits on tort litigation are in place. In a 2003 50-state survey of reporting practices it was found that there was "little difference between systems that provide confidentiality and those that do not."[65] It would appear that healthcare culture and logistics rather than legal activity will stand in the way of even the most secure and best-designed reporting systems.

9

Legal Innovations to Promote Patient Safety—An Introduction

> All systems ... have had to adopt auxiliary measures—information, education, administrative regulation, instinct for self-preservation, technology, market effects (including reputation), professional discipline, and other behavioral influences—to augment the call for accident prevention.[1]

The imaginative CEO of a state hospital association, whose job was to look out for the interests of his member hospitals, had an idea. He invited pairs (more or less) of representatives from the major sectors of the medical malpractice debate to a series of dinner meetings.[2] Gathering together over a period of months were officials and attorneys from the state medical society and the hospital association, defense lawyers, plaintiffs' lawyers, several doctors, a couple of law professors, a judge, and occasionally an insurance actuary.

The CEO launched the meetings by saying that he, for one, recognized his own industry's share of responsibility for the carnage that was being suffered by far too many patients, some of which led to lawsuits. Obliquely, he invited the doctors' representatives to join in his confession, but none took up the offer. No matter. The CEO's float plan was to take them all on a voyage of discovery in search of tort reforms that might improve the litigation environment for doctors and hospitals, while being acceptable, in some ways perhaps even attractive, to plaintiffs' lawyers. The CEO's eventual goal was to take the agreed-upon package to the state's legislature, in the expectation that it would encounter little opposition, and the resulting legal changes would benefit his constituents and perhaps other factions as well.

As the voyage neared its destination—which turned out, as one might expect, to be little more than a collection of inoffensive lowest-common denominators— one of the participants raised the possibility that the group might be able to think of some additional law reforms with the potential to contribute to improving patient safety. The suggestion was greeted with blank looks. *That* type of reform had not previously occurred to those around the table. The hospital association CEO ended the possibility of his dinner group exploring such new directions by declaring, "No. Nothing."

NOTHING?

Clearly, improvement in patient safety is not coming easily. The Institute of Medicine's (IOM) *To Err Is Human* set a goal of rapid improvement: "Given current knowledge about the magnitude of the problem, the committee believes it would be irresponsible to expect anything less than a 50% reduction in errors over five years."[3] Nothing remotely like that occurred.[4] So renewed calls were made for even more dramatic improvement in the *next* five years.[5] Again, in terms of results, little progress ensued. Then the Patient Safety Foundation set a goal of "zero preventable deaths by 2020."[6] Each failed call to action led to exhortations of even greater attainment. Still, no great and widespread improvement in patient safety is in sight.

There are reasons for the healthcare industry's sluggishness in adopting needed safety innovations, and those roadblocks will need to be understood and taken into account as part of the task of drawing up blueprints for progress in patient safety. Among these roadblocks are the lack of a business case for quality and safety[7] and, Hyman and Silver tell us, the culture of medicine, "which embraces values that are antithetical to quality improvement" and has a "tolerance for medical errors."[8] David Studdert and Michelle Mello review what they term "progress in the war on medical errors" and ultimately conclude that "it is questionable whether a typical patient receiving care from a typical health professional in a typical hospital or clinic today is at appreciably lower risk of experiencing a preventable medical injury than they were twenty years ago."[9] More than ambitious pronouncements will be needed.

That does not mean there are no reasons to be hopeful. Periodic reports from the Agency for Healthcare Research and Quality (AHRQ) and elsewhere bring news of scattered improvement.[10] Variability in the practices of healthcare organizations that correlates with safety outcomes suggests that positive changes are possible and that widespread improvements should be achievable.[11] The challenge is to identify or invent methods that lead to improved patient safety, figure out how to make them sustainable, and help healthcare organizations and individuals adopt and maintain the safer practices.

Is there *nothing* law can do to assist in that effort? Is there nothing to be found among the varied tools that law and government have to offer society that can help advance the effort to subdue the epidemic of patient injury and death? In this and the next several chapters, we explore some of the possibilities.

Legal innovations come in wide variety. They fall along a spectrum from direct regulation of specific practices, through a range of indirect influences, through regulation of the larger social-economic environment, which influences the forms and capacities of countless societal activities, including the healthcare system.

When legal tools are operating at their best, most people aren't even aware of what those tools are doing and accomplishing. For example, have you ever thought about what makes it possible to fly across the country or to show two pieces of plastic at a car rental counter and in minutes be put in control of someone else's expensive vehicle for days or weeks?[12] Not only might you steal it, you could do a lot of damage to and with that potentially dangerous machine. And yet the owner is happy to loan it to you. What enables this remarkable transaction between strangers to be a quotidian occurrence is an intricate yet robust network of legal rules connecting businesses, banks, insurers, and governments in a web of interlocking obligations. The law of contracts and banking, and agencies regulating drivers and vehicles and rental car companies, necessarily play a part. If needed, insurance law and tort law can be called upon. And, in the worst of cases, the criminal law can step in. Those regulatory tools enable the marketplace to do its work. Few people ever even notice the legal infrastructure necessary to enable this and many other kinds of transactions. They usually work so well that they are invisible.[13]

Similarly, much of the economic, social, educational, and other spheres of life in our society operate within an infrastructure that is both facilitated and kept in check by law. Without appropriate regulation, free markets could not be free (think, for example, of civil and criminal fraud laws, antitrust laws, and securities laws). Private activity in the United States thrives in part because it is afforded the protections of contract, property, and tort law, as well as constitutional protections. Intellectual property protection facilitates advances in science and technology as well as the arts. When our society is not working as well as we think it could be and should be, we look to law reform as one important way to try to improve it. On these foundations of our semi-regulated society, countless organizations and institutions are built, including the healthcare industry.

That is a rather broad and diluted role for the law to play in patient safety. But, if the healthcare industry had been able to create a system of adequate safety on its own, nothing more than that broad legal infrastructure would be necessary. The longer a problem persists, the bigger it is, and the more unhappy the public becomes about it, the stronger the law's warrant will grow to take more, more focused, and more powerful steps. Are hundreds of thousands of preventable deaths per year enough of a mandate?

SOME GENERAL CONSIDERATIONS

We offer no master plan in this book. What we aim to do is suggest possible directions the law might take, *beyond* the endless tug of war to weaken, or restore, or tweak the malpractice litigation system. We offer illustrations and suggestions; not a complete catalog. Consider this an invitation to a larger conversation.

But First, Some General Considerations. The conversation must be interdisciplinary. Legal policymakers will benefit from collaboration with partners knowledgeable in the same lesson. Economics, statistics, cognitive and behavioral sciences, human factors, and other disciplines, as well as healthcare management, can help.

A fundamental tension exists between traditional medical culture and the innovations necessary to improve safety. The provision of healthcare suffers from variability that makes it less effective and more risky.[14] As research evidence builds and reveals which practices are best for which kinds of patients suffering from what conditions under which circumstances, effective procedures and practices need to be systematized and employed in preference to less effective and less safe procedures. But the culture of medical training and practice creates physicians who are accustomed to exercising their independent judgment unimpeded. Autonomy is incompatible, however, with the filtering out of random and systematic error, just as it is incompatible with the use of evidence-based medicine to steer practice away from less effective and lower-value care toward more effective, higher-value care.[15]

Patient safety advocates are also right in arguing that the health care sector needs a cultural transformation. One commentator cuttingly framed the problem as follows:

> Suppose that an airline's managers and pilots repeatedly resisted installing collision-avoidance systems despite solid evidence of their worth. Suppose, too, that they complained that the radar was not reimbursed adequately, required inconvenient retraining, provided no competitive advantage in attracting passengers at a time when airline profits were low, and (sotto voce) was an insult to pilot judgment. No one would blithely blame "airline culture" for an ensuing disaster, and no one would absolve individual pilots and managers of responsibility for that disaster simply because they never intended for passengers to be harmed.
>
> Health care providers make arguments like these all the time, and they expect them to be taken seriously. Better evidence of attitudes antithetical to patient safety would be hard to find.[16]

Everyone cannot be doing whatever they individually feel is best and at the same time everyone be doing what is best. For quality of care and patient safety to improve, the tension between autonomy and variability will need to be resolved and reduced.

How focused and specific should the law's behavioral guidance be? American legislatures and courts generally avoid directing behavior with specificity—preferring to leave to individuals and organizations the latitude to decide how to accomplish their goals while staying within relatively broad legal boundaries. At times, however, the law can become quite specific. For example, to enable consumers to quickly and easily compare the unit cost of the same product produced by different manufacturers, or different quantities of the same product by the same manufacturer, one state statute directs grocers to post unit prices in statutorily prescribed units, in a specified typeface, in black letters against an orange background defined in angstroms (the wavelength of light reflected from the label). Not much room for variation there. The degree of legal specificity can range from quite broad to quite narrow.

Courts, in contrast to legislatures and regulatory bodies, are even more institutionally committed to avoiding overspecifying what people and organizations should do or not do.[17] As the role of courts continues to decline, we can expect the role of legislatures and regulatory bodies to expand.

Whatever the level of specificity, wherever possible, the lighter the law's touch the better. Behavioral research teaches that the more gently people can be led to the desired behavior change, the more effective and self-sustaining the change will be.[18] In some domains, the mere existence of rules (as an announcement of normative guidelines) is sufficient to bring many or most people along. Where external pressures (be they carrots or sticks) are salient, people attribute their behavior to those exogenous forces, and are less likely to come to own the new behavior. The more behavior change is induced by minimal external pressure, the more it will be attributed to a desire to engage in the new procedures, the more likely that supportive attitudes will form around the new behavior, and the more the adopted changes will become internalized.[19] Over time, if insufficient numbers of people and organizations are making the needed changes, the level of inducement can gradually be increased.

The best legal policies for advancing patient safety will not be self-evident. Innovative laws should be considered provisional; experimentation and evaluation must be regarded as an essential part of the process. What is found to work can be retained and refined; what does not work can and should be replaced. Evidence-based law is as necessary as evidence-based healthcare.[20]

DISCOVER, DISSEMINATE, RECOMMEND, INCENTIVIZE

First, innovations in healthcare that improve the level of patient safety must be discovered. Once they are identified and validated, information about what they are and how to implement them has to be disseminated. Mere spreading of the word might not in itself be sufficient (although sometimes or often it might be). Encouragement in the form of recommendations (people usually want to do what similar, respected others are doing)[21] and incentivization (both carrots and sticks) will often have to be part of what is necessary to improve quality and safety. Can ways be found for the law to be helpful at all of those stages?

Innovation Registry

One helpful role for law and government would be to develop and maintain a registry of healthcare system innovations that have been found to be effective in improving quality and safety. A government health agency could monitor innovative efforts of the nation's healthcare organizations to improve safety—not only those programs that the government has funded, but all such efforts for which data are collected that permit evaluation.[22]

As safer and more effective procedures are discovered and determined to be effective and cost-effective, the law might be able to promote their use simply by placing them on the registry. One thinks of such possibilities as the use of checklists; electronic medical records and health information exchanges; methods for analyzing and learning from adverse events (e.g., root-cause analysis); methods for healthcare teams to work together better (e.g., crew resource management); even more specific methods such as time-out orientation before starting surgery, techniques, and technology for preventing instruments from being retained in surgical patients; and so on.

These innovations can range widely. For example, the American Institute of Architects has identified concerns and proposed principles for the safe design and construction of health care facilities that would contribute to patient safety.[23] If government did no more than to maintain a registry of successful programs, so that they could be replicated by others, that would accelerate advancement in patient safety.

Education and Training

Government could encourage the teaching of what can be expected to become a science of safety as part of the training of healthcare providers. Some of this is already taking place, such as the Hospital Improvement Innovation Networks.[24] Inducements to teach the new knowledge might be entirely unnecessary. But, as a significant subsidizer of medical schools and graduate medical education (training of doctors after they leave medical school), government is in a reasonably good position to encourage medical educational institutions to include the advancement of patient safety in its curriculum.

Research Support and Research

A familiar role for government is to assemble resources and to partner with researchers and stakeholders, investing support in promising research. Appropriate government agencies, institutes, departments, and centers could choose to, or be directed to, devote more of their resources to reducing the incidence of the number three cause of death in the United States. More research on the problem can be encouraged by budgeting more for the research. If you fund it, it will happen.

One federal agency that works with researchers and healthcare organizations specifically to improve patient safety is the AHRQ.[25] Numerous examples exist of the products of AHRQ's own initiatives and those of researchers it has funded. One idea being experimented with is the placement of clinical pharmacists right in emergency departments to improve the medical management of patients with complex conditions and to reduce medication errors.[26] Medications at Transitions and Clinical Handoffs (MATCH) is a medication reconciliation toolkit.[27] As patients move through the healthcare delivery process—from home to hospital and out to skilled nursing facilities or rehabilitation or back home—at each step some medications are added and others subtracted from the prior regimen. On average, there is a 20% discrepancy between the medications a patient should have been prescribed and administered and the medications the patient is actually receiving.[28] MATCH aims to solve that problem.

A major effort of AHRQ is the Patient Safety Culture Survey, currently used by more than 1,000 hospitals, which was designed to help healthcare organizations periodically assess the state of their safety culture, track changes, and evaluate whether changes implemented to improve safety are having the desired effects.

Another major effort of AHRQ has been the development of a program called TeamSTEPPS[29] (Team Strategies and Tools to Enhance Performance and Patient Safety), a healthcare version of "crew resource management," pioneered in the aviation industry.[30] In healthcare as in aviation, the traditional hierarchical culture has too often interfered with detecting and acting to prevent disasters that could have been avoided. TeamSTEPPS is being implemented in hospitals, long-term care facilities, and primary care clinics in the United States and beyond. It aims to improve patient safety by teaching providers how to work with each other more effectively, using such methods as huddles, debriefs, handoffs, and check-backs.

Here is a situation where TeamSTEPPS might be useful. One of your authors spent several days with a hospital's internal training unit. The director explained that one initiative had been teaching nurses how to recognize cardiac arrest, quickly determine which team member was best prepared to take charge of the emergency, and, of course, how to perform defibrillation properly. But when simulations were conducted with physicians participating—although the physicians were less skilled in defibrillation than the nurses—a doctor would nevertheless take charge. The nurses deferred to the doctors, stood by watching as the doctor fumbled around, and allowed the (simulated) patient to die. In answer to a question from your author, the training director explained that most of the nurses were so accustomed to deferring to physicians, and so dreaded any confrontation with a doctor, that letting a patient die was preferable to being yelled at by a doctor. Accordingly, it was realized, everyone needed more than technical knowledge and skill to save patients' lives. They needed to learn how to work more effectively together. This is one of the most important elements of crew resource management, and therefore of TeamSTEPPS.[31]

Some sources of healthcare system error are so clearly within government's responsibility and control that it is government's role to try to design those errors out of the system. For example, the U.S. Food and Drug Administration (FDA) makes the final determination of the names and appearance of medications, including labeling and packaging design.[32] Those confusion-prevention efforts could be improved, borrowing more from cognitive science and other sources of knowledge, and then testing before approving.[33] One study found that up to a quarter of all medication errors resulted from confusion caused by names that sound too similar or look too similar, and a third of them resulted from packaging and labeling confusion.[34] In cases reported to the FDA of such errors,[35] one young man was given clozapine instead of olanzapine and nearly died. A child was given methadone instead of the drug that was prescribed (to treat attention deficit disorder) and did die. A middle-aged woman was hospitalized after taking Flomax®, used to treat symptoms of enlarged prostate, instead of Volmax®, used to relieve bronchospasms. Serzone®, an antidepressant, was mistaken for Seroquel®, used to treat schizophrenia. Iodine was mistaken for Lodine®, a nonsteroidal anti-inflammatory.

Technology

Computer and other technological advances present new opportunities to improve the quality of care and to reduce errors. Information technology is discussed in Chapter 13 of this volume. The limited capabilities of information technology in healthcare were recently described by Regina Barzilay, an MIT computer scientist who works with medical colleagues to develop algorithms that can improve the information that computers can extract from medical imaging. Barzilay commented: "I was really surprised how primitive information technology is in the hospitals. It almost felt that we were in a different century."[36] Such innovations as electronic health records, computerized physician order entry, health information exchanges, and the use of mobile devices, including by patients (eHealth), have started to become familiar parts of the healthcare world. As artificial intelligence moves society toward increased reliance on computer-assisted, or computer-autonomous, decisions and actions, including within healthcare, new opportunities will arise to reduce errors. New ways to make mistakes will also present themselves.[37] Some of these reside in the technology itself. Others emerge through the interaction of humans with technology: when we become too reliant on computers to make decisions for us, we become lazy thinkers and don't bring what we can contribute to the overall task. Law and government can continue to play a part, both in advancing the technologies and in trying to minimize new risks of error by requiring appropriate testing, setting standards, and sometimes approving or rejecting certain approaches or devices.[38]

Other types of technologies, of a noninformation kind, are being developed and will continue to be developed far into the future. Think, for example, of genetically based personalized medicine and robotic surgery. Private investment, research, and development will play a large part, of course. But government institutions, from the National Institutes of Health (NIH) and the Centers for Disease Control and Prevention (CDC) to state universities, will also have roles to play, as funders and researchers as well as facilitators and regulators. The United States has a partnered research and development system.[39] Some technological advances, at some point in the future, will have the potential to make outsized contributions to patient safety. One example is the development of systems for closely monitoring what happens in surgical theaters, so that the causes of harmful outcomes can be identified, understood, and prevented.[40] Google Glass, which was not successful when launched for everyday consumer use, has returned as Google Glass EE (Enterprise Edition) for specialized industrial applications, and its usefulness in medical settings is being explored.[41] Imagine a nurse wearing Google Glass 2.0 entering a patient's hospital room. As soon as the Glass detects the patient's identity, everything the nurse needs to know about that patient would become available "on screen" or on verbal command, without having to touch or swipe or push any buttons. Reminders, checklists, and warnings will be at the ready. If the wrong drug or dose is about to be administered, the Glass will flash a warning. If the patient is being rolled away for a procedure intended for someone else, the Glass would raise a warning. The question for legal policymakers is whether and how the law might facilitate the development of such technological innovations.

Help Industry to Coordinate

Where the industry itself has failed to achieve a needed degree of coordination and consistency, law and government can assist. For example, hospitals have been quite creative in developing emergency codes: code red, code orange, code yellow, paging Doctor Quick, paging Doctor Stork, and so on. But different codes have developed in different hospitals, even hospitals in the same community. Code purple can mean a bomb threat in one hospital, a missing child in another, a patient in need of restraint in another, and so on. Similarly, hospital bracelets come in various colors to alert caregivers to a patient's condition or needs. The colors vary across hospitals. Inconsistencies can lead to confusion and error when caregivers work in different hospitals in the same communities or have moved from a hospital in a different state that employs a different coding system. The law need not dictate the coding system. But the law could assign a government agency the responsibility of bringing together leaders from the healthcare community and facilitate their working together to develop a uniform set of color and word codes. Such facilitation could occur at any level of government or geographic area. Alternatively, in collaboration with health industry officials, a federal or state government agency could promulgate a recommended set of codes, in the expectation that over time those would be adopted by more and more hospitals, with or without external incentives such as ratings by private or government organizations.

Similar coordinating roles for government entities have in fact been used to help identify the safest and most effective drugs, treatments, and other procedures. Beginning in 1977, through its Consensus Development Program (CDP), the NIH sponsored consensus development conferences, meetings of researchers and practitioners to review the relevant evidence and to see where consensus could be reached on what worked best in various areas of diagnosis and treatment. Over 160 consensus statements emerged from these conferences.[42] Their guidance was not imposed through law but had what force it did, in part, simply from its existence and the manner by which it was created. In many instances, the consensus statements were adopted and endorsed by professional organizations or used as the basis for clinical practice guidelines. Over time, as other organizations in and out of government joined the effort to develop evidence-based guidance—among them, the U.S. Preventive Services Task Force, the IOM, AHRQ Comparative Effectiveness Reviews, and the Cochrane Collaboration—the CDP was no longer needed, and in 2013 it was shuttered.[43]

Overcoming Inertia

Mere creation of a list of suggested practices, no matter how strong their basis or how soundly they have been developed, is no assurance that they will be embraced by all, or most, or even a sizable minority of practitioners. The principle of inertia applies to individuals and organizations—or call it the conservation of energy. For individuals as well as organizations, it is easier to keep doing what we have been doing than to learn to do something different. We have interlocking tasks and roles that have come to work well enough for our purposes; change would require us all to restructure, renegotiate and reset those arrangements. Change involves costs of many kinds. We find it easier to do familiar things in familiar ways with familiar people in familiar role-relationships. Even changes that we clearly expect will improve our own lives—never mind the lives of others—we recognize will require us to summon energy and attention to accomplish. The challenge for patient safety reformers is where to find and how to deploy what is necessary to overcome inertia.

An example with interesting parallels to the IOM report and its aftermath can be seen in a report issued by the National Research Council, an arm of the National Academies, that is similar to the IOM. In 2009 the National Research Council issued a report titled *Strengthening Forensic Science in the United States: A Path Forward* (2009). The report summarized research findings indicating that large swaths of the work done in crime laboratories fell far short of being scientifically grounded, empirically tested, or dependably accurate, leading surprisingly often to errors. Those errors accounted for a substantial portion of convictions of innocent people uncovered by postconviction DNA testing. The report called for many reforms, including the creation by Congress of a National Institute of Forensic Science to do all of the things that had not been done successfully in the preceding century of forensic science. What followed has been remarkably little. Inertia, assisted by denial and resistance, has so far prevailed.[44]

A classic illustration of inertia in medical practice is what happened when British researchers first discovered that six months of confinement to bed as a treatment for tuberculosis was no more effective (and far costlier) than allowing patients to remain ambulatory. The new treatment practice did not overtake the old practice for a generation. Only through attrition, as older doctors were gradually replaced by new doctors trained in more recent knowledge, was the old practice replaced by the new.[45] Even today, leaders in evidence-based medicine sometimes say, "Where there is death there is hope."[46] But that reflects a slower pace of change than patients might prefer to see.

Another example is provided by the development by the American Psychiatric Association of evidence-based practice guidelines for the use of electroconvulsive therapy (ECT). The Association issued four major guidelines on the effective use of ECT. A subsequent study looked at how patients in Massachusetts were being treated in the years soon after issuance of those guidelines.[47] The study found that 90% of patients to whom ECT was administered were still receiving it inappropriately—either because it was not an effective treatment for the patient's diagnosis, exceeded the maximum number of treatments that could be effective, was inappropriately administered,[48] or because the patient was a child.

The IOM report did stimulate more research on the problem of medical error. It "was followed by studies that showed huge numbers of medication errors, communication problems in intensive care units (ICUs), gaps in the discharge process, retained sponges in the operating room—in short, everywhere one looked there was evidence of major problems in patient safety."[49] A new healthcare field of patient safety traces its birth to the appearance of the IOM report. As one leader of that new field, Robert Wachter, has said, "prior to the IOM Report, we were doing next to nothing to make patients safer." Dr. Wachter challenged his colleagues to think of any "systems in healthcare that were truly 'hardwired' for safety prior to" the publication of the report. His answer is that there was just one: double-checking blood type before releasing a unit of blood to prevent transfusion errors.[50]

The IOM report proposed a set of reforms to try to rein in the problem of iatrogenic injury, including the creation of a Center for Patient Safety within the AHRQ. The establishment of a nationwide mandatory reporting system that provides for the collection of standardized information about adverse events that result in death or serious harm. The extension by Congress of peer review protections to data related to patient safety and quality improvement that are collected and analyzed by health care organizations. Adding concern for patient safety to the performance standards and expectations for healthcare organizations. Having the FDA increase attention to the safe use of drugs in both pre- and postmarketing processes. Calling for a change in the culture of healthcare organizations to make patient safety a serious part of what they do.

As mentioned earlier in this chapter, the IOM report set a goal of cutting the incidence of errors in half within five years. Commenting at the end of those five years, two leading voices of the patient safety movement were hopeful, but sober: "Although these efforts are affecting safety at the margin, their overall impact is hard to see in national statistics." "[L]ittle evidence exists from any source that systematic improvements in safety are widely available."[51] Subsequent analyses do not yet show a notable downward bending of the injurious error curve.[52]

Restructuring Perverse Incentives

In thinking about how to overcome an industry's inertia, if the first thought is economics—incentives aimed at motivating changed behavior—the second thought needs to be behavioral economics. Incentives can work in unexpected, even counterproductive ways. Moreover, certain incentives currently drive the healthcare industry in ways that tend to work against investment in patient safety.[53] Those perverse incentives could be altered. The law could create incentives (or disincentives) that are contingent upon healthcare organizations meeting (or missing) certain patient safety targets. Healthcare organizations can decide how, exactly, they plan to attain those safety improvements. The law would do no more than specify what the (typically financial) consequences would be of reaching specified levels of infections, falls, deaths, readmissions, or other preventable conditions. In fact, Congress already has launched some efforts of this kind, directing the Centers for Medicare and Medicaid Services to make or reduce payments to providers contingent upon quality and safety performance. Problems of malstructured incentives, recently deployed legal innovations, and other related strategies are discussed in Chapter 10 of this volume.

Clinical Practice Guidelines and Safe Harbors

One legal innovation that might create an incentive to learn about and adopt evidence-based clinical guidelines is that of making practice guidelines safe harbors from claims of liability for malpractice.[54] By adhering to evidence-based safe and effective procedures, providers would be rewarded with additional protection from liability for iatrogenic harm resulting from the treatment/procedure. The argument is that such an incentive would lead more providers to more rapidly adopt those best practices. Practice guidelines have the virtue of being an evolving set of best practices, based heavily on research evidence.[55] The adoption of newer, better, safer practices would be accelerated. On the other hand, safe harbors invite some to change but do not compel any provider to change any practice at all.

Set Standards

One step further is for the law to turn guidelines into enforceable standards. Some specific, focused standards affecting safety already exist. The FDA approves or disapproves drugs and medical devices. Government can set standards for or mandate interoperability of devices, or specify certain uniformities, or packaging, or dosages, or improved naming of medications, all aimed at reducing the risk of errors.

The law need not stop with those more familiar illustrations. Once it is determined, for example, that nurse-to-patient ratios that fall below a certain threshold lead to an increased incidence of patient deaths, hospital-acquired infections, cardiac arrest, pressure ulcers, and other complications,[56] we might consider mandating a minimum ratio. The law does not need to tell the nurses what to do. But by ensuring an adequate number of nurses are on staff, the law helps make it possible for them to do what they already know how to do and want to do. All that remains is to inform the nurses' employers how low a staffing ratio is too low. Hospitals that need to cut corners or want to increase profits would need to look somewhere other than skimping on direct patient care for those cost savings.

What would remain would be the development of means to incentivize compliance, which does not always mean to sanction violations. The law could support the adoption of helpful innovations through training assistance, tax breaks, higher reimbursements, or even direct funding. Those approaches are all carrots, not sticks.

Error Reporting

Reporting of errors and near-misses is considered crucial for advances in patient safety. To change systems so they work more effectively and safely, system redesigners need to know what is leading to errors. Important as it is, getting providers to disclose errors to their healthcare organizations, and organizations to report those errors to larger entities, has proven to be quite a challenge.[57] One study found that "Only 14% of physicians thought information about medical mistakes should be released, while 62% of the public thought that was a good idea."[58]

James Reason, a scholar of error in work organizations, has observed this about the healthcare industry:

> Health care, by its very nature, makes slips, lapses, and mistakes highly likely. Yet, health care professionals—and physicians in particular—are taught very little about the varieties of human fallibility and the conditions that are likely to provoke them. They are raised in a culture of trained perfectibility. After a long, arduous, and expensive education, physicians expect (and are expected) to get it right. Errors are marginalized and stigmatized. They are equated to incompetence. All of this means that unsafe acts—unless they result in patient harm—are hardly discussed or shared with other members of the profession. And this, too, is in stark contrast to commercial aviation, an activity that was predicated from its outset on the assumption that people make mistakes.[59]

Few if any general systems of error reporting in healthcare can be said to be successful.[60] Even when the law protects disclosures from being released beyond a healthcare organization's peer review or patient safety committee, reported errors remain far lower than healthcare officials know they should be. One healthcare worker explained her reasoning to us: no matter how secure and privileged the information in a disclosure is, it can never be as confidential as no disclosure at all.

Failure to disclose errors can be seen as something of a negative tragedy of the commons. Everyone realizes that disclosure of errors is important and that everyone would benefit from what could be done with the shared information. But individuals see their greatest benefits accruing if everyone discloses except themselves. Think of a collection pot that all of us are asked to voluntarily contribute to, which at the end of the year will be used to treat ourselves to a wonderful party. Many will contribute little or nothing, hoping that others will fill the pot. Everyone wants the benefits; few want to make the contributions. This sounds all too familiar. Many solutions to commons dilemmas are theoretically possible, ranging from leaving the solution entirely in the hands of the people who share the commons to the imposition of legally enforceable rules (for example, creating legal regimes of private property). Finding the right solution for the particular circumstances requires ingenuity and experimentation. [61]

Despite past disappointments, the need is great enough that continued experimentation seems justified. Some have suggested borrowing from other industries, such as the Aviation Safety Reporting System (ASRS), a component of the Federal Aviation Agency, though administered independently by NASA.[62] ASRS enables any member of an air crew to file a report from which staff will remove all identifying information after they are satisfied that they have all the information they need to understand what happened. The incident report, therefore, cannot be traced back to the person who filed it. As the ASRS staff acquire insights about how to make air travel safer, they publish them in a newsletter. More urgent findings are communicated directly to airlines, air traffic controllers, manufacturers, and others. A similar system exists in the railroad industry, the Confidential Close Call Reporting System (C^3RS), jointly managed by NASA and the Federal Railroad Administration, in collaboration with railroad carriers and labor organizations.[63]

Experiments with patient safety reporting systems (some modeled after those in the airline and railroad industries, others developed specifically for the healthcare setting) have the potential to contribute to advances in patient safety.[64]

One successful approach is described in detail in Chapter 12 of this volume. In some jurisdictions, government health agencies have the power to grant or withhold authorization to perform certain procedures. By closely monitoring the performance of providers, and exercising their oversight powers wisely, they have been able to elevate the level of quality and safety.

CONCLUSION

Law and government have long played a variety of roles in protecting the public's health. Familiar examples include licensure and discipline of healthcare providers, beginning in the nineteenth century[65]; supporting and initiating a wide range of public health measures, most visibly in the existence of the CDC; assuring safety and effectiveness of drugs and medical devices[66]; subsidizing the training of doctors in medical school and residencies; funding the expansion of hospitals beginning in the 1940s[67]; testing and protecting the nation's vaccine supply[68]; and specific laws to protect the public from communicable diseases.[69]

Recently, states and the federal government have acted to respond to the large number of deaths associated with the opioid crisis, highlighted by a national declaration of a public health emergency.[70] Explaining why the federal government would respond to the opioid crisis with a substantial investment, the chair of the President's Commission on Combating Drug Addiction and the Opioid Crisis stated that "if a terrorist organization was killing 175 [91 from opioids] Americans a day on American soil, what would you be willing to pay to make it stop? I think we'd be willing to do anything and everything to make it stop."[71] If so, we ought to be eager to do even more to counter the persistent epidemic of iatrogenic deaths, which number somewhere between 550 and 1,100 per day. In the next several chapters we explore in greater depth some innovative legal strategies that may more effectively address the harms of preventable medical error.

Patients will benefit if we can move beyond debates about tweaking the tort litigation system and focus instead on what the law could do to measurably improve patient safety. Like all important ideas, these need to be discussed, debated, and evaluated. The most important evaluation, we suggest, is in assessing how well any action with the potential to affect patient safety helps, hurts, or accomplishes nothing.[72] The right legal innovations could get patient safety innovations into motion.

10

Incentives—Good, Bad, and Perverse

> We found clear evidence that reducing harm and improving quality is perversely penalized in our current health care system.[1]

Most economists will advise that things work out best for everyone if each of us must absorb the costs of our actions. If I am free to do anything that pleases me—and any harm, pain, or other burdens I cause by my uninhibited ways are left to fall on others—then I will get to afflict those others with costs they cannot prevent, my own behavior will not improve, and I will continue to make the world a more unpleasant place than I found it (for everyone but myself). Take some things as simple as throwing my garbage out the window instead of disposing of it properly, or ignoring traffic signals, or carelessly knocking people down in my haste to get where I'm going. If, however, doing those things comes with a price attached, and the price reflects the cost to others of what I have done to them, then I can do what pleases me only so long as I'm willing to pay the price. That contingency encourages me to consider whether I really want to pay for the problems I am creating or, instead, decide that I will be happier (and richer) if I rein in my behavior. Either way, I cease making others bear the costs of my externalities.

Most psychologists will offer much the same advice, although their focus will be on the learning rather than on the cost in dollars. If I am exposed to the natural and human-created contingencies of the world, suffering the social and material consequences as well as enjoying the rewards that are brought by my behavior, then my behavior is likely to be shaped into getting along more harmoniously with the world I inhabit.

What does this have to do with the healthcare system? Whatever else our healthcare system is, it also is a web of incentives, disincentives, and perverse incentives. As Dr. Kevin Munjal, working at Mount Sinai Hospital in New York City, observed, "The way we practice is so often affected by the incentives that are created in the system. And the incentives are often about what gets reimbursed, and what doesn't get reimbursed."[2]

The economically oriented analyses provided by physician and legal scholar David Hyman and his colleague Charles Silver offer persuasive accounts of the engines that generate such high levels of patient harm in our healthcare system, as well as the shortcomings of the traditional legal responses. To make their point unmistakable, they titled one of their articles, "Medical Malpractice Litigation and Tort Reform: It's the Incentives, Stupid."[3] We borrowed some of their thoughts earlier and will do so again.

The tort system, when viewed through an economic lens, can be seen as supplementing the more extensive network of incentives and consequences the world provides, certainly including markets, generating economic feedback about the costs of externalities produced by bad drivers, dangerous products, and harmful healthcare systems. Seeing market forces and weak tort law as the problem, Hyman and Silver[4] recommend legal reforms aimed at strengthening those institutions in ways calculated to increase incentives for greater attention to and investment in patient safety. The same things that led to dramatic improvements in the safety of anesthesia practice could lead to improvements elsewhere in healthcare delivery.[5]

To make markets better serve safety goals, they would, for example, tie provider compensation to measurable improvements in outcomes and ensure that patients have the information needed to empower them to distinguish between high-quality and low-quality providers (including publicizing data about those providers). In the absence of the power to choose and sufficient knowledge to inform their choices, consumers are in a poor position to promote safer and better healthcare through their purchasing decisions. Large group purchasing should, at least in principle, be far better able to do so.

To make the tort system more effective, Hyman and Silver recommend rolling back past reforms and then enhancing tort law by allowing premiums for malpractice insurance to rise to better reflect the costs of unsafe healthcare, using caps to reward safety-promoting behavior (e.g., timely reporting of errors, participating in quality and safety surveys of healthcare organizations) and *augmenting* damages for failure to engage in activities that would improve safety. Insurance rates do not provide sufficient incentives because for medical professional liability they are not experience-rated. That is, physicians pay the same premiums as their peers in the same specialty in the same state regardless of how good or bad their own individual performance has been.[6] In addition, Hyuman and Silver would reward adherence to evidence-based practices by permitting their use to serve as an absolute defense in a malpractice claim; rewarding all healthcare workers for reporting quality and safety problems (which reports would be used as evidence in money-generating quasi-fraud actions against the offending organizations and individuals).

Some of those market-oriented reforms are in embryonic form already, advanced by lesser-known provisions of the Patient Protection and Affordable Care Act (ACA). Others, especially the strengthening of tort law, we suspect are unlikely to happen for the same reasons that they were weakened in the first place. Markets for healthcare in the United States are deeply distorted, and not only by the healthcare industry's rent-seeking.[7] The tort system never was, and probably could never become, powerful enough or efficient enough to counterbalance the far larger web of incentives that drive the healthcare industry. Negligently injured patients and their families always brought far too few claims for injuries, and too many lawyers turned away too many cases that they judged to be insufficiently remunerative. Those patterns are woven into the fabric of the American malpractice litigation system. Consequently, the healthcare industry has never had to absorb anything remotely approaching the actual cost of its mishaps and therefore—with the exception of anesthesiology—was never provided with economic incentives sufficient to prompt it to invest in figuring out how to perform its work more safely.[8] That bad situation has been made worse by changes in legal rules that now allow the industry to deflect ever more of the costs of its harmful errors onto the shoulders of patients, families, first-party insurers, and taxpayers.[9]

Substitutes for the inadequate contingencies that have allowed the levels of avoidable injuries and deaths to rise to their current heights must be found, and exploring some of those possibilities is the subject of this chapter. Unless the web of incentives that surrounds the healthcare industry can be redesigned—as Hyman and Silver put it, unless and until "a business case for safety" comes into being—significant decreases in rates of iatrogenic injury and death are not likely anytime soon.

BEHAVIORAL ECONOMICS

Looking at the problem through psychological lenses adds complexity to one's understanding of how to make incentives more effective. As one physician who thinks like a behavioral economist put it, "We're done with simple carrots and sticks."[10] Recognition that people often do not respond in simple, straightforward ways to carrots and sticks led to the birth of behavioral economics. For the most part, the discipline of *behavioral economics* borrows the knowledge of cognitive and social psychology and applies it to decision-making of interest to economists. That people are not the rational, efficient, profit-maximizers of classical economics does not mean that we do not respond to rewards and costs. Rather, to affect behavior, incentives and disincentives are first processed through the prism of human brains. If the departures from rationality are systematic and predictable, then they can be taken into account by policymakers and managers to improve decisions and performance.[11]

For example, sometimes providing incentives for behavior boomerangs, degrading the very performance that it was intended to promote. Suppose a child enjoys drawing pictures and draws lots of them. An adult, hoping to encourage the child to keep drawing and developing art skills, begins to reward the child with a monetary payment for each drawing. Before long, the child's intrinsic motivation for drawing is replaced by the extrinsic reward of money, so that when the payments stop, the child draws less than before the money rewards were introduced. This phenomenon is known as *crowding out*.

Crowding out appears to happen with grownups, in healthcare, as well. A pay-for-performance compensation plan sought to encourage physicians to use specified clinical guidelines, thereby reducing unwanted variability in care and increasing quality outcomes. Under one arrangement, they were offered no incentive payments to animate them to begin using the guidelines. Result: adherence to the guidelines rose slowly and remained at the higher levels achieved. Under an alternative arrangement, providers were given incentive payments to get them started. Result: their use of the guidelines rose rapidly, but when the payments stopped, their use of the guidelines fell below that of the group that received no incentive.[12]

Concepts familiar to behavioral economists, which account for seemingly irrational responses to incentives and are used to design better "decision architecture," include the following.[13]

Inertia. We humans like to keep doing what we've been doing; it's comfortable, we feel competent at it. Learning new behaviors requires effort and the rewards of the new behaviors come later.

Overconfidence bias. We have exaggerated faith in what we already are doing, which adds to the difficulty of changing to something different.

Hyperbolic discounting. Rewards at any distance are psychologically discounted, so they appear to be of low value. That is why we respond more strongly to smaller rewards that can be obtained immediately than to larger rewards that we have to wait for.

Loss aversion, risk aversion. Our fear of losing something we already have is greater than our desire to gain something new. Even if the two are equal in value by more objective measures, they are not psychologically equal in value. In combination with hyperbolic discounting, this means that rewards delivered months or years after the behavior will be less effective in motivating behavior change than smaller rewards delivered promptly. But it also teaches that people work even harder to avoid a small loss in the near term than they will to gain a large reward in the more distant future. Healthcare system managers have put this and the preceding principle to work by *prepaying* providers for performance, while placing those incentive payments at risk of having to be paid back if performance does not meet requirements. Providers will work harder to avoid paying back the reward than they would have worked to obtain it.[14]

Choice overload. When we have too many options from which to choose, we make poorer decisions about those choices, or refrain from making any choice at all. This is a close cousin to cognitive overload: too much information, too many things to decide, leads to errors.

Nudge. To nudge is usually to construct a choice architecture for individual decision makers so that the default is the best choice for most people most of the time, but opting out of the default and making a different choice is readily available when desired. But inertia and choice overload inclines people to stay with the default.[15] The best-known example of this principle in action is to sign up employees automatically for a retirement program that would be best for most of them. They are free to switch to any other available retirement plan they wish to, including none. But by making the default be some retirement plan, many more employees are covered than is the case when the starting point is nothing at all. Nudging has also been found to be hugely effective in regard to organ donation: where a person is automatically designated a potential donor unless she chooses to opt out, the number of donor organs available is vastly greater than in places where a person is not a donor unless she decides to opt in.[16]

Social comparison. The human perceptual and cognitive system works by making comparisons; we do not perceive value, or even physical quantities, such as the amount of ambient light, in absolutes, but only in comparison to something else. In the healthcare context, to motivate providers to achieve certain performance targets (e.g., patients prevented from becoming diabetic), feedback about the numbers achieved does not produce as much beneficial outcome as being able to compare one's performance to that of other providers (and seeing where we stand in relation to those others). But we are even more motivated when we are being compared—not to other providers in general, but—to those we view as similar to ourselves: similar practice, similar experience, same specialty, same general ability level, etc. One study found that feedback to cardiologists using peer-comparison reports was four times as effective as financial incentives in improving mortality rates in their patients.[17]

Cognitive heuristics. A raft of decision shortcuts that our brains evolved for us to use. Under many circumstances, they lead to quick and correct judgments, but with some kinds of decision tasks they lead to systematic errors. This is closely related to System 1 (fast and frugal) versus System 2 (slow and careful) thinking.[18]

Social truth. The phenomenon whereby we believe things to be so because others believe them, or others behave as though they are true, especially if those others are our peers. Objective, empirical reality is less compelling to us than social reality. As social animals, we feel a strong desire to move with our herd or tribe. This is closely related to social norms.[19]

Clinical decision support systems. Systematic, evidence-based guidance in making decisions, these days often using computer algorithms. These have been found to overcome the numerous tendencies toward error in decision-making.[20]

Consider this frustrating example of an effort to improve patient safety by one of the leading patient safety experts in the United States, hindered at every turn by the kinds of phenomena that behavioral economists think about. As discussed further in another chapter,[21] in an effort to reduce what at the time amounted to about 30,000 deaths (two-thirds of them in ICUs) from central line associated bloodstream infections, Dr. Peter Pronovost developed a five-step checklist of clinical best practices.[22] After much struggle against the indifference of administrators and resistance by clinicians, Pronovost was able to mount a demonstration of his approach in the ICU at his home institution, Johns Hopkins. Result: infection rates were brought down nearly to zero. Seeking to scale up use of his protocol, after great difficulty and resistance, Pronovost was able to arrange for 103 hospitals in Michigan to adopt the five-step procedure. After three months of using the protocol, infection rates came down from 2.7 infections per 1,000 catheter-days to zero. (Yes, zero).

Why was it so hard to get hospitals and clinicians to switch to a simple protocol that, data suggested, worked so well?[23] At meetings with medical staffs to plan the adoption of the checklist, little resistance was heard about the procedures per se. But objections did surface about the change of culture, that is, the introduction of a requirement to adhere to clinical guidelines rather than every physician doing as she or he chose. Presumably, there is utility in raising the quality of care and reducing adverse events. But, behaviorally, it proved quite difficult to get people to adopt a simple, slightly new, procedure. Most puzzling, perhaps, even the quality improvement and patient safety communities within the hospitals were reluctant.

Viewed through the lens of behavioral economics, such seemingly odd behavior is more understandable. Inertia, accompanied by overconfidence bias (reinforced by seeing that the great majority of patients did not acquire infections and die) and hyperbolic discounting, made any change seem unnecessarily burdensome and any future gains too small to be worth the effort. Loss aversion made it psychologically unpleasant to give up a well-learned procedure for a new one. What one is already used to doing is more automatic (cognitive System 1); learning to do something new requires more effort and thought (System 2). Moreover, the whole exercise represented loss of some of a professional's customary autonomy. Providers also have a bias toward action, so if all of the materials needed to perform the new procedure properly were not immediately on hand, rather than waiting around for it to be brought from another part of the hospital, they wanted to get on with the catheterization.[24]

Organizations fit better into the classical economic models. Individuals less so. Policy makers can aim incentives and disincentives at healthcare organizations. Then, the managers of those organizations can use the insights and experimental findings of behavioral economics to improve the decisions and practices of the many individuals who carry out the work of the organization.

PERVERSE INCENTIVES

The easiest way to see the impact of incentives on behavior is to look at incentives that push people and organizations in the wrong directions, that is, *perverse* incentives. These motivators of unintended and undesired behavior have been found in countless situations.

For example, under French colonial rule in Vietnam, the government set about to reduce the number of rats in Hanoi by offering a bounty for each rat tail brought in. Rather than leading to the eradication of rats, the program inadvertently set in motion a rat breeding industry.[25]

Closer to healthcare, in early nineteenth-century Britain, executed criminals were the only legal source of cadavers for medical education and training. As the number of medical students and surgeon trainees grew, and with them the need for more cadavers, hospitals and medical schools turned to underhanded suppliers who not only stole freshly buried bodies from graves, but who also created corpses by murdering people. The problem ended when the Anatomy Act of 1832 was passed, permitting the donation of bodies for use in anatomical study and surgical training.[26]

Moving closer in time to modern practice, the perverse effects of the most common payment scheme in American healthcare, fee-for-services, is a frequent topic of concern among health policy analysts. They point out that paying medical professionals primarily for treatment but not for prevention encourages medical conditions to be overlooked until treatment is required. Worse, it discourages prevention because a disease that is prevented means less need for future treatments and fewer fees to be collected. Never mind that prevention would improve the quality of the patient's life. Imagine the creation of an incentive structure that rewards prevention of disease, or preventing small illnesses from turning into large illnesses, when feasible. This is under way as part of the reform known as value-based purchasing of healthcare or pay-for-performance.[27]

Physicians are incentivized to perform services providing the greatest compensation for the least investment of time. Payment contingent on doing things—treatment, procedures, ordering tests, prescribing medication—ensures the doing of more things, including (in the worst cases) some treatments that are unnecessary or even harmful. Undesirable side effects of unnecessary treatments can then, of course, lead to the need for further treatment. Almost all of healthcare's major revenue incentives push in the direction of doing more to earn more.[28]

The centrality of money to the American healthcare industry is difficult to exaggerate.[29] Surgeon and popular author Atul Gawande has observed, "Our systems are incredibly optimized for sending bills. I can send the bill in like three keystrokes. But recording an allergy can be four different screens. So it's not built to set a goal for care and then accomplish it."[30] Elisabeth Rosenthal, formerly an emergency physician and currently editor-in-chief of Kaiser Health News, puts the matter bluntly: "In the past quarter century, the American medical system has stopped focusing on health or even science. Instead it attends more or less single-mindedly to its own profits."[31] Rosenthal has described the system in terms of "rules of the dysfunctional medical market," which include the following.

- More treatment is always better. Default to the most expensive option.
- A lifetime of treatment is preferable to a cure.

- As technologies age, prices can rise rather than fall.
- Economies of scale don't translate to lower prices. With their market power, big providers can simply demand more.
- There is no such thing as a fixed price for a procedure or test.
- There are no standards for billing. There's money to be made in billing for anything and everything.

Americans pay thousands for the same services that cost citizens of other advanced nations hundreds.[32] The U.S. healthcare industry charges more and delivers less than its counterparts in other modern nations.[33] We spend nearly a fifth of our national wealth on healthcare—more than twice as much per capita than the average of all other modern nations, while our "health system generally delivers worse health outcomes than any other developed country."[34]

The existing system has been described as *supply sensitive*, meaning that the patient population magically expands as needed to consume the supply of resources: hospital beds will be filled, operating rooms will be occupied, doctors will keep themselves busy.[35] This leads to great waste as well as increased risks to patients. But it keeps revenue flowing. Supply-sensitive care is a major part of why Americans pay the most to obtain the lowest-quality healthcare overall among modern, wealthy nations.[36]

Relatedly, providing useless treatments persists even after the uselessness of a treatment has been well demonstrated. For example, after research established that spinal fusion rarely did more for a patient than did physical therapy, medication, or the passage of time, the rates of doing the procedure only grew. What finally slowed the practice was insurance companies refusing to pay for it. What medical research knowledge could not accomplish, payment practices did.[37] Much the same has been true of meniscus surgery for aging knees. Repeated studies found that surgery offered no more benefit than a regimen of exercise and physical therapy. The control group in one clinical trial even received fake surgery: full preparations for surgery and shallow cuts that left scars looking just like those of surgery for the condition. Whether it was real surgery, pseudo surgery, or no surgery, patients always reported reduced pain. The *British Medical Journal*, on publishing the most recent study of the nonefficacy of meniscus surgery, editorially commented that the surgery is "a highly questionable practice without supporting evidence of even moderate quality" and that "Good evidence has been widely ignored."[38]

The shortage of primary care doctors and the surplus of specialists (who can charge more for their services) is another product of the existing perverse system of incentives in American healthcare. As we discussed in an earlier chapter, having more specialists than there are patients with problems that require their services leads to more patients receiving services that they do not need. That is supply-sensitive healthcare.

Sometimes *not* having health insurance leads to better care. Newborns with congenital anomalies but without health insurance represent losses to hospitals. So, when they can do it, nonchildren's hospitals transfer those babies to children's hospitals, where they receive better care for their conditions. But similarly afflicted newborns *with* good insurance will be retained by the nonchildren's hospital, so it can collect fees for delivering its lower-quality care to the infant.[39] However, by overburdening children's hospitals with an excess of costly, no-fee-paying cases, the ability of the children's hospitals to provide the superior care that they otherwise could have is reduced. Thus, children in neither type of hospital receive the best treatment possible.

How do patients get to hospitals, anyway? Medicare rules allow payment for ambulance service only if the ambulance takes the patient to a hospital. If the EMTs can resolve the patient's problem on their own, or if they deliver the patient to a more appropriate place, perhaps the patient's primary care doctor or dialysis center, the ambulance company might receive no payment. But if the patient winds up at the most expensive destination, a hospital, then the ambulance service will be paid.

Doctors who administer medications to patients in their offices, such as oncologists and ophthalmologists, purchase and keep those drugs in stock. After administering them, Medicare reimburses the doctors for the cost of the drug plus a 6% bonus. If either of two drugs would serve the patient equally well, although one is much more expensive than the other, who can blame some doctors for choosing the one that will pay them 6% of a large amount rather than 6% of a small amount? And thus, research indicates, more expensive drugs were preferred over less expensive drugs that did the same job.[40] And up go healthcare costs.

Most perversely, when errors occur and harm results, the most common consequence for the healthcare industry is that it makes more money. First, as we have seen in earlier chapters, hospitals are largely insulated from the financial costs of patients' injuries, including those due to negligence.[41] Worse, harmful errors are usually profitable. The logic of the conventional payment system for healthcare is inescapable: do more, get paid more. No matter how a person gets injured—be it a car crash, a fall, a mugging, or an iatrogenic adverse event—if the consequence is an injury that needs medical care, the healthcare industry can charge for it.

Nevertheless, research has been conducted which confirms and quantifies the expected. Medical researcher Sunil Eappen and a number of colleague looked at hospital revenues resulting from 10 major complications befalling patients undergoing nine common surgeries. Around 5.3% of surgical patients were unlucky enough to become victims of one or more of these serious complications. But those patients brought the hospitals in which they were treated a 330% greater profit margin than patients without complications (if they were privately insured; Medicare-insured patients generated 190% greater profits). The researchers noted, "Effective methods for reducing surgical complications have been identified. However, hospitals have been slow to implement them."[42] Who among us would be in a hurry to adopt procedures that will first cost money to implement and then reduce our bottom lines going forward? A co-author, Atul Gawande, commented in the same interview, "The more effective their quality control department is, the more they lose. We're talking about massive amounts of losses if they improve quality."[43] Similar conclusions have been reached by other studies examining how hospital revenues are affected by patient injuries.[44]

News reporting in 2012 indicated that only about 1% of hospitals had installed inexpensive sponge-tracking systems that could reduce the rate of foreign bodies being left during a procedure to nearly zero.[45] Multiply such decisions across the industry, and one sees the effects of the lack of disincentives (weak malpractice system) and the perverse incentives for tolerating iatrogenic injuries.

Intermountain Healthcare, one of the largest hospital systems and healthcare providers in the western United States, has been a leader in finding ways to deliver higher quality care with greater safety.[46] In one study, it found that by giving the right drugs at discharge to patients treated for congestive heart failure, Intermountain saved an additional 300 lives annually and prevented nearly 600 patients from having to be readmitted to the hospital. But making all of those patients better off made Intermountain worse off, because there are fewer opportunities to bill for care. Dr. Brent James, the head of Intermountain's efforts to improve quality, has said, "The health care system is perverse. The payments are perverse. It pays us to harm patients, and it punishes us when we don't."[47] At most hospitals, forgetting to give an antibiotic or giving poor instructions when a patient is discharged creates another chance to bill again if more treatment becomes necessary. Every adverse drug reaction Intermountain avoids deprives it of the revenue it could earn from treating the patient's newly inflicted problems. As Dr. Charles Sorenson Jr., Intermountain's chief operating officer has said, "We are really rewarded for episodic care and maximizing the care delivered in each episode."[48]

Investment in safety, under such contingencies, has little or no payoff. From the perspective of incentives, as long as there is "no business case for safety," patient safety can be expected to improve little and slowly—if it improves at all.

What the Law Could Do

When people and organizations behave in undesirable ways, where are the levers of change? Is it better to scold them and exhort them to swim against the tides of incentives and disincentives? Or do wisdom, fairness, efficiency, and effectiveness suggest we might be better advised to alter the contingencies of benefits and costs to turn them in a better direction? Rather than cursing self-interest, which is deeply bred into all of us, would it not be more advisable to put self-interest to work for the greater good?

Sometimes the law can be surprisingly good at arranging the puzzle pieces of our world so that carrots and sticks and the slippery paths to behavioral destinations are better aligned to produce desirable results. At their best, when webs of legal rules linking behavior to consequences work smoothly and are well woven into the fabric of daily life, they aren't even visible to most people. Law could also be put to work to make patients safer than they now are. What we have in mind, at least for this chapter, are legal reforms that could be (or in some instances already have been) adopted that would change the structure of incentives and disincentives within which healthcare organizations operate. An important word in that sentence is "organizations."

We do not envision the law's incentives as being directed at individual healthcare providers, but rather at the organizations that employ them or permit them to practice within their four walls. The purpose of these incentives would be to counterbalance the failures of the market to provide adequate incentives and the failures of tort law to make up for the market's perverse incentives. In the discussion that follows, we look beyond markets and typical tort incentives, in search of new incentives for safer healthcare.

By directing innovative incentives to the organizational level, the law leaves the industry to figure out how best to do what is needed to produce the results that will lead to greater rewards and fewer costs. The law avoids micromanaging caregivers. Hospitals and other healthcare organizations are free to explore their own safety-promoting solutions and to compete with each other. The research literature on patient safety is aimed at informing organizations of how they can create safer systems. The law would help provide the essential missing ingredients. Furthermore, organizations are more rationally responsive to incentives and disincentives than individual providers are.

INNOVATIVE SOURCES OF INCENTIVES FOR SAFETY

The government is in a position to use taxation and regulation in ways that might create incentives sufficient to lead those in the healthcare industry to think harder about ways to provide its important services more safely, even though such improvements require investment. The following innovative sources of incentives might provide healthcare organizations with the "business case for safety" that they need.

Pigouvian Taxation

The English economist who first recognized the problem of externalities was Arthur Pigou.[49] He was an important English economist who crossed intellectual swords with other important economists, most notably John Maynard Keynes. Born in 1877 on the Isle of Wight, Pigou was a bright young man. He won a scholarship to one of the most elite schools in England, the Harrow School in London, more than 300 years old when he enrolled. At the age of 19 Pigou was admitted to the University of Cambridge as a history student, but his interests were broad enough and deep enough that he won prizes in other fields: the Chancellor's Gold Medal for English verse, the Cobden prize in political economy, the Burney prize in the philosophy of religion, and the Adam Smith prize. In 1908, he became an economics professor at Cambridge, succeeding his former teacher, the eminent economist Alfred Marshall. For three decades, Pigou taught the course in advanced economics, central to the education of economists who would become leading figures around the world. Pigou's moral principles led him to be a conscientious objector during World War I. Instead of killing, he served with a Quaker ambulance unit and insisted on taking the most dangerous assignments.

Pigou described numerous market activities that generated costs to society that were not incorporated into the exchange between buyers and sellers and therefore left third parties picking up the tab for part of the real costs of some products and services. A conceptually simple example would be a factory that piped its toxic wastes directly into the nearest river. One of the costs imposed on downstream users of the river might be that they would have to purify the water that reached them before they could use it safely. The price the factory charged buyers for its products would not include that cost of decontaminating the water, because it was externalized from the cost of production onto others, who were not in on the transaction. If the factory had to find another way to dispose of its toxic wastes, the cost of that disposal would be built into the price of its products. Then the buyers would pay for the real cost of the product, without a subsidy from the public. In addition to such negative externalities (in Pigou's terms, "incidental uncharged disservices"), sometimes there are positive externalities: a market activity that produces social benefits above and beyond what a producer charges ("incidental uncharged services").

Pigou's idea for solving the problem of negative externalities was to tax them in an amount equal to their cost to society. Whatever cost the factory dumping effluents into the river created for its neighbors could be recouped through a tax on the company. A number of economic benefits would result, among them, the price of the product would more fully embody the actual costs of production; the incidental harms could be more efficiently managed; buyers could better judge the value of the product (without the distorting subsidy being involuntarily supplied by downstream neighbors). Facing the actual cost of waste disposal, the factory might be motivated to find innovative ways to make its products with fewer harmful byproducts or find more efficient ways to dispose of the byproducts (thereby lowering its taxes and its products' price, and remaining competitive). Such a tax has come to be called a "Pigovian tax."

The harmful side effects of healthcare could be subjected to Pigovian taxation. At present, tens or hundreds of billions of dollars are externalized by unsafe healthcare practices in the form of harms to patients, the costs of which are not reflected in the price of the services provided, but which are subsidized by unlucky patients, first-party health insurers, disability insurers, and taxpayers. As a result, American society underestimates the already exorbitant cost of its healthcare. Most troubling, from the perspective of patient safety, under the current arrangement the healthcare industry lacks incentives to develop safer procedures, protocols, and systems. Pigovian taxation could go a long way toward making up for the market failures and tort system deficiencies that Hyman and Silver have described. Pigovian taxation would help supply the business case for investment in safety that does not now exist.

Healthcare organizations could be taxed in proportion to the costs of the harms they generate. Call it an "iatrogenic injury tax." Research has already been undertaken to measure the cost of the iatrogenic harms the healthcare industry produces as a byproduct of the good it is paid to do. When the cost of safety externalities becomes important in setting the level of Pigovian taxes on healthcare entities, even more such research would be conducted to make sure they are reasonably accurate. Note, however, that the estimate of externalities need not be perfect and need not reflect all externalities. It need only be correlated with the harms of concern to be beneficial. Once the costs of harm started being internalized, healthcare organizations would be motivated to find ways to deliver healthcare more safely. As each organization developed and adopted safer systems and procedures, its iatrogenic injury tax would begin to fall. Innovative healthcare organizations like Intermountain would no longer find itself having to say that the health care system pays them to hurt patients, punishing them when they don't. Intermountain's accomplishments in patient safety would cause its iatrogenic injury taxes to be low to begin with and further safety improvements would reduce those taxes further.

Pigovian taxation of healthcare organizations would be most easily justified as an exercise in the state recouping what it has had to pay for the healthcare system's harms. But there is no economic or legal reason why such a tax could not be used to recoup the entire cost of such externalities regardless of who is the initial payer. Ultimately, all payers would benefit from increased safety and consequent cost savings. Plus, this benefits patients.

The interesting question is: what should a state do with those additional tax revenues? The wisest and most moral use, we suggest, is for a state to use the funds to provide services and compensation to the victims of harmful medical error. Those are the people whose losses are the basis for the tax, and those are the people whose needs are not being met. A state should resist the temptation to pour the additional revenue into its general fund. The purpose of the tax is to create increased incentives for safety. The expectation, therefore, is that the iatrogenic injury tax would steadily decline as healthcare organizations became safer and safer.

Denial of Payment Programs

One might say that Pigovian taxation of a sort already exists for healthcare in the United States. Programs akin to an iatrogenic injury tax have already begun being implemented by the Centers for Medicare and Medicaid Services (CMS) in the form of denial of payments to healthcare organizations for poor performance in matters of patient safety. Currently, CMS operates several different denial-of-payment programs.

An important difference is that the Pigovian taxation program we described would tax a broad domain of harmful results and leave to healthcare organizations all decisions about what to make safer and how to make them safer. Existing denial-of-payment programs are more targeted, thus giving more direction, but simultaneously allowing managers to find the narrowest range of investments necessary to avoid penalties. Another important difference is that denial of payment can be imposed almost as readily by private health insurers as by government, and some already have.

Unsurprisingly, the industry has protested. When you are accustomed to being paid whether or not you do a job well, and paid even more when you do it poorly, it must be disconcerting to suddenly be told that the payer is going to begin holding you accountable financially for at least some of the damage you do. A prominent hospital executive reportedly "pounded on a table at a Capitol Hill meeting, demanding to know who was responsible for the new law."[50] Spokespersons for the healthcare industry complained that the new accountability rules were "mean-spirited" and that reducing a hospital's payments but not those of the physician who committed the error was unfair.[51] Perhaps in answer to that criticism, CMS later amended the policy to also deny payment to surgeons for certain errors.

Never-Events

"Never-events" is the nickname given to iatrogenic injuries that are regarded as so unambiguous, serious, and preventable that they should never occur. They began life, more formally, as a list of "Serious Reportable Events" developed by the National Quality Forum (NQF) in 2001, the brainchild of NQF's CEO at the time, Dr. Ken Kizer.

The NQF list currently consists of 29 events grouped into seven categories: surgical, product or device, patient protection, care management, environmental, radiologic, and criminal.[52] Among the events on the list are surgery on the wrong body part or wrong patient, wrong surgical procedure, medication errors causing death or serious disability, maternal death or disability in a low-risk pregnancy, infant discharged to the wrong person, sexual assault of a patient, and others.

Backed by a congressional mandate, CMS took the view that what should never occur should never be paid for when it does occur.[53] And so, gradually, CMS has been growing its own list of iatrogenic occurrences for which payment is to be denied to hospitals and other providers. The criteria for placing an iatrogenic event on the list are that it be high cost or high volume; that when present as a secondary diagnosis, it results in assignment of a case to a diagnostic code that has a higher payment; that it could reasonably have been prevented by using evidence-based guidelines; and that it is identifiable based on unique diagnosis codes.[54] At present, CMS's list of no-pay never-events consists of the following.

Category 1—Healthcare Acquired Conditions at Inpatient Hospitals
  Foreign object retained after surgery
  Air embolism
  Blood incompatibility
  Stage III and IV pressure ulcers
  Falls and traumas—including fractures, dislocations, intracranial
    injuries, crushing injuries, burns, electric shock

Catheter-associated urinary tract infection
Vascular catheter-associated infection
Manifestations of poor glycemic control
Surgical site infection—following coronary artery bypass graft, bariatric surgery, or orthopedic procedures
Deep vein thrombosis/Pulmonary embolism—following total knee or hip replacement
Iatrogenic pneumothorax with venous catheterization

Category 2—Other Provider-Preventable Conditions in Any Setting
Wrong surgical or other invasive procedure performed on a patient
Surgical or other invasive procedure performed on wrong body part

Starting in 2008, if one of those injuries occurred, Medicare refused to pay the hospital for the additional cost of care associated with the never-event. It also prohibited the hospital or other provider from charging injured patients for the costs that CMS refused to pay. Charging patients for poor medical care that caused serious injury might strike the reader as surprising. After all, the Leapfrog Group,[55] a consortium of large corporate payers that has advanced a number of safety-oriented initiatives, saw things this way: "It goes without saying that a patient who is a victim of a never event should not have to pay for it. Therefore, the Leapfrog Group asks hospitals to determine, on a case-by-case basis, which costs are directly related to the never event and to waive those costs so that the patient and third-party payer do not receive a bill for those costs."[56] If, dear reader, you thought that healthcare providers were not so shameless as to bill for the wrong-side surgery in addition to the subsequent correct-side surgery, without being told by other industries and government that doing so was callous and greedy, you would be mistaken.[57]

In addition, one might ask, why not deny payment for at least some of the procedures that *caused* the secondary conditions (not just the additional cost of the secondary condition)? And, in 2009, CMS started to do so, ceasing payments to surgeons as well as hospitals for three inexcusable never events: surgery on the wrong patient, on the wrong body part of the right patient, or the wrong procedure.

By not paying for the additional costs of harm, CMS's goal is not so much to save Medicare money as it is to prevent harm from occurring in the first place. (The reduction in Medicare payments to hospitals for never events was been estimated to be less than 0.01% nationally.) By placing a healthcare organization's balance sheet at risk contingent upon harm to patients, an incentive is created to take steps to reduce the risk of those errors. Iatrogenic injuries have been inadvertent profit centers. CMS's "no pay" policy for selected never-events turns those unintended profit centers into losses. Causing an injury for one of the never events costs hospitals money because they do not get reimbursed for something they must nevertheless treat. Consequently—goes the theory—the no-pay-for-never-events policy creates an incentive to invest in prevention, at least of those particular harms. Eventually, the should-never-occur-events might become actual never-events.

The findings of research attempting to detect decreases in patient harm resulting from the program have been mixed.[58] But the studies are few, denial of payment for never events is still young and still developing, so that it and its effects are a moving target. Nonpayment for never-events is expanding in various directions. More providers are affected by what probably will be a growing list of conditions that trigger denials of payment. Denial of payment began with Medicare patients but has been extended to Medicaid beneficiaries. Private insurers—among them Aetna, BlueCross BlueShield, and WellPoint—have followed CMS's lead and refuse to pay for never events of their own choosing. A growing number of states, now more than half, have their own programs requiring hospitals to forego payment for never-event harms. Still, it might not be surprising to find little effect of such a small program (in terms of dollars at risk for any given hospital or provider); some or many hospitals might still judge new investments in safety not to be worth the returns.

Hospital-Acquired Conditions Reduction Program

Compared to the penalties for never events, the ACA has cast some economically similar but far wider nets.[59] One of those nets is the Hospital-Acquired Conditions (HAC) Reduction Program.[60] HAC is a nicely neutral-sounding euphemism for harmful injuries suffered by patients while being cared for in hospitals, injuries that are thought to be preventable by providing patients with higher-quality, safer, evidence-based care.

Studying how hospitals responded to an earlier initiative, the HAC / POA (Present on Admission) program, begun as part of the Deficit Reduction Act of 2005, CMS researchers conducted a series of interviews with hospital personnel. They found that, to avoid payment losses exacted under that program, hospitals implemented: "cultural shifts involving attention, commitment, and support from hospital leadership for patient safety; hiring new staff to assure the accuracy of clinical documentation and POA oversight structures; increased time burden for physicians, nurses, and coders; need to upgrade or purchase new software; and need to collaborate with hospital departments or staff that did not interface directly in the past."[61] These sound like constructive responses to the risk of losing revenue. If nothing else, they show that hospitals do *something* to respond to the risk of losing money. A separate question, though, is whether the steps taken actually reduce the incidence of HACs, or if different actions would be more effective.

Like all of the strategies discussed in this chapter, the HAC Reduction Program is intended to create incentives for hospitals to find ways to reduce hospital acquired conditions. In the several years leading up to the launch of the HAC Reduction Program, one in eight hospital patients suffered a preventable injury, according to a study by the Agency for Healthcare Research and Quality (AHRQ). That study also reported that the incidence of medical errors had decreased by 17% between 2010 and 2013, suggesting that further reductions in HACs were possible.[62]

The HAC Reduction Program requires the Department of Health and Human Services (HHS) to evaluate the patient safety performance of hospitals and to reduce by 1% *all* payments made to the poorest performing 25%. Thus, a hospital that billed Medicare $100 million dollars, but was in that worst-performing quartile, would lose $1 million of revenue. (Actual reductions averaged about half a million dollars to the 25% of hospitals that did suffer reductions in the past few years.) Hospitals for veterans, children, and other select groups, including "critical access hospitals," which serve geographic areas where they are often the only providers, are exempted.

Evaluation of hospitals' performance under the HAC Reduction Program is a complex mix of measures, weightings, and calculations of hospitals' performance in order to be able to rank them "on a continuous spectrum from best performing to worst performing." One purpose of that complexity is to adjust the ratings of hospitals for the risks presented by different patient populations served by the hospitals. Harms that are included in the index on which the rankings are based are the following.[63]

A subset of patient safety indicators developed by AHRQ (termed the Recalibrated PSI 90 Composite measure score, and referred to as Domain 1) is currently composed of the following 10 injury rates for

Pressure ulcer;
Iatrogenic pneumothorax;
In-hospital fall with hip fracture;
Perioperative hemorrhage or hematoma;
Postoperative acute kidney injury;
Postoperative respiratory failure;
Perioperative pulmonary embolism or deep vein thrombosis;
Postoperative sepsis;
Postoperative wound dehiscence; and
Unrecognized abdominopelvic accidental puncture/laceration.

A set of measures of infections developed by the Centers for Disease Control's National Health Safety Network (referred to as Domain 2) is composed of measurement scores for

Central line-associated bloodstream infection;
Catheter-associated urinary tract infection;
Surgical site infection;
Methicillin-resistant staphylococcus aureus bacteremia; and
Clostridium difficile infection.

We should not be surprised if, over time, additional HACs are added (and some, perhaps, subtracted), and the weighting of each element or domain is adjusted as the measures are tweaked in an effort to arrive at increasingly accurate (and thus increasingly fair) rankings.

Penalties for fiscal year (FY) 2015 totaled about $373 million for the 721 hospitals penalized. Of those hospitals, 45% were urban teaching hospitals, a fact that has itself been the basis of criticism of the HAC Reduction Program. If urban teaching hospitals are assumed to be the best (and the safest), then something must be wrong with CMS's measurements of safety. On the other hand, the measures might be on target. The validity of the measures receives continuing attention and, presumably, improvement. Another criticism of the HAC Reduction Program's approach is that the statute requires that the worst-performing quartile of hospitals be penalized whether or not they have shown improvement and regardless of how different the worst-performing hospitals' performance is compared to that of other hospitals (i.e., compared to hospitals just above the cut, which do not suffer payment losses). The difference between some of those above and below the 25% cutoff might be slight. (We hear echoes of our students questioning the fairness of the grades they received and of a Supreme Court justice explaining that "a line has to be drawn somewhere."[64])

For FY 2016, payments were lowered for 758 hospitals, costing them (and saving taxpayers) a total of approximately $364 million.

Loss of revenue is not the only cost these hospitals face. The worst-performing 25% of them have been made public by name, and beginning December, 2017, more detailed data are being posted on CMS's "Hospital Compare" webpage for all to see.

Hospital Readmissions Reduction Program

A third denial-of-payment program is the Hospital Readmissions Reduction Program (HRRP).[65] The HRRP penalizes hospitals that have excessive preventable readmissions for certain conditions. It was launched in FY 2013 with a 1% maximum penalty, which increased each year until reaching its current 3% maximum penalty. Every other year, more conditions were added to the list of those that are monitored and trigger penalties. (See Table 10.1.) The penalty is applied to *all* of a hospital's Medicare charges, not only those of patients who had the procedures being scrutinized. Of the three ACA programs that place hospital revenues at risk contingent on quality and safety, HRRP accounts for the largest proportion of dollars. Whether this program can be thought of as being concerned with iatrogenic harm is debatable, but we include it as a hybrid of quality improvement and safety improvement.

HRRP is aimed, obviously, at reducing the number of patients who are discharged from hospitals only to be readmitted to the same or a different hospital within 30 days—based on the notion that they had not been adequately treated or prepared for discharge the first time around (known as the *index* admission). The phenomenon of readmissions had been studied for decades and was found to occur more frequently among some types of patients and some hospitals and to be quite costly.[66]

Under HRRP, a hospital's readmission rate is risk-adjusted (separately for each of the monitored conditions) to yield a ratio of actual to expected readmissions.

Table 10.1. READMISSIONS MEASURES, MAXIMUM PENALTY, AND DATA PERIODS

Fiscal Year	Readmissions Measures	Maximum Penalty	Data Period
2013	Acute myocardial infarction, heart failure, pneumonia	1%	July 1, 2008–June 30 2011
2014	Same as FY 2013	2%	July 1, 2009–June 30, 2012
2015	FY 2014 measures plus hip/knee replacement, COPD	3%	July 1, 2010–June 30, 2013
2016	Same as FY 2015	3%	July 1, 2011–June 30, 2014
2017	FY 2015 measures plus CABG	3%	July 1, 2012–June 30, 2015

NOTES: CABG = coronary artery bypass grafting. COPD = chronic obstructive pulmonary disease. FY = fiscal year.

SOURCE: Tawnya Bosko, The CMS Hospital Quality Incentive and Penalty Programs: Where Do They Stand? 1(2) MiraMed Focus 1, 5 (Fall, 2015), Table 1. (Reproduced with permission of author.)

These ratios are used to calculate a *readmissions adjustment factor*, which is used to calculate a financial penalty to a hospital for excess readmissions. As you can see in Table 10.1, the data on which these figures are based are sampled from a three-year moving window, which better reflects each hospital's usual performance and avoids penalizing for a single atypical year.

Each year in several recent years (2015, 2016, 2017), nearly 80% of hospitals were penalized. The average penalty assessed against those that were penalized over those years ranged between 0.61% to 0.74%. The proportion of hospitals suffering the maximum (3%) penalty was 1.2%, 1.1%, and 1.8%. And the total dollars not paid by CMS were $428 million, $420 million, and $528 million.[67]

The changes from year to year reflect, in part, the program's evolving list of monitored conditions, which brings some hospitals within the program that had previously been outside of HRRP's purview until procedures were added to the list that those hospitals performed. Various other adjustments might be responsible, as well, so until the program achieves greater stasis, it will be difficult to assess its impact. We can, at least, say that, with about one in five patients who are admitted to hospitals being readmitted within 30 days, readmission is a problem that requires a solution.

The source of the readmission, however, deserves consideration, particularly how much of it is centered in the hospitals. American healthcare is infamous for its fragmentation and lack of continuity. The transition from hospital care to after-hospital care is a major one of those gaps. Among some, perhaps all, of the modern nations that have healthcare systems that outperform ours, a noteworthy difference is that they have healthcare providers whose job is to ensure continuity of care for patients.[68] An older surgeon once told us that throughout his career he rarely knew what happened to patients after the surgery was completed and they left the hospital.

If each piece of the still-not-well-assembled healthcare jigsaw puzzle has little to do with the others, then one potentially important criticism of HRRP is that the hospital has no control over what happens to a patient after the patient is discharged. Patients lacking economic resources or living in unsupportive or unstable circumstances might not be able to follow their discharge instructions, or afford medication, or have help in caring for themselves, even for something so basic as what medication to take and when. Hospitals serving poor populations might be at greater risk of poor readmission ratings, depending on whether and how well CMS takes such factors into account in its calculations. The nursing homes and rehabilitation centers to which some patients are discharged might provide such poor care that the patients do not improve as they would in better facilities. Why, hospital administrators ask, should they be penalized for the failings of other providers, who might be far more responsible for causing patients to deteriorate, necessitating readmission?

In self-defense, some hospitals have hired teams of nurses to check up on discharged patients wherever they go after they leave the hospital. Those nurses visit patients at home to see how they are doing and, if needed, offer assistance and advice. They march into skilled nursing facilities to check on patients, review charts, and question staff. Where they see problems they bring those to the attention of staff, sometimes to the point of instructing those staff on how to better care for the patient. But these "free" after-discharge nursing services last for—you will not be surprised to learn—exactly 30 days. Then those nurses are seen no more. They have new patients to track down, patients who have been out of the hospital for less than 30 days.

This picture reveals several things. Healthcare organizations are capable of adapting to the incentives they are faced with, even to the point of inventing a new nursing specialty. We could say that HRRP obliquely and unintentionally caused a new job, transitional care nurse, to come into being to provide continuity that traditionally did not exist in American healthcare. That these nurses keep an eye on their assigned patients for exactly 30 days shows how precisely hospitals can attune themselves to *their own* needs. This seems to demonstrate how well the incentives are working, even if they are not yet perfect and even if hospital executives feel that their institutions are being treated unfairly. More than anything, though, this suggests the need for scrutiny of healthcare organizations other than hospitals, such as skilled nursing facilities and rehabilitation centers. They need their own business case for investing sufficient effort and resources in quality and safety.

One caution about denial-of-payment programs more generally might be worth considering. Although they seem, at this early stage, to have nudged (shoved?) hospitals in the direction of increased patient safety, could it be that such interventions will not be the best strategy in the long run? If they are succeeding in helping to overcome the inertia of existing systems, so far so good. But once healthcare organizations become focused on the rules imposed by government or private insurers, and obsess about how best to profit under those rules, they might then do nothing else to improve safety beyond whatever level is required to avoid penalties. They might simply wait to see what, if anything, government and insurers demand next. Rather than promoting a "culture of safety" in the healthcare industry, denial-of-payment might be putting large institutional payers in charge of safety, and that might be far from sufficient to accomplish the goal. We do not know whether that is what will happen, but it is something to watch out for.

Enterprise Liability and Enterprise Insurance

A different way to restructure incentives in an effort to stimulate increases in patient safety is to move the financial responsibility for iatrogenic injuries, and perhaps legal responsibility as well, away from individuals (notably doctors) and onto corporate entities (hospitals and other healthcare organizations). A move of this sort has been under discussion for decades. It has never been imposed by law, although it has tended to arise organically in those healthcare organizations where doctors are salaried employees. Some reformers have long suggested that a shift of responsibility along these lines, mandated by state law, would generate several major benefits.

Two principal versions of this shift have been conceived. One, termed *enterprise insurance*,[69] would require hospitals and other concentrations of patient care, to provide liability insurance coverage for all patient care activities taking place within their institution's walls. The insurance provided would cover harms caused by any and every caregiver. Importantly, providers who are not employees of the organization would remain personally legally liable for negligent harm they might cause; lawsuits would be filed against the individual, not against the organization that paid for their liability insurance.

The other version of the shift-to-the-enterprise concept is dubbed *enterprise liability*, signifying that the enterprise not only pays the insurance premiums but also is responsible for all liability.[70] Lawsuits against individual providers would not be permitted; all claims would have to be filed against the enterprise. Under enterprise liability, the law would require all individual healthcare providers to be associated with a healthcare organization—a hospital, a nursing home, a healthcare plan, a private group practice, something. Any of those could be the enterprise that would assume legal responsibility for the torts of the individuals associated with it.

Many details of either of these plans would need to be worked out,[71] but for present purposes, we need get no deeper into the weeds. We want to give the reader a general sketch of the contemplated benefits, and some potential difficulties, of these enterprise-shifting proposals.

One major benefit is that a larger organization can manage insurance costs better than can individuals. It can purchase liability insurance for the group at a lower price than the sum of the individual policies that would have been purchased by the individuals being insured.

More important, as the insurance underwriting cycle periodically takes prices up and down, especially up and out of reach for some individuals, the organization is in a better position to plan for, manage, and smooth out the budgeting for those costs—better able to benefit from soft markets and weather hard markets.[72] Some organizations would even be in a position to self-insure. As the physician director of a major healthcare organization once explained to us, most doctors are still in solo or small practices; they are small businesspeople. The sometimes volatile nature of professional liability insurance can present serious cash flow difficulties to those small businesses. Being able to maintain liability insurance coverage even in the hardest of markets is their number one most unpredictable, and therefore most serious, business challenge. Placing the responsibility for providing that insurance coverage on an enterprise would take a major burden off of individual providers.

Many doctors might be happy knowing that they would never again write a check to pay a malpractice insurance premium or be named as a defendant in a medical malpractice suit. Those unpleasant experiences would be taken over by the enterprise with which they are affiliated. Other doctors would be less pleased, fearing a loss of control over some aspects of their professional lives.

With enterprise liability, when malpractice suits occurred, they would often involve fewer defendants, fewer conflicts among defendants, and fewer lawyers—whenever two or more of those who would have been defendants under conventional tort law had become joined within a single enterprise.

Most important from the viewpoint of encouraging investments in patient safety, enterprise solutions focus the liability and the costs on an organizational unit that is in a better position than any individual is to do something to prevent it.[73] By aiming lawsuits at the organizational level, enterprise solutions put pressure on the people who control those systems. By making the enterprise the financially responsible party, the enterprise gains an incentive to look for ways to be sued less, for less, and to pay lower premiums. A major way to do that is to find ways to reduce the incidence or seriousness of preventable harms, and in so doing the enterprise will increase safety.

For example, the enterprise will probably become fussier about whom it takes responsibility for. Fellow members of a professional group, such as surgeons, often know who the bad apples in their midst are, but currently have virtually no financial incentive to do anything about them.[74] Once their liabilities and their fates are more closely bound, however, it is thought that each will have an interest in making a colleague's work better and safer, keeping the managers of their enterprise well informed, and sometimes parting ways with a too-risky colleague. By refusing to absorb the losses resulting from incompetent and error-prone colleagues, the enterprise's insurance expenses will decline.

Even more beneficial, many of these healthcare enterprises will undertake inquiries into practices that promote higher quality care and greater safety. Rather than each individual having the daunting burden of trying to learn more about everything, committees can focus on different areas of potential improvement. Once better practices are identified, the enterprise could share those better practices by informing or training relevant members of the group. Some enterprises will be in a position to enforce what they have identified as best practices. Hospitals that have introduced new, safer practices, have sometimes found nonemployee physicians to be the most resistant to adopting the new procedures. With financial liability for those doctors shifted to the hospital, the hospital would have an incentive to exercise existing and new leverage.[75]

Where the better and the safer involve changes in technology or physical or organizational arrangements, or changes in staffing ratios or relationships, the enterprise is in a far better position to make those changes than any individual would be, and now the enterprise has the incentive to make those changes. If the enterprise is the hospital, or other center of patient care, it now has an incentive to overhaul its own systems to promote greater safety to lower its own insurance costs. If the enterprise is a group medical practice, the group will have a greater incentive to pressure the hospital to introduce safer systems.

Various objections to enterprise liability or enterprise insurance have been raised and answered.[76] But the most concerning of them is that it might not work. Creating new incentives by imposing new legal or financial responsibility focused at the organizational level could be done, of course. But whether that would bring about the organizational changes—the leadership, the systems, the integration, the training, the shared commitment of healthcare workers—that change the organization's effectiveness, is not at all obvious. The best answer to that concern is probably to make use of the 50 laboratories of legal experimentation that are the United States. If a few states decide to legislate one or another enterprise-shifting strategy, the rest can watch how it is working. Failed efforts can be abandoned; successful ones can be replicated elsewhere.

ET CETERA

Other incentive-restructuring arrangements are possible, of course. Our point here is to suggest that existing incentives often are unhelpful or perverse. They don't do enough to encourage safety, and they do too much to promote excess and risk and are reluctance to invest in safety. Changing the incentive structure that surrounds the delivery of healthcare, if it leads to changes in organizations and systems, is likely to change outcomes for the better for many patients.

11

Systems, Errors, and Responsibility—It's the System's Fault!

The primary objective of system design for safety is to make it difficult for individuals to err.[1]

The healthcare industry recently discovered the *systems approach* to analyzing and improving patient safety. Of course, everyone refers to the healthcare system as a "system." But it has long been regarded as a fragmented, poorly organized, disjointed system. Systems thinking, patient safety experts tell us, recognizes the importance of the matrix of technology, information, actions and inactions of co-workers, lines of communication, upstream planning and design (or lack thereof), and other features of the web in which healthcare workers are embedded. That matrix, as much or more than any individual actor in it, is coming to be viewed as the central axis of errors and the best opportunity for reducing errors, or detecting errors so they can be intercepted before they cause harm. A large part of the problem of patient safety, the healthcare industry has started to realize, is that healthcare evolved into its present condition more or less higgledy-piggledy, like the streets of Boston. Many patient safety experts believe that well-informed, evidence-based *system* redesign is the surest path to improvements in safety.

Medical safety experts can put a date on this discovery: 1994. That is the year that surgeon and patient safety movement leader Lucien Leape published an influential article in the *Journal of the American Medical Association*.[2] In that article, he reiterated the massive problem of preventable iatrogenic injuries and death in healthcare, explained why the culture of medical practice has been unable to stanch the flood of harmful errors, and summarized what he learned about the causes and prevention of errors from other fields, mainly psychology and human factors engineering, and from their applications in other industries.[3] "It seems clear," Leape wrote, "that if physicians, nurses, pharmacists, and administrators are to succeed in reducing errors in hospital care, they will need to fundamentally change the way they think about errors." And that new way of thinking is to comprehend and redesign the larger interconnected system, not just to focus on individual failures.

Healthcare, as Leape makes clear, is a late arrival to the systems revolution. Other industries began to scrutinize themselves from a systems perspective over a century ago, first to increase efficiency and productivity and later to improve safety. Although many forces pressed improvements in industrial safety, the principal means by which it was achieved was through system changes—equipment, organization, prevention of toxic exposure, training—rather than blaming workers as individuals or as members of particular groups (e.g., attributing errors and injuries to workers' ethnicity or national origin), as industry leaders had been insisting. Indeed, much of the conflict between workers and management was a debate over which of them should bear more of the responsibility for the poor health and inadequate safety of employees.[4] Industry argued that "few accidents were due to faulty machinery or inadequate safeguards and that most were the fault of the workers themselves."[5] Progressives, taking the systems perspective, argued that "industry was responsible for most accidents because of its failure to provide safeguards from dangerous machinery"[6]—among other systemic sources of harm.

The casualties of industrialization were likened to victims of an undeclared war.[7] "Speed-ups, monotonous tasks, and exposure to chemical toxins, metallic and organic dusts, and unprotected machinery made the American workplace among the most dangerous in the world."[8] An observer in 1907 described the problem: "Thousands of wage earners, men, women, and children, [are] caught in the machinery of our record breaking production and turned out cripples. Other thousands [are] killed outright.... How many there are, none can say exactly, for we [are] too busy making our record breaking production to count the dead."[9] Concern over working conditions reached a peak in the first decade of the twentieth century, with "contending forces of professionals, government, management, and labor, but also a panoply of journalists, social workers, consumer advocates, environmentalists, and industrialists."[10]

One factor contributing to increased safety in the workplace was a steep increase in the cost of accidents *to businesses* that sprang from the enactment of workers' compensation laws in most states between 1911 and 1921. This greatly heightened their concern for worker safety and produced an enduring decline in workplace accidents and disease from exposure to toxins. As long as the cost of injuries remained on the workers, investment in safety served no business purpose. But once the law started to internalize those losses to the employers, large firms in many industries saw their own benefits in increased safety. (Imagine what changes might develop if the law today instituted a similar reform, a "patient compensation system" that taxed healthcare organizations and providers on an experience-rated basis, thereby creating a fund with which to compensate victims of adverse events, regardless of causation or fault, asking only whether the injury or death occurred in the course of receiving healthcare.)

Companies began to protect workers from dangerous equipment, from power sources, and from toxic substances; searched for risks to abate; and provided protective gear. Corporate safety departments were created, run by engineers and safety committees composed of workers and managers. Private industry established the National Safety Council, partly to advance industry's views of the problem, but also to serve as a clearinghouse of safety information. Federal agencies were established—partly to advance research knowledge through the development of a scientific foundation for safety (e.g., National Institute for Occupational Safety and Health) and partly to enforce evolving safety regulations (e.g., Occupational Safety and Health Administration).

By the end of the twentieth century, the systems approach in relation to accident prevention was familiar in most industries: manufacturing, construction, transportation (most prominently aviation), the military, and others. The rate of workplace injuries had been brought far, far below the levels of a century earlier.

Examples are all around us. You probably have noticed that many instrument displays in cockpits are analog, not digital. That is because researchers long ago found that analog displays are more readily and accurately comprehended by human perception and cognition. Minimizing the risk of misreading or misunderstanding those displays leads to fewer mistakes. The cars we drive will not allow us to start the engine if the car is in gear, or shift out of park if the brake is not depressed. Our cars are beginning to warn us if we begin to drift out of our lane or a vehicle has entered our blind spot. When we design safety into technology, we reduce the need to rely as much on the operator to be aware of everything that needs attention and to do everything that needs to be done to perform a task safely.

Sometimes in the service of the budding corporate interest in safety, sometimes independently, new academic and professional disciplines emerged that took as axiomatic the influence that systems, situations, environment, and organizational structure had on behavior. The American Society of Safety Engineers was founded in 1911. Industrial-organizational psychology traces its origins to that same decade. Other fields developed, among them ergonomics, biomechanics, and human factors engineering. "As it matured, human factors broadened its purview and now focuses on all the circumstances in which errors occur—the equipment, environment, procedures, users, skill levels, training, or generically, the system."[11] Those others have helped various industries to design work tasks, work group interactions, person–technology interfaces, and so on to be safer as well as more efficient and productive. To prevent fingers and hands from being cut off by industrial equipment when a worker has a momentary lapse of awareness of where his hand is, danger was designed out of the machine, for example, by making it necessary to press two buttons, on opposite sides of the machine, compelling fingers to be out of harm's way before the machine could power on. Such design solutions were far more effective than imploring workers to "be careful," "stay alert," "pay attention to what you're doing."

Such fields, long concerned with understanding and modifying human behavior, have also long focused not only on what is found "in" people (such as personality traits or talent or temperament) or on what is put into them (through education and training), but also on the structure, the situation, and the environmental surround in which people do the many things we do in life and work. Social psychology, for example, has traditionally been concerned with the role of "situational" variables in understanding and influencing behavior. One of that field's founders, Kurt Lewin, summed up that perspective in a 1936 book that includes a simple equation positing that behavior is a function of the person and the environment, often operating in interaction with each other.[12] Nearly a century of research that followed has found many ways in which the features of the situations in which people find themselves affect behavior more powerfully than do the characteristics of the individuals in those situations. For example, whether people intervene to help others in distress has been found to be influenced more by features of the situation than by countless attributes of the individuals who are acting (or not acting), such as personality, attitudes, background, demographics, or values (including religious).[13] Daniel Kahneman, the Nobel prize-winning psychologist of behavioral economics fame, has summed up Lewin's insights as suggesting that when looking for a way to change behavior, you will find that the forces pressing behavior forward are overmatched by the forces inhibiting it. Change will come more easily from removing the inhibitory force, and that will usually be most effectively accomplished by changing the environment.

That healthcare managed to avoid systems thinking for the century that it did, although surrounded by such organizational-situational-systems-oriented ferment in academe and in industry, is remarkable in itself.

SYSTEMS THINKING IN HEALTHCARE

A comparison with routine practices in the aviation industry suggests how far behind healthcare is when it comes to prevention of errors. Table 11.1 lists some of the measures undertaken in the aviation industry to ensure safety. These practices do not rely on individuals alone to acquire competence and to perform vital tasks properly. The organization goes to considerable lengths to train employees, maintain their competency (items 1–5, 7, 9), and optimize their interactions with the overall team effort. Those individuals are taught how to work together effectively, not only to prevent disasters but to get the most out of the whole team when unanticipated troubles arise (items 6, 8, 10). Standardized procedures are thought through at a higher level than that of the individual and those standardized procedures are taught, enforced, and ensured (items 7–11). Through management, the organization collectively distributes work among employees so that the dangers of overwork are minimized (item 12) and as an organization evaluates the risks of new procedures before they are attempted (item 13). In healthcare, by contrast, none of these practices is part of the industry's customs.

Table 11.1. PRACTICES TO ACHIEVE COMPETENCY AND MAINTAIN PROFICIENCY IN AVIATION AND MEDICINE

	Aviation	Medicine
1. Training on and checked out before use of new technology	Always	Never
2. Recurrent training in simulator for skill maintenance	Twice a year	Never
3. Competency checks in simulator	Twice a year	Never
4. Emergency training (on both equipment and procedures)	Every year	Never
5. Direct observation and checking of practice	Every year	Never
6. Crew resource management training	Every year	Never
7. Standard-format briefing before any operational phase	Always	Never
8. Standardized communication/phraseology	Yes	Never
9. Standardized procedures for accomplishing tasks	Yes	Never
10. Standardized divisions of labor across team members	Yes	Never
11. Extensive use of checklists	Yes	Some use
12. Duty time limitations and fatigue management	Yes	Never
13. Risk assessment before novel operation	Yes	Never

NOTES: The table is a generalization. Different specialties in medicine make different assumptions and investments in competence, and there also is a slow but gradual move toward more proficiency checking, checklist use, and teamwork and communication training in medicine.

SOURCE: Sidney Dekker, Patient Safety: A Human Factors Approach (2011), at 4, Table 1.1. (Reproduced with permission of publisher.)

Many, probably most, iatrogenic errors can be traced to problems in the complex, fragmented, and disorganized system of healthcare delivery. The implication is that problems could have been prevented by correcting systemic arrangements that heighten the risk of error.[14] Where many systemic problems exist, the cognitive demands on individual practitioners to work safely can be herculean.

Systems thinking makes great sense as a strategy for reducing errors in healthcare. Often, some of the most beneficial error-preventive steps that could be taken are beyond the control of individual doctors, nurses, and other caregivers.[15] Healthcare organizations, not individual providers, choose whether to acquire a computerized prescription ordering system, to upgrade and standardize equipment in operating rooms, to provide for continuity in care, and so on.

Having discovered that they were killing patients at high rates because breathing tubes were sometimes inadvertently placed into the esophagus rather than the trachea, anesthesiologists figured out that they needed to monitor the patient's oxygen saturation in real time so they could detect the problem before, rather than after, brain damage or death occurred.[16] It was the hospitals, not individual anesthesiologists, that had the ability to equip operating rooms with the necessary tools for that job. Many hospitals refused to make that investment, despite the pleas of anesthesiologists. So anesthesiologists pressured them by adopting ethical rules requiring themselves to practice only in hospitals that equipped their operating rooms with such safety devices. With that, they gained the leverage needed to force hospitals to acquire the necessary equipment.

Moreover, individual humans have only so much working memory, only so much perceptual and cognitive capacity, and cannot be aware of and attentive to all critical factors all at one critical moment. To glance at a label in the middle of a surgical procedure and misread it, to momentarily lose sight of the fact that the patient is a child when preparing a dose of anesthesia, to be unaware of the newest and best test for a risky condition, any of which can and have led to disastrous outcomes, are ripe for system-level preventions.

Out of sight of her parents, one-and-a-half year-old Josie King had managed to turn on the hot bathwater and jump into the tub, scalding herself with second and third degree burns over 60% of her body. Later, in the pediatric intensive care unit (ICU) at one of the best hospitals in America, Josie received attentive, loving, skilled, care. After debridement and skin grafts, respiratory support, careful efforts to protect her from the lethal risks of infection and dehydration, and much else, she was found to be improved enough to move to a less intensive unit. She had survived the greatest dangers. But then she died of preventable errors.[17] She suffered cardiac arrest from dehydration after an inappropriate injection of methadone, which added to dehydration started by an infection that had gone untreated, and a doctor's recommendation to return her to the pediatric ICU was ignored. In this tragedy, we can see the system at work, multiple ways that disaster might have been avoided, and some of the system's fragmentation, including failed communication.[18]

Most adverse events involve a combination of both active failures and latent failures. Active failures are the unsafe acts performed by those in direct contact with the patient. Latent conditions are the numerous "resident pathogens" built into or allowed to inhabit the system. The latent conditions could be identified and corrected before they have a chance to lead to adverse events. Sydney Dekker, a human factors and system safety expert, offers this example:

> Suppose that an anesthesiologist has connected a patient to the anesthesia but had to twist the various cables and tubes to fit around the operating table. Now there is a kink in the tube that supplies oxygen. The patient's oxygen saturation quickly becomes problematic [and causes brain damage] before the kink is discovered and corrected.[19]

Systems, Errors, and Responsibility   183

The most immediate cause of this injury is the anesthesiologist's actions in arranging the oxygen tube in a way that put a kink in it. But Dekker outlines numerous other elements of the system that contributed to the problem and that could have been remedied in advance and probably prevented the tragedy:

- The arrangement of the table and the choreography of the surgical and anesthetic teams swarming around it.
- The decision by the manufacturer not to develop kink-resistant tubing.
- The decision by hospital management not to purchase kink-free tubing once it became available.
- That the accident occurred early on a Sunday morning, at the end of a week spent working through a long surgical backlog and after a particularly challenging operation that dragged on the preceding night because of unexpected complications.
- Management's decision not to train the surgical team on assertive communication, which led to the anesthetist's attention not being meaningfully directed to the developing oxygen saturation problem by those who saw the first signs of trouble.
- A preoperative time-out procedure was implemented some time earlier, but was ineffective because team members were never told what exactly each of them was personally supposed to review or remind each other of before an operation.
- The operating theaters in the hospital are located in a structure intended for other purposes.
- The computer interface does not reveal oxygen saturation problems clearly, while various other anesthetic machines in the operating theater all generate loud, underspecified, and intrusive warnings with a history of "crying wolf."
- The hospital had an adverse event reporting system in place, and a nurse anesthetist had previously reported a kink in tubing, but had been reprimanded by the hospital's risk manager for filing the report.

Referring to other contexts, safety systems guru James Reason has described the systems nature of accidents this way: "Rather than being the main instigators of an accident, operators tend to be the inheritors of system defects created by poor design, incorrect installation, faulty maintenance, and bad management decisions. Their part is usually that of adding the final garnish to a lethal brew whose ingredients have already been long in the cooking."[20] Reason's "Twelve Principles of Error Management," which elaborate on this notion, are summarized in Table 11.2.

None of this is to disregard the manifold failings of individuals. Dr. Leape, the leading proponent of the systems approach in patient safety, addressed a national conference of surgeons. "He opened the gathering's keynote speech by looking out over the audience of thousands and asking the doctors to 'raise your hand if you know of a physician you work with who should not be practicing because he

Table 11.2. JAMES REASON'S TWELVE PRINCIPLES OF ERROR MANAGEMENT

1. Human error is both universal and inevitable.
2. Errors are not intrinsically bad.
3. You cannot change the human condition, but you can change the conditions in which humans work.
4. The best people can make the worst mistakes.
5. People cannot easily avoid those actions they did not intend to commit.
6. Errors are consequences, not causes.
7. Many errors fall into recurrent patters.
8. Safety significant errors can occur at all levels of the system.
9. Error management is about managing the manageable.
10. Error management is about making good people excellent.
11. There is no one best way.
12. Effective error management aims at continuous reform not local fixes.

SOURCE: James Reason and Alan Hobbs, Managing Maintenance Error: A Practical Guide (2003), at 101. (Reproduced with permission of publisher.)

or she is dangerous.' Every hand went up."[21] A well-designed and well-functioning system will deal with those problems also, whether by rehabilitating or removing such individuals.

Where systems have been analyzed and redesigned for safety, benefits have been observed. But improvements often require hard work. Officials at Alton Memorial Hospital in Illinois wanted to reduce their medication error rate.[22] In that year, the incident rate for adverse drug events nationally was estimated to be between 2 and 7 per 100 hospital admissions, with an average cost (to patients and insurers) of $4,685 per adverse event.[23] Nearly half of Alton Memorial's medication adverse events were known to be caused by transcription errors: miscopying or omitting physicians' orders. The redesign team hired by Alton had been trained in an engineering approach known as Six Sigma, which requires them to proceed through these steps: *define* a goal, *measure* every relevant aspect of the process, *analyze* what is causing errors, *improve* (redesign) the process, and evaluate (*control*) the effects of the changes.

The team set a goal of reducing transcription errors by 50%. They studied the existing medication ordering process and found that each unit within the hospital had its own medication ordering procedure. Some of those created confusion. Nursing staff frequently interrupted pharmacists about problems such as missing medications. (Interruptions are a major cause of losing focus on the task one is engaged in, leading to errors.) The design team also found that physicians' handwritten orders often were illegible.

The team conceived of several changes that could improve the process:

- Developing a standardized form for ordering medications (thereby eliminating a confusion-inducing prescription form that some units employed).

- Adding 10 lines of space to the new forms to prevent doctors from cramming medication names into a small space, as well as darkening the margins so that doctors would not be tempted to write outside the faxable area.
- Sending intravenous orders to the pharmacy before 6:00 AM so they could be prepared before the day got busy.
- Creating a "missing medication sheet" to fax to the pharmacy rather than informally phoning pharmacists at random times and interrupting them.
- Replacing any fax machines that produced poor copies of orders.
- Working with all hospital units (except the ICU) to design and implement a standard medication order process that met the units' needs.

Interviews with nurses revealed that they wanted quick access to prescriptions, quick pharmacy turnaround, access to patients' medication history, mobility of medication information, a method for double-checking prescriptions, and trustworthiness of the filled prescriptions. To meet those needs, the team created a universal, electronic patient care activity record coupled with a medication administration checking system.

Note that this was not a computer-based order entry system. Had it been, more benefits could have been achieved, including greater oversight and automated warnings when some types of errors were about to be made (drug interactions, dosage errors). Even so, considerable benefits were achieved. To evaluate the impact of their redesign, the team collected data during random audits. The results found that the overall reduction of errors was 90% (far exceeding the project's goal of 50% improvement).

The relative contribution of individual and system factors can be complex and subtle. Michelle Mello and David Studdert[24] analyzed data that came from five malpractice insurance companies located in four regions of the United States (whose insureds were 33,000 physicians, 61 acute care hospitals, and 428 outpatient facilities) consisting of random samples of closed-claim files from each insurer and reviewed by board-certified attending physicians, fellows, or final-year residents in surgery (for surgical claims), obstetrics (for obstetric claims), or internal medicine (for diagnosis and medication claims). Each review took, on average, about an hour-and-a-half to complete.

According to Mello and Studdert, "Individual factors were highly prevalent, contributing to injuries in 96% of the 889 cases involving error." "Judgment errors were the most common type of individual factor, present in 70% of cases."[25] This is a far higher proportion than generally assumed by many advocates of systems approaches to the iatrogenic injury problem,[26] and it suggests that individual failures dominate the landscape of errors. Mello and Studdert note, however, that "system factors . . . were implicated in 56% of injuries."[27] Even more important, they argue that the mistakes made by individuals often were mistakes for which the system can be viewed as having set the stage. "[T]he causality of medical injuries is multifactorial and weblike."

"[I]n analyzing the complex causality typically associated with medical injury, it is difficult to cleanly separate individuals and their failures from the larger environments or systems in which they work."[28] In addition, an average of three separate contributing factors were identified for each error-caused injury, and many had four or more contributing factors.[29] Put simply, there are multiple, interlinked causes of harmful errors, and therefore multiple pathways exist for finding ways to prevent those errors. System fixes are a promising strategy for preventing many of them.

FORCES WORKING AGAINST THE SYSTEMS APPROACH

Despite isolated success stories, the healthcare industry is still in the early stages of adopting systems thinking, and an even earlier stage of doing much of it. One of the most basic of tools, the checklist, is only starting to catch on. Safety specialists spend more time writing about the systems approach and imploring their colleagues and administrators to start redesigning healthcare organizations and procedures from a systems perspective than actually carrying out such transformations. The systems revolution in healthcare remains somewhere beyond the horizon.

Why is medicine so far behind other industries, even though the stakes (for patients) are so high? As Dr. Leape noted, with dramatic understatement, "It is curious . . . that high error rates have not stimulated more concern and efforts at error prevention."[30] Those who have been trying to promote patient safety through systems redesign have suggested a number of explanations.

One is that the horror that produces public outrage has not reached, and cannot reach, the crescendo it would if a similar number of deaths resulted from planes crashing. If healthcare were commercial aviation, two jumbo jets would be going down every day in the United States, killing all on board.[31] But hospital injuries and deaths occur one at a time, quietly, privately. The "unhideability" of plane crashes, and the large clusters of lost lives, ensured that commercial aviation would make itself very close to unfailingly safe or there would be no commercial aviation industry.

Another reason, little discussed by patient safety experts, is economic. As we note elsewhere in this book, no "business case" yet exists for undertaking the expensive challenges of renovating the healthcare nonsystem to make it safer.[32] Earlier we noted that the systems revolution in safety in other industries was prompted in part by the cost of worker injuries being shifted by law onto those businesses. As long as the cost of worker injuries and deaths was borne by the workers and their families, businesses had little incentive to invest in preventing accidents. In healthcare, the incentives problem is even more challenging. Studies have found that errors actually increase healthcare industry revenue.[33] Why would any executive, in any industry, invest millions in a project which, the more successful it is, the more it will reduce future bottom lines?

We agree with safety advocates in healthcare that improvements in patient safety are more likely to be achieved through r-designing systems than by hectoring individuals. Many opportunities for system redesign present themselves—to mention a few major ones: reduce fragmentation in healthcare, reduce diffusion of responsibility, and change incentive structures to create a business case for safety. The tools of applied cognitive psychology and human factors engineering— forcing functions, standardization, simplification, checklists, time-outs, double-checks, etc.—are ready to fill the patient safety cavities of healthcare. But until ways are found to make the systems revolution a reality in healthcare, and for the benefit of patients, systems talk will remain little more than talk.

Adding to the perfect storm blowing against systems reforms is medical culture, which seeks individual control (although not individual accountability),[34] and the eagerness of hospitals and other healthcare organizations to shed responsibility by also giving away control they could exert.[35] In healthcare "[t]here is a strong preoccupation with the autonomy and discretion of its individual actors."[36] Part of the training of doctors is to value their autonomy. They want to choose what they will do and how they will do it. Evidence-based suggestions from consensus committees might be of interest, but directives from above are unwelcome. Physicians resist practicing what is derisively referred to as "cookbook medicine." At the same time, they strive for individual professional flawlessness. As Dr. Leape noted, "Physicians are socialized in medical school and residency to strive for error free practice. There is a powerful emphasis on perfection. . . . In everyday hospital practice, the message is equally clear: mistakes are unacceptable."[37] To acknowledge the high incidence of harmful errors and to recognize that much of that error prevention is beyond their personal control would be akin to admitting a massive professional failure, individually and collectively.[38] But until the organizational aspects of the problem are correctly diagnosed, they cannot be cured.

American hospitals, and healthcare more generally, are almost the antithesis of the systems approach. They are famously fragmented, sometimes chaotic, with what organizational experts regard as peculiarly divergent lines of authority and power—a nonsystem in which we should not be surprised to find errors to be relatively common.[39] The transition out of the hospital and on to the next site for recovery carries considerable risk for failure. In contrast to some European healthcare systems, in the United States, no means has been developed to ensure continuity from one setting to the next. The hospital does not know what is happening to the patient, and the next site—be it a skilled nursing facility, a rehabilitation hospital, or the patient's home—doesn't have access to the information that the hospital did about the patient's needs.[40] In fact, rather than making themselves more capable of organizing their systems to improve coordination, many hospitals have stepped up their fragmentation by engaging with more, rather than fewer, independent contractors—over whom they have limited control.

Imagine an airline where one entity owns the planes, while pilots are independent contractors who apply for "privileges" to fly the planes, which they are routinely granted. The pilots do their jobs more or less as they choose, with the airline having little say in the matter. Periodic renewal of privileges is fairly automatic, except for pilots who have crashed and are probably no longer applying for anything. Further, suppose pilots, not airlines, bring in the customers—another reason to grant flying privileges less than rigorously. When a pilot does crash, his or her insurer, not the airline's, picks up the tab. (Pilots will have worked out a collective deal with their liability insurers such that all pilots who fly the same types of planes and routes pay the same amount in premiums, without regard to differences in risk posed by different pilots.) The result would be that airlines would have little incentive to worry about how well the pilots flew, and little authority to do anything about it anyway.

The great paradox is that safer practices will come from systems, but systems require organizations imposing increased supervision and oversight, and that is something that physicians have traditionally resisted. At the same time, healthcare organizations don't want to assume that level of responsibility and control. Thus, physicians like the usual arrangement because it preserves their autonomy, even though it requires them to be financially responsible for negligent harm they cause. Hospitals like that arrangement because it insulates them from responsibility for the doctors' errors, even though (or perhaps especially because) it denies them control over the work of doctors. Increased control by systematizing organizations implies decreased control by individuals, decreased autonomy, and decreased variation in how providers treat patients. You can't have systems working without individual providers giving up their freedom to do their work as they wish to do it. So no one on either side of the equation is eager to make the changes that safety experts believe are necessary.[41]

One of your authors sat in on a continuing education class for hospital staff, with the focus on advancing the use of TeamSTEPPS to improve patient care.[42] During question-and-answer time, one of the nurses described how at her hospital a newer, safer version of a procedure had been adopted and taught to staff in an effort to bring down infection rates. But an attending physician refused to employ the new procedure, insisting on his right (as an independent contractor) to do things in his own way. What can the staff do, the nurse asked, when a physician insists on using his customary procedure, rather than the newer, safer, evidence-based practice the nursing staff were instructed by the hospital to use? It seems clear that, if the systems approach is to bloom, major changes will need to occur in existing cultures and organizations.

ACCOUNTABILITY AND LIABILITY

In one way, introduction of the systems approach in the healthcare industry has already delivered benefits: rhetorically. Many advocates of the systems approach to solving the problem of iatrogenic injury like to point out that it redirects responsibility for harmful errors away from individual providers. Rather, the errors are the system's fault. As leading patient safety authority Robert Wachter explains, "in most circumstances the doctor or nurse holding the smoking gun is not truly 'at fault,' but [is] simply the last link in a long error chain."[43]

Recall the example earlier in this chapter of the anesthesiologist and the kinked oxygen tube.

The healthcare industry's traditional inclination to "treat . . . quality problems and errors as failings on the part of individual providers" [44] will become a relic of an unenlightened past. Even better, systems thinking leads to the argument that medical malpractice lawsuits must be misguided and unfair. As Dr. Wachter notes, "The modern patient safety movement replaces 'the blame and shame game' with . . . *systems thinking*."[45] If the system is at fault, individual providers are not, and malpractice claims against those providers must be wrongheaded.

Systems talk also pays psychic dividends. If a harmful error was ultimately the system's fault, then the system failed; I did not. In fact, we should all "ultimately move on to a deeper understanding that no one is to blame."[46] People in all kinds of situations look for something, anything, to deflect blame onto. The system is the best of targets. It is everyone, so it is no one. And it can't fight back.

But the systems approach—as opposed to systems rhetoric—cannot mean that there is no responsibility, no accountability, and no liability. Saying "the system did it" does not make no one responsible. The systems approach makes more sense as a suggestion that because major responsibility lies with the system, the accountability belongs to whoever controls (or should control) the system. Presumably, that would be the corporate entity or its officers, directors, and managers. They have the responsibility to design and manage the system, to make it safe, and if it is not safe they have neglected their duties. In other words, the systems approach does not lead to *no* responsibility; it leads to a *refocusing* of responsibility. When a preventable injury occurs, tort claims would be brought against those responsible for the system that caused the injury, or which failed to prevent the injury. That, in turn, would ideally incentivize those managers to improve the system and reduce errors and injuries as part of an iterative process of continuous quality improvement. Workers within the system could obtain their freedom from liability only by giving proper deference to the healthcare organization and its continually improving ways of doing things.

EXPANDING THE VIEW OF THE SYSTEM

We might usefully enlarge the frame through which we view what constitutes the system. Surrounding the healthcare organization and its workers, technology, and activities are larger systems: governments, laws, economies, universities, technological innovation, and other institutions of society. Those, too, have important impacts on health and healthcare. No one today should be surprised to learn that healthcare is a complex, multidisciplinary activity, requiring the efforts of an array of caregivers moved forward increasingly often by an army of researchers and technologists who are themselves supported by the infrastructure of those major societal institutions. Amazing innovations, only a step removed from science fiction, are developed in research laboratories staffed by scientists and others in universities, industry, and government (e.g., the National Institutes of Health) and eventually placed into the hands of healthcare providers to deliver the eventual benefits of those innovations to patients. The importance of those researchers to healthcare is suggested by the facts that for every winner of the Nobel Prize in Physiology or Medicine whose training had been in medicine, five were trained in some other field—biochemistry, biophysics, bio-engineering, cell biology, microbiology, epidemiology, genetics, genetic engineering, molecular biology, virology, or some other discipline. Change will need to come to our present clunky healthcare system if it is to make fully effective use of those innovations. As George Poste (past president for research and development at SmithKline Beecham, founding director of the Biodesign Institute, and currently chief scientist for the Complex Adaptive Systems Initiative at the Arizona State University) has explained:

> Precision medicine is a holistic concept that requires sophisticated integration of diverse functions across the biomedical enterprise. Unfortunately, integration is starkly absent in the landscape of contemporary biomedical research and clinical care. The healthcare ecosystem, from fundamental research to tertiary care, is characterized by isolated silos of specialized expertise, protracted translation of research discoveries to benefit patients, fragmentation and poor coordination of care services, bloated administration and bureaucratic practices and major inefficiencies in the capture and use of information to optimize individual patient care, minimize error and establish best practices.[47]

Thus, the healthcare team at its best involves far more than healthcare organizations and providers, and to work most successfully, they all need to be better organized into an effective and efficient system than they have been conventionally.

One could also count as part of the healthcare team those members of Congress who help create the legal infrastructure of healthcare. For example, those legislators in the 1940s who created the world's most powerful medical research institutes (e.g., National Institutes of Health, National Science Foundation, Centers for Disease Control and Prevention—where innovations are created and tested), and who passed legislation funding the construction of hospitals throughout the country (where the benefits of those advances could be made available to many more Americans).[48] And who, today, are in a position to restructure the legal environment that facilitates the work of private industry to create, develop, and market innovations that can make healthcare safer as well as more effective.

If we expand our view from healthcare to health, we discover still more invisible contributors and begin to see how much more the world we live in is responsible for our health and safety, enabling us to live decades longer than our ancestors of only a few generations ago. Doubtless, it is better not to become sick or injured in the first place—avoiding entirely the discomfort, pain, anxiety, agony, and risk of life-changing disability or even death. Although we are thankful for the caregivers who rescue us from serious illness or injury, those whose efforts saved us by preventing us from ever being exposed to those harms in the first place are all but invisible to us.

Consider, for example, the developers of vaccines.[49] Were we to contract polio or smallpox, we would appreciate the caregivers who came to our rescue. But what of those who develop and manufacture the vaccines that prevent us from ever even contracting those and other deadly and disabling diseases? How many notes of thanks have been sent to those scientists and drug manufacturers for the lives we get to live untroubled by the suffering that would have been wrought by those serious diseases? We don't even know who they are. Their role in keeping us free of disease is barely a part of most people's awareness of what has made our long, healthy lives possible.

The great majority of Americans are even more unaware of those whose contributions were in the nature of advancing public health through prevention. Over the past century-and-a-half, their efforts led to plunging rates of mortality and morbidity from infectious diseases and nearly a doubling of life expectancy. The major killers for thousands of years were diseases such as smallpox, cholera, plague, tuberculosis, and diphtheria, which decimated populations well into the nineteenth century. But the major infectious diseases in the Western world were largely defeated even before the disease vector had been identified, before specific medical treatments had been developed to fight them, before penicillin became available for use with patients (in the mid-1940s), before vaccines had been developed and deployed to prevent them. The death rate from infectious diseases in the United States fell by 75% from 1900 to 1940.

What brought the disease incidence downward so massively were systemic alterations of our environment: sewage disposal, water treatment (including widespread use of chlorination to kill waterborne diseases), food safety (from farm practices to markets, as well as greatly improved refrigeration), organized solid waste treatment, and improved housing (reducing persons-per-room density reduced the spread of diseases, such as tuberculosis). From Figure 11.1, it is evident how great the decline was of disease and death (and increased life expectancy) in the twentieth century owing primarily to public health–related infrastructure improvements undertaken by people we rarely associate with our health—engineers, manufacturers, construction workers, political leaders, lawyers, bankers, and bureaucrats.

Ironically, given the revolution of systems thinking in the patient safety movement, healthcare organizations, especially hospitals, continue to make themselves elusive targets of legal accountability. They minimize their own exposure to liability by making heavy use of independent contractors and outside physicians granted privileges.[50] The result of that organizational structure is that tort litigation has to target an erring actor close in time and space to the harm and seems to overlook the rest of the causal matrix responsible for the iatrogenic harm.

From the viewpoint of those who would like to motivate systems solutions and would prefer to see more accountability aimed at the organization level rather than at individual providers,[51] those arrangements are a significant problem.[52]

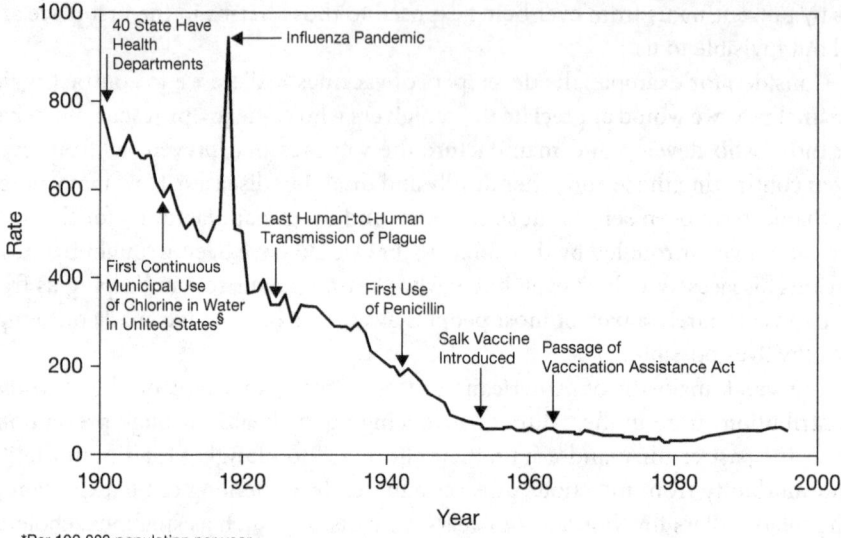

*Per 100,000 population per year.

†Adapted from Armstrong GL, Conn LA, Pinner Rw. Trends in infectious disease mortality in the United States during the 20th century. JAMA 1999:281:61–6.

§American Water Works Association. Water chlorination principles and practices: AWWA manual M20. Denver, Colorado: American Water Works Association, 1973.

Figure 11.1. U.S. death rate, 1900–1999 (per 100,000 population per year).
SOURCE: Centers for Disease Control, A*chievements in Public Health, 1900–1999: Control of Infectious Diseases*, 48(29) MMWR Weekly 621–629 (July 30, 1999), Figure 1.

LEGAL INNOVATIONS TO PROMOTE HEALTH SYSTEMS REFORM

We need to be alert to ways that the law can interact with the healthcare system to encourage systems-oriented solutions in patient safety. As part of the healthcare system's supra-system, one might say, the existing malpractice litigation system already has played a role by creating the impetus for research on iatrogenic harm, leading to the Institute of Medicine's (IOM) report, *To Err Is Human*, in turn stimulating the patient safety movement into being, whose participants overwhelmingly advocate adoption of the systems perspective as a fundamental reform for making healthcare safer.

Law could make more, and more effective, contributions to the larger law–healthcare system. For example, enterprise liability, discussed in the previous chapter, is one way to restructure healthcare organizations to make them the primary (perhaps the exclusive) target of lawsuits. The idea is to change the relationship of providers with the healthcare organizations they work within, shifting responsibility from individual providers to the enterprises they would (be required to) associate themselves with. Healthcare organizations would pay for the damage caused by the errors of those working under their supervision and protection. In response, healthcare organizations would have the incentive to make their systems safer and to require those under their protection to abide by the organizations' patient safety rules and procedures.

Changes in economic incentives in the form of programs denying payment when preventable errors occur have already been introduced into reimbursement policy and show some evidence of stimulating system improvements.[53]

Even more specific regulatory reforms might be considered. For example, certain types of equipment might be required to be present in all operating rooms. (Recall anesthesiologists' discovery of the need to continually monitor surgery patients' oxygen saturation levels and the refusal of some hospitals to purchase the necessary equipment.) If the lack of continuity of care—as a patient moves into, through, and transitions out of the hospital—contributes significantly to dangerously inadequate care,[54] then a new role could be required: individuals assigned the specific task of providing such continuity. Other ways to reduce fragmentation, or its harmful impact, might be identified and well-validated fixes could be legally engineered into the healthcare system. Another possibility is that minimum staffing ratios could be required. Such patchworks of regulation are not ideal, but a small number of them adopted to address problems that account for inordinate shares of harmful errors might be better to have than not have.

The challenge for the future will be for law and policy to figure out what legal innovations would be able to propel, and how far, and at what cost, the transition from risky fragmentation to more coherent, safer, systems.

12

Regulation and Engaged Surveillance

We talk about the interests of the medical profession, the interests of the hospitals, the interests of the nursing homes; but above all else, the whole of the health care system exists for one person, and that's the individual who needs it.[1]

THE SHORTCOMINGS OF GOVERNMENT SAFETY REGULATION

In the abstract, it might be tempting to consider the imposition of substantive government regulations to protect patients from the widespread medical errors that harm hundreds of thousands of Americans each year. There is some precedent for federal intervention to protect consumers from what might be characterized as a major public health threat. This, in large measure, was the basis for the government's determination to impose safety regulations on the automobile industry in the 1960s. The public health case for regulating medicine is, arguably, stronger than that concerning autos, not only because of the size of the problem but because of the ineffectiveness of medical malpractice litigation. As the outstanding malpractice analyst Tom Baker has observed, "The alternative [to malpractice lawsuits] is intrusive government control—maybe not today, but certainly tomorrow."[2] The logic of this observation seems persuasive—when oversight through the courts is unavailing a gap is opened which invites public regulatory intervention. Moreover, the federal government's huge monetary commitment to finance medical treatment through the Medicare and Medicaid programs pushes in the same direction. There are, however, significant reasons to reject government-mandated means-based prescriptive standards (i.e., specifying required practices) as a legal strategy to address medical error.

The Auto Regulation Story

Perhaps the best place to begin in examining why the idea of governmental command and control regulation of medicine should be approached with caution is by looking at what happened when a technology-specifying strategy was adopted in the automobile industry. The passenger car was the result of a series of technical innovations that, in the first decade of the twentieth century, resulted in the manufacture of a reasonably reliable vehicle. From the outset, the automobile was a phenomenal popular success in America. Within three decades the auto industry had become the largest manufacturing business in the country. It did so, in significant part, because in 1908 Henry Ford revolutionized the manufacture and sale of cars with his assembly line production of the relatively inexpensive and durable Model T. The Model T's price put it within reach of middle-class Americans and car ownership became a key indicator of financial and social success. The growth of the auto industry was spurred by the federal government, which in 1916 embarked on the first of many acts to subsidize road building. The government's support for highways made it ever more difficult for other modes of transportation to compete,[3] and by the 1920s the auto had become the dominant form of travel.

The burgeoning auto industry faced a major marketing challenge in the 1920s. Inexpensive functional cars had saturated the market. If the auto business was to continue to expand, replacement sales—that is, the swapping of older models for newer ones—would be crucial.[4] The solution the industry adopted was to design and produce ever larger, faster, longer, and wider cars featuring dramatic styling differences. This had the effect of making older models appear out of date and unfashionable. The styling focus, coupled with dramatically expanding advertising efforts, drew consumer attention away from any consideration of safety. The auto became a status symbol and an expression of individual taste.

As cars flooded onto the roads there was a rapid and dramatic increase in vehicular accidents and deaths. Within 25 years of the first recorded auto fatality (the running down of Henry Biss by an electric taxi in New York City on September 13, 1899) cars had become the leading cause of accidental death in the United States and the leading cause of death, bar none, of young people. For each person killed in an auto accident it has been estimated that at least another 35 were injured.[5] Year by year, the toll of deaths and injuries mounted. The escalation of power, speed, and size afforded drivers a shrinking margin for error. Manufacturers, however, made little effort to compensate for these challenges or design for accidents.

In reaction to the rising tide of accidents car builders argued that the problem lay with bad drivers and poor highways rather than auto design, and they invested substantial effort and resources in convincing the public of this. The industry supported driver education and safety initiatives. It established highway safety organizations like the Auto Safety Foundation,[6] which steered the accident debate in the direction of police enforcement and the punishment of those caught violating traffic rules. According to this approach it was drivers, not cars, who were to blame for accidents and injuries.

This message became gospel as auto manufacture grew into the behemoth of American industry. By the early 1960s, one-sixth of America's workforce labored in auto-related jobs. The auto industry was responsible for 11% of the gross national product. GM was the largest corporation in the United States. Ford was number two, and Chrysler, number five.[7] It was easy to conclude that, accidents notwithstanding, GM President Charles Wilson's braggadocio was justified when he declared, "What's good for General Motors is good for America."[8]

But all was not well for America's drivers or the companies that manufactured their cars. Events in the late 1950s signaled an approaching period of challenge. The Soviet Union launched Sputnik, the first man-made object to orbit the earth, which raised questions about America's technological pre-eminence. In the auto market small foreign imports began to erode the hegemony of the big three American automakers (perhaps big in too many ways).

At this moment accident reports from the roads became increasingly grim. By 1965, the annual highway death toll was nearing 50,000. (If the rate had remained constant, with today's population U.S. auto crash deaths would number about 82,000 per year.) The auto manufacturers' response was to spin the data into a story of rising safety. They argued that there had been substantial safety progress when measured by fatalities per miles traveled.[9] The trouble with this argument, apart from the enormous death and injury toll itself, was that the data were extremely unreliable, a conclusion reached after careful analysis by the U.S. Department of Commerce.[10] The claims of improved safety were built on unconfirmed estimates of miles driven and incomplete accident reports which were neither uniform nor prepared by competent evaluators. Critics forcefully argued that the rising death toll was the real measure of an extremely serious problem (a salient argument in the medical context as well).

America's doctors, in increasing numbers, began to highlight what they described as the nation's leading public health problem: traffic accidents. Medical literature focusing on the problem first appeared in the 1930s. By 1946, the *Journal of the American Medical Association* (JAMA) was moved to publish an editorial calling for traffic accident research to identify methods to protect those riding in cars.[11] The chorus of medical concern continued to grow. In 1954, the American Medical Association (AMA) adopted a resolution calling for greater safety in auto design. In 1957, JAMA published an article entitled "Death on the Highways." It declared: "This is our number one public health problem. We are confronted with a massacre without precedent."[12] All this was somewhat surprising coming as it did from a medical profession that was not keen on government regulation. However, the carnage doctors encountered and treated in emergency rooms and elsewhere triggered a heartfelt and truly public-spirited response.

The story of how the tide turned toward government regulation is a well-known one. Its protagonist was a young lawyer and auto safety advocate named Ralph Nader. In the fall of 1965, he published a book entitled, *Unsafe at Any Speed*, chronicling the dangers posed by American cars, most particularly GM's Corvair. Nader came to the attention of the freshman Senator from Connecticut, Abraham Ribicoff, who proceeded to convene public auto safety hearings. This was, more or less, standard Washington fare—members of Congress had held similarly themed hearings on a number of occasions in the 1950s. Then the story took a dramatic turn. GM was exposed as having hired private detectives to investigate and follow Nader. These operatives appear to have engaged not simply in surveillance but harassment and, perhaps, even efforts at sexual entrapment. When GM's dirty tricks came to light, the news triggered a firestorm of indignation. In the glare of all-out media attention the auto safety inquiry was expanded and the public was invited to embrace the "David" who had taken on GM, the auto "Goliath."

The push for safety regulations might still have been narrowly contained but for the ham-handed response of the Detroit manufacturers. They resisted any government intrusion into their business, forcefully rejecting even a proposal that they fashion voluntary regulations. They continued to deny the risks that the death and accident figures palpably demonstrated. In the political ferment of an activist time, in the wake of the federal government's flexing of its legal muscle in the Civil Rights Act of 1964, a bill took shape that would become the National Motor Vehicle Safety Act of 1966. President Johnson embraced this expansive legislation, declaring at the Act's signing: "[U]ntil now we have tolerated a raging epidemic of highway deaths which has killed more of our youth than all other diseases combined. Through the Highway Safety Act, we are going to find out more about highway disease—and we are going to cure it."[13]

The way to secure greater safety, according to the act, was through federally drafted regulations, many mandating the specifics of safer automobile design and manufacture (in other words, means prescriptions). The president and the legislators who voted for the Act (76–0 in the Senate, 371–0 in the House) felt confident that American science, which having recovered from Sputnik was well on its way to putting a man on the moon, could draft a set of regulatory prescriptions that would produce safer cars. In line with the public health and medical framing of the auto safety campaign, a physician and epidemiologist, Dr. William Haddon, was appointed the first administrator of the new agency, eventually called the National Highway Traffic Safety Administration (NHTSA). His announced aim was, as quickly as feasible, to prepare a set of data-based regulations to improve the safety of the cars that Detroit was building.

NHTSA's initial 23 interim regulations piggybacked on requirements that had been previously fashioned for the Government Services Administration's purchase of a fleet of cars for federal employee use. NHTSA rushed to get these regulations out for the 1968 model year. Industry spokesmen were appalled, calling the regulations "useless," "illegal," and "impossible to meet."[14] None of the Detroit manufacturers agreed to meet more than 10 of the 23 standards. The industry threatened to raise prices, sue to block the regulations, and even shut down assembly lines. In the end, the agency withdrew 3 of the standards, relaxed 14 of them, and adopted 6 with an express willingness to revise them. Despite NHTSA's concessions the automakers sued to block regulations requiring enhanced auto interior safety. The agency's retreat from its interim regulations was blasted by Ralph Nader and his allies. This meant that the agency was now under attack from friends as well as foes. These early skirmishes would pale in comparison to the industry's later assault on NHTSA's 1969 passive restraint (air bag) proposal, a matter we will turn to momentarily.

As the preceding narrative suggests, the safety regulations drafted by NHTSA faced substantial technical, legal, and political resistance. On the technical side the problems were many and challenging. The agency began its regulatory effort by adapting Government Services Administration standards that primarily focused on specified equipment. Regulations that insisted on designated apparatus posed several problems. First, they could only be satisfied by use of the identified gear. Such regulations would not encourage manufacturers to develop new and safer approaches. Once adopted these regulations froze development in place. They insisted on one specific piece of machinery although new and improved items might, over time, become available. To deal with this difficulty, the agency had to devote substantial resources to the repeated review and updating of regulations. This tied down agency staff and narrowed staff focus to what had already been done.

When NHTSA moved beyond off-the-shelf equipment mandates, it faced other hurdles in drafting regulations. The agency needed reliable technical data to identify the most promising safety technologies. Because of its limited budget and the substantial lead time needed for original safety research, the agency had to turn to the industry for performance and cost evaluations of new safety ideas. Predictably, the industry responded with negative appraisals and mountains of data about why what NHTSA wanted was impossible or excessively costly. For the initial 23 interim regulations, the agency received 4,500 pages of technical comments with data attachments. The flood of challenging materials continued with later proposals. The agency frequently had to aim at the lowest common denominator, the least aggressive or innovative safety step to minimize technical challenges. Debates about cost came to dominate many interchanges between regulators and manufacturers.

On those occasions when the agency tried to break out of this technical straitjacket by proposing regulations that identified no technology but a generalized safety goal (performance-based standards), like the introduction of some sort of passive restraints to protect auto occupants, it ran into other difficulties. The NHTSA passive restraint rule, Standard 208, drew vociferous industry complaint. The auto manufacturers claimed that the task, which strongly suggested the introduction of airbags (although it could be accomplished through ignition-disabling interlocked seatbelt systems), was impossible. They did so despite GM's having successfully field-tested airbags in its Oldsmobile Toronados. Manufacturers in 1972 persuaded the federal Sixth Circuit Court of Appeals to suspend implementation of Standard 208 on the grounds that the agency lacked a sufficiently objective basis for enforcing the requirement. It was then sidetracked in the Nixon and Ford administrations (1972–1976) and resurrected only when President Carter (1976–1980) appointed Joan Claybrook, an ardent safety advocate, to head NHTSA. By the fourth year of her tenure, Claybrook managed to get Standard 208 promulgated. The effort, however, came to a grinding halt when the newly installed Reagan administration (1980–1988) demanded the withdrawal of the standard. This administrative decision was overturned by the U.S. Supreme Court, which, on the basis of a lawsuit by the State Farm Insurance Company, found the withdrawal arbitrary and lacking in any technical support whatsoever. The Court's ruling led to a re-evaluation, and, 21 years after first being proposed in 1969, the passive restraint standard went into effect in 1990.

Any regulation drafted by a government agency is vulnerable to political pressure. Senators or congressmen who sit on committees charged with agency oversight or with budgetary authority can demand changes in agency conduct or punish recalcitrant agencies seeking to enforce politically unpopular rules. Alternatively, the Congress, as a body, can vote to repeal a rule. Something of this sort happened with respect to the passive restraint standard. The industry, perhaps in a move calculated to ignite consumer anger, sought to accommodate the passive restraint rule, not by installing airbags (a technology the industry hated) but by using ignition interlock systems that blocked starting cars unless seatbelts were securely fastened. This approach outraged consumers and was perceived as the grossest sort of governmental interference with personal freedom. As the manufacturers may have hoped, popular opinion turned against restraints of any sort (belts or bags), and, in 1974, Congress repealed the passive restraint rule.[15] The agency went back to the idea when Joan Claybrook arrived, and, after a detour to the Supreme Court, Elizabeth Dole, the Reagan administration's Secretary of Transportation, arranged a compromise that led to the eventual acceptance of the passive restraint standard.

The courts too played a role in constraining the development of safety regulations. In evaluating legal challenges to NHTSA standards, courts were inclined to press for the clearest proof of technical feasibility and economic justification. Often the courts' expectations were naïve or ill-informed. In 1972, the Sixth Circuit barred the passive restraint rule opining that the rule was not adequately supported. What the court seemed to be demanding was objective proof of a sort that was beyond the reach of any agency charged with increasing safety.

It is today generally agreed that in the face of industry resistance NHTSA has "effectively given up on rulemaking."[16] Instead it has come to rely on a different device—recall. But that strategy has been marred by surveillance problems that failed to identify, let alone address, major safety problems in cases ranging from malfunctioning Toyota accelerators to GM ignitions. In the late 1960s and early 1970s America led the world in auto safety regulation. Today the National Research Council has concluded, "nearly every high-income country has made more rapid progress [on auto safety] than has the United States in reducing the frequency of road traffic deaths."[17]

Government Guidelines in Medicine

The question that might fairly be asked is whether the auto regulation story sheds significant light on the problems that could arise if the federal government were to get into the business of promulgating prescriptive medical safety standards. First, it should be noted that there are striking similarities between the challenges posed by auto safety in the 1960s and medical safety today. In each case, the development of a powerful, new, and essentially unregulated technology led to the rapid expansion and economic growth of a segment of the U.S. economy. As was the case with auto manufacture, medical care has become a core component of America's financial infrastructure, accounting for more than 17% of the GDP and providing employment for millions of workers.

Medicine's powerful new technology, like that of the automotive industry before it, has produced what the Institute of Medicine, in *To Err Is Human*, described as a public health crisis of enormous proportions. Measured by the metric of death, a tool utilized by analysts in both fields, the medical error problem is several times larger than that experienced on the highways (approximately 25.8 highway fatalities a year per 100,000 population in the 1960s as compared with between 62.5 and 125 medical error–related deaths per 100,000 today). In each case, the true scope of the problem was only identified when a system-wide epidemiological analysis was undertaken that called attention to what had been a decentralized and seldom reported phenomenon.

In both cases, consumers' ignorance thwarted their effective assessment of risks and alternatives. The disparity of information between provider and consumer in each setting undermined any reasonable hope that market forces could, on their own, correct the problem. In each context the industry itself seemed little disposed to provide safety information. Both industries stressed the mantra of independence. With respect to autos this meant perpetuating the belief that if anything went wrong, it was the errant driver's fault and there was nothing warranting regulation. In medicine it has been manifested through a widespread avoidance of safety comparisons (between treaters and between procedures) and insistence on each doctor's freedom to choose whatever course of treatment she or he prefers. In neither industry did a culture of safety grow up as a guiding principle. And each appeared to regard injury and fatality as inescapable by-products of technological progress.

In light of the auto safety experience, one might predict that efforts at making healthcare safer through prescriptive government regulation would fail for the same reasons that auto safety through regulation foundered. Indeed, it already has struggled, and for the same reason: industry pushback. In the late 1980s and early 1990s, the federal government briefly undertook an effort to create and promote government-endorsed practice guidelines. The first step toward these was to assess "outcomes, effectiveness and appropriateness of health care services in order to identify the manner in which diseases, disorders and other health conditions can most effectively and appropriately be prevented, diagnosed, treated and managed clinically."[18] In other words, the government was getting into the business of judging the merits of specific treatment options so it could designate those to be preferred. The government body charged to pursue this task was the Agency for Health Care Policy and Research (AHCPR). It was expected to review surgical and other expensive treatments, not only with respect to medical efficacy but also with an eye to assessing their financial justification.

AHCPR was the idea of medical reformers whose aims were to strengthen the scientific foundation of clinical treatment, shift the basis of treatment decision-making so as to empower patients and curb spending on marginal or ineffective therapies.[19] The last of these goals was particularly attractive to certain members of Congress and the Bush administration (1988–1992) who were concerned about the spiraling cost of Medicare and Medicaid. While AHCPR had no power to prohibit the use of any particular procedure, it was clearly viewed as a means of providing cost/benefit guidance to the agencies charged with deciding questions of government reimbursement for care. Several of those most closely associated with AHCPR had strong ties to the Medicare oversight agency, the Health Care Financing Administration (HCFA). Officials of the White House Office of Management and Budget proposed a cooperative arrangement with AHCPR analysts.

AHCPR was to "develop and periodically review and [update] treatment-specific and condition-specific practice guidelines for clinical treatments."[20] In other words, its final product was to be means prescriptions not unlike those originally promulgated by NHTSA. It was anticipated that these guidelines would be widely disseminated. The initial challenge was to decide which procedures should be scrutinized by panels of experts specifically chosen by AHCPR for the task. To decide this question, the agency set up a "nominations" process. The topics proposed were then scrutinized by AHCPR staff for "high incidence," "significance for the needs of the Medicare and Medicaid programs," "high costs," "controversy or uncertainty about ... effectiveness," "potential to inform and improve patient or provider decision-making," and "availability of scientific data to support ... study or analysis."[21] These selection criteria made it clear that the agency was likely to pursue evaluation of expensive procedures that were unsupported by strong medical evidence where doctors rather than patients seemed to be selecting the treatments to be employed (treatments that were likely to be lucrative for treating physicians and medical facilities). Among early topics of examination were cataract surgery for elderly patients and the use of surgery to address prostate-related urinary complaints. With respect to the former, the panel of experts called for heightened consideration of nonsurgical interventions in light of surgical risks and costs. (Medicare was spending $3.4 billion a year on such surgery.) The cataract guideline was endorsed by the American Academy of Ophthalmology, the American College of Surgeons, the American Nurses Association and the National Society for the Prevention of Blindness.[22] These endorsements notwithstanding, a significant number of cataract surgeons were sharply critical of the guidelines.

In 1993, AHCPR put together a panel of 23 experts to examine the merits of spinal fusion surgery for nonspecific acute back pain.[23] Spinal fusions were, at that time, being performed in more than 100,000 cases a year, frequently within a short time after the onset of symptoms. Their cost to the government was in the billions of dollars annually, a sum increased by the cost of medical devices like pedicle screws (used to help secure spinal segments together) and similar hardware.[24] As in the cataract and prostate cases, the agency approached the question with skepticism about the scientific basis and cost-effectiveness of spinal fusion surgery as a preferred treatment in cases of acute back pain of less than three months in duration.

The panel AHCPR put together had representatives of nearly every discipline called upon to address back pain. While orthopedic surgeons were a part of the panel, they held nothing like a majority position. Some members of the group were declared medical reformers who took a dim view of many surgical interventions.[25] These included Dr. Richard Deyo, a staunch advocate of evidence-based medicine and an outspoken critic of the medical device industry (including the manufacturers of pedicle screws). Chiropractic experts and psychologists who might be expected to prefer nonsurgical interventions were also members of the panel, as was Matthew Liang, a Harvard faculty physician renowned for his critical exploration of gaps in clinical performance and medical care. Not surprisingly, this panel's assessment, one well-grounded in the medical research literature, did not endorse early intervention spinal fusion surgery.[26] It drafted guidelines that urged the use of other, less invasive treatments, particularly during the first month of acute symptoms.

After the preliminary announcement of the panel's proposed guidelines, a significant segment of the orthopedic back surgeon community "went wild."[27] The guidelines were viewed by the surgeons as the first step toward Medicare refusal to pay for any spinal fusion surgeries other than those performed as part of controlled clinical trials. If fusion surgery did not prove superior in these studies, the orthopods feared Medicare might refuse to continue reimbursement, which, in turn, could result in private insurers following suit. Since this sort of surgery was lucrative and widespread, the surgeons faced a serious threat of lost income. Despite support for the guidelines from a range of national organizations including the American Hospital Association, the AMA, and the American Academy of Orthopedic Surgeons, a group of potentially affected treaters began a letter-writing campaign not only against the guidelines (which they called biased and sloppy), but AHCPR as well.[28] A back surgeons' professional group called the North American Spine Society worked to expand the letter-writing effort. The organization created a dedicated lobbying entity called the Center for Patient Advocacy to press its case. The Spine Society was reported to have received substantial support from interested medical device manufacturers.[29] The manufacturers eventually joined the fray directly by suing in court to obtain an injunction against the publication of the guidelines. (Their claim was rejected.)

The surgeons' protests found a receptive audience in the newly elected U.S. House of Representatives in 1994. That was the year when Newt Gingrich, as Speaker of the House, declared the "Contract with America" to cut federal regulation and shrink the size of government. The guidelines and AHCPR proved irresistible targets to the House leadership. Orthopod lobbying was probably not decisive in what happened next (there is mixed testimony on the point), but it certainly facilitated focus on AHCPR. The House proposed a zero budget for the agency and placed it on a "hit list" of 140 programs targeted for elimination.[30]

The agency's allies rallied to its defense. The AMA, Hospital Association, and others worked to save AHCPR. Their pleas were particularly influential with those senators who, in the 1980s, had helped establish the agency in the first place in the hope that it would curb Medicare spending. In the end, the agency survived its near-death experience but suffered a 21% cut in its budget.[31] More important, the new authorizing legislation barred the preparation of further government-sponsored guidelines. As if to underscore the end of the guidelines era, the agency's name was changed to the Agency for Healthcare Research and Quality (AHRQ). What was gone from the agency's name was any reference to "policy," a term associated not only with the guidelines but with the failed Clinton single-payer healthcare initiative rejected several years earlier. For having the temerity to challenge spinal fusion surgery, AHCPR came close to extinction.

AHCPR's guidelines experience serves as a warning about government attempts to fashion substantive means-based medical standards. Like NHTSA's experience in regulating auto safety, government medical rules face the prospect of intense political scrutiny and second-guessing. Such reactions will seldom be driven by the merits (all indications are that the spinal fusion guidelines were scientifically sound, as had been the NHTSA airbag standard), but instead by special interests and the prevailing political ideology. Such guidelines will be vulnerable to political pressures generated by lobbying and interest-group complaint. The ability to defend regulations will depend on the political climate and the strength of elected officials' support. In the current political climate in the United States, it appears that government substantive regulation of medical practice is unlikely to succeed. The situation is made even more difficult when well-heeled health and medical device corporations with a substantial financial stake face a loss of revenue if reforms are adopted. In this setting one can anticipate the expenditure of large sums in an effort to block regulatory action.

The AHCPR episode also suggests that government-endorsed substantive guidelines, prepared by government-selected experts, may be vulnerable to a range of charges including bias and inadequate research. As to the first charge, it is likely that when a drafting panel is put together (especially one concerned with either cost or safety) it is likely to have a mix of disciplines and an agenda. Such panels will always be vulnerable, at least to some extent, to a change of bias. Their vulnerability is enhanced because they do not, necessarily, speak with the voice of the profession. Their lack of specialty-specific authority will make their work more susceptible to challenge. As to the question of data, it is likely that the panels will have neither time nor resources to do original research. Their mission will, inevitably, be to review what has been done by others. This leaves them open to the criticism that they have not seen or done everything possible, but have trusted in secondhand, out-of-date material.

The failure of prescriptive government guidelines can have even more far-reaching consequences. It can undercut scientifically well-founded insights, like those of the spinal fusion panel. Although the fusion guidelines were well supported, after the fight in Congress, they were widely ignored. In the decade after the spinal panel's work was made public, the number of fusion surgeries grew from approximately 100,000 a year to more than 300,000.[32] The Medicare expenditure on this one procedure ballooned to more than $16 billion. A questionable procedure was validated by a political fight, many patients were subjected to unnecessary surgery, and society was saddled with the cost. Moreover, the agency that had challenged the orthopedic status quo had been silenced. It was replaced by an entity that defined its mission as nothing more than to serve as a "clearinghouse." Costs were not trimmed. Patient vulnerability to treater predilection was not curbed. To say that the spinal fusion guidelines experience was a disaster is to dramatically understate.

ENGAGED GOVERNMENTAL SURVEILLANCE

Coupling the insights from the AHCPR experience with those regarding NHTSA provides a serious warning about the wisdom of the government getting directly involved in the business of prescriptive medical regulations (specifying methods of treatment). That does not mean that we should give up all hope of fashioning any sort of safety-enhancing regulations. Rules that mandate techniques are vulnerable. However, an alternative approach that focuses on performance—in other words, fixes measurable outcome goals—may have some promise. Such a regulatory approach, when coupled with effective government surveillance, may avoid the means-based disputes encountered in the auto and orthopedic examples while motivating providers to seek methods to enhance safety.

In recent years the popularity of performance-based regulations has soared as command-and-control approaches have faltered.[33] While we think such initiatives hold considerable promise, a recent episode in the field of automobile regulation provides a note of caution. As a means of reducing the pollution caused by diesel-engine passenger cars, exhaust emission standards were adopted in both the United States and Europe. These did not tell auto manufacturers how to cut emissions (a means prescription) but simply specified emission limits that had to be met. To enforce these standards governments relied on a single screening mechanism—laboratory testing. Volkswagen (VW), a major producer of diesel-powered cars, found an electronic method for subverting the testing process.[34] (VW may not have been the only manufacturer to do so.) The result was that government-mandated emission standards were secretly and illegally evaded for years. When VW's defeat mechanism was discovered (not by government regulators but by academic researchers at West Virginia University's Center for Alternative Fuels, Engines and Emissions)[35] the scandal was enormous, resulting in the corporation being required to pay billions of dollars in fines and damages. For our purposes, the episode underscores the vulnerability of performance-based standards if governmental surveillance is not rigorous and multifaceted. With all this in mind let us turn to an examination of engaged government surveillance programs to enforce medical regulations utilizing performance goals. We will argue that New York State's cardiovascular registry program provides a template for successful safety-enhancing governmental performance standard programs.

Government Surveillance of Medical Matters

Active governmental surveillance of potential threats to health has a long history in the western world. It is said to have begun no later than the fourteenth century when Europe sought to grapple with the threat of the Black Death (or plague).[36] In the 1300s the Venetian Republic established a program whereby it appointed a trio of "guardians" to examine all arriving ships and bar entry to vessels with sick individuals aboard. Later, that effort was expanded to include a quarantine of travelers from plague-stricken areas for 40 days before allowing them entry. The basic elements of engaged surveillance programs have not changed radically since those times. Surveillance of this sort is an instrument of government. It is conducted by government agents. Their purpose is to gather information on threats to public health. In light of their findings, the government decides if steps should be taken to protect the community. The purpose is not simply to gather information but to decide on whether and what steps government should take.

Engaged government surveillance has always presented a variety of challenges. It is often both costly and complex.[37] To be effective the government's agents must be motivated to dig deeply. Their objective must be to tease out health risks. They must be adequately paid and supervised so that their best efforts are made to protect the community. Poor pay or supervision is likely to undermine the vigor of their inquiry and the quality of their assessments. What the examiners are to look for needs clear definition; too broad or vague a set of objectives will yield unreliable assessments. The easiest things to record, like fever among a ship's passengers, or mortality in a treatment facility, are far more likely to yield useful information than appraisal of ambiguous conditions. The data to be gathered must not only be clearly defined but must be gathered in a timely manner so that appropriate protective steps can be taken. It is of little value to get surveillance results after danger has been realized. Surveillance must also be thorough. It is worthless to the community if only half of the plague-infested ships are identified and dealt with.

Engaged surveillance began as a method of combating contagious illness. Its use in modern times has been expanded to address a wide range of public health problems.[38] Its value and efficacy may be enhanced by sharing findings with those whose conduct poses a potential risk. With such information the subjects of scrutiny may be able to remedy or reduce the observed danger. The question remains how to get those whose behavior poses a risk to do something about it. Related to that is the question whether, and to what extent, to share findings with the public, either as a means of helping them protect themselves or encouraging providers to improve their performance.

An Engaged Statistically Based Surveillance Program—New York's Cardiac Treatment Registry

BEFORE THE NEW YORK PROGRAM

Statistically based surveillance of medical care to improve patient safety is not an entirely new idea. Florence Nightingale in the 1850s gathered and publicized London hospital mortality rates with the aim of improving hospital administration and construction.[39] Demonstrating sophistication well beyond that of her peers, Nightingale focused attention on the harm treatment facilities could cause. While she appealed to the medical establishment of her day to make improvements, she also made patient safety a public issue. Without government support or legal authority, however, this effort at statistically driven surveillance could only accomplish whatever safety improvements the medical establishment, perhaps pressured by public opinion, would permit. These were quite limited. The same impediments blocked the reform efforts of America's Dr. Ernest Codman who, in the earliest years of the twentieth century, called for the tracking, recording, and assessment of hospital "End Results," as well as audits of medical performance.[40] His objectives in gathering such data were to identify effective treatment and curtail the activity of those who could not provide it. Codman, although a member of Boston's social and medical elite, was not warmly received in the wake of his criticism of existing practices. Unfortunately, the messenger, as well as the message, was a provocation in Codman's case. By all reports, he was an abrasive egotist, sure of his own superior skill and willing to say so. In response to his campaign, both he and his call for outcome surveillance were branded as unacceptable.

If statistically grounded surveillance was to lead to safety improvement, it was not going to be through employment of a bully pulpit to change minds within the medical establishment. Performance statistics (such as they were) were regularly denigrated as unreliable and uninformative. They were often gathered in a haphazard way and those seeking data often faced substantial challenges as to candor, cost, uniformity, and applicability—barriers that private researchers could seldom overcome. What was necessary if statistical methods were to be used to assess safety and point the way to improvements was a rigorous and compulsory effort conducted under government auspices.

In the United States, the most serious early effort at publicly directed statistical surveillance of patient safety came when the HCFA, in 1986, decided to evaluate coronary artery bypass graft (CABG) surgery programs from across the country. The HCFA's evaluation was based on administrative data submitted by hospitals to the agency to obtain government payment. One might expect that such submissions would be reliable and complete because they were intended to serve as the basis for compensation to those who rendered services to Medicare and Medicaid patients. What the agency set out to determine, based on the data it had, was "observed" and "expected" mortality rates for CABG patients within 180 days of hospital admission.[41] The mortality variable seemed to have the advantage of being a clearly measurable event that might provide valuable insights about the safety of the surgery performed. In 1987, the agency compiled its mortality data with the objective of confidential distribution to "peer review organizations and hospitals."[42] In what would become something of a pattern in government safety surveillance programs, representatives of the media sued the HCFA under the pertinent freedom of information statute to obtain the ratings of all submitting hospitals. The press won the case, received the ratings data, and published them as rankings of hospitals on a nationwide basis. This spurred outraged within the healthcare industry.

The industry attacked the HCFA effort on a variety of grounds. It was argued that the underlying billing data were not designed or suitable for assessment purposes. Billing submissions were said only to be useful for bookkeeping purposes. Although debatable, the point was widely embraced. Of greater persuasive power was the critics' argument that the administrative billing records did not include clinical observations about each patient's condition and vulnerabilities. These factors might independently affect outcomes, separate and apart from the quality and efficacy of the treatment. This absence of "risk adjustment" information was generally agreed to be a major flaw in the HCFA data. The enfeebled patient with diabetes and a history of heart attacks was certainly more likely to succumb, no matter how good a job the medical team did, than the robust patient in the next bed with a relatively simple artery blockage. To make reliable comparisons of mortality-rated performance, adjustments needed to be made for risk factors. This was something that could not be done on the basis of the HCFA data. To make matters worse, once made public, the HCFA evaluations were misused by the press as "rankings." Not only was this unfair in terms of risk differentials but also because, in many cases, the reported variations were not statistically significant—they did not express genuine differences in performance. Health profession anger and complaints led the HCFA to terminate its evaluation effort in 1993 "to prevent its misuse in consumer publications."[43]

The surveillance and ranking of medical providers became even more politically fraught during the early 1990s. The Clinton administration presented a single-payer healthcare plan and incorporated in its operation proposals a requirement for surveillance-based reports on the quality of care.[44] When the Clinton plan went down to defeat, it took the surveillance and ranking idea with it, at least at the national level.

The initiative promoted, but imperfectly implemented, by the HCFA was taken up by several states. The undisputed leader of this effort was New York. In 1987, inspired by the HCFA "precedent,"[45] the New York State Department of Health established a registry for the submission of data on all CABG surgeries performed in the state. This registry required the reporting of clinical data about the condition of each patient and the nature of each procedure (a "patient-level clinical database").[46] This was not administrative or billing data but information designed to identify the risks specific to each patient. It continued the focus on the clearest measure of outcome—patient mortality (although limited to a period of up to 30 days while hospitalized—a problematic limitation later changed). It adjusted mortality rates to reflect the risk factors reported in each case. Its focus was far more fine-grained than its HCFA predecessor. It could provide information not only about provider hospitals but individual doctors, thereby yielding "the first physician-specific mortality report ever published."[47] The program's data were more elaborate and costlier to assemble than any ever gathered before.

REASONS FOR THE ESTABLISHMENT OF THE NEW YORK CABG PROGRAM

Two things that powerfully contributed to the implementation of the New York CABG statistical surveillance program and its eventual extension to include a range of percutaneous (performed by needle puncture rather than scalpel cut) heart procedures were the state's utilization of a certificate of need requirement and the leadership of health department officials willing to use that mechanism to pursue a safety agenda. Certificate of need statutes had been enacted in a number of states in the 1970s. In New York State the law required Department of Health approval of individual facility provision of a wide range of medical services from cardiac surgery to nursing home care. The statute was enacted to encourage high-quality, high-volume care by concentrating delivery of medical services and reducing wasteful duplication. Most states abandoned such regulations but New York retained them—giving the Department of Health authority to require the submission of a great deal of information about the patients treated, the nature of the care provided, and the outcomes achieved. Unsatisfactory outcomes or inadequate reporting could result in suspension, or even revocation, of a certificate of need, barring a provider from continuing to perform such procedures.

The official responsible for overseeing health care in New York was Dr. David Axelrod, who became Commissioner of Health in 1979. His approach to the regulation of care and protection of New Yorkers' safety was strikingly different from that of most who occupied similar positions in other states. He declared that "safety is a political judgement,"[48] and, in his view, the political importance of public safety far outweighed the concerns of industry opponents. He pursued a safety agenda for 12 years under four New York governors from both political parties. Among his efforts to protect New Yorkers was early Department of Health intervention to address the danger posed by toxic pollution at Love Canal. When the industry responsible for the contamination sought access to Department of Health records provided by local residents on a confidential basis to facilitate government investigation, Axelrod fought them, protecting citizen privacy and department inquiry. His agency vigorously pursued polluters including the Xerox Corporation, then one of upstate New York's largest businesses, and promulgated a series of regulations to combat people-endangering pollution. Axelrod took on the big tobacco companies and made New York a leader in restricting public smoking. Concerned by reports regarding medical malpractice he was instrumental in the commissioning of the Harvard study of New York hospitals that documented the enormous scope of medical error and served as the basis of the Institute of Medicine's *To Err Is Human*. His criticism of medical malpractice was not confined to physicians' performance but challenged the legal system that, he felt, compensated few and did little to improve safety. He pushed his department to focus on improving treatment outcomes rather than its traditional function of mandating lists of required equipment. This new approach moved New York away from accreditation along the lines pursued by the Joint Commission which, in Axelrod's view, paid too little attention to the results of the care provided.

In the wake of the HCFA reports on nationwide CABG care, David Axelrod began, in 1988, to focus on heart surgery outcomes in New York. His department observed huge variations among providers in terms of mortality and complication rates—some having as much as a fivefold greater percentage of patients who died within 30 days of hospital admission than others.[49] In response, as he had in so many other contexts, the Commissioner used the authority of the Department of Health to take a series of steps to improve safety. He transformed the cardiac certificate of need program into a "clinical registry," requiring each certificate holder to file detailed clinical reports regularly.[50] These reports were designed with the help of a blue-ribbon panel, the Cardiac Advisory Commission, to facilitate the department's assessment of the quality of care provided by each treatment facility. Again, Axelrod focused on outcomes rather than equipment. He was supported by an unusually skilled and dedicated team of public health academics led by Dr. Edward Hannan of the University of Albany School of Public Health.

The New York Registry—Engaged Statistical Surveillance and Public Disclosure

Each of the 30 or so New York facilities approved to perform CABG surgery (and, later, other heart-related procedures) was, beginning in 1988, required to provide the Department of Health with an ongoing series of reports that included the volume and nature of procedures performed, unadjusted 30-day in-hospital mortality rates (later expanded to death in or out of the treatment facility) and a detailed description, in each patient's case, of pre-existing conditions or complicating factors that could increase the risk of mortality.[51] The Department of Health, under Dr. Hannan's leadership, reviewed, clarified, and audited these data. It then prepared a report that detailed (a) each facility's volume of procedures; (b) unadjusted 30-day mortality rate; (c) expected mortality rate based on state-wide experience; (d) risk-adjusted mortality rate based on the complicating factors reported (the analysis developed with the expert assistance of the Cardiac Advisory Commission); and (e) a determination whether any hospital was significantly outside the norm (based on risk-adjusted performance comparisons). The initial evaluation was provided confidentially to all reporting hospitals in 1989. It confirmed the mortality rate disparities Dr. Axelrod had been concerned about.

In 1990, Hannan and his team published a paper in the JAMA reporting findings derived from the registry data.[52] The paper presented a risk-adjusted mortality rate for each New York hospital but did so without identifying any by name. On the day of the publication of the article, Dr. Axelrod, in keeping with his aggressive approach to public safety, released the names of the hospitals. Public awareness dramatically increased when the *New York Times*, in December 1990, published a list of the hospitals ranked according to their CABG mortality rates. Other news outlets, including the *Wall Street Journal*, followed suit.

The same month, another New York newspaper, *Newsday*, sued the Department of Health under New York's freedom of information law seeking the identity of and mortality rate data for each doctor who performed CABG surgeries reported to the registry. The department fought this request, arguing for the necessity of maintaining confidentiality to encourage accurate reporting as well as claiming that the physician-specific data were likely to be statistically unreliable due to the small number of procedures performed by many of the reporting physicians. The courts were not convinced by these arguments. Citing the public interest in safety information, they ordered disclosure. The Cardiac Advisory Commission strongly opposed disclosure and urged the department to instruct hospitals to de-identify their submissions so that individual doctors' names would not be discoverable.[53] Dr. Axelrod, bucking the sentiment of both his Advisory Commission and the overwhelming majority of the medical profession, ordered the release of the names. After this initial release, subsequent disclosures were, however, limited to those doctors who had performed a large enough number of procedures to permit a statistically trustworthy appraisal of outcomes (at least 200 over a three-year period). The first such surgeon-specific release came in 1992.

Clearly, the most important Department of Health disclosures were the identity of the treating hospitals and doctors whose risk-adjusted mortality rates were much worse than those of their peers. These the department labeled "outliers." That designation had a powerful effect on the providers so labeled. In the earliest data, the hospital with the worst mortality rating was the publicly financed Erie County Medical Center in Buffalo.[54] After the ratings were published, the Cardiac Advisory Committee visited that facility and the hospital voluntarily agreed, in January 1990, to suspend performance of CABG procedures. Before resuming CABG surgery the Medical Center installed a full-time chief of cardiac clinical services, initiated a quality assurance plan to monitor each surgeon's performance, and worked to increase the program's resources. In April 1990, the Medical Center was allowed to resume CABG surgery on a probationary basis. One of the challenges Erie Country Medical Center faced was the low volume of procedures it performed. (The evidence is clear that high volume contributes to safer practice.)[55] Slowly the Buffalo facility was able to safely expand its program and improve its risk-adjusted mortality rate.

The hospital with the second-worst record was Strong Memorial Hospital in Rochester. Through its general director, Paul Griner, it denied that the hospital's care was substandard. Griner contended that the risk-adjusted figures were unreliable and, in Strong Memorial's case, were skewed by a particularly high percentage of very ill patients. He argued: "We appear to be inappropriately indicted because of a disproportionately high percentage of high-risk patients that are not adequately accommodated in the risk factors analysis."[56] Data, however, suggested that the hospital had only two highly skilled CABG surgeons and that when they were unavailable doctors with little training in adult cardiac surgery were pressed into service. These surgeons' mortality rates were quite high. In the wake of these findings, the problematic physicians ceased performing adult CABG procedures, the two skilled practitioners reworked their schedules to accommodate more patients, additional skilled staff were hired, and the mortality rate dropped.[57]

The released information did not simply pinpoint outlier programs but problematic aspects of otherwise sound programs. This was the case with St. Peter's Hospital, the largest private hospital in Albany. Its care for most categories of CABG patients was satisfactory. Its death rate for "emergency" cases was, however, about four times the state average (26% compared to 7%).[58] Again, the program was examined by a Department of Health–assembled team of experts. They concluded that emergency patients were not being adequately "stabilized" before surgery.[59] St. Peter's made changes in the way it delivered emergency surgical care and its death rate plunged.

What all these interventions highlight is the great value and impact of rigorous outside expert surveillance. In each case, classifying a program as an outlier triggered close scrutiny. Examination identified problems that were then addressed. The process led not only to external surveillance but to follow-up internal scrutiny conducted by newly installed staff. It also persuaded institutions to devote increased resources to troubled programs. The critical question is, Why?

At the outset, it should be noted that heart surgery is both a substantial part of major hospital workload (10,000 or more such surgeries are performed in New York per year)[60] and a significant contributor to hospital revenue (up to one-third of revenue by some estimates).[61] What is on the line when suspension or probation looms is a great deal of money. Perhaps even more significant is the professional obloquy feared by physicians associated with outlier programs. As Dr. Ferdinand Vendetti, Jr., of the Albany Medical College put it, "They [doctors] don't want to be outliers. They also want to do the best thing for their patients, so they take this stuff very seriously."[62] Dr. Vendetti's observation is powerfully borne out. All the hospitals identified in the early years of the cardiac surgery program as outliers undertook major steps to improve. On the other hand, those with weak but middling statistics (i.e., somewhat below the median) did not generally make a similar effort.

The registry was also an important source of statistical benchmarking information. The data gathered established statewide safety norms. When a program was substantially outside those norms, a warning flag was raised. This might concern an entire program, as in the case of the Erie County Medical Center, or a single aspect of a program, as with St. Peter's emergency services. In each case the statewide statistical data provided benchmark safety levels and potential modes for improvement.

The "outlier" designation also had a powerful effect on individual doctors. Those so labeled were far more likely than other heart surgeons to terminate their CABG practice in New York. It has been reported that between 1989 and 1992, 27 low-volume surgeons, generally with poor risk-adjusted mortality rates, stopped performing such procedures in the state.[63] The registry data served as ammunition for hospital administrators to end the surgical practice of low-volume physicians who were undermining hospital risk-adjusted mortality rates.[64] In 2006, 15 years into the registry program, Ashish Jha and Arnold Epstein, two Harvard School of Public Health researchers, in a piece published in *Health Affairs* examined the program's impact on surgeons' practice. They found that surgeons with the highest mortality rates "were more likely than others to leave practice of CABG surgery in New York State within two years after the release of [a] report."[65] Twenty percent of the bottom quartile of those evaluated left New York practice within that two-year span as compared to 5% in the top three quartiles.[66]

Digging into these numbers, Jha and Epstein examined the subsequent careers of 31 physicians who left New York cardiac surgery practice between 1989 and 1999. Of that number, two died, four could not be traced, nine took up cardiac surgery outside New York, and seven assumed nonclinical positions. Jha surveyed 18 of the departing surgeons. Ten denied that the registry's reports had any effect. Two others among the 18 said the ratings had "minimal" effect, and six said the registry figures had a "moderate or substantial" effect.[67] It should be noted that two of the departing doctors said that, despite their strong performance records, they were leaving because of perceived pressure "to reject high-risk patients" or because they found New York surgical practice "less enjoyable."[68]

As we have noted, to make the registry program's comparisons effective, mortality data had to be adjusted to factor in the special risks each patient faced. Without such an adjustment, claims like those of Strong Memorial Hospital's general director that it had a disproportionately large number of very ill patients could not be effectively evaluated, and the statistics gathered could not be considered a fair basis for safety comparisons, let alone disciplinary actions like program suspension. The HCFA national program to evaluate CABG surgery safety was undermined because it could not convincingly appraise individual patient risk. To address the challenge New York's expert Cardiac Advisory Committee fashioned a risk-adjustment protocol. That protocol's predictions about mortality independent of the surgery have been found to be "extremely robust over the years"[69] and have been described as "the gold standard among systems of its kind."[70]

To establish and maintain credible comparative evaluations, the registry program had to take a number of other steps. First, it had to be assured that hospital reports were accurate and complete. To insure this the Department of Health established a training program for those designated by each facility as responsible for submissions.[71] Once reports were submitted they were reviewed for reliability by department staff. Their completeness was checked in a number of ways. Since the state keeps a separate record of all hospital discharges, discharge data could be compared to filings with the CABG registry.[72] In this way the Department of Health could protect against cardiac programs losing or disregarding patients. In addition, up to one half of submitting hospitals faced annual audits of a sample of their clinical records to assure accuracy—a step not taken by any other program.[73]

The department also had, as already noted, statewide benchmarks to inform its review. The benchmarks could flag submissions that appeared to exaggerate the risk level among patients at any provider's hospital. This was important because surveillance programs that rely on initial submissions by the regulated may be vulnerable to subversion if those reporting can, with impunity, exaggerate the illness of the patient population. Such exaggeration is frequently referred to as "upcoding"—the inflation of coded risk claims. When statewide benchmarks suggested the possibility of upcoding the Department of Health undertook additional audits. If serious anomalies were found, as was the case on at least two occasions in the early years of the program, the providers were required, at their expense, to have a third party re-evaluate and resubmit their data.[74]

One troubling challenge to the department's program was the temptation among hospitals and doctors to refuse care to the sickest patients because of fears that they might die and thereby adversely affect the caregiver's mortality rating. As already noted, two of the doctors interviewed by Jha and Epstein said they had left New York heart surgery practice because they felt such pressures. This was a more difficult challenge than the submission of distorted data—there would be no file to review if a risky patient was turned away. Over time this challenge led to a push for the exclusion from the registry database of certain categories of risky patients (particularly, those said to be suffering from "shock").[75] We will return to the question of the refusal of care in the next section of this chapter when we review criticisms of the New York registry system.

Professional Backlash Against the Registry Program

It should come as no surprise that some medical professionals, not only in New York but across the country, were intensely critical of the registry program. The criticisms were many and varied but often fell into four categories: first, that the data gathered were inadequate to fairly rate hospital and physician performance; second, that any reporting program was vulnerable to gaming by those reporting; third, that the analyses generated by the registry would be ignored by doctors and patients; and finally, that the registry program threatened the authority of the medical profession.

A criticism voiced about almost every safety initiative examined in this book is that the data gathered simply aren't sufficient to warrant regulatory action. That was certainly the claim regarding the efforts of the registry. Critics argued that the information gathered was an inadequate basis on which to make comparisons between treaters because the risk adjustments made did not fairly reflect the true condition of each patient.[76] Some scholarly critics contended that hospitals and doctors had important clinical data that were not sought by the registry; others, that treaters had more information than could ever be recorded. In either case, it was argued that the absent information was essential to accurate risk assessment.[77] This criticism seems to suggest that sufficient information can never be amassed by those not involved in the treatment process. Pennsylvania doctors facing a reporting system similar to New York's overwhelmingly (79%) believed that the risk adjustment mechanism was inadequate. They were highly skeptical that reports submitted by their peers could ever be sufficiently reliable both because of inadequate inquiry into clinical circumstances and physician resistance to accurate reporting.[78]

Criticism of the New York program was most intense with respect to the comparative ratings of individual doctors. In that context, it was argued that sample sizes were too small and the vagaries of patient populations too great to warrant publicized comparisons between treaters.[79] Based on these concerns some experts opined that it would be 10 or 15 years before anything approaching reliability would be available.[80] In 1994, the General Accounting Office (GAO) prepared a report on statistical surveillance and ranking programs (which it called "report cards") as a healthcare reform.[81] The GAO canvassed medical expert opinion and then outlined professional concerns. It was the experts' view, according to the GAO, that surveillance reports would be based on "inaccurate, misleading or incomplete information"[82] would use measures that failed to "reflect quality" and that "risk adjustment systems may not be reliable."[83]

A second criticism of the CABG surveillance effort, and one we have already noted, was that it was vulnerable to hospital and physician gaming to improve mortality figures, especially by refusing to treat particularly ill patients who were at far greater risk of dying during treatment than others. The consequence of the alleged refusal of surgeons to treat the sickest patients was either to leave them without access to coronary care or force their outmigration to other states for treatment. The press, on several occasions, reported anecdotes of sick patients being turned away.[84] These claims gained some support from surveys among doctors in jurisdictions where ratings were being used.[85] In Pennsylvania, over half of coronary specialists said it was harder to find surgeons for the sickest patients. Similar results were also reported in New York.[86]

No publication had greater impact on the outmigration argument than that produced by a research group at the Cleveland Clinic, in Cleveland, Ohio, which in 1996 published an analysis of the New York patients the hospital had treated.[87] What the prominent Ohio hospital's staff reported was that 5.1% of the facility's patients were from New York State, that these New York patients were older and sicker than the clinic's other patients, that more of them died during the course of treatment, and that these data suggested "increased referrals" from New York doctors afraid to treat the sickest patients because of the registry surveillance and reporting regime.[88]

Apart from the Cleveland Clinic study, perhaps the most influential critique of the New York registry came from David Dranove, Daniel Kessler, and Mark McClellan[89]—all distinguished scholars linked by a skepticism about the role of government in healthcare. A piece they wrote and published in the *Journal of Political Economy* appeared in 2003. The authors seemed intent on pointing out a range of flaws likely to be encountered with any report card scheme. A central argument of the piece was that "mandatory reporting mechanisms inevitably give providers the incentive to refuse to treat more difficult and complicated patients."[90] This selection incentive was said, on the basis of national data regarding the treatment of elderly CABG patients from 1987 to 1994, to have led New York and Pennsylvania surgeons to refuse care to the sickest patients, as well as to promote treatment of less ill patients, resulting in an overall decline in the quality of healthcare for the elderly while increasing medical expenditures. This fundamentally economics-oriented team, however, noted that their findings only measured "short-run responses" and conceded that long-run benefits might be substantial.[91] Despite this concession, it is hard not to view the piece as a warning against early adoption of engaged surveillance and public notification programs.

Another aspect of the gaming concern was that New York doctors were "upcoding" patient risk factors so that when mortality figures were adjusted it would appear that surgeons were more successful than they actually were. In the early days of the New York program (1990–1992), there was an upsurge in risk factor claims especially concerning renal failure and congestive heart failure.[92] These reports were viewed with suspicion by critics and led a number of analysts to conclude that surgeons were exaggerating their patients' illness to improve their safety ratings.

The third point frequently made by skeptical reviewers was that both doctors and patients appeared to ignore the registry data in making treatment decisions. When asked, physician said that they, for the most part, did not consult registry reports to inform referral decisions. Among New York doctors surveyed on the question, 57% said they did not rely on registry data, and 71% said they did not inform their patients of the registry's findings.[93] Pennsylvania cardiologists were even more emphatic in refusing to consider such information—only 10% found it "very important" and less than 10% reported discussing the data with more than 10% of their patients.[94] Patients did not avoid low-rated programs,[95] and there was "no evidence that performance was associated with subsequent change in hospitals' market share."[96]

The widespread and remarkably sharp criticism of the publication of registry evaluations suggests that more was perceived to be at stake in this debate than the technical efficacy of a specific surveillance program. The criticism began in earnest when a national report card approach was being considered and the Clinton healthcare proposal was being debated (1992–1993). What may have been behind the outsized focus on the New York and Pennsylvania reporting programs is suggested in a 2000 JAMA piece by Dr. Martin Marshall and his colleagues, in which the authors observed: "Public disclosure of performance data is a major health policy initiative that represents a potential challenge to health professionals' traditional concept of autonomy."[97] Dr. Marshall and his co-authors went on to decry the paucity of empirical evaluations of reporting systems—relying, it would seem, on a variant of the no-data critique so frequently employed to attack reform proposals. That claim notwithstanding, Marshall's piece had 50 footnotes referencing just about as many articles, suggesting a widely shared medical concern about the intrusion of any evaluative system into what had, theretofore, been the private and infrequently scrutinized domain of the profession.

This concern about autonomy was, in all likelihood, fueled by the fact that the New York system was government run, relying on the certificate of necessity power to enforce its regulations. Conservative critics like Dranove, Kessler, and McClellan were particularly sensitive to government intrusion into the operations of the healthcare system. The autonomy concern was linked by some critics to a hypothesized undermining of patient confidence in physicians' advice. As the author of one *New England Journal of Medicine* article put it, "when any report card is issued, three things can happen to providers: they can appear to be better than, on par with, or worse than their competitors. Since most patients believe that their doctors and hospitals are better than average, the risk of losing patients' confidence is, well, better than average."[98]

The registry and surveillance approach touched on other deep professional concerns as well. It triggered some doctors' paternalistic response that patients do not understand medicine, will never really understand it, and should defer to their physicians on questions about the selection of treaters and therapies. The focus in many of the critiques of the New York and Pennsylvania systems on the lack of consumer use of published evaluations echoes these views and reinforces the claim that medical decisions are best left in doctors' hands.

Of perhaps even greater concern for doctors was the fear that evaluation threatened the hierarchy of authority established in medicine. The source of most medical training is the teaching hospital where young, newly minted doctors learn to practice. Moreover, those institutions are the employers and sources of support for most medical scholars. The upshot of surveillance and reporting is likely to be disclosure of the imperfections of such institutions. Although expressed somewhat differently, this seemed to be the concern of one of the critical articles published in the *New England Journal of Medicine*. That article described teaching hospitals as seeing "a not-so-subtle plot to justify the shifting of costs to patients [who choose to seek such care in hospitals] and to use flawed tools of measurement to drag prestigious but expensive institutions down into apparent mediocrity."[99] Dranove and his colleagues voiced almost identical concerns: "By shifting their practice toward healthier patients, inferior providers make it difficult for report cards to confidently distinguish them from their high-quality counterparts."[100]

Much of the criticism leveled against the New York registry and surveillance program is not well founded. Most critics concede that the system (and its Pennsylvania counterpart) are "well-designed."[101] Criticisms of their predecessor, the HCFA program, informed substantial improvements in New York's and Pennsylvania's approach. The data gathering process was redesigned to be both reliable and thorough—a far cry from HCFA's dependence on billing submissions. Required reports are subjected to cross-checking against other databases like New York's hospital discharge records. An auditing process was, for the first time, introduced to verify, on the basis of clinical records, a sampling of hospital and surgeon submissions. If any irregularities are detected a more thorough audit is required. The most insistently stressed remaining criticism is not about the data themselves but about the invisible effects of the program—particularly refusal to treat the most seriously ill and to force their outmigration. With respect to that question the evidence discussed later in this chapter suggests that it is overstated.

Before we turn to that question, and other issues of gaming, it should be noted that the architects of the New York program have introduced changes in the process to reduce any temptation to refuse care to the very ill. In 2006, the registry stopped including "shock patient" mortality "because of the concern that these patients were not undergoing revascularization as often as it was needed."[102] That was followed in 2010 by the exclusion of patients suffering from an anoxic brain injury.[103] The system has made a number of other adjustments including the extension of reporting requirements to patients who died within 30 days of treatment even if not resident in the hospital. This corrected a weakness in the system that had previously counted only in-hospital deaths and, hence, assigned higher mortality rates to hospitals simply because they held patients longer. The New York methodology, while imperfect, has been subject to constant revision and refinement. Its directors have made an ongoing effort to improve the quality and accuracy of the data. In this case, it appears that the perfect has been used by critics as the enemy of the good, in disregard of the safety progress the program has fostered in New York.

As we have said, the central criticism of the New York system and, indeed, of any system with specified risk-adjustment criteria, is that in one or more ways it will lead to gaming by submitting hospitals and treaters. In the early days of the New York effort there was some evidence that certain institutions yielded to the temptation to cheat. In both 1991 and 1992 the Department of Health found submissions that were substantially out of line with statewide benchmarks and expectations. These submissions led to audits and required revisions. The department's monitoring efforts coupled with routine use of audits and benchmarks appeared to substantially reduce risk-adjustment gaming through the submission of exaggerated risks.

The more serious question, and the one pressed in different ways by both the Cleveland Clinic team and Dranove's economists, was whether New York doctors were avoiding the sickest patients—either sending them out of state or simply refusing to treat them. The easier charge to answer was that made by the researchers from Cleveland. Their study drew its data from Cleveland Clinic records between 1989 and 1993. Edward Hannan, one of the designers of the New York program, demonstrated that this approach was seriously flawed. The first public release of New York CABG data did not occur until late 1990, "so the earliest that hospitals would have been tempted to refer out of state for fear of adverse publicity would have been 1991."[104] This was halfway through the Cleveland Clinic study period. Moreover, the New York outmigration rate, as calculated on the basis of Medicare data, changed little between 1989 and 1993—suggesting that there was no outmigration uptick when public reporting was introduced. Those data, when compared with Medicare reports for other regions, showed New York, both in 1994 and 1999, to have lower outmigration rates than the rest of the country.[105] As the Cleveland group admitted, because theirs was a single institution study, its data alone could not prove a surveillance-and-reporting–inspired outmigration effect. Furthermore, the longstanding effort of the Cleveland Clinic to attract out-of-state patients is well known. The clinic enticed King Kalid bin Abdul Aziz of Saudi Arabia to come to Cleveland for heart surgery. He was joined by other foreign dignitaries including the sheikh of Abu Dhabi. The clinic has fostered outmigration across the United States by partnering with less prestigious hospitals in Illinois, North Carolina, and elsewhere. Its CEO, Dr. Toby Cosgrove, boasted of the hospital's success, saying that its "mission across borders benefits patients worldwide."[106] It seems ironic that clinic researchers were concerned by its recruitment success in near-neighbor western New York (especially in light of Erie County Medical Center's well-documented CABG problems).

Dranove and his colleagues used data regarding Medicare-reimbursed hospitalization in the year before CABG surgery to suggest that New York surgeons were treating less seriously ill patients (ones who were less likely to have been hospitalized in the year before CABG surgery) and turning away higher risk ones. The method Dranove used is "unconventional" as a means of assessing patient health[107] and is designed to skirt surgeon manipulation through inflated risk-adjustment claims. The difficulty is that there is little evidence supporting the assertion that it is a satisfactory measure of patient health at the time of CABG surgery. Using the same Medicare data base (but different metrics) other researchers found that New York's reported risk factor rates were comparable to those of other states both in 1989 (before the registry program began) and 1992 (after it was in operation).[108] Registry architects Mark Chassin and Edward Hannan, responding to the avoidance hypothesis in a 1996 article in the *New England Journal of Medicine*, pointed out that there were no "published reports that document the systematic avoidance of high-risk patients."[109] Dranove notwithstanding, that observation appears accurate.

The remaining source of support for the outmigration hypothesis is the survey responses of cardiologists in New York and Pennsylvania. According to the survey results, there is little doubt that a majority of physicians involved in cardiac care in those states do not like being monitored and having physician performance periodically made public. It should come as no surprise then that they claim, when asked by the survey, that CABG access for the severely ill has declined.[110] Showing their disdain, they also say that they do not believe in the accuracy of the surveillance information, do not use surveillance data in advising patients, and avoid relying on it in the referral process.[111] The surveys inquiring about surgical practice and the use of registries are, in all likelihood, viewed by the doctors responding to them as a referendum on the surveillance effort. It is to be expected that many proud and generally autonomous medical professionals will respond in ways that they believe can undermine the program. Making a similar point, one *New England Journal of Medicine* article noted, "cardiovascular specialists may be questioning the validity of the data in order to vent their displeasure at being monitored."[112] A second possible reason for the survey assertions is that "the respondents may not understand or appreciate" the actual impact of the surveillance program.[113] In this regard it is interesting to note that there was no apparent effort in the surveys to test the respondent's knowledge of program methods or effect on safety.

It is hard to leave the topic of professional backlash without observing three striking ironies. The first is that critics of the New York system and doctors who are surveilled by it have been most attracted to an argument that surveillance is to blame for significant patient harm (through outmigration and nontreatment). The irony here is that the charge has been leveled with little consideration of the range of treatment behaviors that surveillance has corrected. The hypothesized problem is allowed to outweigh the palpable safety gains. A second irony is that when doctors are polled about surveillance they, in essence, say that other doctors and hospitals cannot be trusted to make honest submissions. Besides being a discouraging comment on doctors' perceptions of the integrity of their professional colleagues (one that may, in the main, be wrong), it seems to argue for more rigorous observation, monitoring, and audits. It cannot be sound policy to leave the field to the unscrupulous rather than to supervise them. Finally, attacks on surveillance seem to suggest that doing nothing is preferable to trying to do something. The absence of any effort to provide a constructive alternative is not heartening. In a previous chapter (regarding defensive medicine), we noted that these sorts of arguments depict a medical profession willing and ready to abandon patients in the greatest need, a view we think erroneous and corrosive of trust in caregivers.

THE ACHIEVEMENTS OF THE NEW YORK CABG REGISTRY

There has been a good bit of debate about the impact of the New York registry program. While the evidence is not entirely conclusive, it would appear that the program has had a substantial impact on the quality and safety of heart care in the state. Between 1989 (the beginning of the program) and 1992, in-hospital "crude" (unadjusted) morality declined significantly, from 3.52% to 2.78%. When risk-factor adjustments are considered New York's mortality rate dropped 41% from 4.17% to 2.45%.[114] In 1992, New York had the lowest risk-adjusted CABG mortality rate in the United States. More recently, between 1994 and 1999, New York's mortality rate was a third lower than the aggregated rate for the rest of the country.[115] New York was not the only state to experience improvement in this period. The nation as a whole saw a 19% decrease in mortality between 1987 and 1992.[116] When compared with other jurisdictions, however, New York was clearly a leader in improvement. Using Medicare data, Peterson and his colleagues were able to confirm these points with the over 65 population. In that group New York's 30-day mortality rate dropped much more than was the case elsewhere and New York "was one of the nation's most improved bypass performers between 1987 and 1992."[117] It has been concluded, even by scholarly critics, "that such systems may save lives."[118] The public identification of outliers appeared to have the effect of empowering hospitals to make staffing and practice changes that significantly enhanced safety. The actions undertaken by the Erie County Medical Center, Strong Memorial Hospital, and St. Peter's Hospital all seem to reflect this. The outlier designation also encouraged the departure from cardiac surgery of two groups of high risk surgeons. The first to go were those who performed only a small number of such operations.[119] Data clearly indicated that physicians who performed few procedures were likely to have higher mortality rates. Between 1989 and 1992, 27 such surgeons stopped operating in New York hospitals.[120] Their departure reduced the risks CABG patients faced. These doctors were followed out of the operating theater by a group that had abnormally high mortality rates: "20% of surgeons with patient risk-adjusted mortality in the highest [worst] quartile stopped practicing CABG surgery within 2 years after publication of reports in comparison to roughly 5% of surgeons in the top 3 quartiles."[121] What the registry publication system did was not only give hospitals notice of problems, but also grounds to adopt changes and a public-relations rationale for doing so. This is something quite different from other reporting schemes. The deep concern about being branded an outlier motivates changes that confidential programs cannot.

Among the New York registry's other achievements was the creation of a durable surveillance program that established a standard of excellence—a model that could be referred to by those seeking to foster safety improvement. New York's CABG initiative has been described as "the gold standard" for public reporting.[122] It has become a permanent part of the operations of the Department of Health, assuring long-term public focus on cardiac surgery safety. The registry has adhered to an open files policy that has supplied important data to a wide range of researchers. Some have suggested that the safety improvement experienced in other states was, in part, due to a "spill over" from the New York effort.[123] The registry's durability and accuracy have produced an unbroken stream of feedback to New York hospitals signaling those with problems of the need to improve.

Although New York rank and file cardiologists have regularly voiced their concerns about the registry, its reliance on the advice of the Cardiac Advisory Committee has enhanced its practical effectiveness and credibility. This bridge, forged with the leaders of the profession, has opened the program to expert suggestions for improvements and provided a powerful counterpoint to the charges made by critics. Rules that do not simply flow out of government offices but come with the imprimatur of leading professionals concentrated in the specialty are harder to ignore or overthrow.

Conditions for Success

The New York registry has improved patient heart care in the state. Its achievements are substantial. It provides a valuable model of engaged government surveillance as a tool to improve safety. That said, it is not, in any sense, a panacea. It is an approach that is likely to succeed in improving patient care only if a number of requirements are met.

The registry is narrowly focused. It is only concerned with a well-defined set of cardiac procedures which have the potential of causing death or serious injury. The procedures scrutinized are performed with frequency (more than 10,000 per year) and are an important source of revenue for the institutions that perform them. They are both extremely serious and extremely lucrative. They appear to be viewed by providers as important to financial success and reputation. In 1988, the nation was spending $5 billion a year on bypass surgery and hospitalization for CABG treatment might last as long as 10 days and cost more than $30,000. Such procedures were viewed as a means to "assure the economic survival of some hospitals."[124] This makes them the sort of activity that hospitals care about and invest in. That, in turn, makes public exposure of shortcomings something institutions are likely to take seriously. Being publicly labeled an outlier in such circumstances has the potential of influencing behavior.

The cardiac procedures scrutinized are performed frequently enough to generate useful statistical insights but not in such overwhelming numbers or in so diffuse a manner as to obscure the identity of those providing care (there are only about 30 institutions authorized to perform CABG surgery). In this situation institutional and physician performance can be identified, tracked, and reported. Those who are doing well and those who are not can be readily ascertained. At the same time the group is sufficiently large to provide benchmark statistics.

The outcomes focused on are demonstrably important. They have life and death implications. Concentration on cardiac problems, a leading cause of death in America, can be justified as warranting significant expenditure of public funds—an important point because the process of monitoring reports, auditing records and garnering the highest level of professional input from groups like the Cardiac Advisory Committee is expensive. Mortality-affecting outcomes are the sort of data that governments can reasonably claim an interest in. Government intrusion into the quotidian affairs of medical providers is likely to provoke sustained resistance, negatively affect public support, and generate unmanageable mountains of data. The situation is, arguably, different when the lives of patients are on the line. Life and death consequences are also important because they are the sorts of questions that will capture media attention. They are particularly newsworthy.

It is to be expected that there will be sharp attacks on government surveillance and publication programs like the registry. That has certainly been the case in New York since 1990. A further condition for success is the ability to respond effectively to criticism. To that end, the program must gather demonstrably accurate and useful data. Those data must be openly shared so that analysis can be refined and the program improved. Those in charge must be truly expert and committed to the goal of improving safety through engaged surveillance. New York had the good fortune of having a dedicated and sophisticated team of analysts, headed by Edward Hannan, capable of handling challenges and enabling refinements.

Is the New York Registry a "Report Card"?

Much of the critical literature regarding the New York registry has treated the program as one designed to provide report cards about cardiac care. In one sense this is correct—the registry does generate data that are made public and can be used by consumers to compare the performance of various cardiovascular treatment facilities. But the primary aim of the registry is not the publication of reports providing patients with comparative evaluations of hospitals. It is, according to its directors, a program to "improve their performance."[125] Generally, medical report card programs are not intended to directly drive safety efforts but to guide and empower patients to get "the best performance for the least cost."[126] In theory, this will result in consumer choices that reward those offering the highest quality care and spur competition in the marketplace. There is a substantial body of empirical work suggesting that report card–driven quality efforts seldom work in healthcare.[127] Patients only infrequently refer to such information (particularly in regard to safety).[128] This has been the case in both New York and Pennsylvania where cardiac programs have been the subject of public reports. Patients generally rely on referrals by their personal physicians. And, since the New York and Pennsylvania doctors do not like or use registry-generated reports, the reports have virtually no effect on hospital selection. The entities that do seem to attend to safety information are provider institutions and these seem effectively motivated only when one of their programs is found to be an outlier. It is when public image and professional reputation are jeopardized that institutions react. [129]

What surveillance like that of the New York program can do is supply an audience of healthcare providers with guidance and incentive to improve safety. This is not the case with small variations in "grades" but with major departures from professional norms and the stigma of being branded an outlier. Surveillance-generated information can also provide a roadmap for change. St. Peter's Hospital did a sound job with its heart patients except those in emergent circumstances. The surveillance effort could first inform St. Peter's that it had a serious problem (i.e., it was an outlier on emergencies) and then provide a template for improvement from more successful institutions. The registry, in this case, produced comparative, or benchmark, data of great value in pinpointing a problem and outlining a path to correction. With the advent of electronic health records the potential exists to increase the practice areas in which benchmark guidance is available. The coming of "big data" could make the sort of analysis and comparisons New York has been able to produce because of its painstaking efforts, easier, faster, and cheaper, opening the door to expansion of surveillance programs.

What New York's registry does is relatively straightforward—monitor and improve CABG practice. What report cards are designed to do—inform consumers about the quality of institutional care in some generalized sense—is far more challenging. There are few agreed measures of the quality of care.[130] The information reported is often hard for patients to understand or irrelevant to their perceived needs.[131] When report cards provide global assessments of healthcare institutions they are generally of limited value. A hospital may be good at some things and not others; the same is likely to be true of departments and individual physicians. What makes the New York registry valuable is the narrowness of its focus and communication to an institutional audience.

If data like those from the registry are not meant to serve as report cards and are not attended to by referring physicians, why make the reports public? Part of the answer has already been given in describing provider reaction to being publicly described as an outlier. Improvements like those instituted at the Erie County Medical Center, Strong Memorial Hospital, and St. Peter's Hospital were unlikely to be made without public disclosure. Fear of reputational harm (both in the eyes of the public and members of the profession) seemed to be at work in efforts to overcome the outlier label. Apart from providing institutional motivation, public reporting demonstrates respect for the principles of democracy. In a democracy, citizens have a right to be informed about the behaviors of and risks posed by the institutions that affect their lives. Courts faced with requests under freedom of information statutes have consistently recognized and enforced the public's right to know. Government surveillance can generate valuable information about medical institutions' performance. Whether or not the public at large chooses to avail itself of this information, it should not be kept secret. Only when there is an energetic exchange of information and ideas is there a sound basis for democratic action.

Another Candidate for Government-Engaged Surveillance

The topic of performance-based government regulation should, perhaps, not be left without noting a promising idea being promoted by innovative physicians from hospitals associated with Dartmouth, John Hopkins, and the University of Michigan. This group has persuaded the three hospital systems to adopt a "Volume Pledge"—a promise to restrict the performance of specifically identified risky surgical procedures to facilities and doctors who perform them regularly.[132] The idea is based on the well-established observation, first documented in 1979, that surgeons and hospitals performing a high volume of potentially dangerous surgeries have much safer outcomes than those that do such operations infrequently.[133] More recent analysis, based on a sample of 2.5 million patients treated between 1994 and 1999 for 14 types of procedures (six sorts of cardiovascular operations and eight cancer resectionings) indicate that morality significantly declined as volume increased.[134] While the volume necessary to secure safer results varied, the clear implication was that volume-based experience makes a substantial difference in safety.

Recognizing this critical insight, the three clinical systems have taken a pledge to restrict specific types of risky surgery to those facilities and physicians with substantial experience and to prohibit such surgical activity by those without the requisite background.[135] It has been estimated that as many as 11,000 lives could be saved each year by instituting such a program across the country.[136]

The process of developing and refining lists of surgeries that should be restricted and the experience levels to be required of those who should be permitted to perform them requires further refinement but the implications in terms of safety are clear. By extending the volume principle to exceedingly common elective surgery, analysts have determined that low volume hospitals have a 70% higher mortality rate for knee replacements, a 50% higher rate for hip replacements, and a 20% higher rate for surgical treatment of congestive heart failure and chronic obstructive pulmonary disease.[137]

What government surveillance programs might do in this context involves two distinct steps. The first is to initiate engaged government surveillance of surgeries designated as risky and the mortality rates of facilities performing them. The risk-adjusted data thus gathered should be made available to both the medical profession and the public at large. As in the case of New York's CABG registry program, such information is likely to focus medical profession attention on outlier programs and generate some reputational concerns that may be translated into safety improvements. The data may also help inform referring physicians and consumers about especially risky programs. Although New York's experience on this score has not been particularly encouraging the volume data's impact might be heightened by following Dr. Robert Wachter's suggestion that outlier programs be required to display a "black box" warning like that used with especially dangerous pharmaceutical products.[138]

A second and far more radical step might be considered. There is ample evidence in the operation of the New York CABG program to support imposing limitations on the authority of certain facilities to perform risky surgery. This is what

New York did with certain outliers and might warrant replication by Centers for Medicare and Medicaid Services (CMS) with respect to Medicare and Medicaid reimbursement for such operations. The key criticism of this sort of initiative is that it will deprive patients in rural areas and impoverished communities served by a single provider of access to care. The best solution may not be allowing less skilled doctors to provide potentially dangerous care but to arrange methods for bringing appropriately skilled teams to patients or delivering patients to those teams.[139] In at least some cases, surgeons' criticisms of the volume pledge amounts to little more than the special pleading of doctors who feel their income will be threatened—very much like the effort undertaken by the orthopods who attacked the AHCPR's spinal fusion guidelines. Criticism also appears to have arisen from those who believe that the principle of medical independence warrants allowing every doctor to perform any and all procedures she or he is remotely qualified to undertake.[140] In an era of rapidly accelerating specialization these arguments seem particularly weak. They have been rejected with respect to organ transplant surgery.[141] Finally, critics have claimed that volume does not measure safety and that "quality-based standards" are what is needed.[142] Again, it seems that the opportunity for practical improvement is being attacked in the name of a hypothesized but nonexistent "better."

A program of the sort that focuses on the volume of specified risky surgeries would appear to satisfy the criteria for success we have identified. The program would be narrowly focused on an enumerated set of procedures. These would be identified by frequency of performance and differential mortality risk. The data the government would need for its surveillance would be readily available from Medicare and Medicaid submissions along with death registry data. Finally, the outcome of concern, mortality, is clearly one particularly ascertainable and worthy of government attention.

PRIVATE SAFETY EFFORTS AND THE SURVEILLANCE MODEL

"Sentinel Event" Programs

A number of private initiatives have sought to use surveillance methodologies to improve safety. One of the most prominent of these has been the Joint Commission's effort to get the hospitals it accredits to report "sentinel events" and, with Joint Commission assistance, develop means to prevent them. A sentinel event is "an unexpected occurrence involving death or serious physical or psychological injury, or the risk thereof."[143] Between 1995 and 2004, the Joint Commission program received approximately 3,000 sentinel event reports. Of these, approximately 1,000 did not come from accredited hospitals but from the media or other sources. The volume of reports has been viewed by all observers as absurdly low in light of the number of medical errors established by every study of the problem in the past several decades. The Joint Commission did not make the reports it received public or vigorously investigate them. It did not use its accreditation power to compel safety improvements.[144] In 2002, the National Quality Forum, a private organization dedicated to the improvement of healthcare took up the Joint Commission idea and prepared a list of 27 never-events (later increased to 28) including pressure ulcers, injuries from falls while hospitalized, transfusion of incompatible blood products, and failure to remove foreign bodies from patients at the conclusion of surgery.[145] This provided some needed specificity to the sentinel events concept but did little to improve the flow of reports.

The Joint Commission program illustrated most of the shortcomings the New York cardiac registry was able to avoid in mounting its surveillance program. The Joint Commission effort was not tied to any governmental or other enforcement mechanism. Although the Joint Commission has accreditation power, that power is virtually never used, thereby negating any real leverage the commission might otherwise have had to compel improvements in safety. The New York Department of Health could and did suspend outlier programs. The Joint Commission never did. Moreover, the Joint Commission is dependent for its funding on the hospitals it regulates. The likelihood that it can and will regulate vigorously is remote in the face of this conflict of interest.

The National Quality Forum notwithstanding, the Joint Commission program was not sharply focused. Its sentinel events definition is vague and does not address any particular set of procedures. Its articulated concern is with "unexpected occurrence." What this means is anyone's guess and invites gaming by reporting institutions. Even absent a desire to game the reporting obligation, this requirement is unlikely to produce any substantial number of reports about any particular practice or procedure. Its mandate is as broad as the hospital's entire catalogue of services. It is unlikely that reports will provide sufficient similar-incident information to fix benchmarks or identify better approaches. In the end, the best the Joint Commission could hope for was a string of anecdotes. As the saying goes, "the plural of anecdote is not *data*." In addition to definitional and statistical problems the Joint Commission appeared to do little reviewing or auditing of hospital submissions (or nonsubmissions). Life-threatening mistakes are not the sort of thing hospitals leap to report. The incentives are to avoid disclosure and minimize fault. Without a rigorous effort to independently scrutinize submissions and audit records for missed incidents there is virtually no likelihood of effective surveillance, let alone safety improvement.

The Joint Commission initiative had virtually no impact on healthcare providers. This is not surprising in light of the absence of either accreditation or financial consequences. The only real never-event in the Joint Commission's operation was change-fostering publicity. In the end there was no real reason to report, no assurance that what was reported was accurate, no financial incentive to improve and little hope of generating useful data. Nongovernment surveillance of the Joint Commission type had little chance of doing any better.

After the National Quality Forum's definitional proposals in 2002, a number of states took up the never-events concept and instituted public programs to deny government reimbursement to hospitals for costs related to such events.

Several states went further and instituted reporting programs. These efforts were facilitated by congressional legislation in 2005 in the Patient Safety and Quality Improvement Act, which made provision for patient safety organizations, entities authorized to gather safety problem information on a confidential basis.[146] Despite the reporting and information gathering initiatives, few safety benefits have come out of these efforts. The states that have reporting programs have not provided significant budgetary support for surveillance.[147] This has meant that nothing like the New York registry effort has been undertaken. There are virtually no careful reviews of submissions and few audits (in 2008 only 7 of 27 states with reporting systems authorized any sort of audits at all).[148] In most states the only consequence for a reporting violation is a small fine.[149] There is no public disclosure in most states and no outlier designations.

Limiting Resident Duty Hours to 80 Per Week

The Libby Zion Story has been repeated many times since her death in 1984.[150] She was a college freshman who went to the emergency room of New York Hospital with flu-like symptoms and an odd spasmodic jerking. She was cared for by two young, overworked, undersupervised residents, one with less than a year's experience and the other less than two. They made a series of treatment decisions that a New York jury concluded contributed to her death while she lay manacled to a hospital bed with a fever of 107° and neither of the doctors in attendance. Libby's father, a *New York Daily News* journalist and lawyer, blamed the young doctors but, more emphatically, the medical training system that forced residents to work upwards of 100 hours a week including 30-hour shifts. He vehemently advocated legal changes that would reduce resident hours and, it was hoped, leave treatment decisions in the hands of doctors who were properly supervised and not in the throes of exhaustion. Zion's campaign triggered a political firestorm and led Department of Health Commissioner Axelrod to appoint a blue-ribbon commission headed by Dr. Bertrand Bell (a reform-minded primary care physician) to look into the questions of limiting the number of hours residents could be required to work and the manner in which they would be supervised.

The Bell Commission, as it came to be known, proposed a series of regulations to address the perceived problems of supervision and exhaustion. It suggested a work week limit for residents of an average of 80 hours with no more than 12 continuous hours in the emergency room, no shift exceeding 24 hours, eight-hour rest periods between shifts, at least one day of rest every week, and effective senior physician supervision. These proposed limitations were incorporated into a statute that was enacted by the New York Legislature in 1987.[151] Unlike the New York cardiac registry, no effective surveillance mechanism was established for this program and the only consequence for violation was a small fine. The legislative expectation appeared to be that violations would generally be reported by the victim residents who were to be protected by a whistleblower mechanism in the law. The idea that residents would report their programs and jeopardize their careers (by training program curtailment or career-affecting retaliation) was not realistic.

It should come as no surprise, in light of the residents' situation and the problems we have explored with respect to error reporting, that few complaints were made and New York hospitals generally ignored or gamed their way around the Bell regulation limits. More than 90% of New York hospitals were estimated to be violating the law.[152] In light of news reports about hospital disregard for the limits, the Department of Health undertook a series of "raids" in 1998. These confirmed the scope of the problem and, in turn, led the legislature to increase maximum fines as well as the department's enforcement budget, albeit modestly.

The public concern triggered by the Zion case did not immediately dissipate. In the glare of publicity, the AMA endorsed some restrictions on resident hours[153] and the nongovernmental regulatory body which oversees medical resident training and working conditions, the Accreditation Committee for Graduate Medical Education (ACGME), in 2003, established its own set of restrictions on resident working hours.[154] These were patterned after those enacted in New York. ACGME, however, had an even weaker enforcement mechanism than New York. Although ACGME makes annual inspection visits to upwards of 2,000 teaching hospital programs, these are scripted and formal affairs. They are not geared for a careful audit of program operations, let alone an examination of the specifics of resident working hours. Nor do these visits promote any sort of whistleblowing.

ACGME has displayed little enthusiasm for robust enforcement activity of any sort. As was the case with the Joint Commission, ACGME's clients are the programs it accredits and action against them is likely to provoke multi-institutional backlash.[155] This conflict of interest notwithstanding, the widespread resistance among teaching hospitals to the curbing of resident hours led ACGME to make a show of regulatory enforcement several months after the hours limitations went into effect. It reviewed the working hours of the Johns Hopkins Internal Medicine Residency program and found the program in serious violation of the new limits and initiated the process of withdrawing the program's accreditation.[156] This step, against a highly prestigious program, was supposed to send a message about the seriousness of the regulatory effort. However, the withdrawal of accreditation, if actually carried out, would have harmed the residents it was supposed to protect by interrupting their training and complicating their path to board certification. In the end the enforcement effort was toothless—Johns Hopkins's program was not de-accredited, and the suspension was stipulated to be retroactively lifted if appropriate duty hour adjustments were made.[157]

Despite its tough talk, ACGME did not establish an effective reporting mechanism regarding hours (either by program certification or resident complaint), nor did it institute any sort of rigorous surveillance regime to audit resident hours. Predictably, teaching hospitals went right on requiring a substantially greater than allowed number of work hours from their residents. A 2006 study, published in JAMA, found that 80% of residents were required to work excessive hours.[158] That has continued to be the case despite ACGME's reiteration of its hours limitation rules in 2011. The reasons are not hard to identify. Complaints will be few because residents are likely to hurt themselves if they report their program. ACGME offers no convincing protection to those who would consider complaining.[159] Real enforcement of the ACGME rules would cost teaching hospitals huge sums in staffing expenses and clash with deeply held beliefs among senior physicians about the supposed value of long hours.

The medical profession has advanced a number of arguments against curtailing resident duty hours. It has been suggested that residents only truly understand the diseases they treat if they personally observe the course illness takes in the early days of treatment. This, so the argument goes, can only be accomplished if young doctors are required to work long hours. (What anyone can learn or recall at the end of a 100-hour week and 30-hour shift is open to serious debate.) Long hours are also praised as providing "continuity" of care so that a small and informed team works with each patient. These arguments are not supported by much data. The same may be said of another argument advanced by the profession: that long hours "toughen" young doctors up so that they can deal with a wide array of challenges.[160] Perhaps more to the point, serious hours limitations would cost teaching hospitals substantial sums, by increasing the number of both junior and senior staff required to maintain round-the-clock coverage—expenses these hospitals are not willing or, in some cases, able to afford.

The healthcare industry has also fallen back on its standby objection that the claims about the risks of exhaustion have not been demonstrated empirically. It is quite difficult to accept this argument as anything other than pretextual in light of safety-based hours restrictions on airline pilots (8 hours) and long-haul truckers (10 hours). Even members of Congress have noted the absurdity of assertions that triple-digit working hours make any sense. When the U.S. Navy recently reported safety lapses associated with long hours, Senator John McCain observed: "If we know that somebody's working a 100-hour workweek, I'm not sure we need a study."[161] That said, the hours restrictions have inspired a plethora of studies (709 by one count in 2014).[162] What is striking about many of these is the lengths to which medical analysts have gone to suggest that hours limitations "may" impede, rather than improve, patient safety and "may" interfere with resident education and training.[163] To say that the data against hours restrictions are inconclusive and subject to a wide array of confounds is a substantial understatement (particularly since many studies appear to have assumed changes in hospital resident work schedules had occurred in response to the ACGME rules changes when the reality on the ground is quite different).

In the resident duty hours context it must be said that both public (New York statute) and private (ACGME regulations) efforts have failed to foster substantial change to improve safety. Performance standards unaccompanied by effective surveillance are likely to yield poor results or evasion. In the 80 hours case, providers had little to lose by evasion (mostly modest fines) and a great deal to gain (a pool of inexpensive resident laborers). Moreover, there was no mechanism for public disclosure and no opportunity to trigger the sorts of reputational concerns that can arise from being branded a safety outlier. It is striking that New York, which pioneered effective public surveillance, could not do better on the hours question.

CONCLUSIONS

Government intervention in medical safety surveillance is not a sure-fire cure for medical error. Governments at the federal and state level have used statutes and regulations to promote reporting designed with the hope of getting providers to identify and address a range of problems from never-events to nosocomial infections, all with limited success.[164] But when legally mandated government programs add active surveillance (with auditing, benchmarking and feedback components) they can, as in the case of the New York CABG registry, foster significant safety advances. Experience suggests that a number of legal requirements are critical to safety enhancement through surveillance. First, the surveillance program should be in public rather than private hands. Private efforts like those of the Joint Commission and ACGME seldom appear to result in appreciable safety improvement. Entities like these are simply too beholden to the clientele they regulate. They do not take the tough steps required to pressure reluctant providers to change.

Not only is government involvement essential, it must have both legal leverage to compel compliance and the administrative apparatus to monitor obedience. New York's cardiac registry worked, in part, because the certificate of necessity requirement gave the Department of Health authority to shut down unsafe outlier programs—an authority it showed itself willing to use. More than authority, successful programs need an effective bureaucracy able to review submissions with care, audit programs, follow up on suspicious claims, and develop expertise in the operations of regulated providers. This can be expensive, and few programs have had the sustained budgetary support necessary.

A successful surveillance program must be narrowly tailored in its monitoring mandates. If its focus is too broad, it will not be able to maintain proper oversight or develop effective benchmarks. A diffuse focus spreads resources too thin (there are too many things to scrutinize) and thwarts the development of bureaucratic expertise. The medical activity monitored must be high cost and/or high volume. It has to be the sort of activity that is of financial importance to providers, the sort of thing they will be willing to invest time and money in. It also has to present a serious risk of patient mortality or harm. Less serious problems will be hard to track. The practical and moral objective should be to concentrate on the most serious dangers, something the New York registry was able to do.

Effective government surveillance programs need a steady flow of high-quality information. Regulations must require the submission of such material and the government agency must insist that providers supply it. This means employing the sort of monitoring we have already described. This aspect of surveillance may be getting easier with the rise of electronic health records. These can, if properly configured, provide regulators with real-time access to clinical treatment records for monitoring and review. Legal changes may be required to facilitate access, and expertise may need to be expanded to use such material effectively, but this is an area where the general consensus is that information technology is opening up promising avenues for safety surveillance.[165]

Regulators must insist that performance data be provided on a timely basis. Allowing submissions to be filed after months of delay will not facilitate significant improvement and signals to providers that safety is not critically important.[166] Not only must data be submitted expeditiously but also feedback to providers must be provided in the same way. It is regularly noted that successful safety initiatives feature rapid and useful feedback.[167] Such a process demonstrates that submissions have been attended to and that reporters will benefit from the efforts they are required to make.

Although the most effective surveillance programs must be government operated, there is a serious need for professional medical input through panels of expert advisers in the specialty being overseen.[168] Such groups provide the sort of guidance and expertise that health department bureaucracies cannot hope to duplicate. In the New York registry's case, the Cardiac Advisory Commission was responsible for the development of the respected risk adjustment methodology that made inter-hospital and inter-physician comparisons possible. It also provided the experts who could scrutinize troubled programs and suggest means for them to improve. Beyond their technical contributions, blue ribbon panels signal the profession that its leaders are committed to the effort to improve safety. It is far more difficult to dismiss safety initiatives promoted by the profession's leaders than it is to dismiss health department bureaucrats.

Finally, the surveillance program must be provided with means of making its findings known to the public. This is probably the most controversial aspect of surveillance initiatives but one that experience suggests is critical to success. It is when a provider's lucrative or high-volume practice is identified as an outlier that safety improvements appear most likely to occur. Providers are, generally, extremely slow to make changes when there is little or no threat to reputation. Their calculus seems to change when poor performance is widely broadcast and reputation undermined.

While the clearest path to safety improvement appears to be engaged government surveillance coupled with performance standards, there is a fairly recent counterexample that deserves attention. One of the places where patients face the most serious danger of injury through medical error is the intensive care unit (ICU). Infections acquired in the ICU (nosocomial infections), often induced during the insertion or maintenance of central lines (catheters), sicken tens of thousands of patients a year—in 2006 it was estimated that there were at least 80,000 such infections, of which 20,000 were fatal.[169] ICUs were the places where antibiotic-resistant infections first appeared and where they have been hardest to treat.

In 2003 intensive-care specialist Peter Pronovost of Johns Hopkins Hospital set about testing a five-step program to combat nosocomial infections in ICUs. His plan included scrupulous infection-control steps, a checklist to be followed in all cases by caregivers and closely monitored use of catheters.[170] Pronovost, with the support of the federal AHRQ, persuaded the Michigan Health and Hospital Association to undertake a virtually statewide ICU experiment utilizing the outlined steps (originated at Johns Hopkins). The result was an astounding 66%

drop in the rate of catheter-related bloodstream infections. Doctor Pronovost and his colleagues attributed a significant part of their success to "the existence of an infrastructure—specifically congressional funding to develop and maintain the NNIS [National Nosocomial Infection Surveillance System of the CDC]."[171]

Notwithstanding Pronovost's emphasis on government surveillance, the key to the ICU program's success was his effort, along with that of the Michigan hospitals, to reduce infections by strictly following the specified treatment program and checklist in every case. Since the Michigan results were reported in 2006, the ICU initiative has been successfully repeated in Rhode Island and elsewhere.[172] The evidence of dramatic safety improvement has led a large number of hospitals around the country to change the way they conduct business in the ICU. Despite such results and a recently established CMS Medicare and Medicaid program that reduces government payments to nosocomial infection outlier hospitals,[173] there are regions of the country, especially the deep South (including Louisiana, Mississippi, Alabama, and Arkansas) where change of a demonstrably effective sort has not been adopted.[174] In such circumstances there may be good reason to mandate the course of treatment to be utilized in any case involving Medicare and Medicaid reimbursement. Although this would be means-specifying regulation (coupled with National Nosocomial Infection Surveillance System surveillance), insistence on its use may, because of the supporting evidence and lives at stake, be warranted.

The possible future development of other such protocols and a willingness to mandate their adoption when the evidence warrants, should be recognized as an alternative path to significant safety improvement. The ICU initiative reminds us that no approach has a monopoly on safety improvement. But even the ICU story underscores the critical value of engaged governmental surveillance whether of performance goals or of empirically validated safety protocols.

13

Information Technology

Technology will reinvent healthcare.[1]

23ANDME

Recently, two of the most thoughtful and candid physician observers of medical developments, Robert Wachter and Eric Topol, published books addressing the information technology revolution they perceived to be taking place in medicine.[2] Each acknowledged the challenges such technology was likely to pose. Each also recognized the serious problem presented by medical error and pinned hopes for safety improvement on changes information technology might make in the delivery of patient care. Their aspiration, expressed in very different ways, was that the rise of electronic health records (EHR), artificial intelligence (AI) and radically expanded use of smartphones would improve access to, accuracy of, and outcomes produced by the healthcare system. Both also argued that technology could empower patients to play a more significant part in their own care.

In previous chapters, we have explored the resistance of elements within the healthcare industry to candor and transparency with regard to informed consent and the reporting of treatment errors. Despite this, Dr. Wachter has pinned significant hope for improved safety on medical candor, declaring, with what can only be described as courageous optimism, that "if the arc of history bends toward justice, the arc of medicine bends toward transparency."[3] Taking a different tack, Dr. Topol has tied his hopes for improvement to the power of information technology to sidestep professional control and empower patients in ways that will allow them to pursue and secure better and safer care on their own initiative.

We begin our consideration of the potential impact of information technology by examining a dispute between the genomic testing company, 23andMe, and the U.S. Food and Drug Administration (FDA). Genetic sequencing companies began offering consumers information about their exome (a key protein-coding element of the genome) in the early 2000s. Most of these early providers were not particularly reliable, and many were out to exploit the public's interest in the topic in the wake of the successful completion of the mapping of the human genome in 2003. In 2006, the Government Accountability Office (GAO) investigated a number of the early providers and found that the companies offering direct-to-consumer testing were, in many cases, hawking unproven disease predictions and promoting the purchase of treatments that were nothing more than overpriced multivitamins.[4] In reaction, the FDA and Centers for Disease Control and Prevention (CDC) warned the public against direct-to-consumer genetic testers and advised patients that genetic analysis should only be procured from specialized laboratories at the direction and under the supervision of a doctor.

In 2006, a second wave of genetic testing firms began to operate. These were considered to be more reliable than their predecessors. Among them was a company named 23andMe, which was financed by Silicon Valley tech giants Google and Facebook. Its objective was to provide an array of genetic information directly to customers who purchased its testing kits and provided a sample of saliva for DNA analysis. Though the scientific underpinnings of 23andMe's testing procedure were sound, there was widespread hostility in the healthcare industry to the company's providing customers with analysis asserting a link to various diseases and conditions.

The *Journal of American Medical Association* (JAMA), one of the leading voices of the profession, published an article in 2008 by two medical ethicists about the new genetic testing services.[5] Despite the absence of any indication that the ethicists had specialized technical expertise, their piece was a wholesale attack on direct-to-consumer testing. Its target, among others, was 23andMe. It recognized that such companies "hope to empower consumers to take control of their health,"[6] but appeared to find that objective problematic. The article began by noting that consumer-requested testing was unlawful in a number of states because of legislation mandating the "involvement of a licensed physician."[7] It did not pause to consider the continuing justification of such a requirement in a rapidly developing technological field. It then proceeded to raise questions about the reliability and clinical utility of the new genetic tests. It cited with approval a then-recent article by D. J. Hunter and colleagues, in the prestigious *New England Journal of Medicine*, urging doctors to discourage patients from availing themselves of such services.[8]

The JAMA piece then presented a number of reasons to reject direct-to-consumer initiatives, none of them considering the empirical evidence discussed in this chapter. Primary care physicians were described as having tightly constricted time to devote to patients. The ethicist authors expressed concern that patient acquisition of genetic information would lead to increased requests for counseling and testing, demands that doctors could ill afford to satisfy in light of their busy schedules. The hypothesized demands on physician time were said to be especially troublesome because the clinical value of 23andMe's tests were unproven, and, therefore, one could speculate that questions about them would be unworthy of consideration. The authors went on to argue that the information provided through genetic testing could lead to heightened patient anxiety. That was followed by conjecture that there would be heightened demand for expensive medical follow-up of genetic tests to assuage patient concerns about such illnesses as cancer, heart disease, and Alzheimer's disease. According to the ethicists, the risk is high that there will be an "inappropriate expenditure of healthcare resources" and "a drain on the medical commons.[9]

To avoid these problems, the authors recommended increased government regulation of genetic testing designed, essentially, to limit its availability. They called for the production of large volumes of data to justify any company-claimed inferences about health links to genetic information. They suggested that the medical establishment deserved government funding so that it could conduct high-quality genetic research, reasoning that company data were unlikely to be "an unbiased source of information."[10] (It is interesting that the ethicists were calling for an approach never before employed *even* for the review of potentially life-threatening pharmaceuticals whose approval is generally based on manufacturer-sponsored research.) This furious attack was remarkable for its failure, at any turn, to adduce convincing proof for its concerns and claims. While the authors saw no need to shore up the empirical basis for their criticisms, they were at pains to stress the substantial empirical burden that should be imposed on direct-to-consumer companies. Although it was early in the process of evaluating the merit of providing consumers direct access to genetic information, these critics set out an impossibly demanding template that later critics would repeat throughout the coming debate, no matter what evidence was presented.

A 2009 American Medical Association (AMA) publication, once more with an ethics connection, returned to the direct-to-consumer genetic testing question. In an *American Medical Association Journal of Ethics* piece, Emily Anderson called for heightened government scrutiny of genetic testing companies.[11] Again, the paucity of evidence to demonstrate clinical validity and utility were decried. Added to this criticism was a new point: "physicians' limited knowledge of genetics."[12] This was said to be a problem *for genetic testing companies* because many physicians did not have the training to be of assistance to patients who obtained genetic information on their own initiative. The proposed solution to the information problem was not physician education or referral services but rigorous use of governmental regulatory powers to curtail the flow of information. According to Dr. Anderson, consumers needed protection from information, so much protection that the information should be available only if supported by the highest level of proof and under a doctor's guidance. To assure that this standard was met, the government was urged to closely monitor and regulate all laboratories performing genetic tests. State laws prohibiting direct-to-consumer testing, like those in New York and California, were touted. Heightened FDA scrutiny of genetic testing reports was called for and Federal Trade Commission (FTC) review of advertising claims was promoted. Perhaps driven by a belt-and-suspenders philosophy, Anderson called for enactment of federal legislation that would place the entire industry under constant federal scrutiny and control.

The *Journal of Ethics* piece concluded by highlighting the AMA Board of Trustees report of 2008, which discouraged direct-to-consumer genetic testing and proposed that "testing be made available only under the supervision of a qualified health care professional."[13] This recommendation was made despite AMA recognition that most doctors did not believe themselves fit to provide such supervision. As in previous articles, what was being proposed was a stricter standard of regulation than required with respect to virtually any other industry or practice connected with medical care. The alleged risks that justified this level of protection were the hypothesized possibilities of consumer anxiety and a heightened level of requests for medical advice. Direct-to-consumer delivery of healthcare information was perceived as so threatening that a solution akin to prohibition was proposed for the activity.

Despite the healthcare industry's concerns and objections, 23andMe grew rapidly. It did so notwithstanding a second GAO report, in 2010, critical of the genomic testing industry.[14] By the end of 2010, the company had provided analyses to over 500,000 customers. It appeared to have tapped into an area of substantial consumer concern, one unserved by the medical community. During the same period, research was conducted regarding the critics' claims about patient anxiety and inappropriate use of medical resources. In a 2011 *New England Journal of Medicine* article, Eric Topol and his colleagues found that "the psychological, behavioral and clinical effects of [genetic] risk scanning" hypothesized by direct-to-consumer critics were not significant issues in a group of more than 2,000 recipients of genetic testing information.[15] While this could not be considered the end of the debate (because of the homogeneity of the subjects), it did cast substantial doubt on the critics' conjectures.

The challenge posed to the naysayers' position was heightened by research conducted among primary care physicians. The sampled doctors believed that direct-to-consumer genetic testing reports were understandable and would be helpful in "patient management."[16] The research identified one of the key reasons why caregivers had been slow in adapting to the increased availability of genetic information. The polled physicians indicated their lack of knowledge about genetics. Twenty percent of the 502 respondents had no genetic education whatsoever. Only 22% said "their training in genetics was sufficient to work with their patients who have had genetic testing."[17] This expressed lack of skill appeared to have led some of the surveyed doctors to avoid genetic testing even when specifically suggested by the FDA for "pharmacogenetic" purposes including the fixing of a proper dosage level of the anticoagulant, Warfarin (this despite the fact that 97% of the respondent doctors had prescribed Warfarin in the preceding two years.)[18]

23andMe appeared to be in an enviable position. In 2012 alone, it sold 150,000 kits. Its business was booming and its expanding genetic and personal information data base, provided by customers, virtually all of whom indicated a willingness to participate in medical research, was opening the way to promising avenues of pharmaceutical product development. But all was not well in the management of the company. Its rapid expansion triggered special scrutiny by the FDA, which sought to have the company demonstrate that consumers could understand the nature and limits of the information 23andMe was providing. In the period before November 2013, the FDA held 14 face-to-face meetings with company representatives and exchanged hundreds of written communications with them. The company promised to perform a number of studies but never completed the work.[19] All this appears not to have been a calculated strategy to stonewall the FDA while the company's business boomed, but the result of a breakdown in management as key legal staff departed, and the CEO struggled with a difficult divorce.[20]

For whatever reason, 23andMe did not communicate with the FDA for at least six months during 2013, and on November 22 of that year, the agency sent the company a letter demanding that it "immediately discontinue marketing" its Personal Genome Service, the health report it provided customers concerning 254 diseases and conditions.[21] The FDA acted on the strength of its regulatory authority regarding medical devices, finding that company materials appeared to be dispensing "diagnosis of disease or other conditions."[22] The agency seemed to embrace all of the healthcare industry's criticisms of direct-to-consumer testing, citing concerns about patient misuse and lack of understanding of information supplied (especially such things as the presence of the BRCA gene, which increases the risk of breast and ovarian cancer, as well as the gene affecting the calculation of Warfarin dosage). The FDA seemed to endorse the idea that information should be imparted only when a patient is "under a physician's care,"[23] and only if the company had obtained the FDA's premarketing approvals of the test employed. On December 8, 2013, 23andMe suspended its distribution of the Personal Genome Service to new customers.

Perhaps sensing 23andMe's vulnerability, critics renewed their attacks on an outsider company seeking to provide health information to potential patients. What is remarkable about many of these attacks is that they seemed to disregard the research suggesting that direct-to-consumer genetic information did not pose a threat of harm and that doctors were not well equipped to render genetic services. In December 2013, immediately following the FDA's action, one prominent medical professional critic declared that FDA worries about patient misuse were well-founded "because who knows what individuals will do with information they interpret themselves."[24] This observation is remarkable given what was then known about how patients used that data. One might expect a more nuanced appraisal from a medical genetics expert, which the speaker was, but what was said seemed to reflect an unalterable bias against anything that might come out of a direct-to-consumer service. The same commentator described 23andMe customers as "Caucasian, well educated and economically upscale" and branded their inquiries "recreational genetics."[25] What is particularly noteworthy about this description is its suggestion of frivolity and touristic dabbling by the well-heeled, as if a desire to know about one's health status, genetic predispositions, and current scientific information could never be the proper province of patients.

Interestingly, the story did not end there. While commentators generally noted the fumblings of 23andMe, a number were sharply critical of the philosophy that seemed to underlie the FDA's action. Silicon Valley–based critics decried the government's apparent willingness to squelch technological innovation. Legal critics like University of Chicago professor Richard Epstein ripped what he described as regulatory excess.[26] An editorial in the leading scientific journal, *Nature*, condemned the government's action, declaring, "even if regulators or doctors want to, they will not be able to stand between ordinary people and their DNA for very long."[27]

A short time later, *Nature* published a "Comment" refuting medical critics' and the FDA's unsupported assertions about patient anxiety and alleged misunderstanding of genetic information. The comment argued that the evidence pointed in the opposite direction on these questions and that the FDA's ban "may pose a greater threat to consumer health than the harms it seeks to prevent."[28] In support of this claim it was noted that the FDA's articulated approach might not only stand in the way of providing patients with a wide range of genetic information but threatened other valuable initiatives that might be classified as medical devices by the FDA, including a host of direct-to-patient health apps for smartphones and online tools over which the agency appeared to claim jurisdiction. The comment also pointed out that there were potentially serious constitutional problems with what the FDA was doing because it could interfere with protected commercial speech and bumped up against the U.S. Supreme Court's ruling in *Sorrell v. IMS Health, Inc.*[29] and the Second Circuit's decision in *U.S. v. Caronia*,[30] both emphasizing free speech concerns in the health information context. Perhaps equally influential was a claim voiced in *The New Yorker* magazine,[31] and elsewhere, that the FDA's "selective paternalism" was placing patients in jeopardy by retarding the dissemination of vital genetic information and inhibiting research to identify genetic risks that companies like 23andMe might be in a position to discover with the information provided by their hundreds of thousands of customers.

The case against prohibition of direct-to-consumer genetic testing information was a strong one, and, in 2015, the FDA and the company announced that 23andMe would be allowed to resume providing genetic information to consumers without medical oversight. The change came in February when the testing service announced FDA approval of its distribution directly to customers of test results linked to a rare genetic disorder, Bloom syndrome. This sort of screening has been described as "carrier testing," the identification of those who carry certain genetic traits that could result in serious harm to their offspring.[32] Not only was direct-to-consumer activity to be allowed, the scientific burden of proof the company had to satisfy to offer such testing was minimized. Thus, the door was opened to distribution of an ever-widening range of genetic information to concerned individuals without the oversight of doctors or the healthcare industry. Patients were once again empowered to become the assessors of their own conditions and collectors of critical information about them.

The service 23andMe could provide after it resumed full operations focused on 35 genes that had "carrier status." However, both onlookers and the company's president, Ann Wojcick, saw the FDA's new approach as paving the way for the rapid expansion of the genetic information that could be made available. This was particularly the case because, with a subscriber population approaching one million, 23andMe was in a strong position to identify new correlations as well as take advantage of the accelerating pace of genetic discovery. The company's data have also been recognized as a valuable resource for pharmaceutical research. A number of drug companies have made deals with 23andMe to pursue genetic links to illness. One of the first of these involved Genentech, which has agreed to pay the company up to $60 million in a joint project to analyze the genetic material of up to 12,000 people afflicted with Parkinson's disease, or with family members who were.[33] A similar deal has been made with Pfizer focusing on Crohn's disease.

The direct-to-consumer genetic testing story provides important lessons for efforts to disseminate information to customers that can put them in charge of monitoring their health and addressing potential problems. It suggests the possibility of reducing traditional healthcare's control of certain diagnostic and decision-making processes. As the 23andMe episode illustrates, segments of the industry will fight this sort of shift despite both a lack of background about and genuine engagement with innovative technology. Tools in the holding action against change will include claims that supplying information directly to patients will cause anxiety and that patients are incompetent to manage the necessary response. Those making such claims will not, generally, wait for empirical evidence. They will often rely on anecdote and supposition. Critics will demand that innovators satisfy the highest standards of proof. Even if reliable information is conceded to be available, established medical organizations are likely to call for professional control of its procurement and interpretation. The professional establishment's primary strategy in its effort to retain control will be calls for regulation by the FDA and other government agencies. If 23andMe's story is any indication, medical critics may be able to delay the provision of important information directly to consumers. Why traditional segments of the industry are likely to take this track is something we will examine shortly.

HEALTHCARE INDUSTRY RESISTANCE TO PROVIDING PATIENTS WITH MEDICAL INFORMATION

The example of 23andMe might be dismissed as unrepresentative of the industry's reaction to providing critical health information directly to patients. After all, genetic testing is esoteric and doctors, by their own admission, find it challenging. As it turns out, however, the 23andMe story is paradigmatic of the healthcare industry's reaction to the provision of any diagnostic or treatment-related information directly to consumers without professional oversight. A good example, drawn from the era before the rise of information technology, is the 10-year fight that preceded the marketing of direct-to-consumer home pregnancy tests. The effort to identify a simple and reliable test to determine pregnancy began in the 1920s, utilizing various animals' (rabbits, rats, toads) reaction to hormones in the urine of potentially pregnant women.[34] These tests were slow, expensive, and required skilled technicians. Eventually, a far simpler test was developed to identify the critical pregnancy hormone. In 1967, a product designer at Organon

Pharmaceuticals, Margaret Crane, proposed and designed a home pregnancy test that could be used by any woman who suspected that she was pregnant.[35]

The reaction to this innovative idea was what one might have predicted in light of the 23andMe story. The company delayed development of the home pregnancy test, not on any technical or commercial grounds, but because of its fear that doctors would object. Since doctors were Organon's key customers, anything that might upset them was to be approached warily.[36] Despite such concerns, the commercial potential of a home pregnancy test proved enticing and in 1969 Organon obtained a patent (with Ms. Crane listed as inventor).[37] The product was introduced in Canada in 1970. Efforts to market it in the United States, however, triggered strong regulatory and medical objection. The U.S. Public Health Service opposed the device as did many physicians. Their opposition was premised on the familiar and empirically unsupported arguments that women could not manage either the testing process or the information on their own. They would, it was hypothesized, be gripped by anxiety and would irresponsibly fail to follow up with timely prenatal care. Speaking about the somewhat more elaborate and lengthy test then being introduced into the American market, one prominent Johns Hopkins University physician said, "Pregnancy testing is a very emotional event and people do not do as well as they might. They have a hard time following even relatively simple instructions."[38]

Ten years after the inception of the idea, eight years after the patenting of the device, and six years after its introduction in Canada, in 1977, the home pregnancy test finally arrived in America. The result of the story is, as the saying goes, "history." The tests were wildly popular. Today most pregnancies in the United States are identified by home testing. There has been no wave of anxiety, no evidence of widespread incompetence. Instead, there were simply unwarranted claims that led to delay of patient empowerment.

More recently, the information dissemination disputes have centered on direct patient access, first to laboratory test results and, second, to physicians' notes. Traditionally, patients were denied access to laboratory results. In fact, 13 states, as of 2014, still had laws that barred release of such material to patients, while another seven only allowed access with clinician approval.[39] The rationale, both for the specific laws and the far more pervasive restrictions on access, was very much like that we have already noted. It was argued that patients with unrestricted access to lab results would become anxious about any abnormality, would be unable to understand the import of the information provided, and would bombard physicians with a host of time-consuming questions.[40] As was the case in other settings, these claims were supported by virtually no research.

In 1996, the Health Insurance Portability and Accountability Act (HIPAA)[41] sought to make lab materials available to patients. However, the new legal mandate was ineffective. No more than 6% of patients ever sought access to their lab tests and well-informed observers concluded: "health professionals have erected an invisible but substantial wall" to keep patients out.[42] That wall was maintained with substantial fees for copies of records, prohibition of review unless a clinician was present and lengthy delays in responding to patient requests.[43] Moreover, the original HIPAA rule was not well drafted. It mandated release of records only to "authorized persons." Under the previously noted state laws, that meant the exclusion of patients in 13 states where there was a specific bar to patient access. The result was the same in the seven other states where a clinician's presence was legally mandated. A potential barrier existed in 23 more states because their laws did not specifically "authorize" patients to obtain medical test information.[44]

The HIPAA requirements of 1996 triggered renewed, but yet again ungrounded, assertions about the risks to patients if they were given unfettered access to laboratory information. Doctors continued to speculate that access would cause worry and increase the volume of time-consuming patient questions. Some medical professionals said they saw a threat to the doctor–patient relationship if there was uncounseled disclosure and demanded "evidence showing the positive effect on healthcare safety and quality."[45] These calls disregarded the absence of any evidence supporting a ban as well as the desire patients might have to be candidly informed about their conditions. So things would have been likely to continue but for legal intervention in 2014, when the Department of Health and Human Services (DHHS) revamped its disclosure regulations, the Clinical Laboratory Improvement Amendments, to require generally unrestricted patient access to lab tests, thereby specifically overriding state law restrictions. Once a patient requested such information from a laboratory the new regulations mandated compliance within 30 days.[46] Without these regulations it seems unlikely that access would have been expanded or that the barriers would have been overcome.

The debate about access to doctors' notes, while defined by the same arguments and concerns, has been even more protracted and contentious. In 2015, five years after a widely publicized demonstration program called "Open Notes" was successfully implemented by the Kaiser Permante healthcare system and the Veterans Administration (with more than four million patient users),[47] a poll was conducted to assess doctors' attitudes about patient access to what treating physicians had written about them in their medical records. The poll was conducted on SERMO, perhaps the leading physicians-only social network with approximately 300,000 physician members (approximately 40% of all American doctors).[48] Anonymous answers were submitted by 2,300 doctors to the question: "Should patients have access to their entire medical record—including MD notes, any audio recording, etc.?"[49] The responses showed that a significant segment of the medical profession continued to resist the sharing of information. Access to all records was endorsed by only 34% of those responding. Another 17% said access should never be permitted, and the remaining 49% would allow access only on a case-by-case basis.[50]

Perhaps even more emphatic than the numbers were the remarks made by some respondents. None displays the reasons for some physicians' resistance more clearly than one from "Internal Medicine Doctor," who wrote:

> No they should not have access to their full records, [sic] Many times they contain clinically useful information for patient management that may be offensive but true. Some people can't handle the truth and that will lead to

vilification of the physician. Full access also means generating questions for which there is no time to lecture the patient. I have on more than one occasion been forced to explain as though I could bring all my understanding from years of practice to a patient who recreationally reads about health care. The records remain private property of the physician who generated it [sic] for the care of the patient. If the patient doesn't like that fact then they can go elsewhere. (9 physicians found this comment helpful)[51]

There is an even darker side to medical opposition to note sharing. Doctors' notes are critical to the billing process. If the notes are open to patient scrutiny what could potentially be exposed are the exaggerations some doctors have made to increase the amount they can claim as payment for services reported to have been rendered. Dr. Tom Delbanco, the chief architect of Open Notes, explains: "The final one [reason for physician reluctance to share notes], unspoken and unpleasant, involves truth itself. Provoked by RVUs ["relative value units" used in the Medicare reimbursement formula] and the craziness of payment schemes, patients will see a note that says the clinician did a full exam and discussed multiple issues over the course of 40 minutes when, in fact, they know the 5 minute visit was hands off."[52] Added to this is the concern many doctors feel that their notes might be used against them in framing a medical malpractice claim.[53] Combined, these concerns provide powerful selfish motives to resist any sharing of doctors' notes.

As has frequently been the case with information sharing, the empirical evidence supports dissemination. Dr. Delbanco began the Open Notes program in 2010 with three health care provider networks, 100 doctors, and approximately 25,000 patients.[54] Since then it has grown to cover more than four million patients in many of the finest medical systems in the country, including the Mayo Clinic, the Cleveland Clinic, the Kaiser Northwest system, Beth Israel Deaconess Medical Center in Boston, and the Veterans Administration. The program, which facilitates patient access to virtually all medical records and doctors' notes, has been carefully studied. The evidence demonstrates the benefits such an approach can provide. The data reveal that few patients suffer anxiety after reviewing their doctors' notes. Confusion about content was found to be rare. Participating doctors did not experience an upsurge in patient questioning. Patients reported feeling more "in control of their care," and medication adherence was improved.[55] Virtually every patient queried (99%) wanted the program to continue. Participating doctors noted strengthened relationships with patients, including "enhanced trust, transparency, communications and shared decision making."[56]

Despite the success of Open Notes there remains substantial resistance to information sharing on a wider scale. One indication of this resistance is some institutions' inclination to tightly control the quantity and quality of information provided. What some providers appear to have done is offer patients medical keyholes that permit access to only a restricted set of materials. The result is a cabined view of the treatment process.[57] At the other end of the spectrum are systems that offer what amounts to an information "dump," a repetitive and form-filled mass of little value.[58] In addition to questions about data quality and quantity stand privacy concerns. The movement of information may result in a patient's health records becoming vulnerable to unauthorized disclosure. Thoughtful observers have suggested that privacy questions are particularly worrisome in an era where the hacking of patient information is all too frequent.[59]

THE DEEPER ROOTS OF RESISTANCE TO INFORMATION TECHNOLOGY AND PATIENT PARTICIPATION

We have examined a number of efforts to restrict the flow of medical information to patients. As we have already noted, medical objections have at times been marked by strong emotions and what amounts to an intellectually indefensible double standard—presenting nothing but anecdotal support (if that) for restrictions while demanding extraordinary proof to justify any distribution of information directly to patients. Our sense is that the roots of this dogged and dogmatic resistance go far deeper than the points articulated by those opposing change. The information dissemination revolution made possible by new technologies including EHRs, AI algorithms, and "smart" devices (most particularly smartphones) have begun to threaten healthcare at its intellectual and financial core. It is for these reasons we believe that resistance has been so stubborn, angry, and unlikely to abate without legal intervention.

A number of observers have noted that much of the practice of medicine is not based on data but on "experience."[60] It has been estimated that no more than half the standard therapeutic responses taught in medical school and utilized by practitioners are based on scientific evidence derived from disciplined observation under rigorous experimental conditions.[61] In such a setting, the expertise of long-time practitioners is privileged. It is not, at its heart, scientific—based upon systematic research and carefully gathered evidence applied in a disciplined manner—but subjective and unpredictable.[62] The deaths of upwards of 400,000 patients a year in hospitals due to medical error, the autopsy research findings concerning widespread diagnostic mistakes,[63] and evidence of a range of failures to utilize therapies effectively, or even wash hands, all point toward a flawed system.

Information technology may indicate a way forward. It will make available masses of new data concerning treatment approaches and patient outcomes. As connectivity improves this body of information will grow, facilitating "big data" research that can better assess what works and what doesn't. The pace of research and empirically based findings is likely to accelerate rapidly. It will challenge medicine's "experiential" wisdom and pose a threat to traditional expertise. Doctors and researchers skilled in the new technologies will put substantial pressure on the teachers and teachings of the past. The impact of all this may be profoundly unsettling to established medical hierarchies and learning. A good bit of doctors' anxiety about information technology perhaps finds its basis in this threat to upend traditional bases of treatment and devalue doctors' substantial investments in their training in the "art" of medicine.

Technology not only threatens the basis of knowledge in medicine, it is also likely to weaken physician authority. At present, the doctor is at the center of the treatment process. Her or his superior knowledge establishes a position of power. The patient is highly dependent on the doctor. That dependency is expressed in the patient's docility and efforts to retain the doctor's "good will."[64] The knowledge disparity fosters physician authoritarianism.[65] Information technology tends to undercut this power imbalance.[66] With augmented information, patients can begin to inform themselves of the range of available medical options and identify the considerations that guide treatment. With increased information patients can also enlist the assistance of surrogates to help in decision-making, leaving less to the treater's discretion. All of this is likely to erode physician control and independence of action.

As things presently stand most patients are not in a position to mount such a challenge. In an insightful but concerning 2012 paper, a group of researchers examined the authoritarianism question and found that, even among a group of extremely well-heeled patients, the perception of physician hegemony was dominant. It affected how patients participated in their care and led them to defer to their treaters. The researchers urged a less authoritarian approach but in a disheartening observation suggested that this was likely only if doctors were "provid[ed] adequate reimbursement" for engaging "in shared decision making" with patients.[67] In other words, doctors would have to be *paid* to share decision-making with their patients. This does not bode well for voluntary information sharing or robust patient participation. Nor does it suggest physician openness to such initiatives.

The intellectual challenge posed by information technology reaches even further. When patients have access to their EHRs (including doctors' notes), they will be free to assess their physician's thoughts and mode of expression. With the records in front of them, patients and their surrogates will be able to see not only the shortcomings in their doctors' thinking but even in their grammar and spelling. None of this is likely to enhance physician credibility or authority. A number of doctors have reported feeling compelled to "become more careful" with their writing when they know that patients will have access to it and have viewed this as an untoward constraint.[68]

Perhaps more serious from the healthcare industry's point of view is the likelihood that information technology will reduce income and profits. The range of likely effects is quite broad. At the most fundamental level information is likely to influence patient choices about treatment. Studies suggest that when decisions are shared patients are likely to postpone or refuse elective medical treatment. Patients with adequate information appear to gravitate to less costly and less aggressive treatment strategies.[69] The effect is likely to spread beyond treatment to costly and potentially dangerous tests and imaging techniques. Topol has noted the particular importance of informing patients about the dangers posed by repeated exposure to the radiation used in various advanced imaging processes.[70] All of this is likely to have a considerable effect on the bottom line—certain sorts of elective surgery and high-tech imaging are particularly lucrative for healthcare systems.[71]

It has been estimated that the advent of EHRs in 30% of doctors' offices, a threshold already surpassed, was likely to lead to a significant shifting of work from higher-billing treaters (specialists and physicians) to lower-billing ones (general practitioners and nurses).[72] This "devolution," as it has been called, was estimated to be likely to lead to efficiency gains of between 4% and 9% in doctors' activities, a 4% to 7% shift toward nurse rather than doctor care, and a 2% to 5% move from specialists to general practitioners.[73] Added to these savings are the effects of telemedicine, which facilitates doctor treatment of a large number of patients remotely thereby reducing demand for in-office consultation.[74] As EHR penetration expands, the devolution effect and savings are likely to grow substantially. The implication is that doctors will become less central to the treatment process, and their incomes may reflect that shift. The AMA, perhaps mindful of the threat posed, has vigorously opposed devolution, fighting to preserve the current broad "scope of [physician] practice" rules and requirements[75] (prohibiting less credentialed treaters from undertaking a range of care-related tasks). The FTC, Institute of Medicine, and National Governors Association have all sharply criticized this self-protective financial strategy.

Of perhaps equal significance, the healthcare industry has been alarmed by the financial implications of the analysis by two prominent information-technology-focused critics of medicine: Silicon Valley venture capitalist Vinod Khosla and Harvard Business School theorist Clayton Christensen. While it is not clear whether the predictions of either of these visionaries will come to pass, they have provoked strong reactions in the medical world. Khosla has argued that "[t]echnology will reinvent healthcare"[76] and that forces outside the medical establishment (based both literally and figuratively in Silicon Valley) will lead a revolution that will transform medicine from an art into a science. In addition to insulting the intellectual underpinnings of the healthcare system, Khosla promotes a vision of the world where doctors are substantially less important. He once estimated that machines will be capable of taking over up to 80% of all diagnosis, monitoring, and prescribing.[77]

What this appeared to suggest to Khosla was that the vast majority of doctors might be rendered redundant. Nurses and less extensively trained general practitioners might take their place with the support of AI algorithms and other technologies. What might be left to doctors, in Khosla's view, is the "human aspects" of treatment.[78] Doctors, in large numbers, have been avoiding such hands-on, bedside treatment situations for years.[79] Many in the medical profession have been appalled by Khosla's analysis. It has been described as "spark[ing] outrage."[80] Some physicians claim to have been affected viscerally, declaring themselves "nauseated."[81]

Clayton Christensen is renowned for his writings on the subject of disruptive technologies. While serious questions can be raised about the novelty and applicability of Christensen's theories,[82] he has had great impact on current thinking about business with his argument that simple and cheap technologies can often "disrupt" well-established industries that have committed themselves to ever more elaborate and expensive refinements. Christensen has argued that the medical profession has devoted too many resources to big and expensive technologies, leaving itself vulnerable on the questions of cost and effective service in response to everyday problems. He has suggested that medicine has placed "profits above care" and that hospitals, specialists, and researchers have overshot the level of care needed.[83]

Like Khosla, Christensen anticipates that there will be a devolution of responsibility to lower level treaters and a profound change in established institutions. Christensen's commentary, like that of Khosla, has sent shockwaves through healthcare.[84] Again, like Khosla, Christensen points to the substantial shortcomings of the industry in terms of cost, disorganization, and error. He too has noted the efforts of organized medicine to protect itself from devolution and foreclose inexpensive alternatives like City Physicians walk-in clinics and nurse staffed treatment centers in Walmarts and pharmacy chains.[85]

No institution is more central to big medicine and high health costs than the hospital. According to critics, including Khosla and Christensen, as well as Topol and Wachter, the hospital's central position will be undermined by information technology innovation. Suggesting such a result is to imply the coming decline of the key structure of modern medicine. To reinforce that point, Christensen has described today's large hospitals as money-losing entities ripe for disruption.[86] He sees their unraveling as already underway with mergers, facility closings, and worker layoffs. All of this he describes as a stopgap that cannot correct the hospitals' excessive focus on a costly high-end model of treatment. Khosla sees hospitals as dangerous and poorly managed institutions that will, for the most part, be swept away by the coming technological tide. Dr. Topol emphasizes the appalling death rate caused by medical error and nosocomial infection in today's hospitals. He sees their inability to improve as a harbinger of their marginalization.[87] While not going quite so far as the other three, Dr. Wachter too sees the hospital's decline, especially because of its circumscription of the patient's role.[88] All of these analysts agree that what information technology innovation and patient empowerment signify to traditional healthcare is the overthrow of the way business has been done for decades. This, we believe, explains the depth of professional resistance.

WHAT MAINSTREAM MEDICINE HAS DONE WITH INFORMATION TECHNOLOGY

It is not that medicine has walled itself off from all information technology innovation but rather that it has used innovation overwhelmingly for its own ends and not to empower patients or make significant strides in safety. Wachter has suggested that a key reason for this is that there is no "business incentive" to take the sorts of steps that will move medical care toward patient participation and safety.[89] He illustrates his point by focusing on diagnostic AI algorithms. There are, today, AI systems that can provide substantial assistance with diagnosis—an area that has proven particularly challenging in safety terms. Wachter himself often relies on one such system, called Isabel.⁹⁰ Neither Isabel nor similar systems have been widely adopted as a means of augmenting physician analysis, let alone informing patients. A key reason is money—no way has been found to make a significant profit from a second opinion rendered by a machine. All such input is likely to do is threaten the attending physician's treatment plan. Diagnosis by AI also runs afoul of physician attitudes. Doctors will, on principle, fight being second-guessed by a machine.⁹¹ This is precisely the intellectual stumbling block Khosla emphasized in his critique of modern medicine.

It should be noted as well that both software designers and doctors appear to fear legal liability if AI diagnoses become a significant part of the treatment process. The engineers are worried that they will be sued if their software delivers the wrong answer. Such fears seem wildly exaggerated in light of the decline of medical malpractice, the absence of a treating relationship and the activity of the doctor as "learned intermediary." This is the sort of problem for which there should be a legal fix, a point we will return to at the end of this chapter. Doctors have precisely the opposite fear. They seem to be concerned that AI will show their errors or afford grounds for legal attack. Again, the reality suggests this is a chimerical fear, very like doctors' exaggerated concern about malpractice litigation generally.

Technology has frequently been treated by the healthcare industry as a method of boosting profits. New devices have repeatedly been embraced not because they substantially improve care but because patients and insurers can be charged more for them. Khosla has pointed out that cost-cutting technologies have been resisted in the medical field and that innovation has been rendered subservient to the pursuit of financial return.⁹² To illustrate his point, he highlights the recent move by a number of big hospitals to purchase hugely expensive proton particle accelerators. These machines do not provide substantially improved care but can be billed out at extremely high rates and used as a lure to patients (and physicians) impressed by the latest and most expensive in medical machinery.⁹³

Another way in which technology, particularly information technology, has been bent to the healthcare industry's pursuit of profit is with respect to use of EHR. EHR offers a promising medium for communications about and with patients. Medicine, as we have discussed, has been slow in taking those steps. What it has not been slow in doing is using EHR for billing. Since the 1980s, when such systems began to be installed, the industry has worked hard to perfect their use as billing devices. This has so much been the case that care has taken a back seat to billing as a priority in many such systems. As one observer has put it, "the latter [billing] often trumps the former [care]."⁹⁴ In this view, doctors often write their electronic entries not to document care but to secure maximum insurance payments. In doing so doctors will describe patients as "sicker" than they are.⁹⁵ The EHRs have been turned into a "Christmas tree" on which are hung all the ornaments that will secure the largest possible payout.⁹⁶

Although sharing EHR with patients has been resisted by the profession, doctors in their daily practice have become ever more engrossed by what is presented to them on computer screens. This is so much the case that critics of medicine's turn to technology have suggested that it distracts doctors from human interaction with patients in favor of a focus on the records displayed.[97] Data suggest that doctors spend more time engaged with their computers than they do with their patients and derive more information from EHR records than from the patients they are treating.[98] This trend has grown so significant that critics have voiced serious concerns that physicians' patient skills have atrophied. Arguments have been made that the fault lies with the software companies that design and sell EHR systems. Even though this is but a part of the problem, it suggests that restrictive computer system contracts have undermined treatment decisions and interfered with the flow of information to patients. That said, the customs and practice of medicine have shifted in ways that prioritize the screen over the patient.

EHR AND SAFETY

In its 1999 report *To Err is Human*, the Institute of Medicine called for the development of EHR to enhance patient safety. It reiterated that call in 2004, in its follow-up report, *Patient Safety: Achieving a New Standard for Care*. The idea was that accurate and readily available health records would improve the quality of care, not only by facilitating more effective diagnosis and treatment but also by making such material available both to patients and healthcare providers who subsequently might be called on to provide medical services. The EHR idea was taken up by the Bush administration in 2004, when the president signed an executive order requiring DHHS to work toward the goal of providing most Americans access to electronic records of their healthcare by 2014 and by requiring DHHS and other government agencies to adopt interoperable (i.e. compatible) health information technology standards. While this preliminary work was being done, EHR gained little real-world traction. A reason suggested for this is that coupling EHR and interoperability facilitates patients moving from one treater or healthcare system to another.[99] Creating and providing such material is, in essence, a selfless act. Not only does it hurt business (patients can change providers with the push of a few buttons), but the installation and maintenance costs are extremely high.

So things remained until 2009. In that year, in the wake of the mortgage lending–caused economic meltdown, at the insistence of the Obama administration, Congress enacted the American Recovery and Reinvestment Act. The act created a $700 billion economic stimulus package. The legislation set aside $30 billion to promote the adoption by the healthcare industry of EHR. To achieve this goal, a multipronged, statutorily created incentive program was fashioned, called HITECH.[100] At HITECH's core was a plan to provide up to $9 billion in government funds to hospitals establishing appropriate EHR systems. Participating hospitals had to comply with a specific agenda set forth in a plan entitled "Meaningful Use." Stage 1 of Meaningful Use began in 2011–2012 and was designed to get hospitals to install and rely on EHR systems in treating patients (frequently referred to as electronic capture). By virtually all estimates, it was a resounding success with more than two-thirds of America's 5,000 hospitals satisfying Stage 1 requirements by July 2013, and most of the rest were well on their way to achieving that goal. According to the Centers for Medicare and Medicaid Services (CMS) more than 500,000 healthcare providers (primarily doctors) were, by October 2015, participating in the related Medicare/Medicaid EHR incentive program.[101]

With lavish government support, adoption of EHR systems turned out to be the easy part. The more challenging issue was whether there would be real sharing of data both with patients and with caregivers outside the initial treater system. To secure those goals, in Stage 2 of Meaningful Use, the government specified 17 objectives. These included regulations mandating percentage levels of patient EHR use and similar rules for the sharing of materials with outside healthcare providers (activity frequently referred to as exchange of information). These requirements were mandated to be achieved by 2015 or incentive payments would be reduced. Unfortunately, these requirements were not well crafted. The regulators failed to understand how the treatment process actually works. Requiring *doctors* to get *patients* to use EHR is far more challenging than insisting on its use within the care-giving team.[102] A similar dilemma has arisen with respect to EHR sharing between different healthcare providers. A sharing rule makes sense only where there is firmly established intersystem movement of patients for treatment. For whatever reasons, the second stage of Meaningful Use has not gone smoothly, and the goal of genuine interoperability—the frictionless sharing of diagnostic, treatment and medication records—has not been achieved.

What has been achieved in the shift to EHR, as previously suggested, is the perfection of billing rather than safety. Besides producing the perfect bill, electronic records have drawn doctors' attention away from patients to computer screens. The recording of data has become so pervasive and voluminous that some physicians employ "scribes" to help them transfer their observations and actions into electronic form. EHR has even become an excuse for medical error. When Dallas's Texas Health Presbyterian Hospital committed the medical errors that led to the Ebola crisis described in Chapter 2 of this volume, one of the first things it claimed, albeit erroneously, was that its EHRs system had failed to inform the treating physician of the patient's foreign origin. All of this raises the question of what it will take for EHR to be used in a way that will genuinely improve care.

Despite these problems, a number of experts, beginning with the Institute of Medicine in 1999, have viewed EHR as a valuable tool for improving patient safety. The collection, use, and sharing of reliable and pertinent information can, obviously, improve the coordination of patients' care and cut the risk of error. Electronic systems can do much more. They can be programmed to monitor patient treatment outcomes, en masse, and identify situations in which errors have arisen with frequency.[103] This monitoring, relying on global trigger algorithms, can help pinpoint problem areas. Unfortunately, these applications have not generally been incorporated into EHR systems, despite safety experts calling for such a step since at least 2011.

EHR systems can also be programmed to track patient test results and postprocedure progress. Where data indicate abnormal developments, treaters can be notified through a system of electronic alerts. The same approach can be employed to monitor drug treatment so that dangerous reactions or interactions, as well as erroneous prescriptions, can be avoided or corrected. EHR systems can be reprogrammed, literally overnight, to respond to newly identified dangers. This is what was done in major hospitals around America when it was realized that the travel information that is so important in diagnosing Ebola was not sufficiently salient to attract the treating physician's attention. Finally, EHR can, if made genuinely accessible to patients, provide each with an accurate and up-to-date treatment record facilitating patient inquiry, research and second-opinion seeking.

Most of the potential safety benefits of EHR have yet to be realized. One of the questions we are concerned with in this book is what steps the law might take to foster greater safety through EHR. What virtually all experts in the field agree on is that safety would be enhanced by true interoperability. It is only with the widespread ability to share information that many of EHR's benefits can be secured. Interoperability is not an easy goal to achieve both because of the need to develop a common or shared language of symptoms, treatments and medications and because software vendors and doctors have no financial incentive to facilitate data sharing. Interoperability paves the way for competitor healthcare systems to capitalize on the original treater's work and make another system's patients its own. Moreover, recent experience has demonstrated the value of treatment data, once de-identified, as a saleable commodity to pharmaceutical product developers and others.[104] Some treaters have sought to monopolize these potentially valuable data. Similarly, some software vendors have sought to control their system users' data by encrypting patient information so that it cannot be accessed by anyone other than the medical team delivering care.[105] Once this material has been de-identified, the vendor can offer it for sale. In both cases, interoperability is undermined.

Another set of safety concerns raised by software developers' behavior is connected with the contract terms they have been able to impose on their health system clients. Two of the most problematic of these are developer insistence on nondisparagement and hold-harmless clauses. The first prohibits those using the system from publicly criticizing it. The muzzling of public discussion of flaws impedes the improvement of system safety.[106] A system whose flaws cannot be openly described and discussed is one insulated from accurate appraisal and pressure for improvement. Secrecy increases the risk of product harm. Few examples are more alarming than recent auto manufacturer and parts supplier efforts to hide safety problems. GM kept its ignition problems to itself and hundreds died.[107] Takata did the same with its exploding airbags.[108] Secrecy is antithetical to safety and should have no place in EHR service contracts. Similarly, hold harmless clauses that absolve software makers of all legal liability for the harms their products may cause to patients are deeply troubling. Insulation from legal responsibility undermines the incentive for safety improvement. Protecting software providers from all responsibility literally allows them to behave irresponsibly while their customers, the healthcare providers, shoulder more than their fair share of legal responsibility.

To get substantial safety benefits from electronic records it is necessary to address these flaws in current arrangements regarding the use of EHR systems and between system manufacturers and healthcare entities. Steps that are needed include the revision of HITECH program regulations to require expanded interoperability (phased in over a fixed period in settings where there is regular patient movement between healthcare providers), installation of global trigger safety analysis mechanisms and an end to nondisparagement and hold harmless contract restrictions. Interoperability is technically challenging and offers little financial reward. There is a need for sustained government support to promote the development and adoption of interoperability standards. A logical starting place for government efforts is with those whose care is paid for by the Medicare and Medicaid programs.

In contrast to the interoperability problem, installation of global trigger tools to screen for patterns of medical error presents only limited technical challenges. Safety analysts, writing in 2012 in the *New England Journal of Medicine*, concluded:

> [S]ystems can be programmed to automatically detect easily overlooked and underreported errors of omission, such as patients who are overdue for medication monitoring, patients who lack appropriate surveillance after treatment, and patients who are not provided with follow-up care after receiving abnormal laboratory or radiologic tests results. EHR-based trigger approaches can also be used to detect errors of commission related to preventable adverse drug events, postoperative complications, and misidentification of patients. Organizations must leverage EHRs to facilitate rapid detection of common errors (including EHR-related errors), to monitor the occurrence of high-priority safety events, and to more reliably track trends over time.[109]

The impediment here is less technical than cultural. It challenges providers' reluctance to identify and address errors. Again, it is altered government regulations that can promote improved safety through EHR. Finally, there is a need for the federal government, which paid for the vast expansion in the use of EHR, to prohibit as against public policy, software vendor nondisparagement and hold harmless clauses. These contract restrictions undermine essential safety discussions and unfairly insulate software manufacturers from their own negligence.[110]

There are legal precedents for such government action. When the federal government undertook the Hill–Burton Act[111] to encourage dramatic expansion of U.S. hospital facilities, it not only poured money into hospital construction but insisted that the beneficiaries of government support provide free and reduced fee care to those unable to afford the full cost of treatment.[112] While that requirement has not always been honored, it does provide an example of how government aid to healthcare facilities can be used to improve and extend care. Similar steps are necessary to secure the safety benefits specifically promised when

HITECH was adopted. As to the contractual provisions, courts for decades have refused the enforcement of contractual provisions deemed detrimental to the public health and welfare. Specifically, the courts have prohibited doctors from employing hold harmless or exculpatory clauses with their patients. The same safety rationale should be applied to the exculpatory clauses the software vendors seek to utilize.

It should be noted that EHR introduces its own set of risks. These have been detailed by a number of analysts.[113] The dangers include system crashes (like that experienced by most Rhode Island hospitals when their integrated EHR systems were switched on), malfunctions of the sort that all computer systems experience periodically, software that confuses or misleads users, excessive alerts or alarms that induce user fatigue and work arounds, and system-engendered isolation of caregivers that stifles necessary in-person conversation. To address these problems, some experts have recommended the creation of a federal EHR safety entity to conduct research and recommend improvements. This seems an excellent idea and another that the law can, and should, address.

AI AND SAFETY

The medical effort to utilize AI began in earnest in the 1980s, when various groups sought to develop algorithms to analyze patients' vital signs and symptoms as a means of coming to more reliable diagnoses. The early working groups overstated both the ease of creating such algorithms and their utility in practice. This led, during the 1980s and 1990s, to a substantial backlash in the profession against such efforts, described as the "AI Winter."[114] Recently, the AI project has been reinvigorated. One important change in the effort has been to recast the algorithms as an adjunct to be integrated into the physician's diagnostic process.

There now exist a number of AI systems holding genuine promise of enhancing the accuracy of diagnosis. A system of this sort that we have already mentioned is called Isabel and was developed in England by a nondoctor.[115] The system is named for the daughter of its inventor, Jason Maude, who began his efforts after his three-year old, Isabel, was badly injured due to a failure to correctly diagnose necrotizing fasciitis (a rare disease caused by a bacterial infection that eats away at the patient's flesh). Maude recognized that most doctors have little experience with rare ailments, and if they are to improve their diagnostic efforts, they need to be provided information that can expand their assessment options. That is what Isabel seeks to do by drawing on an expansive data base of medical literature. Isabel is not designed to stand alone but to respond to a physician's careful clinical observations and queries. Isabel is a comparatively "simple" system that requires medical skill to use most effectively.

A very different sort of system is being developed by IBM. That system is called Watson and is a natural language software package programmed to learn as it is exposed to substantial bodies of information.[116] Watson came to prominence when it competed against human champions on the quiz show *Jeopardy*. Americans (including one of the authors and his adult son—both *Jeopardy* junkies) watched in astonishment as Watson trounced the human champs by accurately deciphering and answering linguistically tricky questions and providing (at least most of the time) precise and accurate answers. Among other things, IBM decided to convert this wonderful software into a tool for medical treatment and diagnosis. It turns out that medical treatment is a bit tougher than quiz shows. Watson has been deployed at several leading American cancer centers including Sloan Kettering and the Cleveland Clinic.[117] It has not been used to replace physicians but as their student, to learn how to make clinical judgments most effectively. It has become increasingly sophisticated as it has observed physicians and combined observation with scans of the burgeoning cancer and genetics literatures. Watson is not about to replace doctors any time soon, but it does offer the immediate promise of enhancing physician effectiveness through its information-based supplementation of doctors' diagnoses. It has progressed so far that in the foreseeable future it is likely to be capable of substituting for human doctors "at the low end of complexity."[118] That said, Watson's development has not been trouble-free. A much-trumpeted agreement between a prominent Texas hospital and IBM fell apart in acrimony in 2017, as costs skyrocketed and results lagged.[119]

As with EHR, the question we are interested in is, "What can AI do to improve patient safety?" One aspect of medical work that is said to be in serious need of improvement is diagnosis. Data indicate that between 40,000 and 80,000 deaths per year are related to erroneous diagnoses.[120] Autopsies have found major diagnostic problems in up to one-fifth of the cases examined.[121] While AI cannot promise to eradicate such mistakes, it can dramatically expand the information and options available to the diagnosing physician. A critical part of the present medical diagnostic failure story is "premature closure," doctors settling on an erroneous or incomplete diagnosis early in the process.[122] What AI can do in this context is prompt physicians to keep looking and digging into the patient's problem as new symptoms emerge or are noted. A second aspect of the diagnostic problem is the inclination of many doctors to rely on untrustworthy but prominently featured Internet information provided by interested parties like pharmaceutical manufacturers.[123] Here AI can provide a more measured and balanced assessment that draws on the most reliable information rather than that promoted by interested parties. Recent small-scale research suggests that "clinical support decision tools" appear to offer improved safety not only in diagnosis but as a means "to reduce re-hospitalization and emergency department visits" when effectively coupled with EHRs.[124] Beyond these complementary uses, where AI augments the doctor's own insights, loom future developments where algorithmic analysis may provide a second opinion, one that the patient may seek independently and use to assess the treating physicians' analysis. Such uses seem a ways off but will almost certainly gain significance as AI increases in efficacy. The key here is that patients are likely to need assistance in gaining access to such resources and instruction in their use.

AI has yet to even begin approaching its safety-related potential. In significant part this is due to the attitude among physicians that algorithms are unacceptable as participants in diagnosis and that AI poses a threat to the medical profession. These views, and the resistance they engender to programs like Isabel, present serious impediments to safety improvement through AI. A more subtle barrier is posed by the present approach to the commercialization of AI tools. IBM, along with a number of others, has concluded that the way to make AI, like Watson, profitable is to fashion it into a resource to be consulted by healthcare professionals, not something accessible to patients. It is health system administrators who can be expected, eventually, to be willing to pay for AI assistance, especially if it enhances operational efficiency (limiting the need for expert consultations) and if its commercial appeal grows as a selling point to patients (along the lines of the present craze for robotic surgery). This, in turn, is likely to lead to a de facto medical monopoly on such systems. Were consumers to have ready access to AI resources, these, like other direct-to-patient information sources, might threaten the present medical business model. That reality is likely to retard patient access for quite some time.

Again, there may be legal interventions that can facilitate expanded use of AI and, perhaps, even consumer access. Designers and physician users of AI systems have been deeply concerned that what might be judged to be faulty diagnosis either on the algorithm's part or that of the interpreting doctor, will create an additional basis for tort liability. The Isabel system attempts to circumvent this risk by including a disclaimer that "Isabel is not meant to replace your clinical judgment."[125] To encourage the expanded use of AI systems in diagnosis, the output of such systems should be classified as privileged information barred from use in any legal proceedings. It should be treated in the same way as peer review evaluations of a doctor's performance. (The key difference being that peer review is conducted after treatment has concluded.) To encourage free and candid peer reviews, panel members' evaluations have been classified as off limits and inadmissible in legal proceedings. The same protective approach should be adopted with AI for the very same reason—to promote the most robust evaluation and, thereby, improve medical care.

The question of patient access to AI diagnostic systems presents a different problem. Because AI opinions can challenge a physician's recommendations, lead patients to change care providers, or even raise legal concerns, it is highly likely that treaters will not be keen on providing patients with access. This may not be an easy barrier to overcome. There is, however, precedent for legally mandating access to information that treaters are loath to provide. That is exactly what the informed consent doctrine does. In its original form, it required reluctant physicians to tell each patient about the risks and alternatives to the proposed course of treatment. It would seem a short step from there to require that patients be informed of the contents of any AI analysis employed in the diagnostic or treatment process. Of course, this might prove a disincentive to the use of such systems but assuming their efficiency and commercial appeal, a barrier that might be overcome. In addition, the government might give such systems a boost by requiring their regular use in the rendering of care under programs like Medicare and Medicaid.

SMARTPHONES AND SAFETY

It might be difficult to find two heart specialists with more divergent profiles than former Senate Majority Leader William Frist and outspoken safety crusader and digital researcher Eric Topol. On one topic, however, the two are in substantial agreement, the quality- and safety-enhancing potential of smartphones in the delivery of medical care. Dr. Frist has extolled the virtues of the smartphone as a way to improve American medicine while containing costs.[126] He has stressed the steady expansion of FDA-approved medical uses of smartphones (for glucose monitoring, ultrasound examination, blood pressure measurement and electrocardiograms) and has urged increasing the flow of medical information and patient data. Dr. Topol is even keener on the potential of the smartphone. He has described it as the key "hub" of the future delivery of healthcare.[127] It has, in his view, the potential to generate massive amounts of data regarding both the physiological and psychological condition of virtually any patient. In addition, he has argued that the delivery of medical care at a distance through telemedicine rather than on the basis of physical visits offers the prospect of vastly expanded access and reduced cost.[128]

The key to securing the benefits of smartphone improvement of care according to both men is legal regulation that fosters the growth of technological development and of physician delivery of "virtual" care. The FDA has taken the position that health apps and equipment developed for the smartphone are medical devices that come within its regulatory purview. As in the case of 23andMe, that means that the FDA has to review and be satisfied with their safety. Unlike its restrictive approach to 23andMe, the FDA has responded positively to a number of healthcare augmentations to the smartphone. Included have been those noted by former Senator Frist, as well as an expanding array of vital signs monitors. This is likely to be only the beginning of what phones will be engineered to do. Apple has made an open-source toolkit available for medical research and the pace of innovation is likely to accelerate.[129] The FDA has, in the past, shown caution with new products because of the negative consequences that pharmaceuticals might have. With digital equipment, the risk appears lower in most cases, presenting a situation in which regulators should be encouraged to move more expeditiously. The FDA's approach to products using the smartphone as a platform should be streamlined.

Liberalization of regulation will also be important in encouraging the expansion of telemedical services. There has been a steady growth of such services, averaging between 18% and 30% a year recently.[130] What has stood in the way of even faster growth has been "practice of medicine" restrictions in a number of states requiring that patients initiate treatment with an in-person visit to a physician.[131] This requirement has been promoted by a number of medical societies concerned, it would appear, with competition from telephonic services. The state where this conflict has played out most dramatically is Texas, where legal regulations required face-to-face doctor–patient contact before any diagnosis could be rendered or prescription ordered. A service provider, Teledoc, sued the state over its restrictions and obtained a number of favorable rulings.[132] CMS and the FTC have both supported the expansion of telemedicine and as many as 25 states have, in the last several years, removed legal restrictions on such care. If all protectionist regulations are removed telemedical care is likely to expand rapidly, improving access to diagnosis and treatment as well as reducing costs.

The question remains whether these changes can really improve patient safety. Certainly, getting patients in remote locations timely medical advice will help. Beyond that, there is evidence that when a chain of Massachusetts nursing homes adopted telemedicine for off-hours care, they sent fewer residents to the hospital.[133] Even the State of Texas has had dramatically positive experience with telemedicine. It adopted a telemedicine program to treat prisoners in 1994. That program improved clinical outcomes, saving the state roughly $780 million.[134] All the data we have canvassed suggest that keeping patients away from hospitals when possible is likely to improve safety. The challenge in the nursing home context has been that operators gain little financial benefit from such programs and, therefore, have been slow to adopt them. In addition to the incentives problem, telemedicine presents familiar safety challenges with respect to the delivery of care. Laws in this context need to emphasize the importance of accurate records (in EHR forms that can be shared) and treater availability for monitoring and follow-up care.

DANGERS INTRODUCED BY TECHNOLOGY

While information technology offers a genuine opportunity for safety improvement it also poses a number of risks that need to be recognized and addressed. The availability of an ever-expanding range of imaging technologies and the ease with which they may now be shared has led to an explosion of imaging use. The problem is that many of these techniques expose patients to substantial levels of radiation. Topol suggests that the level of exposure is far too high today and is the cause of perhaps 3% to 5% of the cancers suffered by the population.[135] In light of the risks involved, Topol argues that it is essential that patients be informed of the exposure level of each imaging procedure and that a record of total exposure be maintained for each patient. The challenge is that there are substantial financial incentives to use radiographic imaging technologies and no requirement to track or limit patient exposure. Legal intervention treating this issue as one requiring both detailed informed consent and universal record keeping seems in order.

A second problem posed by the burgeoning use of information technology is protection of patient privacy. The HIPAA restrictions on information sharing, adopted in 1996,[136] have not been particularly effective. The Meaningful Use regulations have sought to improve privacy protection but do not appear to have resulted in substantial improvement, at least according to critics. There is a need to fashion far more rigorous requirements that offer greater protection against hacking and other sorts of intrusion as the volume of EHRs grows.

Interoperability has been one of the key objectives of the EHR project and, as we have argued, will increase the coordination and efficacy of patient care. One of the ways it might be fostered is through the creation of universal patient identification numbers for all Americans. The obvious privacy risks of such an approach, however, led Congress to ban the development of such identifiers.[137] The problem of balancing privacy and effective information sharing for safer care is a tricky one that needs a great deal more legal and legislative work. Another threat to privacy has grown as increasingly sophisticated data mining efforts have focused more frequently on EHR as a source to trace patterns of illness and successful treatment. Although mined materials are generally de-identified, it has been demonstrated that such efforts at anonymity can be defeated and identities discovered. Big data research is an essential tool for the improvement of medical treatment but legally mandated means must be developed to protect the privacy of those whose data are used.

The growth of smartphone vital signs monitoring systems raises another sort of privacy issue. As these technologies improve and become more generally available insurers or healthcare systems may begin to insist on their use as a condition of coverage. In other words, insistence on 24/7 monitoring may become common. The intrusiveness of this sort of surveillance suggests that some legal limits are necessary. The nightmare vision of Orwell's *1984*, with "Big Brother" always watching, pales compared to what might be possible with augmented smartphone technologies that can monitor not only all movements and vital signs but perhaps even emotions or other psychological states through voice analysis and visual scans.[138]

The ascendance of information technology has already resulted in a perhaps excessive physician focus on electronic information rather than that provided by the patient. The expanding flow of information promises to intensify this distraction. It has been repeatedly noted that the brevity of the doctor/patient interaction reduces patient satisfaction and fosters patient searches for information beyond what the physician is willing or able to impart. While patients informing themselves of relevant medical issues is a good thing, the wedge that information technology may drive between doctor and patient is not beneficial. Besides the obvious reduction of useful face-to-face communication (a problem also posed in the doctor/nurse relationship) the decrease in hands-on interactions undermines the physician's skill as an examiner and advisor. Wachter uses a telling analogy. He compares the doctors' problem to that of many young pilots who, when faced with emergencies that cannot be handled by automation, no longer know how to respond or fly the plane.[139] If technology is granted too central a place, it is conceivable that doctors will lose the ability to step in and straighten things out. This is not a legal question but one of immense significance in assuring patient safety.

At the end of the line of concerns about information technology is the cost it will impose on the delivery of healthcare. While touted as a way of improving care, EHR has been expensive to install and operate. The initial costs were deeply subsidized by the federal government. Expenses going forward will add substantially to the cost of treatment. The move to EHR has already proven so costly that it has driven many small and rural hospitals out of business. AI systems and smartphone technologies pose cost challenges as well. Those who succeed in developing these technologies will, undoubtedly, seek to cash in on their achievements. As with the pharmaceutical industry, this could result in a dramatic upward cost spiral. This may not simply impose an additional burden on the public but might price the poor out of the market for the benefits information technology can provide. Appropriate cost controls and access assurance are likely to be needed as a part of the legal response to such innovation.

EPILOGUE

The Path Forward

If you can see things out of whack, then you can see how things can be in whack.[1]

America has a healthcare problem that is little discussed. In its efforts to help us live lives that are as free of disease, pain, and disability as current knowledge enables, our healthcare system also accidentally kills so many of us that it is the third most frequent cause of death for Americans (and the number one cause of accidental death). Not to mention the many nonfatal serious injuries that patients endure.

Using the Institute of Medicine's figures, Sidney Dekker, a human factors expert whose work includes patient safety, has drawn a portrait of what air travel would be like if airlines performed as hospitals do:

> After a flight from, say, New York to Miami with an airplane that carried 150 passengers, only 148 emerge alive. . . . The flight alone caused [death from] a heart attack in one and turbulence-induced blunt-force head trauma in another. Four have developed infections because of being packed inside the hypoxic tube with bad air filtration and cabin crew who refused to wash their hands before serving snacks. Two of these infections are beyond the reach of antibiotics and will debilitate these people for life. One of these passengers has no choice: He will have to remain onboard the airplane for the rest of his life. Two passengers have been poisoned by badly mixed $7 cocktails, which caused permanent liver damage in one and stripped the stomach lining of the other. One has lost a leg from the hip down unnecessarily because it got trapped in the seat in front; another passenger had her common bile duct severed by a snagged seat belt, and yet another has suffered permanent brain damage because of oxygen supply problems near her seat. One child was electrocuted because of a short in the entertainment electronics circuit box

mounted by her left ankle.... And this is not just one flight. It happens on every flight every day, by every airline.[2]

The traditional legal solution is medical malpractice litigation. How much it costs is poorly understood by researchers and greatly exaggerated by healthcare industry lobbyists. Even less well understood is how well or poorly malpractice litigation incentivizes investments in safety—how many deaths and injuries and their associated costs it prevents. But the traditional solution is, by itself, plainly inadequate and has been rendered even more inadequate by recent decades of law reforms. That is apparent from the number of iatrogenic injuries and deaths that occur each year.

What we need is a new kind law reform—laws aimed first, last, and insistently at promoting patient safety. This book has sought to fuel a wide-ranging conversation to explore the possibility of legal innovations that might improve patient safety in a world where neither the healthcare industry nor the legal system have thus far succeeded. We have tried to point a way to a new generation of law and policy, more capable of promoting patient safety. We have explored a number of law-driven and law-related developments, speculated on new possibilities, and hope to have encouraged further thinking along similar lines.

We also encourage experimentation and evidence-based evaluations of innovations. Without such evaluation research, the effort would be seriously incomplete. States, or smaller units within states, can be put to work as the laboratories of legal innovation that we like to claim for our federal system. Different possible solutions must be studied—systematically, empirically, honestly, and, ideally, experimentally. Keep the good ones. Throw away the bad ones. Keep experimenting. Continually improve the safety of healthcare.

NOTES

CHAPTER 1
1. Ross Koppel and Suzanne Gordon, First, Do Less Harm (2012).

CHAPTER 2
1. William J. Mayo, MD, co-founder, Mayo Clinic (1910).
2. U.S. Cong. H. Energy and Commerce Comm., Subcomm. on Oversight and Investigations. *Examining the U.S Public Health Response to the Ebola Outbreak. Hearings, Oct. 16, 2014*, 113th Cong. 2d Sess. Wash.: GPO, 2014 (statement of Dr. Daniel Varga, Chief Clinical Officer, Tex: Health Resources).
3. Sarah Shannon, *Ebola, Team Communication, and Shame: But Shame on Whom?* 15 Am. J. Bioethics 20–25 (2015); Reese Dunklin and Steve Thompson, *ER Doctor Discusses Role in Ebola Patient's Initial Misdiagnosis*, The Dallas Morning News (Dec. 6, 2014), https://www.dallasnews.com/news/news/2014/12/06/er-doctor-discusses-role-in-ebola-patients-initial-misdiagnosis.
4. Id.
5. Press Release, Tex. Health Res., Ebola Update-Events Related to Diagnosis (Oct. 2, 2014).
6. Doreen McCallister, *Nurse Treated for Ebola to Sue Texas Hospital*, The Two-Way: NPR (Mar. 2, 2015), https://www.npr.org/sections/thetwo-way/2015/03/02/390082857/nurse-treated-for-ebola-to-sue-texas-hospital.
7. Manny Fernandez and Dave Philipps, *Death of Thomas Duncan in Dallas Fuels Alarm over Ebola*, New York Times, Oct. 8, 2014, at A1; Bill Chappell and L. Carol Ritchie, *CDC Cites "Breach" in Ebola Protocol As Second Texas Case Emerges*, NPR (Oct. 12, 2014), https://www.npr.org/sections/thetwo-way/2014/10/12/355537175/texas-health-care-worker-tests-positive-for-ebola.
8. Reese Dunklin and Steve Thompson, *ER Doctor Discusses Role in Ebola Patient's Initial Misdiagnosis*, The Dallas Morning News (Dec. 6, 2014), https://www.dallasnews.com/news/news/2014/12/06/er-doctor-discusses-role-in-ebola-patients-initial-misdiagnosis.
9. Transcript, *Gov. Perry Conference Regarding Texas Ebola Case* (CNN television broadcast Oct. 1, 2014).
10. Id.
11. Sarah Shannon, *Ebola, Team Communication, and Shame: But Shame on Whom?*, 15 Am. J. Bioethics 20, 20–25 (2015).

12. Press Release, Tex. Health Res., Ebola Update-Events Related to Diagnosis (Oct. 2, 2014).
13. M.L. Millenson, *Pushing the Profession: How the News Media Turned Patient Safety into a Priority*, 11 BMJ QUAL. SAF. 57, 57 (2002).
14. Jon Swaine, *Texas Hospital Mounts "#PresbyProud" Fightback as Ebola Criticism Mounts*, THE GUARDIAN (Oct. 18, 2014), https://www.theguardian.com/world/2014/oct/18/texas-ebola-hospital-presbyproud-fightback-criticism
15. M. L. Millenson, *Pushing the Profession: How the News Media Turned Patient Safety into a Priority*, 11 BMJ QUAL. SAF. 57 (2002).
16. U.S. Cong. H. Energy and Commerce Comm., Subcomm. on Oversight and Investigations. *Examining the U.S Public Health Response to the Ebola Outbreak. Hearings, Oct. 16, 2014*, 113th Cong. 2d Sess. Wash.: GPO, 2014 (statement of Dr. Daniel Varga, Chief Clinical Officer, Tex: Health Resources).
17. Jessica Dye, *Ebola Lawsuits Would Face High Hurdles in Texas*, REUTERS.COM (Oct. 7, 2014), https://www.reuters.com/article/us-health-ebola-usa-liability-idUSKCN0HW0W920141007.
18. Curtis Skinner and Catherine Evans, *Family of Deceased Ebola Patient Reaches Resolution with Dallas Hospital: Report*, REUTERS.COM (Nov. 12, 2014), https://uk.reuters.com/article/us-health-ebola-usa-texas/family-of-deceased-ebola-patient-reaches-resolution-with-dallas-hospital-report-idUKKCN0IW0PG20141112.
19. Matt Goodman, *How Texas Health Managed Its Ebola Crisis*, D MAGAZINE (Mar. 2015), https://www.dmagazine.com/publications/d-ceo/2015/march/texas-health-ceo-barclay-berdan-ebola-crisis/.
20. Lawrence Altman, *Big Doses of Chemotherapy Drug Killed Patient, Hurt 2d*, NEW YORK TIMES, Mar. 24, 1995, at A00018 (Lehmann); Carol Kepp, *Anatomy of a Mistake: The Tragic Death of Jesica Santillan*, CBS News (Mar. 16, 2003), https://www.cbsnews.com/news/anatomy-of-a-mistake-16-03-2003/ (Santillan).
21. Sarah Shannon, *Ebola, Team Communication, and Shame: But Shame on Whom?* 15 AM. J. BIOETHICS 20 (2015).
22. Norimitsu Onishi and Marc Santora, *Ebola Patient in Dallas Lied on Screening Form, Liberian Airport Official Says*, N.Y. TIMES (Oct. 2, 2014), https://www.nytimes.com/2014/10/03/world/africa/dallas-ebola-patient-thomas-duncan-airport-screening.html.
23. Sarah Shannon, *Ebola, Team Communication, and Shame: But Shame on Whom?*, 15 AM. J. BIOETHICS 20 (2015).
24. Kelly Gilblom et al., *Dead Texas Ebola Patient's Family Questions Hospital Care*, CLAIMSJOURNAL.COM (Oct. 9, 2014), https://www.claimsjournal.com/news/southcentral/2014/10/09/256091.htm.

CHAPTER 3

1. Institute of Medicine, TO ERR IS HUMAN: BUILDING A SAFER HEALTH SYSTEM (Linda T. Kohn et al., eds., 2000).
2. PAUL STARR, THE SOCIAL TRANSFORMATION OF AMERICAN MEDICINE: THE RISE OF A SOVEREIGN PROFESSION AND THE MAKING OF A VAST INDUSTRY, 335–337 (1982)
3. KENNETH ALLEN DEVILLE, MEDICAL MALPRACTICE IN NINETEENTH-CENTURY AMERICA: ORIGINS AND LEGACY, 200–201 (1st ed. 1990).

4. 42 U.S.C. § 1395 (1935); Mark A. Hall, *Institutional Barriers to Healthcare Cost Containment*, 137 U. PENN. L. REV. 431, 446–447 (1988).
5. TOM BAKER, THE MEDICAL MALPRACTICE MYTH, 25–27 (1st ed. 2007) (citing DON HARPER MILLS, DAVID RUBSAMEN and JOHN BOYDEN, REPORT ON THE MEDICAL INS. FEASIBILITY STUDY FOR THE CALIFORNIA MEDICAL ASSOCIATION AND CALIFORNIA HOSPITAL ASSOCIATION (1977)).
6. Medical Injury Compensation Reform Act (MICRA), CAL. CIV. CODE § 3333.2 (2017).
7. TOM BAKER, THE MEDICAL MALPRACTICE MYTH, 2 (1st ed. 2007); The Times Editorial Bd., *Medicare and Medicaid at 50: Successful, Expensive*, THE L.A. TIMES (July 30, 2015) http://www.latimes.com/opinion/editorials/la-ed-medicare-medicaid-50-20150730-story.html.
8. PATRICIA DANZON, MEDICAL MALPRACTICE: THEORY, EVIDENCE AND PUBLIC POLICY (1985).
9. TOM BAKER, THE MEDICAL MALPRACTICE MYTH, 27–30 (1st ed. 2007).
10. TOM BAKER, THE MEDICAL MALPRACTICE MYTH, 27–30 (1st ed. 2007); Troyen A. Brennan et al., *Incidence of Adverse Events and Negligence in Hospitalized Patients*, 324 N. ENG. J. MED. 372–376 (1991).
11. PAUL C. WEILER ET AL., A MEASURE OF MALPRACTICE (1993).
12. Elise C. Becker and Mark Chassin, *Improving the Quality of Healthcare: Who Will Lead?* 20 HEALTH AFF. 164, 165 (2001).
13. Troyen A. Brennan et al., *Incidence of Adverse Events and Negligence in Hospitalized Patients*, 324 N. ENG. J. MED. 372 (1991).
14. Lucian L. Leape, *Scope of Problem and History of Patient Safety*, 35 OBSTET. GYNECOL. CLIN. N. AM. 1 (2008).
15. M.S. Marquis and S. H. Long, *Trends in Managed Care and Managed Competition*, 18 HEALTH AFF. 75, 75 (1999).
16. Employee Retirement Income Security Act (ERISA) 29 U.S. Code § 1144 Other laws (1974).
17. R. J. Blendon et al., *Understanding the Managed Care Backlash*, 17 HEALTH AFF. 80 (1998).
18. *Engalla v. Permanente Medical Group, Inc.*, 15 Cal. 4th 951 (1997).
19. *Mass. Mut. Life Ins. Co. v. Russel*, 473 U.S. 134 (1985); *Metro. Life Ins. Co. v. Massachusetts*, 471 U.S. 724 (1985).
20. Arnold M. Epstein, *Public Release of Performance Data*, 283 JAMA 1884–1885 (2000)
21. Lucian L. Leape, *Errors in Medicine*, 272 J. AM. MED. ASSOC. 1851, 1851 (1994).
22. GEORGE D. LUNDBERG, SEVERED TRUST Why American Medicine Hasn't Been Fixed 171 (2000)
23. Lucian L. Leape, *Scope of Problem and History of Patient Safety*, 35 OBSTET. GYN. CLIN. N AM. 4 (2008).
24. Bradford H. Gray, Michael K. Gusmano, and Sara R. Collins, *AHCPR and the Changing Politics of Health Services Research*, W. Health Aff. 283, 294 (June 25, 2003).
25. Lucian L. Leape, *Scope of Problem and History of Patient Safety*, 35 OBSTET. GYN. CLIN. N AM 4 (2008).
26. Troyen A. Brennan, *The Institute of Medicine Report on Medical Errors-Could It Do Harm?*, 342 N. ENGL. J. MED. 1123 (2000).

27. Lucian L. Leape, *Scope of Problem and History of Patient Safety*, 35 OBSTET. GYN. CLIN. N AM. 4 (2008).
28. Id. at 6.
29. INST. OF MED. COMM. ON QUALITY OF HEALTH CARE IN AM., TO ERR IS HUMAN: BUILDING A SAFER HEALTH SYSTEM (Linda T. Kohn et al. eds., 2000).
30. 10 THE MASS. HEALTH POLICY FORUM, ISSUE BRIEF: MEDICAL ERRORS AND PATIENT SAFETY IN MASSACHUSETTS: WHAT IS THE ROLE OF THE COMMONWEALTH? 3 (2000).
31. Lucian L. Leape, *Scope of Problem and History of Patient Safety*, OBSTET. GYN. CLIN. N AM. 4 (2008).
32. Health Care Quality Improvement Act of 1986 (HCQIA), tit. IV sec. 401 Pub. L. No. 99-660, *amended by* 42 U.S.C. § 11101 (1998).
33. 10 THE MASS. HEALTH POLICY FORUM, ISSUE BRIEF: MEDICAL ERRORS AND PATIENT SAFETY IN MASSACHUSETTS: WHAT IS THE ROLE OF THE COMMONWEALTH? 3 (2000).
34. Id.
35. INST. OF MED. COMM. ON QUALITY OF HEALTH CARE IN AM., TO ERR IS HUMAN: BUILDING A SAFER HEALTH SYSTEM (Linda T. Kohn et al. eds., 2000).
36. Lori B. Andrews, *Medical Error and Patient Claiming in a Hospital Setting* (Am. Bar Found., Working Paper No. 9316, 1993); Ross Wilson et al., *The Quality in Australian Health Care Study*, 163 MED. J. AUSTL. 458 (1995).
37. INST. OF MED. COMM. ON QUALITY OF HEALTH CARE IN AM., TO ERR IS HUMAN: BUILDING A SAFER HEALTH SYSTEM 1 (Linda T. Kohn et al. eds., 2000).
38. Id.
39. ROBERT M. WACHTER AND KAVEH G. SHOJANIA, INTERNAL BLEEDING: THE TRUTH BEHIND AMERICA'S TERRIFYING EPIDEMIC OF MEDICAL MISTAKES 56 (2005).
40. Id.
41. INST. OF MED. COMM. ON QUALITY OF HEALTH CARE IN AM., TO ERR IS HUMAN: BUILDING A SAFER HEALTH SYSTEM 6 (Linda T. Kohn et al. eds., 2000).
42. Maxine M. Harrington, *Revisiting Error: Five Years After the IOM Report, Have Reporting Systems Made a Measurable Difference?* 15 HEALTH MATRIX 329, 330 (citing Robert J. Blendan et al., *Views of Practicing Physicians and the Public on Medical Error*, 347 N. ENGL. J. MED. 1933, 1935 (2002)).
43. Troyen A. Brennan, *Accidental Deaths, Saved Lives, and Improved Quality*, 353 N. ENGL. J. MED. 1405, 1405 (2005).
44. 10 THE MASS. HEALTH POLICY FORUM, ISSUE BRIEF: MEDICAL ERRORS AND PATIENT SAFETY IN MASSACHUSETTS: WHAT IS THE ROLE OF THE COMMONWEALTH? 3 (2000).
45. Lucian L. Leape, *Scope of Problem and History of Patient Safety*, 35 OBSTET. GYN. CLIN. N AM. 5 (2008).

CHAPTER 4

1. Donald Berwick, past Administrator of the Centers for Medicare and Medicaid Services, quoted in Reed Abelson, *In Bid for Better Care, Surgery with a Warranty*, New York Times (May 17, 2007).
2. Medical errors are defined as failure of a planned action to be completed as intended (i.e., error of execution) or the use of a wrong plan to achieve an aim (i.e., error

of planning). An "unintended act (either omission or commission) or an act that does not achieve its intended outcome." (Leape). A "failure of a planned sequence of mental or physical activities to achieve its intended outcome when these failures cannot be attributed to chance." (Reason). Errors do not always lead to harm.
3. Don Harper Mills, *Medical Insurance Feasibility Study*, 128 WEST. J. MED. 360 (1978).
4. Don Harper Mills et al., Report on the Medical Insurance Feasibility Study (1977). See also Don Harper Mills, *Medical Insurance Feasibility Study: A Technical Summary*, 128 WEST. J. MED. 360 (1978).
5. Don Harper Mills et al., Report on the Medical Insurance Feasibility Study (1977).
6. If within the existing system 3 of every 100 negligently injured patients brought claims for compensation, a system that lowered the barriers to such claims could easily bring in 10 or 20 times that number. Moreover, there are three times as many patients who suffer iatrogenic injuries as suffer *negligent* iatrogenic injuries—so multiply by a factor of another 3. Thus, the 3 who currently sued could become 90 or 180 or more.
7. Don Harper Mills, *Medical Insurance Feasibility Study*, 128 WEST. J. MED. 360 (1978). Western Journal of Medicine started life in 1856 as the Transactions of the Medical Society of the State of California. In 1902, it was renamed the California State Journal of Medicine in 1902 and went through several other name changes before being laid to rest in 2002.
8. "Copies of the full report are available from Sutter Publications, Inc., 731 Market Street, San Francisco, CA 94103. Price per copy is $35, plus applicable California state sales tax for California residents. For CMA and CHA members, initial copy price is $15, plus applicable California state sales tax."
9. Knight Steel, *Iatrogenic Disease on a Medical Service*, 32 J. AM. GERIATR. SOC. 445 (1984).
10. PATRICIA M. DANZON, MEDICAL MALPRACTICE: THEORY, EVIDENCE, AND PUBLIC POLICY (1985).
11. Mills saw the value of his data in trying to prevent harm to future patients. See Don Harper Mills, *Medical Lessons from Malpractice Cases*, 183 JAMA 1073 (1963); Don Harper Mills, *Malpractice and the Clinical Laboratory*,144 SCIENCE 638 (1964); Don Harper Mills, *Medical Injury Information: A Preparation for Analysis and Implementation of Prevention Programs*, 236 JAMA 379 (1976); Don Harper Mills, *Medical Peer Review: The Need to Organize a Protective Approach*, 1 HEALTH MATRIX 67 (1991); Orley H. Lindgren, Ronald Christensen, and Don Harper Mills, *Medical Malpractice Risk Management Early Warning Systems*, 54 L. CONTEMP. PROBL. 23 (Spring, 1991).
12. Leon S. Pocincki et al., U.S. Dept. Health, Educ. & Welfare, The Incidence of Iatrogenic Injuries: Report of The Secretary's Comm'n on Medical Malpractice 50 (1973) (Pub. No. (05) 89).
13. PAUL C. WEILER ET AL., A MEASURE OF MALPRACTICE: MEDICAL INJURY, MALPRACTICE LITIGATION, AND PATIENT COMPENSATION (1993).
14. Id., at vii–viii.
15. Id., at 152.
16. Id., at ix. At the time, New York doctors and hospitals paid $1 billion annually in professional liability insurance premiums.

17. Id., at 34–35 (defining adverse event).
18. Id.
19. The number could be misleading because, for example, determining what was negligent and what was not can be a difficult judgment. In litigation, it usually gets sorted out by lawyers and insurance company specialists. In the research, it was done by doctors, and we know that the Harvard reviewers disagreed with each other a fair amount. HMPS, Patients, Doctors, and Lawyers: Medical Injury, Malpractice Litigation, and Patient Compensation in New York, The Report of The HMPS to The State of New York (1990).
20. Eric J. Thomas et al., *Incidence and Types of Adverse Events and Negligent Care in Utah and Colorado*, 38 Med. Care 261 (2000).
21. Centers for Disease Control, Number of Inpatients in Nonfederal, Short-Stay Hospitals, http://www.cdc.gov/nchs/fastats/hospital.htm
22. Office of Inspector General, Department of Health and Human Services, Adverse Events in Hospitals: National Incidence Among Medicare Beneficiaries (2010). Adverse events are judged *preventable* if the outcome would not have occurred had more appropriate care been provided.
23. Paul Weiler et al., A Measure of Malpractice: Medical Injury, Malpractice Litigation, and Patient Compensation (1993).
24. In fact, it has declined, from 37.938 million in 1984 to 34.879 million in 2014.
25. E.g., Virginia Freid and Amy Bernstein, Health Care Utilization Among Adults Aged 55–64 Years: How Has It Changed Over the Past 10 Years? NCHS Data Brief, No. 32 (Mar. 2010).
26. Institute of Medicine, What's Possible for Health Care? (2012). See also Christopher P. Landrigan et al., *Temporal Trends in Rates of Patient Harm Resulting from Medical Care*, 363 N. Engl. J. Med. 2124 (2010); Robert Wachter, Patient Safety, at 10; *Unmistakable Progress, Troubling Gaps*, 29 Health Aff. 165 (2010). As one review put it, "the problem of patient safety has been repeatedly identified in the medical literature since the mid 1950s, but regular surveys concerning patient deaths and injuries resulting from treatment have had almost no effect on current medical practice." L. La Pietra, *Medical Errors and Clinical Risk Management: State of the Art*, 25 Acta Otorhinolaryngol. Ital. 339 (2005).
27. Lucian Leape et al., *Preventing Medical Injury*, 19 Qual. Rev. Bull. 144 (1993); see also C. J. McDonald et al., *Deaths Due to Medical Errors Are Exaggerated in Institute of Medicine Report*, 284 JAMA 93 (2000); Lucian Leape, *Institute of Medicine Medical Error Figures Are Not Exaggerated*, 284 JAMA 95 (2000).
28. And, of course, some have argued that HMPS and the IOM data, as given, overcount the actual deaths and injuries or are not as worrisome as they might seem (e.g., the dead and injured tend to be older patients). These arguments have gained little if any traction in the ongoing research, which confirms or enlarges past findings.
29. Institute of Medicine, To Err is Human: Building a Safer Health System (Linda T. Kohn et al. eds., 2000).
30. Robert M. Wachter, Understanding Patient Safety (2012), at 73.
31. Winta T. Mehtsun et al., *Surgical Never Events in the United States*, 153 Surgery 465 (2013).
32. The NQF initially defined 27 such events in 2002. The list has been revised since then, most recently in 2011 and now consists of 29 events grouped into six

categories: surgical, product or device, patient protection, care management, environmental, radiologic, and criminal.
33. Susanne Hempel et al., *Wrong-Site Surgery, Retained Surgical Items, and Surgical Fires*, 150 JAMA SURG. 796 (2015).
34. Tamara L. Williams et al., *Retained Surgical Sponges: Findings From Incident Reports and a Cost-Benefit Analysis of Radiofrequency Technology*, 219 J. AM. COLL. SURG. 354 (2014).
35. A report from Medicare concurs: "46% to 65% of adverse events in hospitals are related to surgery." Centers for Medicare and Medicaid Services, Fiscal Year 2015 Results for the CMS Hospital-Acquired Condition Reduction Program and Hospital Value-Based Purchasing Program (Dec. 18, 2014).
36. M. A. Healey et al., *Complications in Surgical Patients*, 137 ARCH. SURG. 611 (2002).
37. Shelley S. Magill et al., *Multistate Point-Prevalence Survey of Health Care–Associated Infections*, 370 NEJM 1198 (2014); see also CDC, HAI Data & Stats (2016).
38. Id. The CDC disaggregates those more than 700,000 infections into these types: pneumonia, 157,500; surgical site infections from any inpatient surgery, 157,500; gastrointestinal illness, 123,100; urinary tract infections, 93,300; primary bloodstream infections, 71,900; other, 118,000.
39. Centers for Medicare and Medicaid Services, New Medicare Data Available to Increase Transparency on Hospital Utilization (June 1, 2015).
40. Eyal Zimlichman et al., *Health Care-Associated Infections: A Meta-analysis of Costs and Financial Impact on the U.S. Health Care System*, 173 JAMA INTERN. MED. 2039 (2013).
41. See discussion of handwashing in Chapter 9 in this volume.
42. Michael Kinch et al., *An Overview of FDA-Approved New Molecular Entities (NMEs): 1827–2013*, 19 DRUG DISCOV. TODAY 1033 (2014).
43. JERRY AVORN, POWERFUL MEDICINES: THE BENEFITS, RISKS, AND COSTS OF PRESCRIPTION DRUGS (2005).
44. Hoskie v. United States, 666 F.2d 1353 (l0th Cir. 1981).
45. G. Koren, *Trends of Medication Errors in Hospitalised Children*, 42 J. CLIN. PHARMACOL. 707 (2002).
46. Liz Kowalczyk, *Surgical Error at Tufts Prompts Widespread Changes*, BOSTON GLOBE (Aug. 31, 2014).
47. Karen C. Nanji et al., *Evaluation of Perioperative Medication Errors and Adverse Drug Events*, 124 ANESTHESIOLOGY 25 (2016).
48. D. W. Bates et al., *Incidence of Adverse Drug Events and Potential Adverse Drug Events*, 274 JAMA 29 (1995).
49. INSTITUTE OF MEDICINE, PREVENTING MEDICATION ERRORS (2006).
50. Lisa Sanders, *If the Boy Had Pneumonia, Why Did He Have Odd Sores on His Body?* NEW YORK TIMES MAGAZINE (Oct. 10, 2017).
51. The maxim was coined in the late 1940s by Theodore Woodward, professor at the University of Maryland School of Medicine.
52. See, e.g., JEROME P. KASSIRER ET AL., LEARNING CLINICAL REASONING (2010), which teaches clinical reasoning to medical students: generating and refining diagnostic hypotheses, using and interpreting diagnostic tests, assembling a working diagnosis, examining and applying evidence. The book also contains a discussion of cognitive errors that physicians sometimes fall prey to.

53. INSTITUTE OF MEDICINE, IMPROVING DIAGNOSIS IN HEALTHCARE (2015).
54. Bradford Winters et al., *Diagnostic Errors in the Intensive Care Unit: A Systematic Review of Autopsy Studies*, 11 BMJ QUAL. SAF. 894 (2012).
55. Disclosure of errors, especially to researchers, managers, regulators, is discussed in several later chapters.
56. John J. Harris and Don Harper Mills, *Medical Records and the Questioned Document Examiner*, 8 J. FOREN. SCI. 453 (1963).
57. Knight Steel et al., *Iatrogenic Illness on a General Medical Service at a University Hospital*, 304 N. ENG. J. MED. 638 (1981).
58. Lori B. Andrews et al., *An Alternative Strategy for Studying Adverse Events in Medical Care*, 349 LANCET 309 (1997); Lori B. Andrews, *Studying Medical Error in Situ: Implications for Malpractice Law and Policy*, 54 DEPAUL L. REV. 357 (2004).
59. David C. Classen et al., *"Global Trigger Tool" Shows that Adverse Events in Hospitals May Be Ten Times Greater Than Previously Measured*, 30 HEALTH AFF. 581, 582 (2011).
60. Christine Sammer et al., *Developing and Evaluating an Automated All-Cause Harm Trigger System*, 43 JOINT COMM. J. QUAL. PATIENT SAF. 155 (2017).
61. Id., at 583.
62. Id.
63. Christopher P. Landrigan et al., *Temporal Trends in Rates of Patient Harm Resulting From Medical Care*, 363 N. ENGL. J. MED. 2124 (2010).
64. By this, we refer to one analysis that found a small and not quite statistically significant reduction in preventable harms. The other analyses in the study were even less encouraging.
65. INSTITUTE OF MEDICINE, TO ERR IS HUMAN: BUILDING A SAFER HEALTH SYSTEM (Linda T. Kohn, et al. eds., 2000); Martin Makary and Michael Daniel, *Medical Error—The Third Leading Cause of Death in the U.S.*, 353 BMJ (2016) (online).
66. American Hospital Association, Fast Facts on U.S. Hospitals (2016); Tejal K. Gandhi and Thomas H. Lee, *Patient Safety Beyond the Hospital*, 363 N. ENGL. J. MED. 1001 (2010).
67. Id.
68. INSTITUTE OF MEDICINE, PREVENTING MEDICATION ERRORS (2006).
69. INSTITUTE OF MEDICINE, IMPROVING DIAGNOSIS IN HEALTH CARE (2015). Also see Hardeep Singh et al., *The Frequency of Diagnostic Errors in Outpatient Care: Estimations From Three Large Observational Studies Involving U.S. Adult Populations*, 23 BMJ QUAL. SAF. 727 (2014).
70. Literature reviewed in Jean M. Mitchell, *Assessing Quality Data Reporting by Ambulatory Surgery Centers*, 68 DEPAUL L. REV. 291 (2019).
71. Margaret J. Hall et al., *Ambulatory Surgery Data From Hospitals and Ambulatory Surgery Center: United States, 2010*, 102 NAT. HEALTH STAT. REP. (Feb. 28, 2017).
72. Tara Bishop et al., *Paid Malpractice Claims for Adverse Events in Inpatient and Outpatient Settings*, 305 JAMA 2427 (2011).
73. Office of the Inspector General, DHHS, Adverse Events in Skilled Nursing Facilities: National Incidence Among Medicare Beneficiaries (2014) (OEI-06-11-00370).

74. Although SNFs meet the requirements of Medicare Part A, under the Social Security Act, 90% of SNFs are dually certified as both SNFs and nursing homes (i.e., long-term care providers).
75. DHHS, OIG, Adverse Events in Rehabilitation Hospitals: National Incidence Among Medicare Beneficiaries (2016). In the United States at the time of the study there were 234 rehabilitation hospitals that admitted 139,526 patients, to which Medicare paid $2.4 billion for their services. Skilled nursing facilities, by contrast, numbered 14,948 and admitted 2.4 million patients.
76. Properly informing the patient would have included statements such as "You have no condition that requires the proposed surgery" or "You will be exposed to risk in return for no conceivable benefit."
77. The crime of fraud consists of a knowing misrepresentation of a material fact to a person who relies on the misrepresentation and who consequently suffers a financial loss or other harm from that reliance. The crime of battery (included within assault in some jurisdictions) consists of the voluntary, intentional bringing about of unconsented harmful or offensive contact with a person.
78. Julie Creswell, *A Small Indiana Town Scarred by a Trusted Doctor*, NEW YORK TIMES (Oct. 18, 2015).
79. Id.
80. *Hospital Chain Internal Reports Found Dubious Cardiac Work*, NEW YORK TIMES (Aug. 6, 2012).
81. Id.
82. Julie Creswell and Reed Abelson, *Hospital Chain Said to Scheme to Inflate Bills*, NEW YORK TIMES (Jan. 23, 2014).
83. Walt Bogdanich and Jo Craven McGinty, *Medicare Claims Show Overuse for CT Scanning* (June 17, 2011). Moreover, study after study has shown that doctors who have a financial interest in a service refer more of their patients to that service than do their peers treating patients with the same conditions. See, e.g., U.S. Government Accountability Office, Medicare: Higher Use of Costly Prostate Cancer Treatment by Providers Who Self-Refer Warrant Scrutiny (2013) (radiation for enlarged prostate); U.S. Government Accountability Office, Medicare: Action Needed to Address Higher Use of Anatomic Pathology Services by Providers Who Self-Refer (2013) (pathology labs); Matthew P. Lungren et al., *Physician Self-Referral: Frequency of Negative Findings at MR Imaging of the Knee as a Marker of Appropriate Utilization*, 269 RADIOLOGY 810 (2013) (MRI imaging); Bimal Shah et al., *Association Between Physician Billing and Cardiac Stress Testing Patterns Following Coronary Revascularization*, 306 JAMA 1993 (2011) (cardiac stress testing following bypass or angioplasty).
84. The studies described here are from Nina Mazar, On Amir and Dan Ariely, *The Dishonesty of Honest People: A Theory of Self-Concept Maintenance*, 45 J. MARKET. RES. 633 (2008). For an overview of the related research see DAN ARIELY, THE HONEST TRUTH ABOUT DISHONESTY: HOW WE LIE TO EVERYONE—ESPECIALLY OURSELVES (2013).
85. Interview with Dan Ariely (2012), http://www.npr.org/2012/06/04/154287476/honest-truth-about-why-we-lie-cheat-and-steal
86. David Brooks, *The Moral Diet*, NEW YORK TIMES (June 7, 2012).
87. If anyone knew it had happened.

88. Interview with Dr. Frank Read, NPR, All Things Considered, The Telltale Wombs of Lewiston, Maine (Oct. 8, 2009).
89. Jonathan Bergman et al., *Service Intensity and Physician Income: Conclusions from Medicare's Physician Data Release*, 175 JAMA INTERN. MED. 297 (2015) (finding that physicians reach higher levels of income by ordering more procedures and services per patient rather than by seeing more patients: "These findings suggest that the current health care reimbursement model—fee-for-service—may not be creating the correct incentives for clinicians to keep their patients healthy.").
90. NPR, All Things Considered, The Telltale Wombs of Lewiston, Maine (Oct. 8, 2009).
91. Id.
92. Dr. Robert Keller explained: "We didn't want to talk about money. That's something that we wouldn't want to acknowledge because it would have been a showstopper. I mean, it would have then gone right to the question of greed, and you're not going to keep a doc at the table if you say you're greedy." Id.
93. Gina Kolata, *Why "Useless" Surgery Is Still Popular*, NEW YORK TIMES (Aug. 3, 2016).
94. NPR, All Things Considered, The Telltale Wombs of Lewiston, Maine (Oct. 8, 2009) ("Patients in the high-spending regions were getting about 60 percent more care . . . 60 percent more days in the hospital, twice as many specialist visits. And yet, when we followed patients for up to five years, the mortality rate, whether you were poor, rich, urban or rural . . . if you lived in one of these higher intensity communities, your survival was certainly no better and, in many cases, worse.")
95. The Dartmouth Atlas of Healthcare, http://www.dartmouthatlas.org/
96. The Dartmouth Atlas of Healthcare, Supply-Sensitive Care, http://www.dartmouthatlas.org/keyissues/issue.aspx?con=2937
97. Id.
98. Id.
99. Hospital admissions in the U.S. in 1975 totaled 36,157,000 which is 12 times the number in California at that time, which was 3,011,000.
100. Lucian Leape et al., *Preventing Medical Injury*, 19 QUAL. REV BULL. 144 (1993).
101. Martin Makary and Michael Daniel, *Medical Error—The Third Leading Cause of Death in the U.S.*, 353 BMJ (2016) (online).
102. John T. James, *A New, Evidence-based Estimate of Patient Harms Associated With Hospital Care*, 9 J. PATIENT SAF. 122 (2013).
103. John C. Goodman et al., *The Social Cost of Adverse Medical Events, and What We Can Do About It*, 30 HEALTH AFF. 590 (2011).
104. The Dartmouth Atlas of Healthcare, Supply-Sensitive Care, http://www.dartmouthatlas.org/keyissues/issue.aspx?con=1338
105. A Boeing 747-400 with a three-class layout can hold 416 passengers plus crew. The first to use this analogy in the patient safety context was Lucian L. Leape, *Error in Medicine*, 272 JAMA 1851 (1994). It has frequently been misattributed to the IOM report which, perhaps surprisingly, doesn't use the analogy at all.
106. Something that has gotten the attention of news media, citizens, and government is fear of terrorism within our borders. We pay close attention to those risks, and we invest huge sums to prevent that source of harm to our citizens. The number of fatalities from terrorism, inside the United States, from 2002 through 2016 totals of 190. See National

Consortium for the Study of Terrorism and Responses to Terrorism, Fact Sheet (Oct., 2017), http://www.start.umd.edu/pubs/START_AmericanTerrorismDeaths_FactSheet_Nov2017.pdf. That is an average of under 13 deaths per year. At that rate, it would take more than 30 years to fill one jumbo jet with the victims.
107. Mark R. Chassin, *Is Health Care Ready for Six Sigma Quality?* 76 MILBANK Q. 565, 566–567 (1998). See also Mark R. Chassin, *High-Reliability Health Care: Getting There From Here*, 91 MILBANK Q. 459 (2013).
108. David Hyman and Charles Silver, *The Poor State of Health Care Quality in the U.S.: Is Malpractice Liability Part of the Problem or Part of the Solution?* 90 CORNELL L. REV. 893, 949 (2005).
109. See Martin Makary and Michael Daniel, Medical Error—The Third Leading Cause of Death in the U.S., 353 BMJ (2016) (online).

CHAPTER 5

1. PAUL C. WEILER, HOWARD H. HIATT, JOSEPH P. NEWHOUSE, WILLIAM G. JOHNSON, TROYEN A. BRENNAN, AND LUCIAN L. LEAPE, A MEASURE OF MALPRACTICE: MEDICAL INJURY, MALPRACTICE LITIGATION, AND PATIENT COMPENSATION (1993) (Reporting the Harvard Medical Practice Study [HMPS]). (Harvard University Press, Cambridge, Mass., Copyright © 1993 by the President and Fellows of Harvard College.)
2. This being the core of criminal conduct, it is easy to see why possession and use of recreational drugs, consensual sexual activity, and other victimless crimes are controversial members of the crime category.
3. The lack of a role for morality on the civil side of the law is most clearly evident in contract law, where a person who has entered into a contract but later decides that it is in his or her interest to breach is free to choose whether or not to perform as promised under the terms of the contract. All the defendant has to do to escape from his or her promises is to compensate the plaintiff for the damages that the breach has imposed. A prospective contract defendant can weigh the costs and benefits of performance versus breach, and choose whichever better serves his or her interests. In the eyes of the law, this is a matter of economics, not morality. Note, too, that in this example we have a deliberate, premeditated, intentional contract breach, and the law requires nothing but economic compensation so that the party who has been disadvantaged is restored to the position he or she had bargained for.
4. LEE IACOCCA, IACOCCA: AN AUTOBIOGRAPHY (1984).
5. ROBERT M. WACHTER, UNDERSTANDING PATIENT SAFETY 322 (2012).
6. E.g., Adam Nossiter, *A Mistake, a Rare Prosecution, and a Doctor Is Headed for Jail*, NEW YORK TIMES (Mar. 16, 1995); Sarah Larson, *"Dr. Death" and the Perils of Making Medical Malpractice a Thriller*, NEW YORKER (Oct. 5, 2018).
7. Interestingly, medicine has contractually banned experience rating from malpractice liability insurance policies, heightening the very problem that some healthcare commentators want the tort system to solve.
8. Indeed, the use of negligence as a basis for a criminal conviction is narrowly limited, frowned upon by most legal scholars, and legally controversial. All of that actually suggests how strong the distinction is between what is considered criminal and what is considered tortious: negligent acts are associated with accidents, not crimes, and belong in the world of torts.

9. The major alternative to economic theories of tort law is the theory of corrective justice. *Corrective justice* posits that humans owe a first-order duty to others to refrain from inflicting harm. A second-order duty is to make amends if and when harm is wrongfully inflicted. Only the person (or entity) who violated the first-order duty can, and must, make amends if the balance of justice is to be restored between the injurer and the victim. Consequently, alternatives such as no-fault insurance, or compensation of the victim by government, would fail to achieve what tort law achieves.
10. See, generally, GUIDO CALABRESI, THE COSTS OF ACCIDENTS: A LEGAL AND ECONOMIC ANALYSIS (1970), and RICHARD POSNER, ECONOMIC ANALYSIS OF LAW (9th ed. 2014).
11. Stated more fully: the plaintiff has to prove by a preponderance of the evidence that the pizza delivery driver negligently breached a duty of care that caused injury to the plaintiff. But the focus of the present discussion is the negligence.
12. Brown v. Kendall, 60 Mass. (6 Cush.) 292 (Mass. 1850).
13. United States v. Carroll Towing, 160 F.2d 482 (2d Cir. N.Y. Mar. 17, 1947).
14. That is, the *non*negligent side. JAMES REASON, MANAGING THE RISKS OF ORGANIZATIONAL ACCIDENTS (1997), explains the Johnston Substitution Test:

> Substitute for the (erring) individual someone else coming from the same domain of activity and possessing comparable qualifications and experience. Then ask the following question. "In light of how events unfolded and were perceived by those involved in real time, is it likely that this new individual would have behaved any differently?" If the answer is "probably not" then . . . apportioning blame has no material role to play other than to obscure systemic deficiencies. . . . A useful addition to the substitution test is to ask of the individual's peers: "Given the circumstances that prevailed at that time, could you be sure that you would not have committed the same or similar type of unsafe act?" If the answer again is "probably not," then blame is inappropriate.

15. Richard Posner, *A Theory of Negligence*, 1 J. LEGAL STUD. 29, 33 (1972).
16. Geoffrey Palmer, *New Zealand's Accident Compensation Scheme: Twenty Years On* 44 UNIV. TORONTO LAW J. 223 (1994).
17. Richard Posner, *A Theory of Negligence*, 1 J. LEGAL STUD. 29, 33 (1972).
18. See Chapter 11 of this volume.
19. There are, of course, others involved in the compensation transaction, sometimes including insurers, lawyers, expert witnesses, courts, and others who are paid for their services.
20. Another indication of their pass-through nature is that they constitute income to the business that is reduced dollar-for-dollar as a business expense.
21. Healthcare providers are, in effect, collecting money from their patients and depositing them with a liability insurer which pools them and manages them for later payout to certain patients who have suffered injuries.
22. The patient (or the patient's health insurer) agrees to pay the doctor in exchange for medical care.
23. The fellow servant doctrine prevents an injured worker from collecting damages from an employer when the harmful error was committed by a co-worker.

24. The doctrine of assumption of the risk denies compensation to injured workers who were harmed in the course of an activity which presented obvious risks of injury.
25. "The very effectiveness of new medical technology increases potential liability, because it creates the possibility that someone will negligently deprive the patient of what is now a substantial benefit. Moreover, in modern times, actual liability can also be more frequent. While older medical procedures probably required less physician advertence, the modern patient may be connected to a heart monitor, a brain scanner, a blood-gas analyzer, and a respiration eavesdropper, giving [the physician] twenty-seven interacting dials and a tremendous need for advertence. Negligence . . . increases because these machines round up the mustang risks of disease and domesticate them. Once technology tames disease, there can be relentless legal problems if [the physician] momentarily forgets what he is doing." Mark F. Grady, *Why Are People Negligent? Technology, Nondurable Precautions, and the Medical Malpractice Explosion*, 82 NORTHWEST UNIV. L. REV. 293, 294–295 (1988).
26. See CHARLES L. BOSK, FORGIVE AND REMEMBER: MANAGING MEDICAL FAILURE (2d ed. 2011).
27. See summary of arguments and quotations in Chapter 1 of NEIL VIDMAR, MEDICAL MALPRACTICE AND THE AMERICAN JURY (1997).
28. Mark Galanter, *". . . A Settlement Judge, Not a Trial Judge:" Judicial Mediation in the United States*, 12 J. LAW SOC. 1 (Spring, 1985).
29. Among others, see data reported by TOM BAKER, THE MEDICAL MALPRACTICE MYTH (2005); DAVID ENGEL, THE MYTH OF THE LITIGIOUS SOCIETY (2016); David Hyman and Charles Silver (numerous articles, several of which have been drawn from in this book); Michael J. Saks, *Do We Really Know Anything About the Behavior of the Tort Litigation System—And Why Not?*, 140 U. PENN. L. REV. 1147 (1992); FRANK A. SLOAN AND LINDSEY M. CHEPKE, MEDICAL MALPRACTICE (2008); NEIL VIDMAR, MEDICAL MALPRACTICE AND THE AMERICAN JURY: CONFRONTING THE MYTHS ABOUT JURY INCOMPETENCE, DEEP POCKETS AND OUTRAGEOUS DAMAGE AWARDS (1995).
30. This is not to say that the feedback signals sent are all received with high fidelity and correctly understood. One empirical legal scholar, Theodore Eisenberg, late of Cornell University and founder of the Journal of Empirical Legal Studies, devoted the greater part of his energies to analyzing relevant data and identifying erroneous readings of the system's behavior by those embedded in the system.
31. This response is known as "lumping it." Dictionary definition: "to accept or tolerate a disagreeable situation whether one likes it or not."
32. These are based on the HMPS's New York data.
33. We use the term *opened file* rather than *lawsuit*, because the filing of a lawsuit is not the only reason an insurer will open a file on a case. Notification from an insured that a patient has been seriously injured will lead to a file being opened, even if nothing is ever heard from the patient or the patient's attorney. Although this is probably an overestimate of actual claims, for ease of discussion we assume they are all claims.
34. See studies reviewed in Chapter 4 of this volume.
35. PATRICIA M. DANZON, MEDICAL MALPRACTICE: THEORY, EVIDENCE, AND PUBLIC POLICY 82 (1985), at 23 tbl. 2.4.

36. Marlynn L. May and Daniel B. Stengel, *Who Sues Their Doctors? How Patients Handle Medical Grievances*, 24 L. Soc. Rev. 105 (1990).
37. William L. F. Felstiner et al., *The Emergence and Transformation of Disputes: Naming, Blaming, Claiming*, 15 L. Soc. Rev. 631 (1980–1981).
38. Marlynn L. May and Daniel B. Stengel, *Who Sues Their Doctors? How Patients Handle Medical Grievances*, 24 L. Soc. Rev. 105 (1990).
39. See, e.g., Henry S. Farber and Michelle J. White, *Medical Malpractice: An Empirical Examination of the Litigation Process*, 22 RAND J. Econ. 199 (1991) (noting that plaintiffs' lawyers have a strong incentive to screen prospective plaintiffs and to accept only those cases with a sufficiently high expected value).
40. David A. Hyman, *The Economics of Plaintiff-Side Personal Injury Practice*, 2015 U. Illinois L. Rev. 1563. Also, note that driving up that threshold has led to a statistical illusion. Over time, in many states, the average size of jury awards has increased. Casual observers take that as a reflection of the jury being "out-of-control." Some have argued that reining in those awards requires imposing further obstacles to raise the difficulty and expense of filing cases, of prevailing, and of obtaining compensation. But by raising the cost of entry into the system, such changes would reduce the number of cases by excluding those with less expected value to plaintiffs attorneys, producing a smaller but richer pool of cases leading to even higher trial awards (as well as settlements).
41. Myungho Paik, Bernard Black, and David Hyman, *The Receding Tide of Medical Malpractice Litigation: National Trends*, 10 J. Emp. Legal Stud. 612 (2013) and Mohammad Rahmati et al., *Screening Plaintiffs and Selecting Defendants in Medical Malpractice Litigation: Evidence from Illinois and Indiana*, 15 J. Emp. Legal Stud. 41 (2018) (finding strong evidence of the effects of screening on outcome success).
42. Herbert M. Kritzer, Risks, Reputations, and Rewards: Contingency Fee Legal Practice in the United States 69–74 (2004); Herbert M. Kritzer, *Seven Dogged Myths Concerning Contingency Fees*, 80 Wash. Univ. Law Q. 739, 754–757 (2002); Herbert M. Kritzer, *Contingency Fee Lawyers As Gatekeepers in the Civil Justice System*, 81 Judicature 22, 24 (1997); Herbert M. Kritzer, *Holding Back the Floodtide: The Role of Contingent Fee Lawyers*, Wis. L. Rev. Mar. 1997, at 10, 63.
43. LaRae I. Huycke and Mark M. Huycke, *Characteristics of Potential Plaintiffs in Malpractice Litigation*, 120 Ann. Intern. Med. 792 (1994).
44. Aaron E. Carroll, Parul Divya Parikh, and Jennifer L. Buddenbaum, *The Impact of Defense Expenses in Medical Malpractice Claims*, 40 J. Law Med. Ethics 135 (2012).
45. U.S. Department of Justice, Office of Justice Programs, Bureau of Justice Statistics, Medical Malpractice Insurance Claims in Seven States, 2000–2004 (2007). That means that more cases are resolved by the litigotiation system than appear in the annual reports of the courts.
46. Patricia Danzon, Medical Malpractice: Theory, Evidence and Public Policy (1985).
47. Tom Baker, *Reconsidering the Harvard Medical Practice Study Conclusions about the Validity of Medical Malpractice Claims*, 33 J. Law Med. Ethics 501, 502–506 (2005); Tom Baker, The Medical Malpractice Myth (2005). The main purpose of the Journal of Law, Medicine & Ethics article was to address a complicated debate over the implications of the HMPS. Because that debate is complicated and because the

HMPS data set is one of the smallest for present purposes, we do not address it here. But the interested reader is encouraged to consult the Baker paper.
48. Frank A. Sloan, *Policy Implications*, in SUING FOR MEDICAL MALPRACTICE 219 (Frank A. Sloan et al. eds., 1993).
49. David M. Studdert, Michelle M. Mello, Atul A. Gawande et al., *Claims, Errors, and Compensation Payments in Medical Malpractice Litigation*, 354 NEJM 2024 (2006).
50. One of the first to make this clear with hard data was the economist PATRICIA M. DANZON, MEDICAL MALPRACTICE: THEORY, EVIDENCE, AND PUBLIC POLICY 82 (1985).
51. HARVARD MEDICAL PRACTICE STUDY, PATIENTS, DOCTORS, AND LAWYERS: MEDICAL INJURY, MALPRACTICE LITIGATION, AND PATIENT COMPENSATION IN NEW YORK, THE REPORT OF THE HARVARD MEDICAL PRACTICE STUDY TO THE STATE OF NEW YORK (1990).
52. Saks, M. J. *Enhancing and Restraining Accuracy in Adjudication*, 51 L. CONTEMP. PROBL. 243 (Autumn 1988)
53. David Rottman, *Tort Litigation in The State Courts: Evidence from the Trial Court Information Network*, 14 STATE COURT J. 4 (1990).
54. U.S. Bureau of Justice Statistics, Medical Malpractice Trials and Verdicts in Large Counties, 2001 (NCJ 203098) (April 2004)
55. Setting aside a civil verdict the judge regards as being in error is known as *judgment non obstante veredicto*, or judgment notwithstanding the verdict, or simply JNOV. It is, therefore, not much of an exaggeration to suggest that civil jury verdicts are in essence recommendations offered to the judge.
56. Michael J. Saks, *Do We Really Know Anything About the Behavior of the Tort Litigation System—And Why Not?* 140 U. PENN. L. REV. 1147 (1992).
57. A remaining possibility is that there are cases that ought to have settled but nevertheless transition to the trial stage, but judges and juries are so incapable of understanding the evidence that their verdicts are random. Fortunately for our discussion and for the institution of the trial, this is a possibility that can be ruled out by several lines of triangulating evidence.
58. That is, neither judges nor juries were more likely than the other to find for one party or the other.
59. Harry Kalven Jr., *The Jury, the Law, and the Personal Injury Damage Award*, 19 OHIO ST. LAW J. 158 (1958).
60. Theodore Eisenberg et al., *Judge-jury Agreement in Criminal Cases: A Partial Replication of Kalven and Zeisel's* The American Jury, 2 J. EMP. LEGAL STUD. 171 (2005); Larry Heuer and Steven Penrod, *Trial Complexity: A Field Investigation of its Meaning and its Effects*, 18 L. HUM. BEHAV. 29–51 (1994).
61. Bureau of Justice Statistics, Civil Bench and Jury Trials in State Courts, 2005 (2008), at Tbl 5.
62. The percentage is 26.8% in Bureau of Justice Statistics, Civil Trial Cases and Verdicts in Large Counties, 2001 (2004), at Tbl. 5, and 23% in Cynthia G. Lee and Robert C. LaFountain, *Medical Malpractice Litigation in State Courts*, 18 CASELOAD HIGHLIGHTS 1, Apr. 4, 2011.
63. Compare, ROBERT M, WACHTER, UNDERSTANDING PATIENT SAFETY 324 (2012) ("tort systems inevitably lower the fault-finding bar to allow for easier compensation

of sympathetic victims"; "an unfair match: faced with a heart-wrenching story of an injured patient or grieving family"; "lopsided scales of malpractice justice").
64. David Hyman and Charles Silver, *Medical Malpractice Litigation and Tort Reform: It's The Incentives, Stupid*, 59 VAND. L. REV. 1085 (2006).
65. Thomas B. Metzloff, *Resolving Malpractice Disputes: Imaging the Jury's Shadow*, 54 L. CONTEMP. PROBL. 43, 50 (1991); David M. Studdert and Michelle M. Mello, *When Tort Resolutions Are "Wrong": Predictors of Discordant Outcomes in Medical Malpractice Litigation*, 36 J. LEGAL STUD. 547 (2007).
66. A more difficult challenge would be differences among victims of the same injury that justified inter-individual differences in the value of that loss. As much as we all might value our hearing, Beethoven's loss was almost certainly more devastating.
67. See David Baldus et al., *Improving Judicial Oversight of Jury Damages Assessments: A Proposal for the Comparative Additur/remittitur Review of Awards for Nonpecuniary Harms and Punitive Damages*, 80 IOWA L. REV. 1109 (1995) and Michael J. Saks et al., *Reducing Variability in Civil Jury Awards*, 21 L. HUM. BEHAV. 243 (1997).
68. Also, arguably, it presents an empirical as well as a legal challenge.
69. Roselle L. Wissler et al., *Decision-Making about General Damages: A Comparison of Jurors, Judges, and Lawyers*, 98 MICH. L. REV. 751 (1999). The prediction equation for ratings by jurors had a multiple correlation squared (R^2) of 0.72, compared to those of trial judges ($R^2 = 0.69$), plaintiffs' lawyers ($R^2 = 0.78$), and defense lawyers ($R^2 = 0.75$).
70. Id.
71. The suggestions of Baldus et al., Wissler et al., and others—namely, to maintain databases of injuries–circumstances–awards and provide relevant information to jurors and judges to give them some guidance in reaching award decisions—would strengthen vertical equity and reduce horizontal inequity. The challenge, course, is whether enough cases can be found that permit apples-to-a-basket-of-apples comparisons.
72. Thomas H. Cohen, U.S. Dept. of Justice, Bureau of Justice Statistics, Medical Malpractice Trials and Verdicts in Large Counties 2001, at 1 (Apr. 2004); David M. Studdert et al., *Are Damages Caps Regressive? A Study of Malpractice Jury Verdicts in California*, 23 HEALTH AFF. 54 (2004).
73. Frank Sloan and Stephen van Wert, *Costs of Injuries*, in SUING FOR MEDICAL MALPRACTICE 139, 139 (Frank A. Sloan et al. eds., 1993). The findings contrast with familiar claims that malpractice awards are excessive and must be capped.
74. See discussion of this problem and empirical studies cited in Michael J. Saks, *Do We Really Know Anything About the Behavior of the Tort Litigation System—And Why Not?* 140 U. PENN. L. REV. 1147 (1992) and Frank Sloan and Stephen van Wert, *Costs of Injuries*, in SUING FOR MEDICAL MALPRACTICE 139 (Frank A. Sloan et al. eds., 1993).
75. Frank Sloan et al. (eds.), SUING FOR MEDICAL MALPRACTICE (1993).
76. Bear in mind that plaintiffs who lose their cases owe their lawyers no fee (so those cases are investments that are all loss for the attorneys who took them) and, for reasons we previously reviewed, medical malpractice litigation is one of the riskiest areas in which plaintiffs attorneys can work (meaning they are easy cases in which to lose money if the attorney is not smart and careful). For a more extensive discussion

of the economics of attorney fees and related policy issues, see Sloan and Chepke, 2008, Chapter 6.
77. For example, a classic study of settlements in litigation found:

> The evaluation of the routine case is strongly affected by understandings common to both adjusters and attorneys concerning an appropriate relationship between settlement and the degree of injury as measured by medical bills. This can be termed the formula method of evaluation. The hospital and physicians' bills are totaled and are multiplied by an arbitrary coefficient—typically from two to five, depending on the practice of the area—to yield an agreeable figure for the intangibles of the case, the pain and suffering and inconvenience. With represented claimants, a figure of three times the medical bills is sometimes described as allocating one-third to the lawyer, one-third to the physician, and one-third to the claimant. H. LAURENCE ROSS, SETTLED OUT OF COURT 107-8 (1980).

78. A growth function often illustrated in advertisements by investment companies, urging people to begin saving early for retirement.
79. Michael J. Saks, *Do We Really Know Anything About the Behavior of the Tort Litigation System—And Why Not?* 140 U. PENN. L. REV. 1147 (1992) and Allan Raitz et al., *Determining Damages*, 14 L. HUM. BEHAV. 385 (1990).
80. See NEIL VIDMAR, MEDICAL MALPRACTICE AND THE AMERICAN JURY: CONFRONTING THE MYTHS ABOUT JURY INCOMPETENCE, DEEP POCKETS AND OUTRAGEOUS DAMAGE AWARDS (1995) and Roselle L. Wissler et al., *The Impact of Jury Instructions on the Fusion of Liability and Compensatory Damages*, 25 L. HUM. BEHAV. 125 (2001).
81. See Eleanor D. Kinney and William P. Gronfein, *Indiana's Malpractice System: No-Fault by Accident?* L. CONTEMP. PROBL. (Winter–Spring 1991), at 169, 172–174. In the late 1980s, mean awards were about $400,000 in Indiana compared to about $300,000 in Michigan and Ohio.
82. This is a further indication, as we commented earlier, that judges have a great deal of control over civil jury trial outcomes when they wish to exercise it.
83. Michael J. Saks, *Do We Really Know Anything About the Behavior of the Tort Litigation System—And Why Not?* 140 U. PENNS. L. REV. 1147 (1992); Neil J. Vidmar, Felicia Gross and Mary Rose, *Jury Awards for Medical Malpractice and Post-verdict Adjustments of Those Awards*, 48 DEPAUL L. REV. 265, 280, 298 (1998); NEIL VIDMAR, MEDICAL MALPRACTICE AND THE AMERICAN JURY: CONFRONTING THE MYTHS ABOUT JURY INCOMPETENCE, DEEP POCKETS AND OUTRAGEOUS DAMAGE AWARDS 261 (1995); David A. Hyman et al., Tort Reform and the Pretrial Litigation Process: Evidence From Texas Medical Malpractice Cases, 1988–2003 (finding that post-verdict "haircuts" are common and large); Neil Vidmar, Juries and Jury Verdicts in Medical Malpractice Cases: Implications for Tort Reform in Pennsylvania (Jan. 28, 2002) (unpublished manuscript, on file with Neil Vidmar).
84. Charles Silver et al., Policy Limits, Payouts, and Blood Money: Medical Malpractice Settlements in the Shadow of Insurance," 5 UC Irvine L. Rev. 559 (2015) ("out of pocket payments by physicians were rare and usually small").

85. Why? One of us has informally asked attorneys who specialize in malpractice, and has never received a convincing response. Perhaps the closest one has been the suggestion that collection is an entirely different expertise, which they lack, so they do not undertake it and are unwilling to delegate that to a different attorney.
86. If the earliest stages of claiming were thought of as though we were evaluating a biomedical screening test, then (using the HMPS New York State data) the opening of insurance claim files would have a specificity of 0.99 (meaning that of those cases that were excluded by the system as involving no negligent injury, 99% were correctly excluded; that is, 99% true negatives). Sensitivity (detecting negligence when negligence is present, in other words, the true positive rate) would be somewhere between 0.17 (if the final HMPS negligence designations were employed as the criterion) and 0.74 (if any determination of the presence of negligence in a case by any reviewer were taken as the criterion). The sensitivity data are unavoidably volatile because so few claim files emerged from the 30,121 hospital records examined: only 47 in all.
87. Ashley M. Votruba and Michael J. Saks, *Medical Adverse Events and Malpractice Litigation in Arizona: By-the-Numbers,* 45 ARIZ. ST. LAW J. 1537 (2013). The values have been rounded for ease of comprehension.
88. Of the HMPS New York State data that were the result of negligence and that provided determinable injuries, 50% ranged from "moderate [injury], recovery [in] 1–6 months" to death, and half of those were deaths.
89. DEBORAH R. HENSLER ET AL., COMPENSATION FOR ACCIDENTAL INJURIES IN THE UNITED STATES (1991).
90. Ashley M. Votruba and Michael J. Saks, *Medical Adverse Events and Malpractice Litigation in Arizona: By-the-Numbers,* 45 ARIZ. ST. LAW J. 1537 (2013).
91. David A. Hyman and Charles Silver, *Five Myths of Medical Malpractice,* 143 CHEST 222 (2013).
92. In addition to data presented earlier in this chapter, see, e.g., id., ("[A]n enormous fraction of patients who are harmed by medical negligence either make no effort to recover damages or cannot find lawyers willing to take their cases"), and PATRICIA DANZON, MEDICAL MALPRACTICE: THEORY, EVIDENCE AND PUBLIC POLICY (1985) (noting that her evidence "supports the belief that small malpractice claims are often barred from recovery because of the high fixed costs of participating in the legal process.").

CHAPTER 6

1. Peter H. Schuck, *Tort Reform, Kiwi-Style,* 27 YALE L. POLICY REV. 187 (2008).
2. The Ethicist (column), New York Times (May 17, 2017).
3. See, e.g., Michelle Mello et al., *Communication-and-Resolution Programs: The Challenges and Lessons Learned from Six Early Adopters,* 33 HEALTH AFF. 20 (2014); Allen Kachalia et al., *Effects of a Communication-and-Resolution Program on Hospitals' Malpractice Claims and Costs,* 37 HEALTH AFF. 1836 (2018); and the interestingly named CANDOR program, promoted by the Agency for Healthcare Research and Quality, https://www.ahrq.gov/professionals/quality-patient-safety/patient-safety-resources/resources/candor/introduction.html
4. CAROL TAVRIS AND ELLIOT ARONSON, MISTAKES WERE MADE (BUT NOT BY ME): WHY WE JUSTIFY FOOLISH BELIEFS, BAD DECISIONS, AND HURTFUL ACTS (2015).

5. Id.
6. Of cases deemed negligent adverse events in the HMPS, fewer than 3% became claims for compensation. *All* claim files opened (those not meeting the HMPS's criteria plus those that did) equaled only 17% of valid claims that could properly have been brought. Of all patients, only 0.16% (that's16 one-hundredths of 1%) had claim files opened on their cases.
7. Externalities—costs created by an economic transaction that are displaced onto third parties rather than being borne by the parties benefitting from the transaction—are discussed in greater depth in Chapters 5 and 11 of this volume.
8. Evidence of liability not clear enough, losses not high enough. Joanna Shepherd, *Uncovering the Silent Victims of the American Medical Liability System*, 67 VAND. L REV 151 (2014) ("In fact, over half of the attorneys responded that they will not accept a case unless expected damages are at least $250,000, even for a case they are almost certain to win on the merits.").
9. One interesting reason is the nature of the case mix that reaches the jury: because malpractice defendants are more reluctant than other tort defendants to settle, stronger defense cases go to trial than occur in other types or tort cases.
10. A correlation of about $r = 0.70$.
11. Very recent exceptions have emerged, creating duties to inform third parties (family members of a patient) of certain genetic risks that are diagnosed.
12. David A. Hyman, *Medical Malpractice and the Tort System: What Do We Know and What (If Anything) Should We Do About It?*, 80 TEX. L. REV. 1639 (2001–2002).
13. See New Zealand's reforms, discussed later in this chapter.
14. It is beside the point to also say that the lawyers on both sides are working for money, because all of us, whatever we do, are doing that to earn our livings—in addition to whatever other goals we might have.
15. Tom Baker, *Blood Money, New Money, and the Moral Economy of Tort Law in Action Blood Money*, 35 L. SOC. REV 275 (2001) (emphasis added).
16. Alexander B. Lemann, *Coercive Insurance and the Soul of Tort Law*, 105 GEORGETOWN LAW J. 55 (2016) (noting that "virtually all car accidents (95.8%) currently result in settlements between insurance companies" and that "the standardization of this process has been a project of insurance companies for almost as long as the car has been used for transportation").
17. A national study by the RAND Corporation of all kinds of nonfatal accidental injuries found that the tort system returned to victims only about four cents on every dollar of loss. The rest was paid by various sources, although mostly by the victims and their families. DEBORAH R. HENSLER ET AL., COMPENSATION FOR ACCIDENTAL INJURIES IN THE UNITED STATES (1991).
18. "Marginal" here means greater precaution than would otherwise have occurred.
19. Michael J. Saks, *Do We Really Know Anything About the Behavior of the Tort Litigation System—And Why Not?* 140 U. PENN. L. REV. 1147, 1287 (1992).
20. Ann G. Lawthers, *Physicians' Perceptions of the Risk of Being Sued*, 17 J HEALTH POLIT. POLIC. 463 (1992); PAUL WEILER ET AL., A MEASURE OF MALPRACTICE: MEDICAL INJURY, MALPRACTICE LITIGATION, AND PATIENT COMPENSATION (1993), at 124–125.
21. Once we set aside auto crash cases, only 34.5% of tort defendants overall are individuals; in medical malpractice cases, 38.5% of defendants are individuals.

Thomas H. Cohen, Tort Bench and Jury Trial in State Courts, 2005, Bureau of Justice Statistics Bulletin, Table 2 (November, 2009) (NCJ 228129). (According to court statistics staff at the National Center for State Courts, these are the most recent data available on the subject.)
22. Sarah Verschoor, *IU Freshman Rescued after Surviving Three Days in Cave*, INDIANA DAILY STUDENT (Sept. 21, 2017), http://www.idsnews.com/article/2017/09/iu-freshman-found-after-surviving-three-days-in-a-cave
23. Id.
24. For more on this subject, see Chapter 11 of this volume.
25. See, generally, Gary T. Schwartz, *Reality in the Economic Analysis of Tort Law: Does Tort Law Really Deter?*, 42 UCLA L. REV. 377, 381–387 (1994); DON DEWEES ET AL., EXPLORING THE DOMAIN OF ACCIDENT LAW: TAKING THE FACTS SERIOUSLY (1996).
26. This is a point that has been made repeatedly by competent researchers. See, e.g., W. Jonathan Cardi et al., *Does Tort Law Deter?* 9 J EMP. LEGAL STUD. 567 (2012).
27. MICHAEL J. MOORE AND W. KIP VISCUSI, COMPENSATION MECHANISMS FOR JOB RISKS 133 (1990); James R. Chelius, *Liability for Industrial Accidents: A Comparison of Negligence and Strict Liability Systems*, 5 J. LEGAL STUD. 293, 303–306 (1976).
28. Michelle J. White, *An Empirical Test of the Comparative and Contributory Negligence Rules in Accident Law*, 20 RAND J. ECON. 308 (1989). Traditional contributory negligence denies a plaintiff all recovery if the plaintiff's own negligence contributed to the accident; comparative negligence reduces the damages paid to the plaintiff in proportion to the plaintiff's share of the responsibility for the accident. See also Frank A. Sloan, Bridget A. Reilly, and Christoph Schenzler, *Effects of Tort Liability and Insurance on Heavy Drinking and Drinking and Driving*, 38 J. LAW ECON. 49, 49 (1995) (finding, similarly, that "switching from contributory to comparative negligence increased binge drinking").
29. Alma Cohen and Rajeev Dehejia, *The Effect of Automobile Insurance and Accident Liability Laws on Traffic Fatalities*, 47 J. LAW ECON. 357, 382 (2004) (about 10% more fatalities with no-fault rules); J. David Cummins, Richard D. Phillips, and Mary A. Weiss, *The Incentive Effects of No-Fault Automobile Insurance*, 44 J. LAW ECON. 427, 427 (2001) (more fatalities with no-fault); A. Richard Derrig et al., *The Effect of Population Safety Belt Usage Rates on Motor Vehicle-Related Fatalities*, 34 ACCIDENTS ANAL. PREVENT. 101 (2002) (no significant difference); Paul Zador and Adrian Lund, *Re-analysis of the Effects of No-Fault Auto Insurance on Fatal Crashes*, 53 J. RISK INS. 226, 235 (1986) (fewer fatalities with no-fault); S. Paul Kochanowski and Madelyn V. Young, *Deterrents Aspects of No-Fault Automobile Insurance: Some Empirical Findings*, 52 J. RISK INS. 269 (1985) (no significant difference); M. Elisabeth Landes, *Insurance Liability and Accidents: A Theoretical and Empirical Investigation of the Effect of No-Fault Accidents*, 25 J. LAW ECON. 49, 50 (1982) (more fatalities with no-fault); Frank A. Sloan et al., *Tort Liability Versus Other Approaches for Deterring Careless Driving*, 14 INT. REV. L. ECON. 53, 66–67 (1994) (an 18% increase in fatalities with no-fault rules).
30. Geoffrey Palmer, *New Zealand's Accident Compensation Scheme: Twenty Years On* 44 UNIV. TORONTO LAW J. 223 (1994); Peter H. Schuck, Tort Reform, Kiwi-Style, 27 YALE L. POL. REV. 187 (2008–2009); FRANK A. SLOAN AND LINDSEY M. CHEPKE, MEDICAL MALPRACTICE (2008).

31. The benefits include hospital and medical costs; wage replacement, starting only one week after injury, at a rate of 80% of average weekly earnings; rehabilitation and transportation costs; lump sum payments for permanent loss or impairment; and entitlements for surviving spouses and children.
32. Geoffrey Palmer, *New Zealand's Accident Compensation Scheme: Twenty Years On* 44 UNIV. TORONTO LAW J. 223 (1994); Peter H. Schuck, Tort Reform, Kiwi-Style, 27 YALE L. POL. REV. 187 (2008–2009).
33. FRANK A. SLOAN AND LINDSEY M. CHEPKE, MEDICAL MALPRACTICE 302 (2008).
34. George J. Annas, *The Patient's Right to Safety—Improving the Quality of Care through Litigation Against Hospitals*, 354 NEW ENGL. J. MED. 2063 (2006).
35. Id.
36. Peter Davis et al., *Adverse Events in New Zealand Public Hospitals I: Occurrence and Impact*, 115 NEW ZEAL. MED. J. (2002). The New Zealand adverse event rates were comparable to those of Australia and the United Kingdom.
37. Michael L. Smith, *Deterrence and Origin of Legal System: Evidence from 1950–1999*, 7 AM. L. ECON. REV. 350 (2005).
38. W. Jonathan Cardi et al., *Does Tort Law Deter?*, 9 J. EMP. LEGAL STUD. 567 (2012).
39. JERRY AVORN, POWERFUL MEDICINES: THE BENEFITS, RISKS, AND COSTS OF PRESCRIPTION DRUGS 23–38 (2004).
40. In what the researchers say is the only experimental study on the subject, W. Jonathan Cardi et al., *Does Tort Law Deter?* 9 J. EMP. LEGAL STUD. 567 (2012), presented 717 first-year law students at 13 law schools with nine diverse scenarios, each involving activities that risked harm to persons or property. Participants were randomly divided into groups that were informed that any resulting harm might lead either to a "significant criminal fine" or to a tort suit or that neither criminal nor civil liability could follow from accidental harm in the scenarios. Participants were asked to imagine themselves in each scenario and to indicate how likely they were to engage in the activity under the circumstances described. The risk of criminal sanctions for inadvertently causing harm reduced the likelihood of engaging in the activity for six of the nine scenarios, but the risk of tort liability reduced the likelihood for only one of the activities. This simulation study is as close as one is likely to get to an apples-to-apples comparison on the deterrence question. But this approach presents some problems of its own, most important, the extent to which what people say they would do predicts what they would actually do.
41. Ann G. Lawthers, *Physicians' Perceptions of the Risk of Being Sued*, 17 J. HEALTH POLIT. POLIC. 463 (1992); PAUL WEILER ET AL., A MEASURE OF MALPRACTICE: MEDICAL INJURY, MALPRACTICE LITIGATION, AND PATIENT COMPENSATION (1993).
42. Emily R. Carrier et al., *Physicians' Fears of Malpractice Lawsuits are not Assuaged by Tort Reforms*, 29 HEALTH AFF. 1585 (2010).
43. Allen Kachalia and Michelle M. Mello, *New Directions in Medical Liability Reform*, 364 NEJM 1564 (2011).
44. Zenon Zabinski and Bernard S. Black, The Deterrent Effect of Tort Law: Evidence from Medical Malpractice Reform (February 15, 2015). Northwestern Law & Econ Research Paper No. 13-09. Available at http://dx.doi.org/10.2139/ssrn.2161362

45. Id. See also Rand Institute for Civil Justice, Is Better Patient Safety Associated With Less Malpractice Activity? Evidence from California (2010) ("Our results showed a highly significant correlation between the frequency of adverse events and malpractice claims"; "Nearly two-thirds of the variation in malpractice claiming against surgeons and nonsurgeons can be explained by changes in safety.")
46. Michael D. Frakes and Anupam B. Jena, *Does Medical Malpractice Law Improve Health Care Quality?*, 143 J. PUBLIC ECON. 142 (2016).
47. F.W. Cheney, A*SA Closed Claims Project—Where Have We Been and Where Are We Going?*, 57 AM. SOC. ANESTHESIOLOG. NEWSL. 8 (1993). See also Ellison C. Pierce, Jr., *The Development of Anesthesia Guidelines and Standards*, 16 QUALITY REV. BULL. 61 (1990).
48. David A. Hyman and Charles Silver, *The Poor State of Health Care Quality in the U.S.: Is Malpractice Liability Part of the Problem or Part of the Solution?*, 90 CORNELL L. REV. 893 (2005), argue that "two major factors forced [the anesthesiologists'] hand: malpractice claims and negative publicity. . . . Anesthesiologists worked hard to protect patients because of malpractice exposure, not in spite of it."
49. See Chapter 7 of this volume.
50. ROBERT M. WACHTER, UNDERSTANDING PATIENT SAFETY xiii, xiv (2012). Dr. Wachter states that the *only* hard-wired safety measure he is aware of, pre-IOM report, is the prevention of transfusion errors by double-checking before releasing a unit of blood.
51. PAUL WEILER ET AL., A MEASURE OF MALPRACTICE: MEDICAL INJURY, MALPRACTICE LITIGATION, AND PATIENT COMPENSATION (1993).
52. David M. Studdert and Michelle M. Mello, *When Tort Resolutions Are "Wrong": Predictors of Discordant Outcomes in Medical Malpractice Litigation*, 36 J. LEGAL STUD. 547 (2007).
53. PAUL WEILER ET AL., A MEASURE OF MALPRACTICE: MEDICAL INJURY, MALPRACTICE LITIGATION, AND PATIENT COMPENSATION 75 (1993): "[W]hile the absolute number of unfounded claims is considerably larger than the absolute number of valid claims, the pattern shows that the chances that any one doctor will be sued are far greater if negligent treatment has occurred than if it has not. To return to our traffic analogy, even though more drivers may be ticketed by police after going through green than red lights, the reason is that far more drivers go through green lights in the first place. With that difference controlled for, the odds that a careless driver will get a ticket, or that a careless doctor will be sued, are far greater than the odds faced by their careful counterparts." And further, "As we shall see in Chapter 6, however cloudy the malpractice signal might appear to doctors, both the reality and the perception of that signal have a pronounced tilt in the proper direction."
54. Id. (emphasis supplied).
55. Had they run an analysis counting cases which had been evaluated as having some indicia of negligent tort, the error rate would be seen as smaller. See Michael J. Saks, *Medical Malpractice: Facing Real Problems and Finding Real Solutions*. Review of Weiler et al., A Measure of Malpractice: Medical Injury, Malpractice Litigation, and Patient Compensation (Harvard University Press, 1993), 35 WILLIAM MARY L. REV. 693 (1994); Tom Baker, *Reconsidering the Harvard Medical Practice Study Conclusions about the Validity of Medical Malpractice Claims*, 33 J LAW MED. ETHICS 501 (2005).

56. That 22 is a likelihood ratio, one type of measure of the accuracy of a test. Medical students are taught that likelihood ratios great than 10 are very good. https://www.med.emory.edu/EMAC/curriculum/diagnosis/lr%27s.htm
57. See data in Chapter 4 of this volume.
58. David M. Studdert and Michelle M. Mello, *When Tort Resolutions Are "Wrong": Predictors of Discordant Outcomes in Medical Malpractice Litigation*, 36 J. LEGAL STUD. 547 (2007).
59. Id. Our calculation, based on data in their Table 2.
60. A single Pap tests fails to detect disease 50% of the time.
61. Ashley N. D. Meyer et al., *Physicians' Diagnostic Accuracy, Confidence, and Resource Requests: A Vignette Study*, 173 JAMA INTERN MED. 1952 (2013).
62. Charles Friedman et al., *Do Physicians Know When Their Diagnoses Are Correct? Implications for Decision Support and Error Reduction*, 20 J. GEN. INTERN. MED. 334 (2005).
63. John D. Whited et al., *Primary Care Clinicians' Performance for Detecting Actinic Keratoses and Skin Cancer*, 157 ARCH. INTERNAL MED. 985 (1997).
64. Pierre Leichner et al., *A Study of the Reliability of the Clinical Oral Examination in Psychiatry*, 29 CAN. J. PSYCHIATR. 394 (1984).
65. GERD GIGERENZER, CALCULATED RISKS: HOW TO KNOW WHEN NUMBERS DECEIVE YOU (2002).
66. PAUL WEILER ET AL., A MEASURE OF MALPRACTICE: MEDICAL INJURY, MALPRACTICE LITIGATION, AND PATIENT COMPENSATION (1993).
67. David M. Studdert and Michelle M. Mello, *When Tort Resolutions Are "Wrong": Predictors of Discordant Outcomes in Medical Malpractice Litigation*, 36 J. LEGAL STUD. 547 (2007).
68. Relevant evidence is discussed, e.g., in Chapter 5 of this volume and in TOM BAKER, THE MEDICAL MALPRACTICE MYTH (2005), Chapter 4.
69. Relevant evidence is discussed in the present chapter and in id.
70. Relevant evidence is discussed, e.g., in David A. Hyman and Charles Silver, *Five Myths of Medical Malpractice*, 143 CHEST 222 (2013); and in TOM BAKER, THE MEDICAL MALPRACTICE MYTH (2005), Chapter 3.
71. Relevant evidence is discussed, e.g., in the present chapter; in David A. Hyman and Charles Silver, *Five Myths of Medical Malpractice*, 143 CHEST 222 (2013); in David A. Hyman and Charles Silver, *Medical Malpractice Litigation and Tort Reform: It's the Incentives, Stupid*, 59 VAND. L. REV. 1085 (2006); and in Bernard Black et al., *The Association between Patient Safety Indicators and Medical Malpractice Risk: Evidence from Florida and Texas*, 3 AMER. J. HEALTH ECON. 109 (Spring, 2017) (studying hospital adverse events and malpractice claim rates in Florida and Texas and finding strong correlation between Patient Safety Indicators and malpractice claim rates, "evidence that malpractice claims leading to payouts are not random events. Instead, hospitals that improve patient safety can reduce malpractice payouts"); and in Rand Institute for Civil Justice, Is Better Patient Safety Associated with Less Malpractice Activity? Evidence from California (2010) ("Our results showed a highly significant correlation between the frequency of adverse events and malpractice claims"; "Nearly two-thirds of the variation in malpractice claiming against surgeons and nonsurgeons can be explained by changes in safety").

72. E.g., ROBERT WACHTER AND KAVEH SHOJANIA, INTERNAL BLEEDING: THE TRUTH BEHIND AMERICA'S TERRIFYING EPIDEMIC OF MEDICAL MISTAKES (2004). See also Michelle M. Mello and David M. Studdert, *Deconstructing Negligence: The Role of Individual and System Factors in Causing Medical Injuries*, 96 GEO. LAW J. 599, 605 (2007–2008). When possible, however, plaintiffs' attorneys prefer to sue organizations, if only for their deeper pockets. But the healthcare industry is organized—partly as a result of the evolution of medical practitioner culture, partly as a strategy by hospitals—in ways that make lawsuits against organizations, especially hospitals, difficult. See note 21 of the present chapter and accompanying text, as well as Chapter 11 of this volume.
73. Relevant evidence is discussed, e.g., in Chapter 5 of this volume; TOM BAKER, THE MEDICAL MALPRACTICE MYTH (2005), Chapter 4; and David M. Studdert and Michelle M. Mello, *When Tort Resolutions Are "Wrong": Predictors of Discordant Outcomes in Medical Malpractice Litigation*, 36 J. LEGAL STUD. 547 (2007).
74. Relevant evidence is discussed, e.g., in Chapter 5 of this volume and TOM BAKER, THE MEDICAL MALPRACTICE MYTH (2005), Chapter 4.
75. Relevant evidence is discussed, e.g., in Chapter 5 of this volume; David A. Hyman and Charles Silver, *Five Myths of Medical Malpractice*, 143 CHEST 222 (2013); and TOM BAKER, THE MEDICAL MALPRACTICE MYTH (2005), Chapter 4.
76. Relevant evidence is discussed, e.g., in David A. Hyman and Charles Silver, *Five Myths of Medical Malpractice*, 143 CHEST 222 (2013).
77. Relevant evidence is discussed, e.g., in David A. Hyman and Charles Silver, *The Poor State of Health Care Quality in the U.S.: Is Malpractice Liability Part of the Problem or Part of the Solution?*, 90 CORNELL L. REV. 893 (2005).
78. Relevant evidence is discussed, e.g., in Chapter 7; in David A. Hyman and Charles Silver, *Five Myths of Medical Malpractice*, 143 CHEST 222 (2013); and in TOM BAKER, THE MEDICAL MALPRACTICE MYTH (2005), Chapter 6.
79. Relevant evidence is discussed, e.g., in the present chapter.
80. Relevant evidence is discussed, e.g., in Chapter 5 of this volume. See also, e.g., ROBERT M. WACHTER, UNDERSTANDING PATIENT SAFETY (2012) (commenting that "it is remarkable how little money actually ends up in the hands of the victims and their families").
81. See MICHAEL L. MILLENSON, DEMANDING MEDICAL EXCELLENCE: DOCTORS AND ACCOUNTABILITY IN THE INFORMATION AGE 72 (1999).
82. But see David A. Hyman and Charles Silver, *The Poor State of Health Care Quality in the U.S.: Is Malpractice Liability Part of the Problem or Part of the Solution?*, 90 CORNELL L. REV. 893 (2005) (reviewing literature indicating that fear of litigation had increased, not reduced, disclosure).
83. PAUL WEILER ET AL., A MEASURE OF MALPRACTICE: MEDICAL INJURY, MALPRACTICE LITIGATION, AND PATIENT COMPENSATION (1993).
84. Wayne Oliver and Jeffrey Segal, To Reduce Healthcare Costs Eliminate, Don't Reform, Malpractice System, TheHill.com (October 23, 2014). Available at http://thehill.com/blogs/congress-blog/healthcare/221533-to-reduce-healthcare-costs-eliminate-dont-reform-malpractice
85. Ellen Wertheimer, *Calling It a Leg Doesn't Make It a Leg*: Doctors, Lawyers, and Tort Reform*, 13 ROGER WILLIAMS L. REV. 154, 154 (2008).

86. Randall R. Bovbjerg, *Patient Safety and Physician Silence*, 25 J. LEGAL MED. 505 (2004).
87. PATRICIA M. DANZON, MEDICAL MALPRACTICE: THEORY, EVIDENCE, AND PUBLIC POLICY 23 (1985).
88. Susan Forray and Eric Wunder, Patient Compensation Systems Evolve—But Are No Less Worrisome (PIAA Online Report, Inside Medical Liability) (February, 2017).
89. See, e.g., ADAM SMITH, THE WEALTH OF NATIONS 152 (1776) ("People of the same trade seldom meet together, even for merriment and diversion, but the conversation ends in a conspiracy against the public, or in some contrivance to raise prices.")
90. Randall Bovbjerg and Robert Berenson, *Enterprise Liability in the Twenty-First Century*, in Sage and Kersh (eds.) MEDICAL MALPRACTICE AND THE U.S. HEALTH CARE SYSTEM (2006), at 230.
91. Myungho Paik, Bernard Black, and David Hyman, *The Receding Tide of Medical Malpractice Litigation: National Trends, Part I*, 10 J EMP. LEGAL STUD. 612 (2013); see also Michelle Mello et al., *The Medical Liability Climate and Prospects for Reform*, 312 JAMA 2146 (2014).
92. Allen Kachalia and Michelle M. Mello, *New Directions in Medical Liability Reform*, 364 NEJM 1564 (2011).
93. FRANK A. SLOAN AND LINDSEY M. CHEPKE, MEDICAL MALPRACTICE (2008), Chapter 5.
94. Several methods of creating less malevolent limits on awards have been proposed. See, e.g., David C. Baldus et al., *Improving Judicial Oversight of Jury Damages Assessments: A Proposal for the Comparative Additur/Remittitur Review of Awards for Nonpecuniary Harms and Punitive Damages*, 80 IOWA L. REV. 1109 (1995) (damages scaling); Randall Bovbjerg et al., *Valuing Life and Limb in Tort: Scheduling "Pain and Suffering,"* 83 NORTHWESTERN UNIV. L. REV. 908 (1989) (damages scheduling); PAUL WEILER ET AL., A MEASURE OF MALPRACTICE: MEDICAL INJURY, MALPRACTICE LITIGATION, AND PATIENT COMPENSATION (1993) (finding savings from lower-level injuries and higher-level income earners); or at least indexing caps to inflation. See further discussions in FRANK A. SLOAN AND LINDSEY M. CHEPKE, MEDICAL MALPRACTICE (2008); Catherine M. Sharkey, *Unintended Consequences of Medical Malpractice Damages Caps*, 80 NY UNIV. L. REV. 391 (2005); David M. Studdert et al., *Are Damages Caps Regressive? A Study of Malpractice Jury Verdicts in California*, 23 HEALTH AFF. 54 (2004).
95. Zenon Zabinski and Bernard S. Black, The Deterrent Effect of Tort Law: Evidence from Medical Malpractice Reform (February 15, 2015). Northwestern Law & Econ Research Paper No. 13-09. Available at http://dx.doi.org/10.2139/ssrn.2161362
96. Anne Krueger, *The Political Economy of the Rent-Seeking Society*, 64 AM. ECON. REV. 291 (1974).
97. Michael J. Saks, Daniel Strouse and N.J. Schweitzer, *A Multi-attribute Utility Analysis of Legal Policy Responses to Medical Adverse Events*, 54 DEPAUL L. REV. 277 (2005) (in the symposium, "Starting Over? Redesigning the Medical Malpractice System").
98. David A. Hyman and Charles Silver, *The Poor State of Health Care Quality in the U.S.: Is Malpractice Liability Part of the Problem or Part of the Solution?*, 90 CORNELL L. REV. 893 (2005). See also Joanna C. Schwartz, *A Dose of Reality for Medical Malpractice Reform*, 88 NY UNIV. L. REV. 1224 (2013).

99. E.g., Michelle Mello and Troyen Brennan, *Deterrence of Medical Errors: Theory and Evidence for Malpractice Reform*, 80 TEX. L. REV. 1595 (2002); PAUL WEILER ET AL., A MEASURE OF MALPRACTICE: MEDICAL INJURY, MALPRACTICE LITIGATION, AND PATIENT COMPENSATION (1993).

100. Michael J. Saks, Daniel Strouse and N. J. Schweitzer, *A Multi-attribute Utility Analysis of Legal Policy Responses to Medical Adverse Events*, 54 DEPAUL L. REV. 277 (2005) (in the symposium, Starting Over?: Redesigning the Medical Malpractice System).

101. ROBERT WACHTER AND KAVEH SHOJANIA, INTERNAL BLEEDING: THE TRUTH BEHIND AMERICA'S TERRIFYING EPIDEMIC OF MEDICAL MISTAKES (2004).

102. We are thinking particularly of arguments concerning defensive medicine (see Chapter 7 of this volume) and disclosure of errors (see David A. Hyman and Charles Silver, *The Poor State of Health Care Quality in the U.S.: Is Malpractice Liability Part of the Problem or Part of the Solution?*, 90 CORNELL L. REV. 893 (2005).)

103. Peter H. Schuck, *Tort Reform, Kiwi-Style*, 27 YALE L. POLIC. REV. 187 (2008–2009).

CHAPTER 7

1. David A. Hyman & William Sage, *Do Health Reform and Malpractice Reform Fit Together?* (American Enterprise Institute Health Policy Working Paper 2011-02, Apr. 11, 2011).

2. Laurence R. Tancredi and Jeremiah A. Barondess, *The Problem of Defensive Medicine*, 200 SCIENCE 879 (1978). STEDMAN's MEDICAL DICTIONARY defines defensive medicine as, "diagnostic or therapeutic measures conducted primarily as a safeguard against possible subsequent malpractice liability." A more economically sensitive definition given by Frank A. Sloan and John H. Shadle, *Is There Empirical Evidence for "Defensive Medicine"? A Reassessment*, 28 J. HEALTH ECON. 481 (2009), sees defensive medicine as care for which expected cost exceeds expected benefit.

3. David M. Studdert et al., *Defensive Medicine Among High-Risk Specialist Physicians in a Volatile Malpractice Environment*, 293 JAMA 2609 (2005).

4. Richard Abel, Stephen Daniels, Philip Howard, Peter Schuck, and G. Marc Whitehead, *Public Discontent: The Debate Goes Beyond Tort Law*, 81 ABA J. 70 (Aug. 1995).

5. We say "most of the costs" because some very large healthcare organizations and some government facilities self-insure, and their liability expenditures are not reflected in the insurance data we cite. For example, "Medical professionals employed by federal agencies, such as the U.S. Department of Veterans Affairs, do not need malpractice coverage since the federal government self-insures against liability claims. State and local governments in some instances may also provide liability protection for medical employees." Insurance Information Institute, Understanding Medical Malpractice Insurance, at https://www.iii.org/article/understanding-medical-malpractice-insurance

6. Data are from 2017. Malpractice premiums are from A.M. Best, U.S. Property/Casualty—2017 Direct Premiums Written by Line. http://www.ambest.com/review/displaychart.aspx?Record_Code=274410. Healthcare expenditures are from Centers for Medicare and Medicaid Services, National Health Expenditure Highlights 2017. https://www.cms.gov/research-statistics-data-and-systems/statistics-trends-and-reports/nationalhealthexpenddata/nhe-fact-sheet.html.

7. All else equal, one might expect an industry that constitutes 17.9% of the GDP to cause more or less 17.9% of the damage and pay more or less 17.9% of the cost of those damages (through its liability insurance premiums). Yet the healthcare industry generates far more than its share of the damage while paying a little over a tenth of its "share" of victim reimbursement costs for those harms. (The math: 2.4/17.9 = 0.09 = less than one-tenth.)
8. Philip K. Howard, *Legal Malpractice*, Wall St. J. (Jan. 27, 2003) at A16.
9. David A. Hyman and Charles Silver, *The Poor State of Health Care Quality in the U.S.: Is Malpractice Liability Part of the Problem or Part of the Solution?*, 90 Cornell L. Rev. 893 (2005).
10. David A. Hyman and Charles Silver, *Believing Six Improbable Things: Medical Malpractice Legal Fear*, 28 Harv. J. Law Pub. Pol. 107 (2004).
11. U.S. Department of Health and Human Services, Addressing the New Health Care Crisis: Reforming the Medical Litigation System to Improve the Quality of Health Care (2003).
12. ATRA Press Release, Citing 'Defensive Medicine' Costs, ATRA Backs H.R. 5, http://www.atra.org/newsroom/citing-defensive-medicine-costs-atra-backs-hr-5 (last visited September 29, 2016).
13. Jackson Healthcare Study #1. See Physicians on Medical Liability Reform Options: An Online Quantitative Research Study (Jackson Healthcare, Dec. 5, 2012), archived at http://perma.cc/KTB8-L68K; Jackson Healthcare Study #2, Gallup and Jackson Healthcare, Physicians on Medical Liability Reform Options: An Online Quantitative Research Study (Jackson Healthcare, Dec. 5, 2012), archived at http://perma.cc/KTB8-L68K. Their figures were arrived at by asking doctors to guestimate what percentage of the procedures that they and their colleagues order are motivated by concerns about malpractice litigation. Their average responses were 26-% to 34% which, when multiplied by the total national healthcare bill, produces those numbers.

    This guestimate was picked up by then-congressman (later, Secretary of DHHS, briefly in 2017) Tom Price and repeated in a press release. Tom Price, Press Release, Gallup: 26% of Health Care Dollars Spent to Fend Off Trial Bar (Republican Study Committee, Feb 22, 2010), archived at http:// perma.cc/L2G5-GCUU. ("[P]hysicians estimated that 21 percent of everything they do can be attributed to the practice of defensive medicine."). Price was the Secretary of DHHS briefly in 2017.
14. Wayne Oliver and Jeffrey Segal, *To Reduce Healthcare Costs Eliminate, Don't Reform, the Malpractice System*, The Hill Blog (Oct. 23, 2014). http://thehill.com/blogs/congress-blog/healthcare/221533-to-reduce-healthcare-costs-eliminate-dont-reform-malpractice.
15. See Chapter 11 of this volume.
16. Ann G. Lawthers et al., *Physicians' Perceptions of the Risk of Being Sued*, 17 J. Health Polit. Pol. L. 463 (1992).
17. Anupam B. Jena et al., *Physician Spending and Subsequent Risk of Malpractice Claims: Observational Study*, 351 BMJ h5516 (2015) (finding that higher levels of physician spending were associated with reduced risk of subsequent malpractice claim). Said to be the first study to show this effect. Molly Walker, *'Defensive Medicine' Pays Off, Study Suggests* (Nov. 6, 2015) https://www.medpagetoday.com/practicemanagement/medicolegal/54498

18. Bronislaw Malinowski, *Magic, Science and Religion*, in Joseph Needham (ed.) SCIENCE, RELIGION AND REALITY (1925).
19. These are the overall averages for all players, all teams in major league baseball for the 2018 season.
20. See Chapter 4 of this volume.
21. We review the literature later in this chapter.
22. C-sections carry their own risks to the mother, including postoperative adhesions, incisional hernias (which could require further surgery), and wound infections, with the rate of adverse outcomes being slightly than that of vaginal deliveries. Safe Prevention of the Primary Cesarean Delivery, American Congress of Obstetricians and Gynecologists and the Society for Maternal-Fetal Medicine (March 2014). With the declining effectiveness of antibiotics, infection becomes an increasingly serious problem. In response to the lawyer's statement, this author waited in vain for someone in the audience to stand up and say something like: We are the doctors, not you. We work for the patients, not for you. We are not going to practice medicine in a manner calculated to make life easier for our insurers and our lawyers.
23. Atul Gawande, *The Cost Conundrum*, NEW YORKER (June 1, 2009).
24. Nested within this cost–benefit judgment there is, no doubt, another cost–benefit judgment, pertaining to the patient.
25. Fraud is the purposeful misrepresentation of a material fact, knowing that the fact is false or misleading, relied on by the victim, and resulting in some pecuniary harm to the victim.
26. The crime of reckless endangerment consists in a perpetrator recklessly (meaning: being consciously aware of the risk) exposing a victim to a substantial risk of imminent death or physical injury. A needless biopsy, surgery, or perhaps even exposure to radiation could be viewed as constituting the requisite harm.
27. AMA Code of Medical Ethics (2001).
28. Not unless you took so seriously the obligation to be truthful that you felt compelled to inform the world about the misdeeds of yourself and your colleagues. But if you felt that strongly, why not just stop doing it?
29. Colonel Frank W. Kiel, *Medical Malpractice Claims Against the Army*, 75 MIL. L. REV. 1 (1977).
30. Don Harper Mills, *Information Please*, 6 J LEGAL MED. 255 (1985).
31. Bradley G. Wertman, *Why Do Physicians Order Laboratory Tests?* 243 JAMA 2080 (1980).
32. Note, *The Medical Malpractice Threat: A Study of Defensive Medicine*, 1971 DUKE LAW J. 939.
33. Richard P. Bergen, *Defensive Medicine Is Good Medicine*, 228 J. AM. MED. ASSOC. 1188 (1974).
34. Jackson Healthcare Study #1. See *Physicians on Medical Liability Reform Options: An Online Quantitative Research Study* (Jackson Healthcare, Dec. 5, 2012), archived at http://perma.cc/KTB8-L68K.
35. Jackson Healthcare Study #2, Gallup and Jackson Healthcare, Physicians on Medical Liability Reform Options: An Online Quantitative Research Study (Jackson Healthcare, Dec. 5, 2012), archived at http://perma.cc/KTB8-L68K.
36. David M. Studdert et al., *Defensive Medicine Among High-Risk Specialist Physicians in a Volatile Malpractice Environment*, 293 JAMA 2609 (2005).

37. Tara Bishop et al., *Physicians' Views on Defensive Medicine: A National Survey*, 170 ARCH. INTERN. MED. 1081 (2010).
38. Jonas B. Green, *The Malpractice Muddle*, 29 HEALTH AFF. 2355 (2010).
39. See the subsection "Beyond Inadvertence," in Chapter 4 of this volume.
40. See the previous subsection in this chapter, "Why Would Anyone Admit to Engaging in Defensive Medicine?"
41. See Insurance Fraud in America: Current Issues Facing Industry and Consumers, Report produced for Hearing Before the Subcommittee on Consumer Protection, Product Safety, Insurance, and Data Security of the Committee on Commerce, Science, and Transportation, United States Senate, 115th Congress, First Session (Aug. 3, 2017); Coalition Against Insurance Fraud. https://www.insurancefraud.org/statistics.htm#13; National Association of Insurance Commissioners. https://www.naic.org/cipr_topics/topic_insurance_fraud.htm; FBI, What We Investigate, Health Care Fraud. https://www.fbi.gov/investigate/white-collar-crime/health-care-fraud.
42. The $933 billion (in current dollars) calculated by the Jackson Health System is more than 23 times as much as $40 billion. See the previous subsection in this chapter, "A Tool for Advocacy."
43. Yet many of those same serious students of the topic emerge from their search where they started: pretty sure that defensive medicine occurs—based, obviously, on something other than sound research evidence. It is as if they are saying: it's got to be there, we just can't find good evidence of it.
44. See, e.g., Atul Gawande, *America's Epidemic of Unnecessary Care*, NEW YORKER (May 11, 2015); Jonathan Bergman et al., *Service Intensity and Physician Income: Conclusions from Medicare's Physician Data Release*, 175 JAMA INTERN. MED. 297 (2015); Ity Shurtz, *Malpractice Law, Physicians' Financial Incentives, and Medical Treatment: How do they Interact?*, 57 J. LAW ECON. 1 (Feb. 2014) (finding that physicians are performing fewer procedures that incur expenses and increasing services that are deemed more profitable to execute; when procedures become more profitable to perform, the financial incentives often will offset the malpractice liability concerns of providing the service).
45. U.S. CONGRESS, OFFICE OF TECHNOLOGY ASSESSMENT, DEFENSIVE MEDICINE AND MEDICAL MALPRACTICE (July 1994) (OTA-H—6O2), at 13.
46. Diane E. Hoffman and Bradley Herring, Report to the Maryland Health Services Cost Review Commission on Defensive Medicine (revised) (Feb. 15, 2015).
47. For example, "Does fear or threat of malpractice liability influence whether you use additional diagnostic or therapeutic procedures?" and "How often do you practice defensive medicine?"
48. Robert Rosenthal, *File Drawer Problem and Tolerance for Null Results*, 86 PSYCHOL. BULL. 638 (1979).
49. Theodore D. Sterling, *Publication Decisions and Their Possible Effects on Inferences Drawn from Tests of Significance—or Vice Versa*, 54 J. AM. STAT. ASSOC. 30 (1959). This problem likely is one of the reasons for the "replication crisis" that is being experienced in biomedical, economic, and other areas of research, where published findings cannot be replicated. Research communities in various fields are hard at work trying to solve this problem.
50. See, e.g., David M. Studdert et al., *Defensive Medicine Among High-risk Specialist Physicians in a Volatile Malpractice Environment*, 293 JAMA 2609 (2005) (finding

93% of physicians in high risk specialties during a period of increasing insurance costs in one state, reporting they engaged in defensive practices, a third of whom who even recommended unnecessary invasive procedures). Massachusetts Medical Society, Investigation of Defensive Medicine in Massachusetts (2008), available at http://www.ncrponline.org/PDFs/Mass_Med_ Soc.pdf (finding 84% of respondents reporting that they engaged in defensive practices). Gallup and Jackson Healthcare, Physicians on Medical Liability Reform Options: An Online Quantitative Research Study (Jackson Healthcare, Dec. 5, 2012), archived at http://perma.cc/KTB8-L68K (finding in the Gallup–Jackson study that 75% of surveyed physicians reported practicing defensive medicine, primarily "to avoid being named in a potential lawsuit;" and finding 92% in an earlier survey conducted by Jackson alone).

51. This is not to say that survey research cannot be more useful for some other purposes, such as asking someone to look at a product and say who they believe manufactured it (as in trademark infringement litigation). See, e.g., Shari Seidman Diamond, *Reference Guide on Survey Research*, in FEDERAL JUDICIAL CENTER, REFERENCE MANUAL ON SCIENTIFIC EVIDENCE, 359–424 (3rd ed. 2011).
52. Id.
53. In reviewing direct physician surveys conducted up through the 1990s, OTA complained of response rates under 50% creating unacceptable risks unrepresentativeness and bias. U.S. CONGRESS, OFFICE OF TECHNOLOGY ASSESSMENT, DEFENSIVE MEDICINE AND MEDICAL MALPRACTICE (July, 1994) (OTA-H—6O2). Since then, response rates seem to have fallen further. For example, in the Massachusetts Medical Society, Investigation of Defensive Medicine in Massachusetts (2008) (available at http://www.ncrponline.org/PDFs/Mass_Med_ Soc.pdf) study, only 23.6% of sampled doctors responded. A study by researchers at Children's Hospital of Philadelphia, reported at an annual meeting of the American Academy of Orthopaedic Surgeons, had an 11% response rate (of 640 surgeons solicited, 72 replied.) With an especially highly motivated population during an especially highly motivating time period, David M. Studdert et al. were able to achieve a 65% response rate; David M. Studdert et al., *Defensive Medicine Among High-Risk Specialist Physicians in a Volatile Malpractice Environment*, 293 JAMA 2609 (2005).
54. ROGER TOURANGEAU ET AL., THE PSYCHOLOGY OF SURVEY RESPONSE (2000).
55. In the classic experiment on this effect, a wheel of fortune was spun, which (unbeknownst to the research participants) was set to stop randomly at either 10 or 65. Participants were asked whether the percentage of African nations in the UN was greater or smaller than that number. Then they were asked to estimate the percentage of nations in the UN that were African. Those participants whose wheel had stopped on 10 generated lower estimates (25% on average) than participants whose wheel stopped at 65 (45% on average). Amos Tversky and Daniel Kahneman, *Judgment under Uncertainty: Heuristics and Biases*, 185 SCIENCE 1124 (1974). This phenomenon has been replicated in numerous experiments on a wide variety of different estimation topics.
56. John M. Darley and C. Daniel Batson, *"From Jerusalem to Jericho": A Study of Situational and Dispositional Variables in Helping Behavior*, 27 J. PERSONALITY SOC. PSYCHOL. 100 (1973). In their experiment, volunteer seminary students at Princeton

University were sent across campus to record an ad, which they were to improvise along the way, explaining why they were pursuing their careers. Half were assigned to talk about the practical benefits of a career as a minister; the other half were assigned to talk about service to others. Each of those halves was further subdivided, with half given a recording time that allowed a leisurely walk to the studio and the other half an appointment they would have to hustle to not to be late.

Along the way, an actor who feigned illness was lying by the path, pleading for help. Most of the seminarians who were unrushed time stopped to help, but most of those who were in a hurry passed by the stricken person. That seemingly trivial variable (being in a hurry or not) was the major predictor of whether they offered help or not, rather than factors we or they would expect to matter, such as personality, backgrounds, attitudes, and beliefs related to religious commitment, service to others, and so on. But when asked what led them to help or not, participants in such studies are usually clueless about what really drove their actions (or inaction).

Relatedly, as Jonathan Haidt has made famous through his metaphor of the "emotional dog and its rational tail," when we are required to offer reasons for our behavior, we are remarkably skilled at formulating rational-sounding explanations that might have nothing to do with the actual drivers of our behavior, which even the behaver is not sure of. Jonathan Haidt, *The Emotional Dog and Its Rational Tail: A Social Intuitionist Approach to Moral Judgment*, 108 PSYCHOL. REV. 814 (2001).

57. Marist Institute for Public Opinion at Marist College, Poughkeepsie, N. (Dec. 1997).
58. Jackson Healthcare, Quantifying the Cost of Defensive Medicine, at https://www.jacksonhealthcare.com/media-room/surveys/defensive-medicine-study-2010.aspx
59. Id.
60. U.S. CONGRESS, OFFICE OF TECHNOLOGY ASSESSMENT, DEFENSIVE MEDICINE AND MEDICAL MALPRACTICE (July, 1994) (OTA-H—6O2), at 74.
61. For example, in a different context, if asked whether they felt that criminals receive sentences from courts that are too long, too short, or about right, most people answer that the sentences are too short. But when given descriptions of specific crimes and asked what they feel the proper sentence would be for that particular crime, people recommend on average *lower* sentences than what the courts actually give. Loretta J. Stalans and Shari S. Diamond, *Formation and Change in Lay Evaluations of Criminal Sentencing: Misperception and Discontent*, 14 L. HUM. BEHAV. 199 (1990).
62. Id.
63. Id.
64. Id.
65. Id.
66. Paul Jesilow, *The Effects of Fraud on the Evaluation of Health Care*, 13 HEALTH CARE ANAL. 239 (2005).
67. *How [Medicare] Scams Distort Medical Science*, AARP BULL. 18 (June, 2016).
68. JERRY AVORN, POWERFUL MEDICINES: THE BENEFITS, RISKS, AND COSTS OF PRESCRIPTION DRUGS 23–38 (2004).
69. Id.

70. A. Russell Localio et al., *Relationship Between Malpractice Claims and Caesarean Delivery*, 269 J. AM. MED. ASSOC. 366 (1993) (using New York State hospital claims data for 1984); Lisa Dubaya et al., *The Impact of Malpractice Fears on Cesarean Section Rates*, 18 J. HEALTH ECON. 491 (1999) (using national birth data from 1990–1992, found that where malpractice premiums were higher, cesarean rates were higher, primarily for patients in lower socioeconomic strata); Karna Murthy et al., *Association Between Rising Professional Liability Insurance Premiums and Primary Cesarean Delivery Rates*, 10 OBSTET. GYN. 1264 (2007) (for Illinois obstetricians, higher rates of primary cesarean delivery were associated with higher medical liability insurance premiums for Illinois obstetricians-gynecologists).

71. Katherine Baicker and Amitabh Chandra, *Medicare Spending, the Physician Workforce, and Beneficiaries' Quality of Care*, HEALTH AFF. w184–w197 (published online Apr. 7, 2004; 10.1377/hlthaff.w4.184) (no increase in cesareans with higher malpractice premiums); Beomsoo Kim, *The Impact of Malpractice Risk on the Use of Obstetrics Procedures*, 36 J. LEGAL STUD. S79 (2007) (found cesarean rates not to be sensitive to malpractice risk); David Dranove and Yasutora Watanabe, *Influence and Deterrence: How Obstetricians Respond to Litigation against Themselves and Their Colleagues*, 12 AM. L. ECON. REV. 69 (2010) (using micro-data, found a short term hospital-wide increase in cesarean rates in response to malpractice suits against them or their colleagues, and an upsurge in the use of cesareans by the responsible physician, but these effects disappeared in a short time); Janet Currie and W. Bentley MacLeod, *First Do No Harm? Tort Reform and Birth Outcomes*, 123 QUART. J. ECON. 819 (2008) (finding that replacing the traditional rule of joint and several liability with proportional share liability for all defendants reduced complications of labor and c-sections, but that the introduction of noneconomic damages caps *increased* the rate of cesareans); Michael Frakes, *Defensive Medicine and Obstetric Practices*, 9 J. EMP. LEGAL STUD. 457 (2012) (no relationship to c-sections, but finding a noneconomic damage cap was associated with a reduction in the utilization of episiotomies during vaginal deliveries).

72. A. Dale Tussing and Martha A. Wojtowycz, *Malpractice, Defensive Medicine, and Obstetric Behavior*, 35 MED. CARE 172 (1997).

73. Daniel P. Kessler and Mark McClellan, *Do Doctors Practice Defensive Medicine?* 111 QUART. J. ECON. 353 (1996).

74. Allowing juries to learn whether the injured patient had other insurance sources to cover his or her loses.

75. Daniel P. Kessler and Mark McClellan, *Malpractice Law and Health Care Reform: Optimal Liability Policy in an Era of Managed Care*, 84 J. PUB. ECON. 175 (2002).

76. Congressional Budget Office, U.S. Gen. Accountability Office, Medical Malpractice Accountability: Implications of Rising Premiums on Access to Health Care, Rep. No. GAO-03-836, at 29 (2003).

77. Congressional Budget Office (2006), Medical Malpractice Tort Limits and Health Care Spending, at http://www.cbo.gov/ftpdocs/71xx/doc7174/04-28-MedicalMalpractice.pdf. This finding should not be too surprising. Under the traditional rule, liability insurers of hospitals often covered the costs of all defendants, or all damages were assessed against the physician defendant who was judged to

be principally responsible for the harm. Under the reform, however, plaintiffs are compelled to name more defendants and to seek judgments against all of them in order to recover the full amount of damages that the court found the injured patient to be entitled to. Any defensive strategies that were being undertaken would, if anything, increase.

78. Id. Later, the director of Office of Management and Budget, Douglas W. Elmendorf, responded to a query in a Letter to Senator Orrin G. Hatch (Congressional Budget Office, Oct. 9, 2009), archived at http://perma.cc/P7KS-SQE8 ("CBO Report"), explaining that their data suggested that a package of tort reforms including a $250,000 cap on noneconomic damages; $500,000 cap on punitive damages; modification of the collateral source rule; shortening of the statute of limitations; and replacement of joint and several liability with a proportionate share allocation rule—would reduce total national healthcare spending attributable to utilization of services (by inference, attributable to defensive medicine) by about 0.3%—equal at that time to about $5.4 billion per year).
79. Katherine Baicker and Amitabh Chandra, *The Effect of Malpractice Liability on the Delivery of Health Care*, 8 FORUM HEALTH ECON. POLIC. 4 (2006).
80. Katherine Baicker et al., *Malpractice Liability Costs and the Practice of Medicine in the Medicare Program*, 26 HEALTH AFF. 841 (2007).
81. Frank A. Sloan and John H. Shadle, *Is There Empirical Evidence for "Defensive Medicine"? A Reassessment*, 28 J. HEALTH ECON. 481 (2009).
82. J. William Thomas et al., *Low Costs of Defensive Medicine, Small Savings from Tort Reform*, 29 HEALTH AFF. 1578, 1582–1583 (2010).
83. Leonard J. Nelson III et al., *Medical Liability and Health Care Reform*, 21 HEALTH MATRIX 443 (2011).
84. Ronen Avraham et al., *The Impact of Tort Reform on Employer-Sponsored Health Insurance Premiums*, 28 J. LAW ECON. ORG. 657 (2012).
85. Darius N. Lakdawalla and Seth A. Seabury, *The Welfare Effects of Malpractice Liability*, 32 INT. REV. L. ECON. 356, 365 (2012).
86. Myungho Paik et al., *Will Tort Reform Bend the Cost Curve? Evidence from Texas*, 9 J. EMP. LEGAL STUD. 173 (2012).
87. Myungho Paik et al., *Damage Caps and Defensive Medicine, Revisited*, 51 J. HEALTH ECON. 84 (2017).
88. Ali Moghtaderi et al., Damage Caps and Defensive Medicine: Reexamination with Patient Level Data (2017), working paper available at https://papers.ssrn.com/sol3/papers.cfm?abstract_id=2816969 (2017).
89. Douglas W. Elmendorf, Letter to Senator Orrin G. Hatch (Congressional Budget Office, Oct. 9, 2009), archived at http://perma.cc/P7KS-SQE8.
90. Darius N. Lakdawalla and Seth A. Seabury, *The Welfare Effects of Malpractice Liability*, 32 INT. REV. L. ECON. 356, 365 (2012).
91. By definition, therefore, not defensive practices.
92. Janet Currie and W. Bentley MacLeod, *First Do No Harm? Tort Reform and Birth Outcomes*, 123 QUART. J. ECON. 819 (2008).
93. Zenon Zabinski and Bernard S. Black, The Deterrent Effect of Tort Law: Evidence from Medical Malpractice Reform (February 15, 2015). Northwestern Law & Econ Research Paper No. 13-09. Available at http://dx.doi.org/10.2139/ssrn.2161362

94. Michael D. Frakes and Jonathan Gruber, Defensive Medicine: Evidence from Military Immunity (2018) National Bureau of Economic Research, http://www.nber.org/papers/w24846
95. Michael D. Frakes and Jonathan Gruber, Defensive Medicine: Evidence from Military Immunity, National Bureau of Economic Research, Working Paper 24846 (2018), http://www.nber.org/papers/w24846
96. Perhaps this reflects the restraining hand of managed care.
97. Lying to patients and insurers.
98. Subjecting patients to needless tests and treatments.
99. Enriching themselves by redistributing wealth from patients, insurers, and taxpayers to themselves.
100. See Chapter 4 of this volume.
101. President Barack Obama seems to have been at least somewhat persuaded: "I don't believe malpractice reform is a silver bullet, but I have talked to enough doctors to know that defensive medicine may be contributing to unnecessary costs." Barack Obama, Remarks by the President to a Joint Session of Congress on Health Care (speech, Washington, DC, Sept. 9, 2009), available at www.whitehouse.gov/the_press_office/remarks-by-the-president-to-a-joint-session-of-congress-on-health-care/.
102. Myungho Paik et al., *Damage Caps and Defensive Medicine, Revisited*, 51 J HEALTH ECON. 84 (2017).
103. Michelle M. Mello et al., *National Costs of the Medical Liability System*, 29 HEALTH AFF. 1569 (2010).
104. "Mello and her coauthors relied heavily on Kessler and McClellan, whose findings generally fall on the very high end of those studies that have found a positive association between liability forces and health-care costs." Michael D. Frakes, *The Surprising Relevance of Medical Malpractice Law*, 82 U. CHICAGO L. REV. 317 (2015), at n. 79.
105. See studies summarized in earlier notes.
106. Michelle M. Mello et al., *National Costs of the Medical Liability System*, 29 HEALTH AFF. 1569 (2010).
107. One recent study that offers a peek at the benefit side of the equation is Zenon Zabinski and Bernard S. Black, The Deterrent Effect of Tort Law: Evidence from Medical Malpractice Reform (February 15, 2015). Northwestern Law & Econ Research Paper No. 13-09. Available at http://dx.doi.org/10.2139/ssrn.2161362 (finding that the adoption of caps, the most popular reform, seems to initiate a decline in patient safety measured by Agency for Healthcare Research and Quality's patient safety indicators).
108. One could say "dangerously" high. When one of every five dollars a society spends is spent on healthcare, trending ever upward, much of it wasteful, that society has far less to invest in many other, more productive, activities.
109. James J. Mongan et al., *Options for Slowing the Growth of Health Care Costs*, 358 N. ENGL. J. MED. 1509 (2008).
110. Michael D. Frakes, *The Surprising Relevance of Medical Malpractice Law*, 82 U. CHICAGO L. REV. 317 (2015). See also J. William Thomas et al., *Low Costs of Defensive Medicine, Small Savings From Tort Reform*, 29 HEALTH AFF. 1578, 1582–1583 (2010) (concluding that "defensive medicine practices exist and are widespread, but their impact on medical care costs is small.") and Michelle M. Mello

and Troyen A. Brennan, *Deterrence of Medical Errors: Theory and Evidence for Malpractice Reform*, 80 TEXAS L. REV. 1595, 1629 (2002) (commenting that defensive medicine "has long been invoked by chronic defendants . . . as a rationale for enacting tort reform. However, the over deterrence rhetoric has not been firmly grounded in fact. Most defensive-medicine studies have failed to demonstrate any real impacts on medical practice arising from higher malpractice premiums").

111. Margot Sanger-Katz, *A Fear of Lawsuits Really Does Seem to Result in Extra Medical Tests*, NEW YORK TIMES (July 23, 2018). ("Mr. Gruber said the paper's estimates were best viewed as a kind of ceiling for the effects of more realistic reforms." "Any law that limits the cases where patients can sue, or the amount of money they can collect, is likely to lower medical use in the hospital by less than the 5 percent they measured in their study.")

112. Adjusting Mello et al.'s total of $45.6 billion of defensive medicine costs into 2016 dollars ($50.8 billion) and dividing that by total national spending on healthcare in 2016 ($3.3 trillion) yields 1.5%.

113. See Jonathan Skinner and Elliott S. Fisher, Reflections on Geographic Variations in U.S. Health Care iii (Dartmouth Institute for Health Policy & Clinical Practice, Mar 31, 2010), archived at http://perma.cc/8CZK-MV2B (finding that, if all regions of the U.S. could safely reduce care to the level observed in low spending regions with equal quality, healthcare cost savings of 20% to 30% could be achieved—but concluding that that is an underestimate because even the low-cost regions employ some wasteful practices that could be safely eliminated).

114. David A. Hyman and Charles Silver, *The Poor State of Health Care Quality in the U.S.: Is Malpractice Liability Part of the Problem or Part of the Solution?* 90 CORNELL L. REV. 893 (2005).

115. Accountable Care Organizations (Updated) Health Affairs (Aug. 13, 2010) https://www.healthaffairs.org/do/10.1377/hpb20100813.757461/full/ and David Muhlestein et al., Recent Progress in the Value Journey: Growth of ACOs And Value-Based Payment Models in 2018, Health Affairs Blog (Aug. 14, 2018) https://www.healthaffairs.org/blog

116. Emily R. Carrier et al., *Physicians' Fears of Malpractice Lawsuits are not Assuaged by Tort Reforms*, 29 HEALTH AFF. 1585 (2010). ("We found high levels of malpractice concern among both generalists and specialists in states where objective measures of malpractice risk were low. We also found relatively modest differences in physicians' concerns across states with and without common tort reforms.")

117. Id. Carrier et al. propose several possible explanations for their finding that doctors are insensitive to something that they are thought to be quite concerned about. The most paradoxical of them is the possibility that reform advocates have them confused: "Advocacy efforts by medical professional societies in support of tort reform may contribute to this problem by conveying the impression that most or all states and specialties are in crisis and require additional legal protection." If so, it is the extreme and undifferentiated complaining of their supplicants that has created a situation that prevents reforms from being able to change the very thing (wasteful spending) that supposedly prompts the supplication.

118. David A. Hyman & William Sage, Do Health Reform and Malpractice Reform Fit Together? (AEI Health Policy Working Paper 2011-02) (Apr. 1, 2011), available at http://www.aei.org/paper/100209

119. Ann G. Lawthers et al., *Physicians' Perceptions of the Risk of Being Sued*, 17 J. HEALTH POLIT. POL. L. 463 (1992).
120. Marshall Kapp, *Medical Error Versus Malpractice*, 1 DEPAUL J. HEALTH CARE L. 751 (1997).
121. Hal Scherz & Wayne Oliver, *Defensive Medicine: A Cure Worse Than the Disease*, FORBES (Aug. 27, 2013).
122. Rather than the image promoted by healthcare industry lobbyists of frightened providers who cause their patients expense and place them at risk, eagerly violating laws and ethical principles, merely to reduce the chances the provider will face the annoyance of a lawsuit.
123. See Michael D. Frakes, *The Surprising Relevance of Medical Malpractice Law*, 82 U. CHICAGO L. REV. 317 (2015).
124. Katherine Baicker and Amitabh Chandra, *Defensive Medicine and Disappearing Doctors?* 28 REGULATION 24 (2005).

CHAPTER 8

1. CHARLES L. BOSK, FORGIVE AND REMEMBER: MANAGING MEDICAL FAILURE, 2nd ed. (University of Chicago Press, 2003).
2. INSTITUTE OF MEDICINE, TO ERR IS HUMAN: BUILDING A SAFER HEALTH SYSTEM 89 (Linda T. Kohn et al., eds., 2000).
3. Id. at 86.
4. CHARLES L. BOSK, FORGIVE AND REMEMBER: MANAGING MEDICAL FAILURE 114 (2nd ed. 2003).
5. INSTITUTE OF MEDICINE, TO ERR IS HUMAN: BUILDING A SAFER HEALTH SYSTEM 102 (Linda T. Kohn et al, eds., 2000).
6. Id. at 94–97.
7. Id. at 95.
8. THE MASSACHUSETTS HEALTH POLICY FORUM, ISSUE BRIEF: MEDICAL ERRORS AND PATIENT SAFETY IN MASSACHUSETTS: WHAT IS THE ROLE OF THE COMMONWEALTH? (Wendy K. Mariner et al. eds., 2000).
9. ROBERT M. WACHTER AND KAVEH G. SHOJANIA, INTERNAL BLEEDING: THE TRUTH BEHIND AMERICA'S TERRIFYING EPIDEMIC OF MEDICAL MISTAKES 286–288 (2005).
10. Lucian L. Leape, *Errors in Medicine*, 272 J. AM. MED. ASSOC. 1851, 1851 (1994).
11. Lucian L. Leape, *Reporting of Adverse Events*, 347 N. ENGL. J. MED. 1633, 1634–1637 (2002).
12. Id. at 1637.
13. Troyen A. Brennan, *Accidental Deaths, Saved Lives, and Improved Quality*, 353 N. ENG. J. MED. 1404, 1406 (2005); Lucian L. Leape and Donald Berwick, *Five Years After To Err Is Human*, 293 J. AMER. MED. ASSOC. 2384, 2388 (2005); Peter Provonost et al., *Framework for Patient Safety and Improvement*, 119 CIRCULATION 330, 331–334 (2009).
14. Troyen A. Brennan, *Accidental Deaths, Saved Lives, and Improved Quality*, 353 N. ENGL. J. MED. 1404, 1406 (2005)
15. Robert M. Wachter, *Patient Safety at Ten: Unmistakable Progress, Troubling Gaps*, 29 HEALTH AFF. 165, 167 (2010).
16. Id. at 167; Troyen A. Brennan, *Accidental Deaths, Saved Lives, and Improved Quality*, 353 N. ENGL. J. MED. 1404, 1408 (2005).

17. 13 THE MASS. HEALTH POLICY FORUM, ISSUE BRIEF: MEDICAL ERROR REPORTING, PROFESSIONAL TENSIONS BETWEEN CONFIDENTIALITY AND LIABILITY 6 (2001).
18. Lucian L. Leape, Reporting of Adverse Events, 347 N. ENGL. J. MED. 1633 (2002); ROBERT M. WACHTER AND KAVEH G. SHOJANIA, INTERNAL BLEEDING: THE TRUTH BEHIND AMERICA'S TERRIFYING EPIDEMIC OF MEDICAL MISTAKES 273 (2005).
19. Id. at 283–284.
20. Id. at 285–287.
21. Troyen A. Brennan, *Accidental Deaths, Saved Lives, and Improved Quality*, 353 N. ENGL. J. MED. 1404, 1406 (2005).
22. Christopher P. Landrigan et al., *Temporal Trends in Rates of Patient Harm Resulting from Medical Care*, 363 N. ENGL. J. MED. 2124, 2130 (2010); Peter Pronovost et al., *Framework for Patient Safety and Improvement*, 119 CIRCULATION 330, 335–336 (2009); ROBERT M. WACHTER AND KAVEH G. SHOJANIA, INTERNAL BLEEDING: THE TRUTH BEHIND AMERICA'S TERRIFYING EPIDEMIC OF MEDICAL MISTAKES 281–286 (2005); Lucian L. Leape, *Reporting of Adverse Events*, 347 N. ENGL. J. MED. 1633 (2002).
23. 13 THE MASS. HEALTH POLICY FORUM, ISSUE BRIEF: MEDICAL ERROR REPORTING, PROFESSIONAL TENSIONS BETWEEN CONFIDENTIALITY AND LIABILITY 5 (2001).
24. CHARLES L. BOSK, FORGIVE AND REMEMBER: MANAGING MEDICAL FAILURE 114–116 (2nd ed. 2003).
25. ROBERT M. WACHTER AND KAVEH G. SHOJANIA, INTERNAL BLEEDING: THE TRUTH BEHIND AMERICA'S TERRIFYING EPIDEMIC OF MEDICAL MISTAKES 277 (2005), citing Edgar Pierluissi et al., *Discussions of Medial Errors in Morbidity and Mortality Conferences*, 290 J. AM. MED. ASSOC. 2838, 2838–2842 (2003).
26. KENNETH ALLEN DEVILLE, MEDICAL MALPRACTICE IN NINETEENTH-CENTURY AMERICA: ORIGINS AND LEGACY 200–201 (1st ed. 1990).
27. Leigh Ann Lauth, *The Patient Safety and Quality Improvement Act of 2005: An Initiative for Sham Peer Review in the Health Care Setting*, 4 IND. HEALTH LAW J. 151, 164–165 (2007).
28. ROBERT M. WACHTER AND KAVEH G. SHOJANIA, INTERNAL BLEEDING: THE TRUTH BEHIND AMERICA'S TERRIFYING EPIDEMIC OF MEDICAL MISTAKES 301 (2005).
29. R. J. Blendon et al., *Views of Practicing Physicians and the Public on Medical Errors*, 347 N. ENGL. J. MED. 1993 (2002).
30. ROBERT M. WACHTER AND KAVEH G. SHOJANIA, INTERNAL BLEEDING: THE TRUTH BEHIND AMERICA'S TERRIFYING EPIDEMIC OF MEDICAL MISTAKES 23 (2005).
31. Id. at 301.
32. Id.
33. Id. at 304.
34. Id. at 309.
35. Id. at 312.
36. FRANK A. SLOAN AND LINDSEY M. CHEPKE, MEDICAL MALPRACTICE 165 (1st ed. 2008).
37. Troyen A. Brennan, *Accidental Deaths, Saved Lives, and Improved Quality*, 353 N. ENGL. J. MED. 1405, 1405–1409 (2005).
38. THE MASSACHUSETTS HEALTH POLICY FORUM, ISSUE BRIEF: MEDICAL ERROR REPORTING, PROFESSIONAL TENSIONS BETWEEN CONFIDENTIALITY AND LIABILITY 18 (2001).

39. Id. at 15 (Dana-Farber's pharmacy director resigned, the resident physician was suspended from practice for three years, 16 nurses agreed to sanctions, and the hospital settled privately with the victim's family).
40. ROBERT M. WACHTER AND KAVEH G. SHOJANIA, INTERNAL BLEEDING: THE TRUTH BEHIND AMERICA'S TERRIFYING EPIDEMIC OF MEDICAL MISTAKES 251–262 (2005).
41. ROBERT M. WACHTER AND KAVEH G. SHOJANIA, INTERNAL BLEEDING: THE TRUTH BEHIND AMERICA'S TERRIFYING EPIDEMIC OF MEDICAL MISTAKES 274–275 (2005).
42. Id. at 259–261; Joanna C. Schwartz, *A Dose of Relief for Medical Malpractice Reform*, 88 NYU L. REV. 1224, 1241 (2013).
43. *Camden-Clark Mem'l Hosp Corp. v. Nguyen*, 807 S.E. 2d 747 (W. Va. 2017); *Fahlen v. Sutter Central Valley Hospitals*, 58 Cal. 4th 655 (Ca. 2014); Leigh Ann Lauth, *The Patient Safety and Quality Improvement Act of 2005: An Initiative for Sham Peer Review in the Health Care Setting*, 4 IND. HEALTH LAW J. 151, 167–168 (2007).
44. MICHAEL L. MILLENSON, DEMANDING MEDICAL EXCELLENCE 90 (1999).
45. Leigh Ann Lauth, *The Patient Safety and Quality Improvement Act of 2005: An Initiative for Sham Peer Review in the Health Care Setting*, 4 IND. HEALTH LAW J. 151, 169–170 n. 14 (2007).
46. *Rodgers v. Lenox Hill Hosp.*, 626 N.Y.S.2d 137 (N.Y. App. Div. 1995); *Gillispie v. RegionalCare Hosp. Partners, Inc.*, 892 F.3d 585 (3rd Cir. 2018); *Camden-Clark Mem'l Hosp. Corp. v. Nguyen*, 807 S.E.2d 747 (W. Va. 2017).
47. Edgar Pierluisi et al, *Are Medical Errors Discussed in Morbidity and Mortality Conferences?* 290 JAMA 2838 (2007).
48. TOM BAKER, THE MEDICAL MALPRACTICE MYTH 80 (1st ed. 2005).
49. ROBERT M. WACHTER AND KAVEH G. SHOJANIA, INTERNAL BLEEDING: THE TRUTH BEHIND AMERICA'S TERRIFYING EPIDEMIC OF MEDICAL MISTAKES 278 (2005).
50. CHARLES L. BOSK, FORGIVE AND REMEMBER: MANAGING MEDICAL FAILURE 191 (2nd ed. 2003).
51. Id.
52. William M. Sage, *Bridging the Relational-Regulatory Gap: A Pragmatic Information Policy for Patient Safety and Medical Malpractice*, 59 VAND. L. REV. 1263, 1299 (2006).
53. THE MASS. HEALTH POLICY FORUM, ISSUE BRIEF: MEDICAL ERROR REPORTING, PROFESSIONAL TENSIONS BETWEEN CONFIDENTIALITY AND LIABILITY 16 (2001).
54. William M. Sage, *Bridging the Relational-Regulatory Gap: A Pragmatic Information Policy for Patient Safety and Medical Malpractice*, 59 VAND. L. REV. 1263, 1307 (2006).
55. Id at 1286.
56. Id.
57. Leigh Ann Lauth, *The Patient Safety and Quality Improvement Act of 2005: An Initiative for Sham Peer Review in the Health Care Setting*, 4 IND. HEALTH LAW J. 151, 166 (2007).
58. THE MASS. HEALTH POLICY FORUM, ISSUE BRIEF: MEDICAL ERROR REPORTING, PROFESSIONAL TENSIONS BETWEEN CONFIDENTIALITY AND LIABILITY 9 (2001).
59. ROBERT M. WACHTER AND KAVEH G. SHOJANIA, INTERNAL BLEEDING: THE TRUTH BEHIND AMERICA'S TERRIFYING EPIDEMIC OF MEDICAL MISTAKES 288 (2005).

60. Robert M. Wachter, *Patient Safety at Ten: Unmistakable Progress, Troubling Gaps*, 29 HEALTH AFF. 165, 166 (2010).
61. THE MASS. HEALTH POLICY FORUM, ISSUE BRIEF: MEDICAL ERROR REPORTING, PROFESSIONAL TENSIONS BETWEEN CONFIDENTIALITY AND LIABILITY 16–17 (2001).
62. Id. at 17.
63. Id. at 16.
64. George J. Annas, *The Patient's Right to Safety—Improving the Quality of Care Through Litigation Against Hospitals*, 354 N. ENGL. J. MED. 2063, 2065 (2006).
65. Barry R. Furrow, *Medical Mistakes: Tiptoeing Toward Safety*, 3 HOUSTON J. HEALTH L. POLIC. 181, 203 n. 162 (2003).

CHAPTER 9

1. Peter H. Schuck, *Tort Reform, Kiwi-Style*, 27 YALE L. & POLICY REVIEW 187 (2008).
2. One of your authors was a member of the hospital association's ad hoc committee.
3. INSTITUTE OF MEDICINE, TO ERR IS HUMAN (Linda T. Kohn et al., eds., 2000).
4. Maxine Harrington, *Revisiting Medical Error: Five Years after the IOM Report, Have Reporting Systems Made a Measurable Difference?* 15 HEALTH MATRIX 329 (2005).
5. Lucian L. Leape and Donald M. Berwick, *Five Years After to Err Is Human What Have We Learned?* 239 JAMA 2384 (2005).
6. At https://patientsafetymovement.org/about/
7. David Hyman and Charles Silver, *Healthcare Quality, Patient Safety, and the Culture of Medicine*, 46 N. ENGL. L. REV. 417 (2012) ("indeed, sometimes, there is a business case for lower quality").
8. Id.
9. David M. Studdert and Michelle M. Mello, *In from the Cold? Law's Evolving Role in Patient Safety*, 68 DEPAUL L. REV. 421 (2019).
10. AHRQ, *Saving Lives and Saving Money: Hospital-Acquired Conditions Update: Interim Data from National Efforts to Make Care Safer, 2010–2014*, at https://www.ahrq.gov/professionals/quality-patient-safety/pfp/interimhacrate2014.html and AHRQ, *Declines in Hospital-Acquired Conditions Save 8,000 Lives and $2.9 Billion in Costs, 2014–2016* (2018), at https://www.ahrq.gov/news/newsroom/press-releases/declines-in-hacs.html.
11. Bernard Black et al., *The Association Between Patient Safety Indicators and Medical Malpractice Risk: Evidence From Florida and Texas*, 3 AM. J. HEALTH ECON. 109 (Spring 2017) (finding large variations in PSIs, from county to county and from hospital to hospital [within counties], suggesting that hospitals should be able to improve safety at an acceptable cost since some of their peer hospitals had done so).
12. Our appreciation goes to Robert Charrow, General Counsel, U.S. Department of Health and Human Services (as of this writing) for the example.
13. It is, of course, when things go wrong that we start to notice.
14. E.g., Katy Backes Kozhimannil et al., *Cesarean Delivery Rates Vary Tenfold Among US Hospitals; Reducing Variation May Address Quality And Cost Issues*, 32 Health Aff. 527 (2013); Josh Ferguson, *Reducing Unwanted Variation in Healthcare Clears the Way for Outcomes Improvement*, at https://www.healthcatalyst.com/Reducing-Variation-in-Healthcare-to-Boost-Improvement.
15. SHARON E. STRAUS ET AL., EVIDENCE-BASED MEDICINE (4TH ED. 2010).

16. David Hyman and Charles Silver, *The Poor State of Health Care Quality in the U.S.*, 90 CORNELL L. REV. 893 (2005) (quoting Michael L. Millenson, *The Silence*, 22 HEALTH AFF. Mar.–Apr. 2003), at 110.
17. Daniel P. Kessler (ed.), REGULATION VS. LITIGATION: PERSPECTIVES FROM ECONOMICS AND LAW (2010).
18. ROBERT B. CIALDINI, INFLUENCE: SCIENCE AND PRACTICE (5TH ED. 2008); RICHARD H. THALER AND CASS R. SUNSTEIN, NUDGE (2008).
19. Edward L. Deci et al., *Facilitating Internalization*, 62 J. PERSONALITY 119 (1994)
20. Donald T. Campbell, *Methods for the Experimenting Society*, 12 AM. J. EVAL. 223 (1991); William N. Dunn (ed.), THE EXPERIMENTING SOCIETY: ESSAYS IN HONOR OF DONALD T. CAMPBELL (Policy Studies Review Annual) (1997).
21. See ROBERT B. CIALDINI, INFLUENCE: SCIENCE AND PRACTICE (5TH ED. 2008).
22. This is not to say that only law and government can perform this service. But government health agencies are well situated to do it, or to facilitate private efforts to develop and maintain such a registry. An example of a far larger project is the Cochrane organization, which is strongly independent while collaborating with and being funded by both governments and private firms. See www.cochrane.org.
23. John C. Reiling, *Creating a Culture of Patient Safety through Innovative Hospital Design*, in K. Henriksen et al. (eds.), ADVANCES IN PATIENT SAFETY: FROM RESEARCH TO IMPLEMENTATION, VOL. 2: CONCEPTS AND METHODOLOGY (2005).
24. See, Centers for Medicare and Medicaid Services, Partnerships for Patients, at www.PartnershipforPatients.cms.gov.
25. AHRQ is a diluted form of a predecessor agency, the Agency for Health Care Policy and Research (AHCPR), discussed in Chapter 12 of this volume.
26. Agency for Healthcare Research and Quality, AHRQ Patient Safety Research Spurs Development of 100 Emergency Department Pharmacies (Jul 2013), https://www.ahrq.gov/news/newsroom/case-studies/cquips1305.html
27. See AHRQ website; developed by Kristine Gleason, RPh, of Northwestern Memorial Hospital.
28. Id.
29. Agency for Healthcare Research and Quality, About TeamSTEPPS, at https://www.ahrq.gov/teamstepps/about-teamstepps/index.html. The effectiveness of TeamSTEPPS is still under study: compare the findings of Taylor Sawyer et al., *Improvements in Teamwork During Neonatal Resuscitation after Interprofessional TeamSTEPPS Training*, 32 NEONATAL NETW. 26–33 (2013) to those of Greg L. Stewart et al., *Empowering Sustained Patient Safety*, 30 J. NURS. CARE QUAL. 240–246 (2015).
30. Originally termed "cockpit resource management" and originated by NASA psychologist John Lauber.
31. The nurses' behavior had its counterpart in aviation, where it is even more remarkable. Lower-ranking crew members refrained from correcting the errors of higher-ranking members, even as the plane was heading into a fatal failure and it was the crews' own lives that would be lost.
32. FDA, Center for Drug Evaluation and Research, Division of Medication Error Prevention and Analysis.
33. FDA, Contents of a Complete Submission for the Evaluation of Proprietary Names: Guidance for Industry (2016).

34. Adrienne Berman, *Reducing Medication Errors Through Naming, Labeling, and Packaging*, 28 J. MED. SYST. 9 (2004).
35. Id.
36. Interviewed in Richard Harris, Training A Computer to Read Mammograms as Well as a Doctor, NPR (Apr. 1, 2019).
37. Ross Koppell, *Uses of the Legal System that Attenuate Patient Safety*, 68 DEPAUL L. REV. 273 (2019).
38. See National Science Foundation, Division of Information and Intelligent Systems, https://www.nsf.gov/funding/pgm_summ.jsp?pims_id=503305
39. For example, since the end World War II, the federal government has supplied approximately half of the funding for basic research. Science, Data Check: U.S. Government Share of Basic Research Funding Falls Below 50%, (Mar 9, 2017), http://www.sciencemag.org/news/2017/03/data-check-us-government-share-basic-research-funding-falls-below-50
40. Nathan Cortez, *A Black Box for Patient Safety?* 68 DEPAUL L. REV. 239 (2019).
41. Steven Levy, Google Glass 2.0 is a Startling Second Act, https://www.wired.com/story/google-glass-2-is-here/.
42. NIH Consensus Development Program, Retirement of the National Institutes of Health Consensus Development Program, https://consensus.nih.gov/.
43. Id.
44. Paul C. Giannelli, *Forensic Science: Daubert's Failure,* 68 CASE WEST. R. L. REV. 869 (2018).
45. A. L. COCHRANE, EFFECTIVENESS & EFFICIENCY: RANDOM REFLECTIONS ON HEALTH SERVICES (1972).
46. Sir Iain Chalmers, co-founder of the Cochrane Collaboration, commenting on the long resistance of older physicians to evidence-based medicine: "So one way you can look at it is where there is death there is hope, as a cohort of doctors who rubbished it moved into retirement and then death, the opposition disappeared." Freakonomics Radio (Podcast), Bad Medicine, Part 1: (Drug) Trials and Tribulations, at http://freakonomics.com/podcast/bad-medicine-part-1-drug-trials-tribulations/.
47. Alice R. Benedict and Michael J. Saks, *The Regulation of Professional Behavior: Electroconvulsive Therapy in Massachusetts*, 1987 J. PSYCHIATR. L. 247 (1987).
48. Placement of electrodes was bilateral.
49. ROBERT M. WACHTER, UNDERSTANDING PATIENT SAFETY 3 (2012).
50. Id., at xiii, xiv.
51. Lucian L. Leape and Donald M. Berwick, *Five Years After To Err Is Human What Have We Learned?* 239 JAMA 2384 (2005).
52. Christopher Landrigan et al., *Temporal Trends in Rates of Patient Harm Resulting from Medical Care*, 363 N. ENGL. J. MED. 2124 (2010).
53. See generally David A. Hyman and Charles Silver, *Medical Malpractice Litigation and Tort Reform: It's the Incentives, Stupid*, 59 VANDERBILT L. REV. 1085 (2006).
54. See Peter Orszag, *Malpractice Methodology*, NEW YORK TIMES A39 (Oct. 21, 2010).
55. But see Ivan Oranksy and Adam Marcus, Trump Administration is Shutting Down Practice-guidelines Clearinghouse for Doctors (Jun 13, 2018), at www.statnews.com

56. E.g., Linda H. Aiken et al., *Hospital Nurse Staffing and Patient Mortality, Nurse Burnout, and Job Dissatisfaction*, 288 J. AM. MED. ASSOC. 1987 (2002); Jack Needleman, *Nurse-staffing Levels and Quality of Care in Hospitals*, 346 N. ENGL. J. MED. 1415 (2002).
57. E.g., Kathleen Mazor et al., *Primary Care Physicians' Willingness to Disclose Oncology Errors Involving Multiple Providers to Patients*, 25 BMJ QUAL. SAF. 787 (2016)
58. Robert M. Wachter and Kaveh G. Shojania, INTERN. BLEED. (2005), at 63.
59. James Reason, *Foreword*, in Albert W. Wu (ed.), THE VALUE OF CLOSE CALLS IN IMPROVING PATIENT SAFETY (2011).
60. See Chapter 8 of this volume.
61. ELINOR OSTROM, GOVERNING THE COMMONS: THE EVOLUTION OF INSTITUTIONS FOR COLLECTIVE ACTION (2015).
62. FAA Advisory Circular 00-46E.
63. https://c3rs.arc.nasa.gov/information/summary.html
64. PRONOVOST ET AL., IMPROVING THE VALUE OF PATIENT SAFETY REPORTING SYSTEMS, ADVANCES IN PATIENT SAFETY: NEW DIRECTIONS AND ALTERNATIVE APPROACHES (2008), Rockville, MD, Agency for Healthcare Research and Quality.
65. PAUL STARR, SOCIAL TRANSFORMATION OF AMERICAN MEDICINE (1982).
66. FDA (in operation since 1906).
67. Hill-Burton Act (discussed in PAUL STARR, THE SOCIAL TRANSFORMATION OF AMERICAN MEDICINE, 1982).
68. See Centers for Disease Control and Prevention and Department of Health and Human Services (National Vaccine Program Office).
69. 42 U.S.C. § 264.
70. Determination that a Public Health Emergency Exists, signed October 26, 2017, by Acting DHHS Secretary Eric D. Hargan. Each day, according to the CDC, 91 Americans die from opioid overdoses. https://www.cdc.gov/drugoverdose/epidemic/index.html
71. NPR, Opioid Commission Delivers Recommendations (Nov 2, 2017), https://www.npr.org/2017/11/02/561524873/opioid-commission-delivers-recommendations
72. E.g., see Chapter 6 of this volume, discussing research on the effects of tort reforms.

CHAPTER 10

1. Sunil Eappen, Senior Vice President for Medical Affairs and Chief Medical Officer, Brigham and Women's Hospital, quoted in Harvard T. H. Chan School of Public Health, "Patients With Surgical Complications Provide Greater Hospital Profit-Margins" (Press Release, April 26, 2013).
2. Zoe Chase (interviewer), How Perverse Incentives Drive Up Health Care Costs (Jan 16, 2014), at https://www.npr.org/2014/01/16/262946913/how-perverse-incentives-drive-up-health-care-costs
3. David A. Hyman and Charles Silver, *Medical Malpractice Litigation and Tort Reform: It's the Incentives, Stupid*, 59 VANDERBILT L. REV. 1085 (2006). See also David A. Hyman and Charles Silver, *Healthcare Quality, Patient Safety, and the Culture of Medicine*, 46 N. ENG. L. REV. 417 (2012); David A. Hyman and Charles Silver, *The Poor State of Health Care Quality in the U.S.: Is Malpractice Liability Part of the Problem or Part of the Solution?* 90 CORNELL L. REV. 893 (2005).

4. Id., and David A. Hyman and Charles Silver, *Medical Malpractice Litigation and Tort Reform: It's the Incentives, Stupid*, 59 VANDERBILT L. REV. 1085 (2006).
5. See discussion in Chapter 6 of this volume.
6. See Chapter 5 of this volume. Consequently, doctors who cause fewer negligent adverse events subsidize their colleagues who cause more.
7. The economist's term for unproductive manipulation of laws and markets by an industry to increase the industry's profits without offering more or better products or services.
8. Id.
9. See Chapter 6 of this volume
10. Anne-Marie Audet, How Behavioral Economics Can Advance the Design of Effective Clinician Incentive Programs, Health Affairs Blog (2015), at http://healthaffairs.org/blog/2015/09/15/how-behavioral-economics-can-advance-the-design-of-effective-clinician-incentive-programs/
11. DAN ARIELY, PREDICTABLY IRRATIONAL (2009).
12. DOUGLAS E. HOUGH, IRRATIONALITY IN HEALTH CARE: WHAT BEHAVIORAL ECONOMICS REVEALS ABOUT WHAT WE DO AND WHY (2013) (see Anomaly 20: "Why does physician adherence to clinical guidelines decline when financial incentives are removed?")
13. See, e.g., id.
14. Id.
15. RICHARD H. THALER AND CASS R. SUNSTEIN, NUDGE: IMPROVING DECISIONS ABOUT HEALTH, WEALTH, AND HAPPINESS (2008).
16. Id.
17. See Peer Comparative Reports: https://www.aeaweb.org/articles.php?doi=10.1257/aer.103.7.2875.
18. DANIEL KAHNEMAN, THINKING, FAST AND SLOW (2013).
19. ROBERT B. CIALDINI, INFLUENCE: THE PSYCHOLOGY OF PERSUASION (2006).
20. James C. Cox et al., *Higher Quality and Lower cost from Improving Hospital Discharge Decision Making*, 131 J. ECON. BEHAV. ORG. 1 (2016).
21. See Chapter 12 of this volume.
22. These are the five steps: (a) wash hands with soap and water or alcohol gel, (b) wear sterile gloves, hat, mask, gown and completely cover patient with sterile drapes, (c) avoid placing the catheter in the groin, (d) clean the insertion site with chlorhexidine antiseptic, (e) remove catheters when no longer needed (don't leave in longer than needed).
23. PETER J. PRONOVOST AND& ERIC VOHR, SAFE PATIENTS, SMART HOSPITALS (2010).
24. DOUGLAS E. HOUGH, IRRATIONALITY IN HEALTH CARE: WHAT BEHAVIORAL ECONOMICS REVEALS ABOUT WHAT WE DO AND WHY (2013) (see Anomaly 22: "Why do tens of thousands of patients die each year in the United States from central line-associated bloodstream infections—even though a simple five-step checklist used by physicians and nurses could reduce the number by two-thirds?")
25. Michael G. Vann, *Of Rats, Rice, and Race: The Great Hanoi Rat Massacre, an Episode in French Colonial History*, 4 FRENCH COL. HIST.191 (2003).

26. Lisa Rosner, The Anatomy Murders: Being the True and Spectacular History of Edinburgh's Notorious Burke and Hare and of the Man of Science Who Abetted Them in the Commission of Their Most Heinous Crimes (2009).
27. Vijay Govindarajan and Ravi Ramamurti, Reverse Innovation in Health Care: How to Make Value-Based Delivery Work (2018).
28. Elisabeth Rosenthal, An American Sickness: How Healthcare Became Big Business and How You Can Take It Back (2017).
29. David A. Hyman, *Follow the Money: Money Matters in Health Care, Just Like in Everything Else*, 36 Am. J. Law Med. 370 (2010).
30. Interview Apr. 25, 2018, on http://freakonomics.com/podcast/atul-gawande/
31. Elisabeth Rosenthal, An American Sickness (2017).
32. Over half of the debt listed for collection on credit reports is attributable to medical bills. Beth Pinsker, *How to Cope with Old Medical Debt*, Reuters (July 9, 2018). Available at https://www.reuters.com/article/us-money-debt-medical/how-to-cope-with-old-medical-debt-idUSKBN1JZ2KK
33. Elizabeth Docteur and Robert A, Berenson, How Does the Quality of U.S. Health Care Compare Internationally? (Urban Institute, 2009); Austin Frakt, *Medical Mystery: Something Happened to U.S. Health Spending After 1980*, New York Times (May 134, 2018) ("The spending began soaring beyond that of other advanced nations, but without the same benefits in life expectancy."); Irene Papanicolas et al., *Health Care Spending in the United States and Other High-Income Countries*, 319 JAMA 1024 (2018); and Steven H. Woolf and Laudan Aron (eds.), U.S. Health in International Perspective: Shorter Lives, Poorer Health (National Research Council and Institute of Medicine, 2013).
34. Elisabeth Rosenthal, An American Sickness 3 (2017).
35. Dartmouth Atlas Project, Supply-Sensitive Care (2007). Discussed in more detail in Chapter 4 of this volume.
36. The Commonwealth Fund, New Survey (July 10, 2014). Also see Elizabeth Docteur and Robert A, Berenson, How Does the Quality of U.S. Health Care Compare Internationally? (Urban Institute, 2009); Steven H. Woolf and Laudan Aron (eds.), U.S. Health in International Perspective: Shorter Lives, Poorer Health (National Research Council and Institute of Medicine, 2013).
37. E.g., Sohail K. Mizra and Richard A. Deyo, *Systematic Review of Randomized Trials Comparing Lumbar Fusion Surgery to Nonoperative Care for Treatment of Chronic Back Pain*, 32 Spine 816 (2007) and Hiroyuki Yoshihara and Daisuke Yoneoka, *National Trends in the Surgical Treatment for Lumbar Degenerative Disc Disease: United States, 2000 to 2009*, 15 Spine J. 265 (2015).
38. Teppo L. N. Järvinen and Gordon H. Guyatt, *Arthroscopic Surgery for Knee Pain*, 354 BMJ i3934 (2016).
39. Loren Berman et al., *The Paradoxical Effect of Medical Insurance on Delivery of Surgical Care for Infants With Congenital Anomalies*, 45 J. Ped. Surgery 38 (2010).
40. Peter B. Bach, *Indication-Specific Pricing for Cancer Drugs*, 312 JAMA 1629 (2014). See also, Alison Kodjac, Medicare Looks To Cut Drug Costs By Changing How It Pays Doctors (Mar. 9, 2016), https://www.npr.org/sections/health-shots/2016/03/09/469792479/medicare-looks-to-cut-drug-costs-by-changing-how-it-pays-doctors

("As it is now, Dr. Patrick Conway, chief medical officer for the CMS, called the reimbursement structure 'perverse.'")

41. Michelle M. Mello et al., *Who Pays for Medical Errors? An Analysis of Adverse Event Costs, the Medical Liability System, and Incentives for Patient Safety Improvement*, 4 J. EMP. LEGAL STUD. 835 (2007).
42. Sunil Eappen et al., *Relationship Between Occurrence of Surgical Complications and Hospital Finances*, 309 JAMA 1599 (2013).
43. Patients with surgical complications provide greater hospital profit-margins, Harvard T. H. Chan School of Public Health (press release, Apr. 16, 2013).
44. Dan C. Krupka et al., *The Impact on Hospitals of Reducing Surgical Complications Suggests Many Will Need Shared Savings Programs with Payers*, 31 HEALTH AFF. 2571 (2012) (hospitals earn substantially higher revenue when surgical patients suffer complications than when they do not); Michelle Mello et al., *Who Pays for Medical Errors? An Analysis of Adverse Event Costs, the Medical Liability System, and Incentives for Patient Safety Improvement*, 4 J. EMP. LEGAL STUD. 835 (2007); Marlene R. Miller et al., *Patient Safety Events During Pediatric Hospitalizations*, 111 PEDIATRICS 1358 (2003) (hospitalized pediatric patients who suffered preventable injuries were charged between two and twenty times as much, and had between two and eighteen times the risk of mortality).
45. Anahad O'Connor, *No Sponge Left Behind: Strategies for Surgery*, NEW YORK TIMES (Sep. 25, 2012).
46. David Leonhardt, *Making Healthcare Better*, NEW YORK TIMES MAGAZINE (Nov. 3, 2009).
47. Reed Abelson, *Hospitals Say They're Penalized By Medicare for Improving Care*, NEW YORK TIMES (Dec. 5, 2003).
48. Id.
49. ARTHUR C. PIGOU, THE ECONOMICS OF WELFARE (1920). See also W. J. Baumol, *On Taxation and the Control of Externalities*, 62 AM. ECON. REV. 307 (1972); Robert E. Kohn, *The Limitations of Pigouvian Taxes as a Long-Run Remedy for Externalities: Comment*, 101 QUART. J. ECON. 625 (1986); G. Tullock, *Excess Benefit*, 3 WATER RESOURC. RES. 643 (1967).
50. Arnold Milstein, *Ending Extra Payment for "Never Events"—Stronger Incentives for Patients' Safety*, 360 N. ENGL. J. MED. 2388 (2009).
51. Id.
52. National Quality Forum, List of SREs, http://www.qualityforum.org/Topics/SREs/List_of_SREs.aspx
53. John Crist, *Never Say Never: "Never Events" in Medicare*, 20 HEALTH MATRIX 437 (2010).
54. Deficit Reduction Act, P.L. 109-171 § 5001(c)(1), Social Security Act (SSA), § 1886(d)(4)(D), 42 U.S.C. § 1395ww(d)(4)(D). Obviously, this approach is not fudge-proof if a provider or hospital are determined to defraud the system.
55. The Leapfrog Group is a consortium of Fortune 500 companies and other large private and public health care purchasers whose principal focus is to actively promote patient safety.
56. Leapfrog Hospital Survey Factsheet: Never Events (April 1, 2017), at www.leapfroggroup.org/survey.

57. JoNel Aleccia, More States Shred Bills for Awful Medical Errors, NBC News (August 12, 2008), http://www.nbcnews.com/id/26081421
58. Teresa M. Waters et al., *Effect of Medicare's Nonpayment for Hospital-Acquired Conditions: Lessons for Future Policy*, 175 JAMA INTERN. MED. 347 (2015) (data from 1,381 hospitals, finding denial of payment system to be associated with improvements in rate of central line-associated bloodstream infections and catheter-associated urinary tract infections (conditions for which better hospital processes are known to produce better outcomes), but not associated with improvements in hospital-acquired pressure ulcers or injurious falls [conditions for which there is less evidence that changing hospital processes leads to better outcomes]); Grace M. Lee et al., *Effect of Nonpayment for Preventable Infections in U.S. Hospitals*, 367 N. ENGL. J. MED. 1428 (2012) (finding no effect on central catheter-associated bloodstream infections, catheter-associated UTI, or ventilator-associated pneumonia); Caroline P. Thirukumaran et al., *Impact of Medicare's Nonpayment Program on Hospital-acquired Conditions*, 55 MED. CARE 447 (2017) (finding decline in incidence of catheter-associated urinary tract infections among hospitals with relatively high Medicare populations, and other measured declines); Jereen Z. Kwong et al., *Effect of Medicare's Nonpayment Policy on Surgical Site Infections Following Orthopedic Procedures*, 38 INFECT. CONT. HOSP. EP. 817 (2017) (significant reduction in relative risk of infection for both Medicare and non-Medicare patients).
59. The ACA has a third incentive program, the Value-Based Purchasing (VBP) Program, which aims to reward hospitals for providing better care (higher quality care), not merely for greater quantities of care. See the CMS pamphlet, Hospital Value-Based Purchasing (ICN 907664) (Sept. 2015). Although VBP is expected to increase safety, if only be reducing the amount of low-value and no-value treatment patients receive, it covers such broad territory that we will not be discussing it as part of our consideration of innovative incentives designed to reduce iatrogenic harm.
60. Section 3008 of the ACA. Beginning in Fiscal Year (FY) 2015 (i.e., discharges beginning on Oct. 1, 2014).
61. Asta Sorensen et al., *HAC-POA Policy Effects on Hospitals, Other Payers, and Patients*, 4 MEDICARE MEDICAID RES. REV. (2014).
62. AHRQ, 2013 Annual Hospital-Acquired Condition Rate and Estimates of Cost Savings and Deaths Averted From 2010 to 2013 (Oct. 2015) (AHRQ Publication No. 16-0006-EF), at http://www.ahrq.gov/professionals/quality-patient-safety/pfp/index.htm
63. CMS, Hospital-Acquired Condition Reduction Program Fiscal Year 2018 Fact Sheet.
64. Ballew v. Georgia, 435 U.S. 223 (1978) (Powell, concurring).
65. Established by Section 3025 of the Patient Protection and Affordable Care Act (2010), as an addition to section 1886(q) of the 1965 Social Security Act. See https://www.cms.gov/medicare/medicare-fee-for-service-payment/acuteinpatientpps/readmissions-reduction-program.html
66. See CMS, Report to Congress: Promoting Greater Efficiency in Medicare (2007).
67. Cristina Boccuti and Giselle Casillas, Aiming for Fewer Hospital U-Turns: The Medicare Hospital Readmission Reduction Program (Kaiser Foundation Issue Brief) (March 10, 2017). http://www.kff.org/medicare/issue-brief/aiming-for-fewer-hospital-u-turns-the-medicare-hospital-readmission-reduction-program/

68. NATIONAL RESEARCH COUNCIL AND INSTITUTE OF MEDICINE, U.S. HEALTH IN INTERNATIONAL PERSPECTIVE: SHORTER LIVES, POORER HEALTH (2013).
69. Tom Baker, *Medical Malpractice Insurance Reform: "Enterprise Insurance" and Some Alternatives*, in William M. Sage and Rogan Kersh (eds.), MEDICAL MALPRACTICE AND THE U.S. HEALTH CARE SYSTEM (2006).
70. Randall R. Bovbjerg and Robert Berenson, *Enterprise Liability in the Twenty-first Century*, in William M. Sage and Rogan Kersh (eds.), MEDICAL MALPRACTICE AND THE U.S. HEALTH CARE SYSTEM (2006); Tom Baker, *Medical Malpractice Insurance Reform: "Enterprise Insurance" and Some Alternatives*, in William M. Sage and Rogan Kersh (eds.), MEDICAL MALPRACTICE AND THE U.S. HEALTH CARE SYSTEM (2006); William M. Sage, *Enterprise Liability and the Emerging Managed Health Care System*, 60 LAW CONTEMP. PROBL. 159 (Spring, 1997).
71. For example, providers in solo or small practices might not easily be able to associate themselves with a larger "enterprise," so they might have to be an exception, and continue as conventionally. Alternatively, such practitioners who were attracted to the idea of enterprise liability might form their own enterprises.
72. For an explication of the liability insurance underwriting cycle, see TOM BAKER, THE MEDICAL MALPRACTICE MYTH (2005).
73. Id.
74. See, e.g., MARTY MAKARY, UNACCOUNTABLE: WHAT HOSPITALS WON'T TELL YOU AND HOW TRANSPARENCY CAN REVOLUTIONIZE HEALTH CARE (2012). See also Alice R. Benedict and Michael J. Saks, *The Regulation of Professional Behavior: Electroconvulsive Therapy in Massachusetts*, 15 J. PSYCHIATR. L. 247 (1987) ("while 41% of the statewide sample of psychiatrists [surveyed] reported knowing a colleague who, they believed, prescribed or administered ECT inappropriately, only 17% indicated that they advised their colleague of that concern, and only 2% reported their concerns to an appropriate official or body for corrective action.").
75. Recall our earlier discussion of the variation in healthcare practices. That variation itself bespeaks shortcomings that are not conducive to high levels of quality and safety.
76. Randall R. Bovbjerg and Robert Berenson, *Enterprise Liability in the Twenty-First Century*, in William M. Sage and Rogan Kersh (eds.), MEDICAL MALPRACTICE AND THE U.S. HEALTH CARE SYSTEM (2006); Tom Baker, *Medical Malpractice Insurance Reform: "Enterprise Insurance" and Some Alternatives*, in William M. Sage and Rogan Kersh (eds.), MEDICAL MALPRACTICE AND THE U.S. HEALTH CARE SYSTEM (2006); William M. Sage, *Enterprise Liability and the Emerging Managed Health Care System*, 60 L. CONTEMP. PROBL. 159 (Spring 1997).

CHAPTER 11

1. Lucian L. Leape, *Error in Medicine*, 272 J. AM. MED. ASSOC. 1851 (1994).
2. Lucian L. Leape, *Error in Medicine*, 272 JAMA 1851 (1994).
3. Id.
4. "[T]he exploitation of labor is measured not only in long hours of work and lost dollars but also in shortened lives, high disease rates, and painful injuries." David Rosner and Gerald Markowitz (eds.), DYING FOR WORK: WORKERS' SAFETY AND HEALTH IN TWENTIETH-CENTURY AMERICA ix (1981). "[T]he problem of safety and health was near the surface in many labor struggles." Id., at x.

5. Id. at xv.
6. Id.
7. B. Reeve, *The Death Roll of Industry*, 17 CHARITIES COMMONS 791 (1907).
8. David Rosner and Gerald Markowitz (eds.), DYING FOR WORK: WORKERS' SAFETY AND HEALTH IN TWENTIETH-CENTURY AMERICA xi (1981).
9. B. Reeve, *The Death Roll of Industry*, 17 CHARITIES COMMONS 791 (1907).
10. David Rosner and Gerald Markowitz (eds.), DYING FOR WORK: WORKERS' SAFETY AND HEALTH IN TWENTIETH-CENTURY AMERICA xi (1981).
11. SYDNEY DEKKER, PATIENT SAFETY: A HUMAN FACTORS APPROACH 37 (2011).
12. KURT LEWIN, PRINCIPLES OF TOPOLOGICAL PSYCHOLOGY (1936).
13. JOHN M. DARLEY AND BIBB LATANÉ, THE UNRESPONSIVE BYSTANDER: WHY DOESN'T HE HELP? (1970); John M. Darley and C. Daniel Batson, *"From Jerusalem to Jericho": A Study of Situational and Dispositional Variables in Helping Behavior*, 27 J. PERSONALITY SOC. PSYCHOL. 100 (1973).
14. E.g., INSTITUTE OF MEDICINE, TO ERR IS HUMAN: BUILDING A SAFER HEALTH SYSTEM (2000); Lucian L. Leape, *Error in Medicine*, 272 JAMA 1851(1994); PATRICE L. SPATH, ERROR REDUCTION IN HEALTH CARE: A SYSTEMS APPROACH TO IMPROVING PATIENT SAFETY (2d ed. 2011); ROBERT M. WACHTER, UNDERSTANDING PATIENT SAFETY (2012).
15. Id.
16. Ellison C. Pierce, Jr., *The Development of Anesthesia Guidelines and Standards*, 16 QUAL. REV. BULL. 61 (1990),
17. SORREL KING, JOSIE'S STORY: A MOTHER'S INSPIRING CRUSADE TO MAKE MEDICAL CARE SAFE (2009).
18. Steven H. Woolf et al., *A String of Mistakes: The Cascade Analysis in Describing, Counting, and Preventing Medical Errors*, 2 ANN. FAM. MED. 317 (2004).
19. SYDNEY DEKKER, PATIENT SAFETY: A HUMAN FACTORS APPROACH (2011).
20. JAMES REASON, HUMAN ERROR 173 (1990).
21. MARTY MAKARY, UNACCOUNTABLE 4 (2012).
22. SOREN BISGAARD, SOLUTIONS TO THE HEALTHCARE QUALITY CRISIS: CASES AND EXAMPLES OF LEAN SIX SIGMA IN HEALTHCARE 85 (2009).
23. David W. Bates et al., *The Costs of Adverse Drug Events in Hospitalized Patients*, 277 JAMA 277 (1997).
24. The underlying data were originally reported in David M. Studdert et al., *Claims, Errors, and Compensation Payments in Medical Malpractice Litigation*, 354 N. ENGL. J. MED. 2024 (2006). The reanalysis of interest is in Michelle M. Mello and David M. Studdert, *Deconstructing Negligence: The Role of Individual and System Factors in Causing Medical Injuries*, 96 GEORGETOWN LAW J. 599 (2007–2008).
25. Id., at 605.
26. E.g., ROBERT M. WACHTER, UNDERSTANDING PATIENT SAFETY 25 (2012) (suggesting that most errors are of the automatic, unintended kind ["slips"] rather than the result of conscious processes ["mistakes"]).
27. Michelle M. Mello and David M. Studdert, *Deconstructing Negligence: The Role of Individual and System Factors in Causing Medical Injuries*, 96 GEORGETOWN LAW J. 599, 605 (2007–2008).
28. Id., at 601.
29. Id., at 601.

30. Lucian L. Leape, *Error in Medicine*, 272 JAMA 1851, 1854 (1994).
31. The analogy of iatrogenic patient deaths to airline crashes seems to have originated with Leape, id., who gave the figure at three jumbo jets crashing every two days.
32. See Chapter 10 of this volume.
33. Id.
34. David Hyman and Charles Silver, *Healthcare Quality, Patient Safety, and the Culture of Medicine*, 46 N. ENG. L. REV. 417 (2012).
35. See Chapter 7 of this volume and the following discussion regarding the structure of the industry, which protects larger organizational units from being accountable for liability.
36. SYDNEY DEKKER, PATIENT SAFETY: A HUMAN FACTORS APPROACH 28 (2011).
37. Lucian L. Leape, *Error in Medicine*, 272 JAMA 1851, 1854 (1994).
38. There are exceptions, of course, which function more as organized, coherent systems of care, and their record of safety generally is better than that of most other healthcare organizations. Well-known examples are the Mayo Clinic, the Cleveland Clinic, and Intermountain Healthcare.
39. E.g., Ross Koppel and Suzanne Gordon (eds.), FIRST, DO LESS HARM (2012); ROBERT M. WACHTER, UNDERSTANDING PATIENT SAFETY (2012); SYDNEY DEKKER, PATIENT SAFETY: A HUMAN FACTORS APPROACH (2011); Lucian L. Leape, *Error in Medicine*, 272 JAMA 1851 (1994); MICHAEL L. MILLENSON, DEMANDING MEDICAL EXCELLENCE (1999); and other works on harmful errors in healthcare.
40. A remarkable 20% of all patients discharged from hospitals suffer adverse events after being discharged. Alan J. Forster et al., *The Incidence and Severity of Adverse Events Affecting Patients After Discharge from the Hospital*, 138 ANN. INTERN. MED. 161 (2002). The annual cost of hospital readmission is around $30 billion. H. Joanna Jiang et al., Healthcare Cost and Utilization Project, Nationwide Frequency and Costs of Potentially Preventable Hospitalizations, 2006, Statistical Brief #72, at 1–2 (2009). As many as half of the patients rehospitalized within thirty days after a medical (as opposed to a surgical) discharge to the community showed no sign of having seen a doctor in an office visit between the time of discharge and the time of rehospitalization. Medicare Payment Advisory Commission. Even those with unplanned rehospitalizations following surgical discharge were overwhelmingly rehospitalized not for surgical complications but for a different medical condition, and those rehospitalizations were lengthier than primary hospitalizations for non-postsurgery Medicare beneficiaries with the same diagnosis. See C. Moore et al., *Medical Errors Related to Discontinuity of Care from an Inpatient to an Outpatient Setting*. 18 J. GEN. INTERN. MED. 646 (2003). Countries that rate highest in various measures of healthcare quality and safety also have more continuity of care.
41. See., e.g., SYDNEY DEKKER, PATIENT SAFETY: A HUMAN FACTORS APPROACH 5 (2011) ("Dramatic improvements in safety ... have been correlated with a gradual reduction in actor autonomy—particularly through standardization and procedures." Resistance to "this in healthcare has gone hand in hand with the idea that physicians are unique craftspeople whose exercise of skill is about situational insight, deftness, contextual sensitivity, mastery, and prowess.")
42. For discussion of TeamSTEPPS, see Chapter 9 of this volume.
43. ROBERT M. WACHTER, UNDERSTANDING PATIENT SAFETY 322 (2012).
44. Id., at 446.

45. Id., at 21.
46. Id., at 324.
47. George Poste, *The Complex Strategic Landscape for Precision Medicine: Cost, Convergence, Culture, Computing and Creative Destruction*, JOURNAL OF PRECISION MEDICINE (2017). Available at https://www.thejournalofprecisionmedicine.com/archive-manager/the-complex-strategic-landscape-for-precision-medicine-cost-convergence-culture-computing-and-creative-destruction/.
48. Hill-Burton Act (discussed in PAUL STARR, THE SOCIAL TRANSFORMATION OF AMERICAN MEDICINE, 1982).
49. CDC, 14 Diseases You Almost Forgot About (Thanks to Vaccines). At https://www.cdc.gov/vaccines/parents/diseases/child/14-diseases.html?s_cid=bb-vaccines-Child-HP01-NCIRD.
50. Again, as noted earlier, there are exceptions—healthcare organizations where all caregivers are employees, and the organization does not evade responsibility for the torts of its employees.
51. Id.
52. For a view that the problem inheres in substantive tort law, rather than the business relationships in healthcare organizations, see Michelle M. Mello and David M. Studdert, *Deconstructing Negligence: The Role of Individual and System Factors in Causing Medical Injuries*, 96 GEORGETOWN LAW J. 599, 601, 620 (2007–2008) (arguing that "doctrinal realignment" (not changes in organizational arrangements) is the move necessary to correct a "heavy focus on individual liability"). On the other hand, tort lawyers generally choose organizations over individuals as their defendants. Even in the healthcare context, fewer than 40% of defendants in medical malpractice cases are individuals. Thomas H. Cohen, Tort Bench and Jury Trial in State Courts, 2005, Bureau of Justice Statistics Bulletin, Table 2 (Nov. 2009) (NCJ 228129). That percentage can be expected to shrink further as more physicians become employees of hospitals and other healthcare organizations.
53. These, too, were discussed in greater detail in the preceding chapter.
54. Carlton Moore et al., *Medical Errors Related to Discontinuity of Care from an Inpatient to an Outpatient Setting*, 18 J. GEN. INTERN. MED. 646 (2003).

CHAPTER 12

1. David Axelrod, past New York State Health Commissioner, quoted in MICHAEL L. MILLENSON, DEMANDING MEDICAL EXCELLENCE (1999).
2. TOM BAKER, THE MEDICAL MALPRACTICE MYTH 114 (2007).
3. JOEL E. EASTMAN, STYLING VS. SAFETY: THE AMERICAN AUTOMOBILE INDUSTRY AND THE DEVELOPMENT OF AUTOMOTIVE SAFETY, 1900–1966 xii (1984).
4. Id. at 23.
5. JERRY L. MASHAW AND DAVID L. HARFST, THE STRUGGLE FOR AUTO SAFETY 43 (1990).
6. JOEL E. EASTMAN, STYLING VS. SAFETY: THE AMERICAN AUTOMOBILE INDUSTRY AND THE DEVELOPMENT OF AUTOMOTIVE SAFETY, 1900–1966 144 (1984).
7. JERRY L. MASHAW AND DAVID L. HARFST, THE STRUGGLE FOR AUTO SAFETY 50 (1990).
8. Id. at 2.

9. Joel E. Eastman, Styling vs. Safety: The American Automobile Industry and the Development of Automotive Safety, 1900–1966 156 (1984).
10. Id. at 59.
11. The medical literature discussed in the text is described in: Michael R. Lemov, Car Safety Wars: One Hundred Years of Technology, Politics, and Death (2015).
12. Id. at 105.
13. Jerry L. Mashaw and David L. Harfst, The Struggle for Auto Safety 5 (1990).
14. Michael R. Lemov, Car Safety Wars: One Hundred Years of Technology, Politics, and Death 115 (2015).
15. Id. at 154.
16. Id. at 12.
17. Id. at 15.
18. 42 U.S.C. § 1320b-12(a)(1)(A) (2003).
19. John. A. Wennberg, *AHCPR and the Strategy for Health Care Reform*, 11 Health Aff. 67, 67 (1992).
20. 42 U.S.C. § 1320b-12(a)(1)(A) (2003).
21. Agency for Health Care Policy and Research Nominations of Topics for Evidence-Based Practice Centers (EPCs), 62 Fed. Reg. 229, 63345 (Nov. 28, 1997).
22. Warren E. Leary, *Options to Cataract Surgery Stressed*, New York Times, Feb. 26, 1993, at A15.
23. Stanley J. Bigos, O. Richard Bowyer and G. Richard Braen, *Acute Low Back Problems in Adults, AHCPR Clinical Practice Guidelines, No. 14*, Agency for Health Care Policy and Research (AHCPR) (Dec. 1994), http://www.ncbi.nlm.nih.gov/books/NBK52408/.
24. Shannon Brownlee, *Newtered*, The Washington Monthly: Special Healthcare Issue 27, 32 (Oct. 2007).
25. Richard A. Deyo, *Problems Worth Attacking May Attack Back*, in Lessons Learned in Changing Healthcare 71, 74 (Paul Batalden ed., 2010).
26. Id.; Stanley J. Bigos, O. Richard Bowyer and G. Richard Braen, *Acute Low Back Problems in Adults, AHCPR Clinical Practice Guidelines, No. 14*, Agency for Health Care Policy and Research (Dec. 1994), http://www.ncbi.nlm.nih.gov/books/NBK52408/.
27. Shannon Brownlee, *Newtered*, The Washington Monthly: Special Healthcare Issue 27, 28 (Oct. 2007).
28. Richard A. Deyo, *Problems Worth Attacking May Attack Back*, Lessons Learned in Changing Healthcare 71, 74 (Paul Batalden ed., 2010).
29. Id.; Shannon Brownlee, *Newtered*, The Washington Monthly: Special Healthcare Issue 27, 28 (Oct. 2007) (discussing injunction sought by pedicle screw manufacturer to prevent release of the panel's guidelines).
30. Bradford H. Gray, Michael K. Gusmano and Sara R. Collins, *AHCPR and the Changing Politics of Health Services Research*, W3 Health Aff. 283, 294 (June 25, 2003).
31. Id. at 295.
32. Shannon Brownlee, *Newtered*, The Washington Monthly: Special Healthcare Issue 27, 30–31 (Oct. 2007).

33. Cary Coglianese, *The Limits of Performance-Based Regulation*, 50 U. MICH. J. LAW REFORM 525 (2017); Cass R. Sunstein, Simpler: The Future of Government 11–12 (2013).
34. Clifford Atiyeh, *Everything You Need to Know about the VW Diesel-Emissions Scandal*, CAR AND DRIVER (Oct. 24, 2017), https://blog.caranddriver.com/everything-you-need-to-know-about-the-vw-diesel-emissions-scandal/.
35. Andrew Wendler, *How Volkswagen Got Busted for Skirting EPA Emission Standards*, CAR AND DRIVER (Sept. 21, 2015), https://blog.caranddriver.com/how-volkswagen-got-busted-for-gaming-epa-diesel-emissions-standards/.
36. S. Declich and A.O. Carter, *Public Health Surveillance: Historical Origins, Methods and Evaluation*, 72 BULL. WORLD HEALTH ORGAN. 285, 285 (1994).
37. Id. at 293.
38. Id. at 295.
39. E.C. Kudzma, *Florence Nightingale and Healthcare Reform*, 19 NURS. SCI. Q. 61, 61–64 (2006).
40. Ernest A. Codman, *A Study in Hospital Efficiency: As Demonstrated by the Case Report of the First Five Years of a Private Hospital*, reprinted in 471 CLIN. ORTHOP. RELAT. RES. 1778, 1778–1783 (2013).
41. UNITED STATES GENERAL ACCOUNTING OFFICE, HEALTH CARE REFORM: "REPORT CARDS" ARE USEFUL BUT SIGNIFICANT ISSUES NEED TO BE ADDRESSED, REPORT TO THE CHAIRMAN, COMMITTEE ON LABOR AND HUMAN RESOURCES, U.S. SENATE 12 (Sept. 1994).
42. Id.
43. Cephas P. Swamidoss, Sorin J. Brull, Gail Watrous and Paul G. Barash, *Health-Care Report Cards and Implications for Anesthesia*, 88 ANESTHESIOLOGY 809, 812 (1998).
44. Arnold Epstein, *Sounding Board: Performance Reports on Quality—Prototypes, Problems, and Prospects*, 333 N. ENGL. J. MED. 57, 57 (1995)
45. Edward L. Hannan et al., *The New York State Cardiac Registries*, 59 J. AM. COLL. CARDIOL. 2309, 2309 (2012).
46. Id.
47. Jesse Green and Neil Wintfeld, *Report Cards on Cardiac Surgeons—Assessing New York State's Approach*, 332 N. ENGL. J. MED. 1229, 1229 (1995).
48. Peter J. Millock, *David Axelrod, M.D.: His Impact on the Law and Public Policy*, 14 NYSBA HEALTH LAW J. 64, 65 (Winter 2009).
49. Edward L. Hannan et al., *The New York State Cardiac Registries*, 59 J. AM. COLL. CARDIOL. 2309, 2309 (2012).
50. Id.
51. Id. at 2310.
52. Edward L. Hannan et al., *Adult Open Heart Surgery in New York State. An Analysis of Risk Factors and Hospital Mortality Rates*, 264 JAMA 2768, 2768–2774 (1990).
53. Edward L. Hannan et al., *The New York State Cardiac Registries*, 59 J. AM. COLL. CARDIOL. 2309, 2310 (2012).
54. Mark R. Chassin, *Achieving And Sustaining Improved Quality: Lessons from New York State and Cardiac Surgery*, 21 HEALTH AFF. 40, 42 (2002).
55. Id. at 43.
56. Lawrence K. Altman, *Heart-Surgery Death Rates Decline in New York*, NEW YORK TIMES, Dec. 5, 1990, at B10.

57. Mark R. Chassin, *Achieving And Sustaining Improved Quality: Lessons from New York State and Cardiac Surgery*, 21 HEALTH AFF. 40, 43–45 (2002).
58. Id. at 43.
59. Edward L. Hannan et al., *The New York State Cardiac Registries*, 59 J. AM. COLL. CARDIOL. 2309, 2311 (2012).
60. Cathleen F. Crowley, *Getting to the Heart of a Life, Death Matter*, TIMES UNION (Dec. 31, 2012), http://www.timesunion.com/local/article/Getting-to-the-heart-of-a-life-death-matter-4154751.php.
61. Robert Kolker, *Heartless*, NEW YORK MAGAZINE (Mar. 7, 2013), http://nymag.com/nymetro/health/features/14788/.
62. Cathleen F. Crowley, *Getting to the Heart of a Life, Death Matter*, TIMES UNION (Dec. 31, 2012), http://www.timesunion.com/local/article/Getting-to-the-heart-of-a-life-death-matter-4154751.php.
63. Id.
64. Mark R. Chassin, *Achieving And Sustaining Improved Quality: Lessons from New York State and Cardiac Surgery*, 21 HEALTH AFF. 40, 43 (2002).
65. Ashish K. Jha and Arnold M. Epstein, *The Predictive Accuracy of the New York Coronary Artery Bypass Surgery Report-Card System*, 25 HEALTH AFF. 844, 849–850 (2006).
66. Id.
67. Id. at 850.
68. Id.
69. Mark R. Chassin, *Achieving And Sustaining Improved Quality: Lessons from New York State and Cardiac Surgery*, 21 HEALTH AFF. 40, 47 (2002).
70. Jesse Green and Neil Wintfeld, *Report Cards on Cardiac Surgeons – Assessing New York State's Approach*, 332 N. ENGL. J. MED. 1229, 1229 (1995).
71. Mark R. Chassin et al., *Benefits and Hazards of Reporting Medical Outcomes Publicly*, 334 N. ENGL. J. MED. 394, 395 (1996).
72. Id. at 396.
73. Board, Editorial, *A National Survey of Medical Error Reporting Laws*, 9 YALE J. HEALTH POL. L. ETHICS 201, 217 (2009).
74. Mark R. Chassin et al., *Benefits and Hazards of Reporting Medical Outcomes Publicly*, 334 N. ENGL. J. MED. 394, 396 (1996).
75. Robert Kolker, *Heartless*, NEW YORK MAGAZINE (Mar. 7, 2013), http://nymag.com/nymetro/health/features/14788/.
76. David Dranove et al., *Is More Information Better? The Effects of "Report Cards" on Health Care Providers*, 111 J. POL. ECON. 555, 556 (June 2003); Arnold M. Epstein, Editorial, *Public Release of Performance Data*, 283 JAMA 1884, 1885 (2000); Eric C. Schneider and Arnold M. Epstein, *Influence of Cardiac-Surgery Performance Reports on Referral Practices and Access to Care—A Survey of Cardiovascular Specialists*, 335 N. ENGL. J. MED. 251, 251 (1996).
77. Id.
78. Id.
79. Ashish K. Jha and Arnold M. Epstein, *The Predictive Accuracy of the New York Coronary Artery Bypass Surgery Report-Card System*, 25 HEALTH AFF. 844, 852 (2006).

80. United States General Accounting Office, Health Care Reform: "Report Cards" Are Useful but Significant Issues Need to Be Addressed, Report to the Chairman, Committee on Labor and Human Resources, U.S. Senate 4 (Sept. 1994).
81. Id.
82. Id.
83. Id. at 40.
84. Robert Kolker, *Heartless*, New York Magazine (Mar. 7, 2013), http://nymag.com/nymetro/health/features/14788/; Jesse Green and Neil Wintfeld, *Report Cards on Cardiac Surgeons—Assessing New York State's Approach*, 332 N. Engl. J. Med. 1229, 1229 (1995); M.J. Byer, *Faint Hearts*, New York Times, Mar. 21, 1992, at A23.
85. Eric C. Schneider and Arnold M. Epstein, *Influence of Cardiac-Surgery Performance Reports on Referral Practices and Access to Care—A Survey of Cardiovascular Specialists*, 335 N. Engl. J. Med. 251, 251 (1996).
86. Martin N. Marshall et al., *The Public Release of Performance Data*, 283 JAMA 1866, 1872 (2000).
87. Nowamagbe A. Omoigui et al., *Outmigration for Coronary Bypass Surgery in an Era of Public Dissemination of Clinical Outcomes*, 93 Circulation 27, 27 (1996).
88. Id.
89. David Dranove et al., *supra* note 75.*Is More Information Better? The Effects of "Report Cards" on Health Care Providers*, 111 J. Pol. Econ. 555, 556 (2003) (The three authors cited in the text were joined by Mark Satterthwaite.).
90. Id. at 581.
91. Id. at 584.
92. Jesse Green and Neil Wintfeld, *Report Cards on Cardiac Surgeons—Assessing New York State's Approach*, 332 N. Engl. J. Med. 1229, 1230 (1995).
93. Amanda S. Xi, *State of the Art and Science—The Next Generation of Physician Report Cards*, 17 AMA J. Ethics 647, 647–650 (2015).
94. Eric C. Schneider and Arnold M. Epstein, *Influence of Cardiac-Surgery Performance Reports on Referral Practices and Access to Care—A Survey of Cardiovascular Specialists*, 335 N. Engl. J. Med. 251, 251 (1996).
95. Id.; Ashish K. Jha and Arnold M. Epstein, *The Predictive Accuracy of the New York Coronary Artery Bypass Surgery Report-Card System*, 25 Health Aff. 844, 845 (2006).
96. Eric C. Schneider and Arnold M. Epstein, *Influence of Cardiac-Surgery Performance Reports on Referral Practices and Access to Care—A Survey of Cardiovascular Specialists*, 335 N. Engl. J. Med. 251, 251 (1996).
97. Martin Marshall et al., *The Public Release of Performance Data: What Do We Expect to Gain? A Review of the Evidence*, 283 JAMA 1866, 1873 (2000).
98. Thomas H. Lee et al., *A Middle Ground on Public Accountability*, 350 N. Engl. J. Med. 2409, 2410 (2004).
99. Id. at 2409.
100. David Dranove et al., *Is More Information Better? The Effects of "Report Cards" on Health Care Providers*, 111 J. Pol. Econ. 555, 557 (June 2003).
101. Jesse Green and Neil Wintfeld, *Report Cards on Cardiac Surgeons – Assessing New York State's Approach*, 332 N. Engl. J. Med. 1229, 1229 (1995).

102. Edward L. Hannan et al., *The New York State Cardiac Registries*, 59 J. Am. Coll. Cardiol. 2309, 2313 (2012).
103. Id.
104. Id. at 2312.
105. Id.
106. Zack Budryk, *Toby Cosgrove Reveals the Secret to Cleveland Clinic's Care Delivery Transformation*, FierceHealthcare (June 22, 2015), https://www.fiercehealthcare.com/healthcare/toby-cosgrove-reveals-secret-to-cleveland-clinic-s-care-delivery-transformation; Brandon Glenn, *Cleveland Clinic Opens Saudi Arabia Office to Focus on Medical Education*, MedCityNews (Jan. 23, 2012), https://medcitynews.com/2012/01/cleveland-clinic-opens-saudi-arabia-office-to-focus-on-medical-education/.
107. Edward L. Hannan et al., *The New York State Cardiac Registries*, 59 J. Am. Coll. Cardiol. 2309, 2312 (2012).
108. Eric D. Peterson et al., *The Effects of New York's Bypass Surgery Provider Profiling on Access to Care and Patient Outcomes in the Elderly*, 32 J. Am. Coll. Cardiol. 993, 996 (1998).
109. Mark R. Chassin et al., *Benefits and Hazards of Reporting Medical Outcomes Publicly*, 334 N. Engl. J. Med. 394, 397 (1996).
110. Eric C. Schneider and Arnold M. Epstein, *Influence of Cardiac-Surgery Performance Reports on Referral Practices and Access to Care—A Survey of Cardiovascular Specialists*, 335 N. Engl. J. Med. 251, 254 (1996).
111. Id. at 251.
112. Id. at 254.
113. Id.
114. Edward L. Hannan et al., *The New York State Cardiac Registries*, 59 J. Am. Coll. Cardiol. 2309, 2311 (2012).
115. Id. at 2312.
116. Eric D. Peterson et al., *The Effects of New York's Bypass Surgery Provider Profiling on Access to Care and Patient Outcomes in the Elderly*, 32 J. Am. Coll. Cardiol. 993, 998 (1998).
117. Id.
118. Jesse Green and Neil Wintfeld, *Report Cards on Cardiac Surgeons—Assessing New York State's Approach*, 332 N. Engl. J. Med. 1229, 1229 (1995).
119. Mark R. Chassin et al., *Benefits and Hazards of Reporting Medical Outcomes Publicly*, 334 N. Engl. J. Med. 394, 397 (1996).
120. Id.
121. Edward L. Hannan et al., *The New York State Cardiac Registries*, 59 J. Am. Coll. Cardiol. 2309, 2313 (2012).
122. Ashish K. Jha and Arnold M. Epstein, *The Predictive Accuracy of the New York Coronary Artery Bypass Surgery Report-Card System*, 25 Health Aff. 844, 844 (2006).
123. Eric D. Peterson et al., *The Effects of New York's Bypass Surgery Provider Profiling on Access to Care and Patient Outcomes in the Elderly*, 32 J. Am. Coll. Cardiol. 993, 999 (1998).
124. Richard L. Madden, *Small Hospitals Vie to Offer Heart Surgery*, New York Times, Mar. 10, 1988

125. Mark R. Chassin et al., *Benefits and Hazards of Reporting Medical Outcomes Publicly*, 334 N. ENGL. J. MED. 394, 397 (1996).
126. UNITED STATES GENERAL ACCOUNTING OFFICE, HEALTH CARE REFORM: "REPORT CARDS" ARE USEFUL BUT SIGNIFICANT ISSUES NEED TO BE ADDRESSED, REPORT TO THE CHAIRMAN, COMMITTEE ON LABOR AND HUMAN RESOURCES, U.S. SENATE 12 (Sept. 1994).
127. Martin Marshall et al., *The Public Release of Performance Data: What Do We Expect to Gain? A Review of the Evidence*, 283 JAMA 1866, 1867 (2000).
128. David W Baker et al., *The Effect of Publicly Reporting Hospital Performance on Market Share and Risk-Adjusted Mortality at High-Mortality Hospitals*, 41 MED. CARE 729, 729–740 (2003).
129. Arnold M. Epstein, *Public Release of Performance Data*, 283 JAMA 1884, 1885 (2000).
130. UNITED STATES GENERAL ACCOUNTING OFFICE, HEALTH CARE REFORM: "REPORT CARDS" ARE USEFUL BUT SIGNIFICANT ISSUES NEED TO BE ADDRESSED, REPORT TO THE CHAIRMAN, COMMITTEE ON LABOR AND HUMAN RESOURCES, U.S. SENATE 4 (Sept. 1994).
131. Martin Marshall et al., *The Public Release of Performance Data: What Do We Expect to Gain? A Review of the Evidence*, 283 JAMA 1866, 1867 (2000).
132. David R. Urbach, *Pledging to Eliminate Low-Volume Surgery*, 373 N. ENGL. J. MED. 1388, 1388 (2015).
133. H.S. Luft et al., *Should Operations Be Regionalized? The Empirical Relation Between Surgical Volume and Morality*, 301 N. ENGL. J. MED. 1364, 1364–1369 (1979).
134. John D. Birkmeyer et al., *Hospital Volume and Surgical Mortality in the United States*, 346 N. ENGL. J. MED. 1128, 1128–1137 (2002).
135. Steve Sternberg, *Hospitals Move to Limit Low-Volume Surgeries*, U.S. NEWS (May 19, 2015), https://www.usnews.com/news/articles/2015/05/19/hospitals-move-to-limit-low-volume-surgeries.
136. Andrea K. McDaniels, *Complications More Likely When Doctors Don't Do Enough Surgeries, Study Says*, BALTIMORE SUN (May 29, 2015), http://www.baltimoresun.com/health/maryland-health/bs-hs-low-volume-surgery-20150520-story.html.
137. Id.
138. Steve Sternberg, *Risks are High at Low-Volume Hospitals*, U.S. NEWS (May 18, 2015), https://www.usnews.com/news/articles/2015/05/18/risks-are-high-at-low-volume-hospitals
139. David R. Urbach, *Pledging to Eliminate Low-Volume Surgery*, 373 N. ENGL. J. MED. 1388, 1390 (2015).
140. Sandra G. Boodman, *Major Hospitals Restrict High-Risk Surgeries to Experienced Docs*, MEDCITY NEWS (Apr. 27, 2016), https://medcitynews.com/2016/04/hospitals-high-risk-surgeries/.
141. *See* 42 C.F.R. §§ 405, 408, and 498 (Requirements for Approval and Reapproval of Transplant Centers).
142. Riley Schatzle, *The Volume-Outcome Debate: The Results Are In. Or Are They?*, MEDELITA (May 11, 2016), https://www.medelita.com/blog/volume-outcome-healthcare-debate/.
143. Joint Commission Sentinel Event Policy and Procedures, https://www.jointcommission.org/.

144. Leigh A. Lauth, *The Patient Safety and Quality Improvement Act of 2005: An Invitation for Sham Peer Review in the Health Care Setting*, 4 IND. HEALTH L. REV. 151 (2007).
145. Press Release, National Quality Forum, National Quality Forum Updates Endorsement of Serious Reportable Events, HEALTHCORE (Nov. 15, 2006).
146. Patient Safety and Quality Improvement Act, 42 U.S. Code §§ 299b-21-26.
147. Board, Editorial, *A National Survey of Medical Error Reporting Laws*, 9 YALE J. HEALTH POL. L. 201, 205 (2009).
148. Id.
149. Id. at 216.
150. Barron H. Lener, *A Case That Shook Medicine*, WASHINGTON POST (Nov. 28, 2006), http://www.washingtonpost.com/wp-dyn/content/article/2006/11/24/AR2006112400985.html.
151. 10 NYCRR [Dept. of Health] § 405.4.
152. Esther B. Fein, *Flouting Law, Hospitals Overwork Novice Doctors*, NEW YORK TIMES (Dec. 14, 1997), http://www.nytimes.com/1997/12/14/nyregion/flouting-law-hospitals-overwork-novice-doctors.html/.
153. Jennifer F. Whetsell, *Changing the Law, Changing the Culture: Rethinking the 'Sleepy Resident' Problem*, 12 ANN. HEALTH L. 23, 55 (2003).
154. Id. at 27 n. 17
155. Thomas R. McLean, *The 80-Hour Work Week*, 26 J. LEGAL MED. 339, 357 (2005).
156. Id. at 356.
157. Id. at 356 n. 112.
158. Barron H. Lener, *A Case That Shook Medicine*, WASHINGTON POST (Nov. 28, 2006), http://www.washingtonpost.com/wp-dyn/content/article/2006/11/24/AR2006112400985.html.
159. Kyle M. Fargen, *Are Duty Hour Regulations Promoting a Culture of Dishonesty Among Resident Physicians?* 5 J. GRAD. MED. EDUC. 553, 553–555 (2013); Brian L. Drolet, *Surgical Residents' Perceptions of 2011 Accreditation Council for Graduate Medical Education Duty Hour Regulations*, 148 JAMA SURG. 427, 427–433 (2013).
160. Jennifer F. Whetsell, *Changing the Law, Changing the Culture: Rethinking the "Sleepy Resident" Problem*, 12 ANN. HEALTH L. 23, 66–67 (2003).
161. Eric Schmitt, *Navy Returns to Compasses and Pencils to Help Avoid Collisions at Sea*, NEW YORK TIMES, Sept. 28, 2017, at A11.
162. Najma Ahmed et al., *A Systematic Review of the Effects of Resident Duty Hour Restrictions in Surgery: Impact on Resident Wellness, Training, and Patient Outcomes*, 259 ANN. SURG. 1041, 1043 (2014).
163. Jennifer F. Whetsell, *Changing the Law, Changing the Culture: Rethinking the 'Sleepy Resident' Problem*, 12 ANN. HEALTH L. 23, 55 (2003).
164. Linda McKibben et al., *Guidance on Public Reporting of Healthcare-Associated Infections: Recommendations of the Healthcare Infection Control Practices Advisory Committee*, 33 AM. J. INFECT. CONTROL. 217, 217–226 (2005).
165. Chanu Rhee et al., *Objective Sepsis Surveillance Using Electronic Clinical Data*, 37 INFECT. CONTROL HOSP. EPIDEMIOL. 163, 163–171 (2016); Thomas R. Frieden, *Maximizing Infection Prevention in the Next Decade: Defining Unacceptable*, 31 INFECT. CONTROL HOSP. EPIDEMIOL. S1, S1–S3 (2010).

166. Board, Editorial, *A National Survey of Medical Error Reporting Laws*, 9 YALE J. HEALTH POL. L. 201, 218 (2009).
167. Linda McKibben et al., *Guidance on Public Reporting of Healthcare-Associated Infections: Recommendations of the Healthcare Infection Control Practices Advisory Committee*, 33 AM. J. INFECT. CONTROL. 217, 222 (2005).
168. Id. at 223.
169. Peter Pronovost et al., *An Intervention to Decrease Catheter-Related Bloodstream Infections in the ICU*, 355 N. ENGL. J. MED. 2725, 2726 (2006).
170. Id. at 2726–2727.
171. Id. at 2730.
172. Kelly M. Pyrek, *Checklists, Culture of Accountability are Reinvigorating the Patient Safety Movement*, INFECTION CONTROL TODAY (Apr. 18, 2011), http://www.infectioncontroltoday.com/articles/2011/04/checklists-culture-of-accountability-are-reinvigorating-the-patient-safety-movement.aspx.
173. Peter Pronovost, *A National Initiative To Reduce Central Line-Associated Bloodstream Infections: A Model For Reducing Preventable Harm*, HEALTH AFFAIRS BLOG (Sept. 23, 2013), http://healthaffairs.org/blog/2013/09/23/a-national-initiative-to-reduce-central-line-associated-bloodstream-infections-a-model-for-reducing-preventable-harm/.
174. Hallie Levine, *Zero Tolerance for Deadly Hospital-Acquired Infections*, CONSUMER REP. (Nov. 21, 2016), https://www.consumerreports.org/hospital-safety/hospital-acquired-infections-zero-tolerance/.

CHAPTER 13

1. Vinod Khosla, founder, Khosla Ventures, writing in *"20-Percent Doctor Included" & Dr. Algorithm: Speculations and Musings of a Technology Optimist*, Khosla Ventures 2 (Sept. 16, 2016).
2. ROBERT WACHTER, THE DIGITAL DOCTOR: HOPE, HYPE, AND HARM AT THE DAWN OF MEDICINE'S COMPUTER AGE (2015); ERIC TOPOL, THE PATIENT WILL SEE YOU NOW: THE FUTURE OF MEDICINE IS IN YOUR HANDS (2015).
3. ROBERT WACHTER, THE DIGITAL DOCTOR: HOPE, HYPE, AND HARM AT THE DAWN OF MEDICINE'S COMPUTER AGE 171 (2015);
4. United States General Accounting Office (GAO), *Direct-to-Consumer Genetic Tests Misleading Test Results Are Further Complicated by Deceptive Marketing and Other Questionable Practices*, TESTIMONY BEFORE THE SUBCOMMITTEE ON OVERSIGHT AND INVESTIGATIONS, COMMITTEE ON ENERGY AND COMMERCE, H.R. 1 (July 22, 2010).
5. Amy L. McGuire and Wylie Burke, *Raiding the Medical Commons: An Unwelcome Side Effect of Direct-to-Consumer Personal Genome Testing*, 22 J. AM. MED. ASSOC. 2669 (2008).
6. Id. at 2669.
7. Id.
8. D.J. Hunter et al., *Letting the Genome Out of the Bottle—Will We Get Our Wish?* 358 N. ENGL. J. MED. 105 (2008).
9. Amy L. McGuire and Wylie Burke, *Raiding the Medical Commons: An Unwelcome Side Effect of Direct-to-Consumer Personal Genome Testing*, 22 J. AM. MED. ASSOC. 2669, 2670 (2008).

10. Id.
11. Emily E. Anderson, *Direct-to-consumer personal genome services: need for more oversight*, 11 VIRTUAL MENTOR 701 (2009).
12. Id. at 701.
13. Id. at 705.
14. United States General Accounting Office, *Direct-to-Consumer Genetic Tests Misleading Test Results Are Further Complicated by Deceptive Marketing and Other Questionable Practices*, TESTIMONY BEFORE THE SUBCOMMITTEE ON OVERSIGHT AND INVESTIGATIONS, COMMITTEE ON ENERGY AND COMMERCE, H.R. 1 (July 22, 2010).
15. Cinnamon S. Bloss et al., *Effect of Direct-to-Consumer Genomewide Profiling to Assess Disease Risk*, 364 N. ENGL. J. MED. 524 (2011).
16. Barbara A. Bernhardt et al., *Incorporating Direct-to-Consumer Genomic Information into Patient Care: Attitudes and Experiences of Primary Care Physicians*, 9 PER. MED. 683, 687 (2012).
17. Id. at 686.
18. Id.
19. Letter from Alberto Gutierrez, Director, Office of Invitro Diagnostic Device Evaluation and Safety Center for Device and Radiological Health, to Anne Wojcicki, CEO, 23andMe, Inc. (Nov. 22, 2013) (on file with www.fda.gov).
20. Christina Farr, *23andMe Lost Its Chief Legal Counsel Months Before FDA's Legal Crackdown*, VENTUREBEAT (Dec. 24, 2013), https://venturebeat.com/2013/12/24/23andme-lost-its-chief-legal-counsel-months-before-fdas-legal-crackdown/; Leah Fessler, *The CEO for 23andMe Says Every Company Should Hire One Woman for Every Man*, QUARTZ AT WORK (Feb. 6, 2018), https://work.qz.com/1191990/23andme-ceo-anne-wojcicki-says-every-company-should-hire-one-woman-for-every-man/.
21. Id.
22. Id.
23. Id.
24. Knowledge@Wharton, *The FDA vs. 23andMe: A Lesson for Health Care Entrepreneurs*, WHARTON BUSINESS SCHOOL, UNIVERSITY OF PENNSYLVANIA (Dec. 18, 2013), http://knowledge.wharton.upenn.edu/article/fda-vs-23andme-lesson-health-care-entrepreneurs/. (quoting Reed Pyeritz, Professor of Medicine and Chief of the Division of Medical Genetics at the Perelman School of Medicine at the University of Pennsylvania).
25. Id.
26. Richard Epstein, *The FDA Strikes Again: Its Ban on Home Testing Kits Is, as Usual, Likely to Do More Harm Than Good*, POINT OF LAW (Nov. 27, 2013), http://www.pointoflaw.com/archives/2013/11/t.php.
27. Editorial, *The FDA and Me*, 504 NATURE 7, 8 (2013).
28. Robert C. Green and Nita A Farahany, *Regulation: The FDA Is Overcautious on Consumer Genomics*, 505 NATURE 286, 286 (2014).
29. Sorrell, et al. v. IMS Health Inc., et al., 564 U.S. 552 (2011).
30. United States v. Caronia, 703 F.3d 149 (2nd Cir. 2012).
31. David Dobbs, *The F.D.A. vs. Personal Genetic Testing*, THE NEW YORKER (Nov. 27, 2013), https://www.newyorker.com/tech/elements/the-f-d-a-vs-personal-genetic-testing.

32. Matthew Herper, *What 23andMe's FDA Approval Means for the Future of Genomics*, FORBES (Feb. 20, 2015), https://www.forbes.com/sites/matthewherper/2015/02/20/what-23andmes-fda-approval-means-for-the-future-of-genomics/#431efbb65ffb.
33. Id.
34. Jane E. Brody, *Personal Health: Do-It-Yourself Pregnancy Tests Have Advantages, but Need Care*, NEW YORK TIMES, Feb. 1, 1978, at 11.
35. Pagan Kennedy, *Could Women Be Trusted With Their Own Pregnancy Tests?* NEW YORK TIMES, July 31, 2016, at SR1.
36. Id.
37. Id.
38. Jane E. Brody, *Personal Health: Do-it-yourself pregnancy tests have advantages, but need care*, NEW YORK TIMES, Feb. 1, 1978, at 11.
39. Michael J. Young et al., *Direct-to-Patient Laboratory Test Reporting Balancing Access With Effective Clinical Communication*, 312 J. AM. MED. ASSOC. 127, 127 (2014).
40. Kate Christensen and Valerie M. Sue, *Viewing Laboratory Test Results Online Patients' Actions and Reactions*, 5 J. PARTICIPAT. MED. (2013).
41. 29 U.S. Code § 1181; 42 U.S.C. § 300gg; 42 U.S.C. § 1320d
42. Tom Delbanco and Jan Walker, *Modern Healthcare: Patients Should Have Easier Access to Their Doctors' Medical Notes*, OPEN NOTES (Nov. 7, 2011), https://www.opennotes.org/news/modern-healthcare-patients-should-have-easier-access-to-their-doctors-medical-notes/.
43. Tom Delbanco et al., *Open Notes: Doctors and Patients Signing On*, 153 ANN. INTERN. MED. 121 (2010).
44. Michael J. Young et al., *Direct-to-Patient Laboratory Test Reporting Balancing Access With Effective Clinical Communication*, 312 J. AM. MED. ASSOC. 127, 128 (2014).
45. John Lumpkin, *Making Sense of the Debate Over Patient Access to Medical Information*, HEALTH CARE BLOG (Feb. 14, 2012), http://thehealthcareblog.com/blog/2012/02/14/making-sense-of-the-debate-over-patient-access-to-medical-information/.
46. Michael J. Young et al., *Direct-to-Patient Laboratory Test Reporting Balancing Access With Effective Clinical Communication*, 312 J. AM. MED. ASSOC. 127, 128 (2014).
47. Mike Miliard, *OpenNotes: "This Is Not a Software Package, This Is a Movement,"* HEALTHCARE IT NEWS (Jan. 8, 2015), https://www.healthcareitnews.com/news/opennotes-not-software-package-movement. (The M.D. Anderson Cancer Center and Mayo Clinic also implemented open notes broadly); Jan Walker et al., *The Road Toward Fully Transparent Medical Records*, 370 N. ENGL. J. MED. 6, 7 (2014).
48. Dan Munro, *New Poll Shows Two-Thirds of Doctors Reluctant to Share Health Data With Patients*, FORBES. (June 8, 2015), https://www.forbes.com/sites/danmunro/2015/06/08/two%E2%80%92thirds-of-doctors-are-reluctant-to-share-health-data-with-patients/.
49. Id.
50. Id.
51. Id.
52. Id.
53. Tom Delbanco et al., *Open Notes: Doctors and Patients Signing On*, 153 ANN. INTERN. MED. 121, 124 (2010).
54. Id. at 122.

55. Tom Delbanco et al., *Inviting Patients to Read Their Doctors' Notes: A Quasi-Experimental Study and a Look Ahead*, 157 ANN INTERN MED. 461 (2012).
56. Id. at 466.
57. Ken Terry, *Patient Records: The Struggle for Ownership*, MEDICAL ECONOMICS (Dec. 10, 2015), https://www.medicaleconomics.com/health-law-policy/patient-records-struggle-ownership; Robert Wachter, THE DIGITAL DOCTOR: HOPE, HYPE, AND HARM AT THE DAWN OF MEDICINE'S COMPUTER AGE 264 (2015).
58. ROBERT WACHTER, THE DIGITAL DOCTOR: HOPE, HYPE, AND HARM AT THE DAWN OF MEDICINE'S COMPUTER AGE 184 (2015).
59. Dan Munro, *New Poll Shows Two-Thirds of Doctors Reluctant to Share Health Data With Patients*, FORBES. (June 8, 2015), https://www.forbes.com/sites/danmunro/2015/06/08/two%E2%80%92thirds-of-doctors-are-reluctant-to-share-health-data-with-patients/.
60. David M. Culter, *Why Medicine Will Be More Like Walmart*, MIT TECHNICAL REVIEW (Sept. 20, 2013), https://www.technologyreview.com/s/518906/why-medicine-will-be-more-like-walmart/; Vinod Khosla, *The Reinvention of Medicine: Dr. Algorithm V0-7 and Beyond*, TECH CRUNCH (Sept. 22, 2014), https://techcrunch.com/2014/09/22/the-reinvention-of-medicine-dr-algorithm-version-0-7-and-beyond/. See also Steve Dubner, *Transcript: Bad Medicine, Part 1: The Story of 98.6*, FREAKONOMICS (Nov. 20, 2016), http://freakonomics.com/podcast/bad-medicine-part-1-story-98-6/ (describing the hostility with which medical professionals responded to the Cochrane Collaboration, "the first organization to really systematize, compile, and evaluate the best evidence for given medical questions").
61. Vinod Khosla, *"20-Percent Doctor Included" & Dr. Algorithm: Speculations and Musings of a Technology Optimist*, KHOSLA VENTURES 2–4 (Sept. 16, 2016), https://www.khoslaventures.com/wp-content/uploads/20-Percent-Doctor-Included.pdf.
62. Id. at 4.
63. Id. at 18–20.
64. Dominick L. Frosch et al., *Authoritarian Physicians And Patients' Fear Of Being Labeled 'Difficult' Among Key Obstacles To Shared Decision Making*, 31 HEALTH AFF. 1030, 1032 (2012).
65. Id. at 1033.
66. Id. at 1035.
67. Id.
68. ROBERT WACHTER, THE DIGITAL DOCTOR: HOPE, HYPE, AND HARM AT THE DAWN OF MEDICINE'S COMPUTER AGE 177 (2015).
69. Dominick L. Frosch et al., *Authoritarian Physicians And Patients' Fear Of Being Labeled "Difficult" Among Key Obstacles To Shared Decision Making*, 31 HEALTH AFF. 1030, 1035 (2012).
70. ERIC TOPOL, THE PATIENT WILL SEE YOU NOW: THE FUTURE OF MEDICINE IS IN YOUR HANDS 145 (2015).
71. Id. at 145–152.
72. Jonathan P. Weiner et al., *The Impact of Health Information Technology and e-Health on the Future Demand for Physician Services*, 32 HEALTH AFF. 1998, 2001 (2013).
73. Id.
74. Rena Xu, *The Doctor Will See You Onscreen*, THE NEW YORKER (Mar. 10, 2014), https://www.newyorker.com/business/currency/the-doctor-will-see-you-onscreen.

75. Eric Topol, The Patient Will See You Now: The Future of Medicine is in Your Hands 163 (2015).
76. Vinod Khosla, *"20-Percent Doctor Included" & Dr. Algorithm: Speculations and Musings of a Technology Optimist*, Khosla Ventures 2 (Sept. 16, 2016), https://www.khoslaventures.com/wp-content/uploads/20-Percent-Doctor-Included.pdf.
77. Id. (Khosla reasserted this point in 2017, most particularly with respect to radiologists who, he said, will be obsolete in five years because "there's no reason a human should be doing it."); Christina Farr, *Here's Why One Tech Investor Thinks Some Doctors Will Be "Obsolete" in Five Years*, CNBC (Apr. 7, 2017), https://www.cnbc.com/2017/04/07/vinod-khosla-radiologists-obsolete-five-years.html.
78. Id.
79. Robert Wachter, The Digital Doctor: Hope, Hype, and Harm at the Dawn of Medicine's Computer Age 53–55 (2015).
80. Matt Marshall, *Vinod Khosla Says Technology Will Replace 80 Percent of Doctors—Sparks Indignation*, Venture Beat (Sept. 2, 2012), https://venturebeat.com/2012/09/02/vinod-khosla-says-technology-will-replace-80-percent-of-doctors-sparks-indignation/.
81. Id.
82. Jill Lepore, *The Disruption Machine*, The New Yorker, June 23, 2014, at 2.
83. Clayton M. Christensen et al., *Will Disruptive Innovations Cure Health Care?*, Harvard Bus. Rev. (Sept.–Oct. 2000), https://hbr.org/2000/09/will-disruptive-innovations-cure-health-care.
84. See, e.g., Jason Hwang and Clayton M. Christensen, *Disruptive Innovation in Health Care Delivery: A Framework for Business-Model Innovation*, 27 Health Aff. 1329 (2008).
85. Id.
86. Clayton M. Christensen et al., *Will Disruptive Innovations Cure Health Care?*, Harvard Bus. Rev. (Sept. - Oct. 2000), https://hbr.org/2000/09/will-disruptive-innovations-cure-health-care.
87. Eric Topol, The Patient Will See You Now: The Future of Medicine is in Your Hands 183–193 (2015).
88. Robert Wachter, The Digital Doctor: Hope, Hype, and Harm at the Dawn of Medicine's Computer Age 258–260 (2015).
89. Id. at 108.
90. Id. at 110.
91. Id. at 108.
92. Vinod Khosla, *"20-Percent Doctor Included" & Dr. Algorithm: Speculations and Musings of a Technology Optimist*, Khosla Ventures 102–103 (Sept. 16, 2016), https://www.khoslaventures.com/wp-content/uploads/20-Percent-Doctor-Included.pdf.
93. Id. at 103.
94. Robert Wachter, The Digital Doctor: Hope, Hype, and Harm at the Dawn of Medicine's Computer Age 8 (2015).
95. Id. at 39–41.
96. Id.
97. Abraham Verghese, *Treat the Patient, Not the CT Scan*, New York Times, Feb. 27, 2011, at WK10.

98. ROBERT WACHTER, THE DIGITAL DOCTOR: HOPE, HYPE, AND HARM AT THE DAWN OF MEDICINE'S COMPUTER AGE 24–25 (2015). (quoting Arnold Relman, retired editor of the *New England Journal of Medicine*).
99. Id. at 215–216.
100. Health Information Technology for Economic and Clinical Health (HITECH) Act, Pub. L. No. 111-5, Title XIII, 123 Stat. 226 (2009).
101. CENTERS FOR MEDICARE & MEDICAID SERVICES, *Data and Program Reports*, https://www.cms.gov/regulations-and-guidance/legislation/ehrincentiveprograms/dataandreports.html.
102. ROBERT WACHTER, THE DIGITAL DOCTOR: HOPE, HYPE, AND HARM AT THE DAWN OF MEDICINE'S COMPUTER AGE 209 (2015).
103. Dean F. Sittig and Hardeep Singh, *Electronic Health Records and National Patient-Safety Goals*, 367 N. ENGL. J. MED. 1854, 1857 (2012); Ashish K. Jha and David C. Classen, *Getting Moving on Patient Safety—Harnessing Electronic Data for Safer Care*, 365 N. ENGL. J. MED. 1756, 1757 (2011).
104. Jamie Cattell et al., *How Big Data Can Revolutionize Pharmaceutical R&D*, MCKINSEY & COMPANY (Apr. 2003), https://www.mckinsey.com/industries/pharmaceuticals-and-medical-products/our-insights/how-big-data-can-revolutionize-pharmaceutical-r-and-d (noting that "applying big-data strategies to better inform decision making could generate up to $100 billion in value annually across the US health-care system, by optimizing innovation, improving the efficiency of research and clinical trials, and building new tools for physicians, consumers, insurers, and regulators to meet the promise of more individualized approaches.")
105. Jerry Maynor, *Leveraging Electronic Health Record Data for Marketing Research*, PM360 (July 1, 2012), https://www.pm360online.com/leveraging-electronic-health-record-data-for-marketing-research/(noting the importance of privacy considerations and data availability).
106. ROBERT WACHTER, THE DIGITAL DOCTOR: HOPE, HYPE, AND HARM AT THE DAWN OF MEDICINE'S COMPUTER AGE 88–90 (2015).
107. Micheline Maynard, *The $2 Billion Toll of GM's Defect Coverup*, FORBES (Sept. 17, 2015), https://www.forbes.com/sites/michelinemaynard/2015/09/17/the-2-billion-toll-of-gms-defect-coverup/
108. Hiroko Tabuchi, *Takata Saw and Hid Risk in Airbags in 2004, Former Workers Say*, NEW YORK TIMES (Nov. 6, 2014), https://www.nytimes.com/2014/11/07/business/airbag-maker-takata-is-said-to-have-conducted-secret-tests.html; Press Release, Department of Justice, Takata Corporation Agrees to Plead Guilty and Pay $1 Billion in Criminal Penalties for Airbag Scheme (Jan. 13, 2017).
109. Dean F. Sittig and Hardeep Singh, *Electronic Health Records and National Patient-Safety Goals*, 367 N. ENGL. J. MED. 1854, 1857 (2012).
110. Ross Koppel and David Kreda, *Health Care Information Technology Vendors' "Hold Harmless" Clause: Implications for Patients and Clinicians*, 301 J. AM. MED. ASSOC. 1276 (2009).
111. Hospital Survey and Construction Act ("Hill–Burton Act"), Pub. L. No. 79-725, § 2, 60 Stat. 1041 (1946) (as amended 42 U.S.C. §§ 291-291o (1976)).
112. Hill–Burton Act, 42 U.S.C. § 291(e) ("that the State plan shall provide for adequate hospitals, and other facilities for which aid under this part is available, for all

persons residing in the State, and adequate hospitals (and such other facilities) to furnish needed services for persons unable to pay therefor").

113. Dean F. Sittig and Hardeep Singh, *Electronic Health Records and National Patient-Safety Goals*, 367 N. ENGL. J. MED. 1854 (2012); Linda Harrington et al., *Safety Issues Related to the Electronic Medical Record (EMR): Synthesis of the Literature from the Last Decade, 2000-2009*, 56 J. HEALTHCARE MANAG. 31 (2011).

114. Vimla L. Patel et al., *The Coming of Age of Artificial Intelligence in Medicine*, 46 ARTIF. INTELL. MED. 5, 8 (2009).

115. ROBERT WACHTER, THE DIGITAL DOCTOR: HOPE, HYPE, AND HARM AT THE DAWN OF MEDICINE'S COMPUTER AGE 106–109 (2015).

116. Id. at 111–113.

117. Angela Townsend, *Cleveland Clinic, IBM Launch New Watson Project to Find New Treatment Options for Cancer Patients*, CLEVELAND.COM (Oct. 29, 2014), www.cleveland.com/healthfit/index.ssf/2014/10/cleveland_clinic_ibm_to_begin.html.

118. ROBERT WACHTER, THE DIGITAL DOCTOR: HOPE, HYPE, AND HARM AT THE DAWN OF MEDICINE'S COMPUTER AGE 112 (2015).

119. David H. Freedman, *A Reality Check for IBM's AI Ambitions*, MIT TECH. REV. (June 27, 2017), https://www.technologyreview.com/s/607965/a-reality-check-for-ibms-ai-ambitions/.

120. D.E. Newman-Toker and P.J. Pronovost, *Diagnostic Errors—The Next Frontier for Patient Safety*, 249 J. AM. MED. ASSOC. 1060, 1060 (2009).

121. K.G. Shojania et al., *Changes in Rates of Autopsy-Detected Diagnostic Errors Over Time: A Systematic Review*, 289 J. AM. MED. ASSOC. 2849 (2003).

122. Vinod Khosla, *"20-Percent Doctor Included" & Dr. Algorithm: Speculations and Musings of a Technology Optimist*, KHOSLA VENTURES 2–4 (Sept. 16, 2016), https://www.khoslaventures.com/wp-content/uploads/20-Percent-Doctor-Included.pdf.

123. Julian De Freitas et al., *Vulnerabilities to Misinformation in Online Pharmaceutical Marketing*, 106 J. ROYAL SOC. MED. 184 (2013).

124. Kate Monica, *Clinical Decision Support Tools Reduce Re-Hospitalizations*, EHR INTELLIGENCE (Feb. 7, 2017), https://ehrintelligence.com/news/clinical-decision-support-tools-reduce-re-hospitalizations.

125. ROBERT WACHTER, THE DIGITAL DOCTOR: HOPE, HYPE, AND HARM AT THE DAWN OF MEDICINE'S COMPUTER AGE 110 (2015).

126. William H. Frist, *Connected Health and the Rise of the Patient-Consumer*, 33 HEALTH AFF. 191 (2014).

127. ERIC TOPOL, THE PATIENT WILL SEE YOU NOW: THE FUTURE OF MEDICINE IS IN YOUR HANDS 5 (2015).

128. Id. at 165–172.

129. Matthew Herper, *In Big Shift, 23andMe Will Invent Drugs Using Customer Data*, FORBES (Mar. 12, 2015), https://www.forbes.com/sites/matthewherper/2015/03/12/23andme-enters-the-drug-business-just-as-apple-changes-it/#7538d4eb2cb3.

130. Drew Laing, *Telemedicine Causing Controversy in Some U.S. States*, NEXTECH (June 9, 2016), www.nextech.com/blog/telemedicine-causing-controversy-in-some-u.s.-states.

131. Eric Wicklund, *Texas Takes Heat for Its Telemedicine Restrictions*, mHEALTH INTELLIGENCE (Jan. 7, 2016), https://mhealthintelligence.com/news/texas-takes-heat-for-its-telemedicine-restrictions. *See also* Brian Dear, *Crossing the Line: A*

Legal Argument for Interstate Online Therapy, iCouch: Therapy Simple (May 15, 2017), https://simple.icouch.me/blog/crossing-the-line-a-legal-argument-for-interstate-online-therapy (discussing how the practice of medicine is interstate commerce, which can be regulated by Congress.)
132. Id.
133. Rena Xu, *The Doctor Will See You Onscreen*, The New Yorker (Mar. 10, 2014), https://www.newyorker.com/business/currency/the-doctor-will-see-you-onscreen.
134. Eric Wicklund, *Texas Takes Heat for Its Telemedicine Restrictions*, mHealth Intelligence (Jan. 7, 2016), https://mhealthintelligence.com/news/texas-takes-heat-for-its-telemedicine-restrictions.
135. Eric Topol, The Patient Will See You Now: The Future of Medicine is in Your Hands 113–118 (2015).
136. The Standards for Privacy of Individually Identifiable Health Information (Privacy Rule), The Health Insurance Portability and Accountability Act of 1996 (HIPAA), 45 CFR §§ 160 and 164.
137. Oct. 21, 1998, Pub. L. 105-277, Title V, § 516 ("None of the funds made available in this Act may be used to promulgate or adopt any final standard under section 1173(b) of the Social Security Act (42 U.S.C. 1320d–2(b)) providing for, or providing for the assignment of, a unique health identifier for an individual (except in an individual's capacity as an employer or a health care provider), until legislation is enacted specifically approving the standard"). But see Mary Butler, *Congress Eases Ban on Patient Identifier Development in Spending Package*, J. AHIMA (May 17, 2017), journal.ahima.org/2017/05/17/congress-eases-ban-on-patient-identifier-development-in-spending-package/ (discussing Congress's loosening of an almost 20-year ban on unique patient identifiers).
138. Vinod Khosla, *"20-Percent Doctor Included" & Dr. Algorithm: Speculations and Musings of a Technology Optimist*, Khosla Ventures 33 (Sept. 16, 2016), https://www.khoslaventures.com/wp-content/uploads/20-Percent-Doctor-Included.pdf.
139. Robert Wachter, The Digital Doctor: Hope, Hype, and Harm at the Dawn of Medicine's Computer Age 275 (2015).

Epilogue
1. Theodor Seuss Geisel (Dr. Seuss), quoted in Miles Corwin, *Author Isn't Just a Cat in the Hat*, The Los Angeles Times (Nov. 27, 1983).
2. Sidney Dekker, Patient Safety: A Human Factors Approach, 33–34 (2011).

INDEX

Tables and figures are indicated by *t* and *f* following the page number

For the benefit of digital users, indexed terms that span two pages (e.g., 52–53) may, on occasion, appear on only one of those pages.

Accident Compensation Corporation, 82
accident law. *See* medical accident subspecies of tort law; tort law
accidents, 72. *See also* medical accidents
 systems nature of, 183–84
accountability and liability, 188–89
acute myocardial infarction (AMI), 116
adverse events. *See also specific topics*
 defined, 27
 disaggregating, 32 (*see also* healthcare-associated infections)
  diagnosis, 36–38
  medication, 34–36
  treatment, 32–33
Agency for Health Care Policy and Research (AHCPR), 17, 201–4
 spinal fusion guidelines, 17, 202–5, 224–25
Agency for Healthcare Research and Quality (AHRQ), 17, 20–21, 138, 142–43, 204, 231–32. *See also* Patient Safety Indicators (PSI) instrument
 Center for Patient Safety, 147
airplane travel. *See* aviation
ambulance service, Medicare payment for, 161
American Hospital Association, 134–35
American Medical Association (AMA), 11–12, 105, 197, 235, 236
 AHCPR and, 203, 204

Code of Medical Ethics, 104–5
 National Patient Safety Foundation (NPSF) and, 17–18
 opposition to devolution, 245
 Patient Compensation System (PCS) and, 94
 on tort law, 92
American Psychiatric Association, 147
anchoring (heuristic), 110
anesthesiologists, 85–86, 182–83
Annenberg Center for Health Sciences, meetings at, 17–18
Ariely, Dan, 44
Aronson, Elliot, 38
artificial intelligence (AI) diagnostic systems, 233, 257–58
 diagnostic algorithms, 245, 246–47
 doctors' fear of, 246–47
 and safety, 246–47, 252–54
assumption of the risk, 58, 273n24
attorney filtering of cases, 61–62
 portion of cases that they reject, 62
attorneys advising doctors how to practice (defensive) medicine, 103
auditing of medical records, 213, 217, 222, 226
automobile regulation, 195–200, 205–6. *See also* National Highway Traffic Safety Administration
automobiles, 60
autonomy of health professionals, 216–17

availability heuristic, 110
aviation
    error reporting in, 126–28
    medicine and, 127, 128, 186, 259–60
        practices to achieve competency and maintain proficiency in, 180, 181*t*
Aviation Safety Reporting System (ASRS), 127–29, 150
Avraham, Ronen, 117
Axelrod, David, 27, 209–11

back pain, 202–3
Baicker, Katherine, 117
Baker, Tom, 78–79, 195–96
Barzilay, Regina, 144
Batson, C. Daniel, 290n55
battery, 42, 104, 269n77
Bazell, Robert, 19
behavioral economics, 155–58
Bell Commission, 227–28
Black, Bernard, 85–86
blaming (the other person or entity), 61
Bosk, Charles L., 131, 134
Brennan, Troyen A., 20, 47, 130–31, 132
Bush, George W., 20–21
bypass surgery. *See* coronary artery bypass grafting

CABG. *See* coronary artery bypass grafting
California Medical Association and California Hospital Association (CMA/CHA), 93–94
    CMA/CHA study, 24–26, 47
caps. *See* damages caps
Cardiac Advisory Committee, 210–11, 213, 221
cardiac arrest, 143
cardiac procedures, 15–16, 116. *See also* cardiovascular surgery
    tort reform and, 117, 118
    unnecessary, 43, 224
cardiac treatment registry. *See* coronary artery bypass grafting (CABG) registry
cardiovascular disease, 116
cardiovascular surgery, 220–21. *See also* coronary artery bypass grafting
    unnecessary, 224

Carrier, Emily, 122
carrier status, 238–39
carrier testing, 238
Cavar, Lucas, 80–81
Center for Patient Safety of AHRQ, 147
Centers for Medicare & Medicaid Services (CMS), 147–48, 165, 168, 170, 171, 172, 224–25, 232, 255–56
    denial-of-payment programs, 165, 166
    list of no-pay never-events, 166–67
    "no pay" policy for selected never-events, 147–48, 167–68, 171
cesarean sections (C-sections), 103, 115, 118, 288n21, 291–92n70
Chandra, Amitabh, 117
charitable immunity doctrine, 58
charts. *See* medical records
Chassin, Mark, 15–16, 49, 219
choice overload, 156
Christensen, Clayton, 245–46
claiming (recompense), 61
Claybrook, Joan, 199–200
clinical scenario surveys. *See under* defensive medicine: types of studies on
Clostridium difficile (*C. difficile*), 34
Codman, Ernest, 207
cognitive heuristics, 157
compensation. *See also specific topics*
    securing, 78–80
"complications." *See* surgical/procedural complications
computerized medical records. *See* electronic health records
computer tomography (CT) scans, unnecessary, 43–44, 46–47
Consensus Development Program (CDP), 145–46
conspiracy of silence, 125, 134
coronary artery bypass grafting (CABG), 171*t*
coronary artery bypass grafting (CABG) registry, New York's, 223, 224–25, 226–27, 230, 231
    achievements, 220–21
    conditions for success, 221–22
    engaged statistical surveillance and public disclosure, 210–14

Index 329

professional backlash against the program, 214–20
before the program, 207–9
reasons for establishment of, 209–10
as a "report card," 222–23
corrective justice, theory of, 272n9
Cosgrove, Toby, 218
Crane, Margaret, 239–40
"crew resource management," 143
criminal fraud, 104. *See also* fraud
criminal law vs. tort law, 52–54, 80, 271n8, 281n40
criminal prosecution, 42–43, 94, 281n40
crowding out, 155–56

damages caps, 70, 71, 85, 95–96, 117–18, 292–93n77 *See also* noneconomic damages caps
noneconomic, 12, 15, 95, 116, 118
Danzon, Patricia, 12–13, 25–26
Darley, John M., 290n55
Dartmouth Atlas, The, 46–47
Dartmouth Institute for Health Policy and Clinical Practice, 45, 46–47, 224
death. *See also specific topics*
defensive medicine and patient mortality, 118
portion of adverse events that cause, 28t, 28–29, 30, 32–34, 39–40, 41
U.S. death rate, 191, 192f
deaths caused by medical care, 47–49. *See also specific topics*
from diagnostic errors, 37–38, 40
goal of "zero preventable deaths," 138
in hospitals, 25, 28t, 30, 32–34, 37–38, 39–40, 47
from medication errors, 41
in outpatient care, 40–42
preventable/avoidable, 31, 47, 121
savings from deaths prevented, 121
decision architecture, 156–57
designing better, 156
decision support systems, clinical, 157
defensive medicine, 117
benefits, 121
costs, 100, 106, 107, 108–9, 110, 111–12, 116, 117, 121–22

David Hyman and Charles Silver on, 122
definitions, 99, 103, 108–9, 286n2
goal of, 104
Michelle Mello on, 120–21
nature of, 99–100
and patient mortality, 118
"positive" vs. "negative," 108
reasons for admitting to engaging in, 101, 104–7
reasons for engaging in, 101–4, 105–6
scope of the term, 103–4
as a tool for advocacy, 100–1
tort reform and, 106, 116, 122, 294n109
types of studies on, 109
clinical scenario surveys, 109, 112–13
direct physician surveys, 109–12
multivariate statistical analyses, 109, 114–19
what we do and do not know about, 99–100, 107–9, 120–21
"Defensive Medicine Is Good Medicine" (Bergen), 105–6
Dekker, Sydney, 182–83, 259–60
Delbanco, Tom, 242
denial-of-payment programs, 165–66, 168, 170, 172–73
Department of Health, Education and Welfare (HEW), 26
Department of Health and Human Services (DHHS/HHS), 89, 126, 169, 241, 248
deterrence, 75
general, 85–86
meanings of the term, 54, 80
vs. retribution, 78
in tort vs. criminal law, 54
deterrent value of tort law, 56, 78–79, 80, 84, 85–86, 87
anecdotal evidence on the, 86–87
deterrence as purpose of tort law, 54, 78–79, 80
empirical studies of tort deterrence, 81–82, 84–85
organizations, individuals, and the, 80–81
overdeterrence, 86–87
(*see also* defensive medicine)

"devolution," 245, 246
Deyo, Richard, 203
diagnosis, 86. *See also* artificial intelligence (AI) diagnostic systems; misdiagnosis
diagnostic procedures, unnecessary. *See* unnecessary diagnostic procedures
disability caused by adverse events, 28*t*, 28–29
    permanent, 25, 28*t*, 28–29, 30, 93–94
disability insurance, 72
dishonesty. *See also* fraud
    experiments examining, 44
doctors
    "good" vs. "bad," 53 (*see also* "rotten apple" doctors)
    refusing to treat the sickest patients, 214, 215, 217–18 (*see also* outmigration of patients)
doctors' fears
    of artificial intelligence (AI) diagnostic systems, 246–47
    of malpractice litigation, 84–85, 99, 122–23 (*see also* defensive medicine)
    tort reform and, 99, 122
Dranove, David, 215, 216–17, 218, 219
Duncan, Thomas Eric, 5–9

Eappen, Sunil, 161–62
Ebola virus disease
    diagnosis, 250
    EHR systems and, 249, 250
    medical errors and, 249
    Thomas Duncan and the Dallas crisis, 5–9, 37, 249
education of healthcare providers, 142–50
electroconvulsive therapy (ECT), 147
electronic capture, 248–49
electronic health records (EHRs), 243
    benefits of, 38, 223, 230, 233, 244, 245, 248–49, 250, 253, 257
    safety, 39–40, 248–52, 253
    and billing, 245, 247, 249
    costs of moving to, 248–49, 257–58
    criticisms of, 247–48, 257
    and "devolution," 245, 246

EHR sharing between healthcare providers, 7, 249, 256
EHR systems, 9, 39–40, 247–50, 251, 252
Eric Duncan's EHR, 5, 7
funding for, 248–49
objectives, 248–49, 257
patients' access to their, 244, 247–48, 249
prevalence, 245
and privacy, 250–51, 256–57
risks associated with, 38, 252
the shift to and adoption of, 233, 245, 247–49
Employee Retirement Security Act (ERISA), 14
enterprise liability and enterprise insurance, 173–75, 192–93, 307n71
Epstein, Arnold, 212–13
Epstein, Richard, 237–38
error, medical
    confronting and deflecting the costs of harm, 15–18
    defined, 264–65n2
    discovering and ignoring a problem, 12–13
    incidence and magnitude of the problem, 47–49
    tolerance for, 138
    types of, 32*t*, 32
"Error in Medicine" (Leape), 16, 177–78, 270n105 *See also* Leape, Lucian
error reporting, 149–50
    acquiring and using safety reports in healthcare, 128–31
    in aviation, 126–28
    cultural barriers to, 131–35
ethics, medical
    defensive medicine and, 104–5
    genetic testing and, 234–36
externalities, 79–80, 153, 154, 163–65, 272n17
    defined, 272n17, 279n7

Federal Aviation Administration (FAA), 126–27, 150
Federal Trade Commission (FTC), 235, 245, 255–56

Index

fellow servant doctrine, 58, 272n23
file drawer problem, 109
Food and Drug Administration (FDA) and 23andMe, 236–39, 255
Forgive and Remember: Managing Medical Failure (Bosk), 131, 134
Frakes, Michael D., 86, 118–19, 121
fraud, 107, 114, 120. *See also* upcoding
  billing for needless services as, 104
  defensive medicine and, 104–5, 107, 114, 119–20, 122
  defined, 269n77, 288n24
  duty to report, 104–5
  insurance, 107
  Medicare and, 114
  unnecessary treatment as, 42, 107, 120 (*see also* unnecessary treatment)
fraudulent billing, 114
fraudulent changes in medical records, 38
Frist, William, 255

Galanter, Marc, 59–60
Galbraith, John Kenneth, 89
Gawande, Atul A., 64, 103, 113, 123, 159, 161–62
General Accounting Office (GAO) report on statistical surveillance and ranking programs, 214–15
genetic testing, 233–36, 237, 239–40. *See also* 23andMe
Gingrich, Newt, 203–4
Glass. *See* Google Glass EE
global trigger algorithms, 249
Global Trigger Tool, 39–40, 47, 49
global trigger tools, 251
Google Glass EE (Enterprise Edition), 144–45
governmental surveillance
  engaged, 205–25
  of medical matters, 206
government guidelines in medicine, 201–5
government safety regulation. *See also* legal innovations
  shortcomings of, 195–205
Griner, Paul, 211
Gruber, Jonathan, 118–19, 121

Haddon, William, 198
Haidt, Jonathan, 290n55
Hannan, David L., 210, 218, 219, 222
Harvard Medical Practice Study (HMPS), 26–27, 87
  findings, 33, 35, 37, 87–89
  HMPS approach to records review, 31
Health, Education and Welfare, U.S. Department of, 26
Health and Human Services. *See* Department of Health and Human Services
healthcare-associated infections (HAIs)
  acquired in ICUs, 231–32
  costs, 34
  epidemiology, 33–34
  prevention, 34, 303n22
Health Care Financing Administration (HCFA), 202, 207–9, 210, 213, 217. *See also* coronary artery bypass grafting (CABG) registry
healthcare organizations, 80–81, 162–63. *See also* incentives: innovative sources of
health care sector, need for cultural transformation in, 140
Health Information Technology for Economic and Clinical Health Act. *See* HITECH program
health insurance, 14. See also *Report on the Medical Insurance Feasibility Study*
  coverage and quality of medical care, 160–61
  insurance fraud, 107
health insurance companies. *See also* managed care
  refusal to pay/denial of payment, 160
Health Insurance Portability and Accountability Act of 1996 (HIPAA), 18, 134, 240–41, 256
health maintenance organizations (HMOs), 14
Health Management Associates (HMA), 43
health systems reform, legal innovations to promote, 192–93
HITECH program, 248–49, 251
honesty. *See* dishonesty

Hospital-Acquired Conditions (HAC) Reduction Program, 168–70
hospital-acquired infections. *See* healthcare-associated infections
Hospital Corporation of America (HCA), 43
Hospital Readmissions Reduction Program (HRRP), 170–73
hospital records. *See* medical records
hospitals. *See also specific topics*
   beyond, 40–42
   teaching, 43–44, 170, 217 (*see also* resident duty hours)
Howard, Philip, 100–1
Hyman, David A., 96
   on the culture of medicine, 138
   on defensive medicine, 122
   on malpractice cases, 67–68, 100–1, 154
   on malpractice insurance, 154
   on medical error (rates), 49, 138, 154
   on physician habits and beliefs and lawsuit risk, 122–23
   on safety, 154, 155
   on tort law and communication in healthcare industry, 96
   on tort reform, 122, 154
hyperbolic discounting, 156

Iacocca, Lee, 53
iatrogenic harm, 12, 265n6
   defined, 12
iatrogenic injury tax, 165
Improving Diagnosis in Healthcare (IOM report), 37
inadvertence, beyond. *See* unnecessary treatment
incentives (for safety), 153–55. *See also* perverse incentives
   innovative sources of, 163–75
   what the law could do, 162–63 (*see also* legal innovations)
income/earnings, estimating the value of future lost, 69, 70*f*
Indiana University Caving Club, 80–81
individual factors contributing to injuries, 185–86
inertia, 156. *see also under* legal innovations: to promote patient safety
infections, 191, 192*f See also* Ebola virus disease; healthcare-associated infections
   misdiagnosis, 36–38
information technology, 144–45. *See also* artificial intelligence (AI) diagnostic systems; electronic health records
   dangers introduced by, 256–58
   deeper roots of resistance to, 243–46
   what mainstream medicine has done with, 246–48
injuries. *See also* error; *specific topics*
   stages of emotionally processing, 61
   studies of, based on patient records, 26–31
innovations, legal. *See* legal innovations
Institute of Medicine (IOM), 17–18, 126–27, 130–31
   reports, 36, 37, 40, 48 (see also *To Err Is Human*)
intensive care units (ICUs), 147, 157–58
   infections acquired in, 231–32
   misdiagnoses and missed diagnoses in, 37–38
intentional harm, 53, 80. *See also* unnecessary treatment
Intermountain Healthcare, 162, 165
Internal Bleeding: The Truth Behind America's Terrifying Epidemic of Medical Mistakes (Wachter and Shojania), 93, 132, 233
Isabel (AI system), 246–47, 252
ischemic heart disease (IHD), 116

Jackson HealthCare, 111
Jackson Health System, 100–1
James, Brent, 162
James, John, 47
Jena, Anupam, 86
Jha, Ashish, 212–13
Johns Hopkins University School of Medicine, 157–58, 224, 231–32
   Internal Medicine Residency program, 228

Johnson, Lyndon Baines, 198
joint and several liability vs. proportionate share liability, 116–17, 292n70, 292–93n77
Joint Commission on Accreditation of Healthcare Organizations (JCAHO/Joint Commission), 18, 225–26, 228
    impact, 226, 230
    never-event program, 134–35, 225–26
    sentinel event program, 18, 20, 125–26, 134–35, 225–26
    shortcomings and limitations, 134–35, 209–10, 226
    voluntary reporting program, 134–35
judge-jury concordance (trial verdicts), 66–67
judgment errors, 185–86

Kachalia, Allen, 95, 96
Kahneman, Daniel, 180
Kessler, Daniel, 116, 117, 215, 216–17
Keynes, John Maynard, 163–64
Khosla, Vinod, 245, 246, 247
King, Josie, 182
Kizer, Ken, 32–33

Lakdawalla, Darius N., 117–18
lawsuits. *See also* litigotiation process; *specific topics*
    vs. opened files, 273n33
Leape, Lucian L.
    on analogy between the airline industry and medicine, 127, 128
    Aviation Safety Reporting System (ASRS) and, 127, 128
    on medical error (rates), 13, 16, 47, 128, 177–78, 183–84, 186, 187, 264–65n2
    systems approach and, 177–78, 183–84
Leapfrog Group, 18, 167
legal innovations. *See also* government safety regulation; incentives: what the law could do
    to promote health systems reform, 192–93
    to promote patient safety, 137–39, 150–51 (*see also* error reporting)
    clinical practice guidelines and safe harbors, 148
    discover, disseminate, recommend, incentivize, 141–50
    education and training, 142
    general considerations, 139–41
    helping industry to coordinate, 145–46
    innovation registry, 141–42
    overcoming inertia, 146–47
    research support and research, 142–44
    restructuring perverse incentives, 147–48
    setting standards, 148–49
    technology, 144–45
Lehman, Betsy, 16, 17, 132–33
Lester, Mark, 6–7
Lewin, Kurt, 180
liability insurance, 71. *See also* enterprise liability and enterprise insurance; medical malpractice insurance
liability insurance premiums, 100, 105, 117. *See also* medical malpractice insurance premiums
Liang, Matthew, 203
Libby Zion Law, 227–28
litigation, medical malpractice, 2, 15, 86. *See also* medical malpractice cases
    costs, 100
    diminishing, 9
    doctors' perceptions and fears of, 84–85, 99, 122–23 (*see also* defensive medicine)
    Michelle Mello on, 64, 65*f*, 87, 88–89, 120–21
    vs. no-fault system, 12, 94, 135–36 (*see also* no-fault compensation system)
    proposal to remove it from conventional courts, 100–1
    tort reform to curtail, 20–21
    viewed by doctors as greatest problem facing medicine, 131–32
litigation system, tort, 51–52, 66. *See also* tort law; *specific topics*
    behavior of the, 76–78
    according to the healthcare industry, 89–92

global comparisons, 83
and healthcare costs, 105
industry's (critical) pronouncements about, 89–91
and safety of healthcare, 80
securing reimbursement for losses suffered by victims of injury, 78–80
targeting the right events, 87–89
litigotiation process, elements of, 59–60, 71–73
adjustments following verdicts, 71
attorney filtering of cases, 61–62
compensation awards, 68–71
initiation of claims by victims, 60–61
pretrial disposition, 62–66 (*see also* settlement)
physician ratings of evidence and probability of payment to plaintiff, 64, 65*f*
trials, 65–66
verdicts, 66–68
little-rotten-apples problem, 18, 44–45
locality rule, 58–59, 86
loss aversion, 156
"lumping it," 51–52, 273n31
Lundberg, George, 16

Magliozzi, Bob, 42
Magliozzi, Ray, 42
Malinowski, Bronislaw, 102
malpractice. *See* medical malpractice
malpractice reform. *See* medical malpractice reform(s)
managed care, 14–15
and defensive medicine, 116, 117, 122
manslaughter, 53
Marshall, Mark, 216
Massachusetts, 27, 135
MATCH (Medications at Transitions and Clinical Handoffs), 142–43
Maude, Isabel, 246–47, 252
McCain, John, 229
McClellan, Mark, 116, 117, 215, 216–17
Medicaid. *See* Centers for Medicare & Medicaid Services
medical accidents, 54, 77–78
incidence, 127

medical accident subspecies of tort law, 58–59
medical error. *See* error
"medical facts" strategy, 15–16
Medical Injury Compensation Reform Act of 1975 (MICRA), 12, 15
medical malpractice, 131–33
incidence, 27–30
Medical Malpractice: Theory, Evidence and Public Policy (Danzon), 12–13, 25–26
medical malpractice cases. *See also* litigation
organizational defendants in, 80
resolution of, 63, 65–66
"medical malpractice crisis"
of early 1970s, 12, 23–24
of mid-1980s, 26
medical malpractice insurance, 78. *See also* enterprise liability and enterprise insurance; no-fault compensation system
insurance reforms, 91*t*
medical malpractice insurance claims, 29, 62–64
medical malpractice insurance companies, 29
malpractice settlements and, 65–66, 67–68
refusal to pay/denial of payment, 42, 165–66
for never events, 168
medical malpractice insurance policies, 65–66
medical malpractice insurance premiums, 15, 23–24, 100, 121, 154. *See also* liability insurance premiums
of anesthesiologists, 86
and defensive medicine, 117
factors that influence, 100, 114, 117, 154
patient safety, 86
physician refuse to settle, 65–66
tort reform, 15, 95, 154
Medicare and, 114, 117
"Medical Malpractice Litigation and Tort Reform: It's the Incentives, Stupid" (Hyman and Silver), 154
medical malpractice reform(s), 71, 95–96, 101. *See also* tort reform(s)

Index 335

economic impact, 101, 121
first-generation (promoted by healthcare organizations), 90–91, 91*t*, 95
second-generation (opposed by healthcare organizations), 90–91, 92*t*, 95
medical malpractice trials, 66
  compensation awards, 68–71
  verdicts/outcomes, 66–68, 128
medical records. *See also* electronic health records; Health Insurance Portability and Accountability Act of 1996
  auditing, 213, 217, 222, 226
  errors and injuries kept out of, 31, 38
  false information in, 43
  fraudulent changes in, 38
  keeping detailed and accurate, 105–6, 108
  limitations, 38
  patient access to, 240–42, 244, 247–48, 249 (*see also* genetic testing; Health Insurance Portability and Accountability Act of 1996; information technology)
  privacy and, 242–43
  reviews of, 35, 37, 38–40, 41, 47, 62, 114, 209–10, 218
  studies of medical errors and injuries based on, 26–31
medical resident work hours. *See* resident duty hours
Medicare, 11–12, 42–44, 202. *See also* Centers for Medicare & Medicaid Services
  costs/payments/spending, 34, 41, 42–43, 47, 117, 161, 167–68, 202
  tort reform and, 116–17, 118
  defensive medicine and, 104, 116
  fraud and, 114
  "never" list, 34
  refusal to pay, 167, 203
  skilled nursing facilities (SNFs) and, 41
Medicare/Medicaid EHR incentive program., 248–49
medication, 34–35, 39, 104
medication errors, 34–36, 39, 143–44, 184–85
  deaths caused by, 35–36, 41, 48
  incidence, 35–36, 40, 41, 48
  in outpatient care, 40, 41, 48
  prevention, 34–36, 41, 142–44
Medications at Transitions and Clinical Handoffs (MATCH), 142–43
"medicolegal concerns," 105
Meier, Joseph, 5, 7
Mello, Michelle M., 96
  on defensive medicine, 120–21
  on malpractice litigation, 64, 65*f*, 87, 88–89, 120–21
  on medical error, 64, 88, 138, 185–86
  on tort reform, 95
military treatment facilities (MTF), 119
Mills, Don Harper, 12, 23, 24–26, 38, 105
misdiagnosis. *See also* diagnosis
  in ICUs, 37–38
  of infections, 36–37
Mistakes Were Made (But Not by Me) (Tavris and Aronson), 38
Mongan, James, 121
mortality. *See* death
mortality and morbidity (M&M) conferences, 125–26, 131, 134
multivariate statistical analyses. *See under* defensive medicine: types of studies on
Munjal, Kevin, 153–54
myocardial infarction. *See* acute myocardial infarction

Nader, Ralph, 198–99
naming, blaming, and claiming (stages), 61
naming a harm (stage), 61
NASA (National Aeronautics and Space Administration), 17–18, 127, 150
National Highway Traffic Safety Administration (NHTSA), 198–200, 202, 204, 205
National Institutes of Health (NIH), 145–46
National Motor Vehicle Safety Act of 1966, 198
National Patient Safety Foundation (NPSF), 17–18

National Practitioner Data Bank (NPDB), 18, 32–33, 132, 134
National Quality Forum (NQF), 17–18, 166, 225–27
National Research Council, 146, 200
negative externalities, 164. *See also* externalities
negligence, 55–56, 58, 59. *See also specific topics*
   as a basis for criminal conviction, 271n8
   defining, 55, 59
negligent adverse events and claims in New York State, 29*t*, 29
negligent iatrogenic injuries, 265n6 *See also specific topics*
never-event program, Joint Commission, 134–35, 226
never-events, 129–31, 225–27
   CMS's list of no-pay, 166–67
   defined, 166
   incidence, 32–33
   nonpayment and denial of payment for, 167–68
   origin of the term, 32–33
   overview, 166–68
New York's cardiac treatment registry. *See* coronary artery bypass grafting (CABG) registry
New Zealand
   abolition of tort liability, 56, 82–83, 84, 135–36
   error disclosure and reporting in, 82–83, 135–36
   patient safety in, 83, 84
Nightingale, Florence, 207
Nissen, Steven, 43
no-fault approaches, 92*t*
no-fault auto insurance, 82, 83–84
no-fault compensation system, 24, 28–29, 82, 92*t*, 94. *See also* New Zealand: abolition of tort liability
   advantages, 96
   cost burden, 24, 25
   and doctors disclosing errors, 135–36
   legislation to enact, 12, 94
   and the number of compensated patients, 25
   tort law and, 55, 56, 272n9

no-fault program, efforts to enact, 12
noneconomic damages, 68, 69
noneconomic damages caps, 12, 15, 95, 116, 118
no-pay-for-never-events policy, 167–68
North American Spine Society, 203
nosocomial infections. *See* healthcare-associated infections
nudge, 156–57
nurses, 148–49
   transitional care, 172
nursing homes, 172, 256. *See also* skilled nursing facilities

Obama, Barack, 294n100
observing patient care, directly, 38–39
occupational safety. *See* workplace safety
opened file, 273n33, 274n40
OpenNotes, 241, 242–43
organizations. *See* healthcare organizations
Organon Pharmaceutical, 239–40
Orwell, George, 257
outmigration of patients, caused by refusal to treat them, 215, 217, 218, 219. *See also* doctors: refusing to treat the sickest patients
outmigration rates, 218
overconfidence bias, 156

Paik, Myungho, 118, 120
"pain-and-suffering" awards, 69. *See also* noneconomic damages
Patient Compensation System (PCS), 94, 178–79
Patient Protection and Affordable Care Act (ACA), 154–55, 168, 170
patients, providing medical information to. *See also* medical records: patient access to
   deeper roots of resistance to information technology and patient participation, 243–46
   healthcare industry resistance to, 239–43
Patient Safety: Achieving a New Standard for Care (IOM report), 248
Patient Safety and Quality Improvement Act, 226–27

Patient Safety Culture Survey, 143
Patient Safety Foundation, 138
Patient Safety Indicators (PSI) instrument, 85–86. *See also* Recalibrated PSI 90 Composite
peer review, 26, 125–26, 134, 147, 254
Perry, Rick, 6
perverse incentives, 158–62, 163, 175
   defined, 158–59
   restructuring, 147–48
Peterson, Eric D., 220–21
physician surveys. *See under* defensive medicine: types of studies on
Pigou, Arthur C., 163–64
Pigovian taxation, 163–66
Posner, Richard, 56–57
Poste, George, 189–90
pregnancy tests, home, 239–40
prepaying providers for performance, 156
Present on Admission (POA) Program, HAC's, 168
pretrial disposition. *See* settlement
prevention, 75. *See also specific topics*
   motivation for, 79, 80 (*see also* deterrence)
priming (psychology), 111
privacy, medical records and, 242–43, 250–51, 256–57. *See also* Health Insurance Portability and Accountability Act of 1996; information technology
private safety efforts and the surveillance model, 225–29
Pronovost, Peter, 157–58, 231–32
proportionate share liability, 116–17, 292n70, 292–93n77
punitive damages, 54

readmissions adjustment factor, 170–71
Reason, James, 149, 183
   principles of error management, 183, 184*t*
Recalibrated PSI 90 Composite, 169
reckless endangerment, 104, 288n25 *See also* manslaughter
records. *See* medical records
regulation. *See* government safety regulation

rehabilitation hospitals, 41
remittitur, 71
rent-seeking, 96, 154–55
report card programs, medical, 214–15, 216, 222–23
"report cards," 214–15, 216–17
   limitations and lack of efficacy, 215, 217, 222–23
   purpose, 223
Report on the Medical Insurance Feasibility Study, 24–26
reputation, professional, 131–32, 133, 221, 222–23
reputational concerns, 67, 133, 134, 223, 224, 229, 231
research (support), 142–44. *See also specific topics*
resident duty hours, limited to 80 per week, 227–29
res ipsa loquitur ("the thing speaks for itself"), 128
responsibility, refocusing of, 189
retained surgical instruments, 32–33, 147
Ribicoff, Abraham, 198
risk assumption. *See* assumption of the risk
risk aversion, 156
Rosenthal, Elisabeth, 159–60
"rotten apple" doctors, 18, 44–45. *See also* doctors: "good" vs. "bad"

Sage, William M., 122–23, 134
Santillan, Jesica, 8, 132–33
Scherz, Hal, 122–23
Schuck, Peter, 97
Seabury, Seth A., 117–18
self-dealing, 103, 120
"self-insurance," 57, 174
self-report studies. *See under* defensive medicine: types of studies on
Semmelweis, Ignaz, 133
sentinel events
   defined, 225–26
   Joint Commission's sentinel event program, 18, 20, 125–26, 134–35, 225–26
sepsis, 34
Serious Reportable Events, NQF's list of, 166

settlement (litigation), 66, 67–68, 77
   degree of injury and, 277n77
   overview, 62–66
several liability. *See* joint and several liability vs. proportionate share liability
Shadle, John, 108–9, 117
Shojania, Kaveh, 93, 132
should-never-occur-events, 167–68
silence, 134
   conspiracy of, 125, 134
Silver, Charles
   on the culture of medicine, 138
   on defensive medicine and tort law, 122
   on malpractice cases, 67–68, 100–1
   on malpractice insurance, 154
   on medical error (rates), 49, 138, 154
   on safety, 154, 155
   on tort reform, 122, 154
Six Sigma, 184
skilled nursing facilities (SNFs), 41, 48, 172. *See also* nursing homes
Sloan, Frank, 108–9, 117
smartphones and safety, 255–56
Smith, Michael, 83, 84
social comparison, 157
social psychology, 180
social truth, 157
Sorenson, Charles, Jr., 162
spinal fusion, 160, 205
   AHCPR guidelines, 17, 202–5, 224–25
   lack of efficacy, 160, 203
   Medicare refusal to pay for, 203
strict liability, 55. *See also* no-fault compensation system
strict locality rule, 58–59
Studdert, David M.
   on malpractice litigation, 64, 65*f*, 87, 88–89
   on medical error, 64, 88, 138, 185–86
superstition and superstitious behavior, 102
supply-sensitive care, 46–47, 160
   defined, 46–47
surgical instruments, retained, 32–33, 147
surgical/procedural complications, 51–52, 148–49. *See also specific topics*

incidence, 33
methods for reducing, 161–62
result in greater profit for hospital, 161–62
surgical procedures, 32–33. *See also* anesthesiologists; coronary artery bypass grafting; unnecessary surgical procedures
   outpatient, 48
   restriction of and government-engaged surveillance of risky, 224–25
surveillance, governmental. *See* governmental surveillance
surveillance model, private safety efforts and the, 225–29
system redesign, 149, 155, 177–78, 184, 185, 186, 187. *See also* health systems reform
systems approach (to analyzing and improving safety), 177, 179, 185–86. *See also* Leape, Lucian; systems thinking in healthcare
   accountability and liability, 188–89
   contrasted with American hospitals and healthcare, 187
   expanding the view of the system, 189–91
   forces working against the, 186–88
   introduction of, in healthcare industry, 188–89
   responsibility in the, 189
systems factors implicated in injuries, 185–86
systems nature of accidents, 183–84
systems thinking in healthcare, 180–86, 189. *See also* systems approach
   expanding the view of the system, 189–91

Tavris, Carol, 38
teaching hospitals, 43–44, 170, 217. *See also* resident duty hours
TeamSTEPPS29 (Team Strategies and Tools to Enhance Performance and Patient Safety), 143
technology, 144–45, 233. *See also* information technology
   medical, and liability, 273n25

Thomas, J. William, 117
To Err Is Human: Building a Safer Health System (IOM report), 18–21, 125–27, 201
  critics of, 20
  factors that led to, 87, 192, 209–10
  findings, 30–31
  goals set by, 138, 147
  National Research Council's report and, 146
  patient safety movement inspired by, 19, 87, 147, 192
  proposals made in, 125, 126, 147, 248
  research inspired by, 147
Topol, Eric, 233, 236, 244, 246, 255, 256
tort actions, impact of the right kind of, 86
tortfeasors, 54, 57, 58, 80, 87
tort law, 52. *See also* litigation system; medical accidents; *specific topics*
  changes in, as applied to healthcare industry, 95–96
  vs. criminal law, 52–54, 80, 271n8, 281n40
  economic analysis, 54–57
  evaluating the studies of its effects on safety, 83–84
  the healthcare industry's love–hate relationship with, 93–95
  origins and nature of, 52–54
  purposes, 54, 78–79, 80
tort litigation system. *See* litigation system; tort law
tort reform(s), 8, 15, 20–21, 27. *See also* damages caps; medical malpractice reform(s)
  David Hyman on, 122, 154
  defensive medicine and, 106, 116, 122, 294n109
  direct vs. indirect, 116
  impact of, 85, 96, 116, 118, 122, 294n109 (*see also* defensive medicine)
    on healthcare providers' fear, 99, 122
    on malpractice insurance premiums, 15, 95, 154
    on medical spending, 116, 118, 120
    negative effects, 2, 9, 90–91
    on treatment practices, 117, 118 (*see also* defensive medicine)
  vs. managed care, 116 (*see also* managed care: and defensive medicine)
  "third wave" (2002–2005), 118
training of healthcare providers, 142–50
transitional care nurse, 172
treatment, unnecessary. *See* unnecessary treatment
"triggers," 39
23andMe, 233–35, 236–40
  FDA and, 236–39, 255

unnecessary diagnostic procedures, 43–44. *See also* computer tomography (CT) scans; defensive medicine
unnecessary surgical procedures, 42, 45–46, 48–49, 224. *See also* spinal fusion
unnecessary treatment, 42–44, 45–47, 48–49
  as fraud, 42, 107, 120
upcoding, 213–14, 216
U.S. Department of Health, Education and Welfare (HEW), 26

vaccines, 192f
  developers of, 191
Value-Based Purchasing (VBP) Program, 306n59
Varga, Daniel, 7–8
Vendetti, Ferdinand, Jr., 212
Volkswagen (VW), 205–6
volume pledge, 224–25

Wachter, Robert M., 132, 275–76n63
  on hospitals, 246
  on information technology, 233, 246–47, 257
  Internal Bleeding: The Truth Behind America's Terrifying Epidemic of Medical Mistakes, 93, 132, 233
  malpractice, litigation, and, 132, 189
  on safety, 93, 147, 189, 233, 282n50
  on systems thinking, 188–89

"war on medical errors," 138
Watson (computer), 252–53
Weiler, Paul, 87
Wennberg, Jack, 45–46
Wertheimer, Ellen, 93
Wojcick, Ann, 238–39

workplace safety, 178–79
   factors contributing to improvements in, 178–79

Zabinski, Zenon, 85–86
Zion, Libby, 227, 228